Dementia

Contemporary Neurology Series:

Fred Plum, M.D. and Fletcher H. McDowell, M.D., *Editors-in-Chief*

Dementia

CHARLES E. WELLS, M.D./Editor
Professor of Psychiatry and Neurology
Vice-Chairman, Department of Psychiatry
Vanderbilt University School of Medicine
Nashville, Tennessee

Edition 2

 F. A. DAVIS COMPANY, PHILADELPHIA

Library of Congress Cataloging in Publication Data

Main entry under title:

Dementia.

Includes bibliographies and index.
1. Dementia. I. Wells, Charles E., 1929–[DNLM: 1. Psychosbs,
Organic. WM220 D376] RC386.2.D44 1977 616.8'9 77-7103
ISBN 0-8036-9221-8

Preface

Since the first edition of this book, the importance of dementia has been signaled not only by its recognition as a growing public health problem, but also by the increasing attention accorded it by medical investigators. Several books and innumerable other publications dealing with dementia and closely related topics have appeared. The sheer volume of newly published material makes it obvious that no one book can completely cover the subject. Still, in this second edition, many of the previously covered topics have been enlarged and updated, and new, timely, and important topics have been added.

I am grateful to the contributors who labored to make this edition a significant statement of our current state of knowledge concerning dementia; to Doctors Fred Plum, Fletcher McDowell, Gunter Haase, and Marc Hollender who read all or portions of the manuscript and offered helpful criticisms and suggestions; to Mrs. Christine Young, Medical Editor of the F. A. Davis Company, for her perceptive critiques and truly professional assistance; to Mrs. Reba Moore for her untiring administrative and secretarial assistance without which this task would not have been accomplished; and to Anne Dennison, Darlene French, Mary Lynn Green, Linda Hardy, and Kaye Wight who types and retyped portions of the manuscript.

Charles E. Wells, M.D.

Contributors

Joseph H. Allen, Jr., M.D.
Professor of Radiology and Chief, Section of Neuroradiology, Vanderbilt University School of Medicine, Nashville, Tennessee

Stanley H. Appel, M.D.
Professor of Neurology and Biochemistry and Chief, Division of Neurology, Duke University School of Medicine, Durham, North Carolina

A. Lee Bahr, M.D.
Assistant Professor of Radiology, Johns Hopkins University School of Medicine, Baltimore, Maryland

Denton C. Buchanan, Ph.D.
Assistant Professor of Psychiatry (Clinical Psychology), Vanderbilt University School of Medicine, Nashville, Tennessee

Gunter R. Haase, M.D.
Professor of Neurology, University of Pennsylvania School of Medicine; Director, Department of Neurology, Pennsylvania Hospital, Philadelphia, Pennsylvania

A. Everette James, Jr., Sc.M., M.D.
Professor and Chairman, Department of Radiology and Radiological Sciences, Vanderbilt University School of Medicine, Nashville, Tennessee

Richard T. Johnson, M.D.
Eisenhower Professor of Neurology and Professor of Microbiology, Johns Hopkins University School of Medicine, Baltimore, Maryland

Robert Katzman, M.D.
Professor and Chairman, Department of Neurology, Albert Einstein College of Medicine of Yeshiva University, New York, New York

James Lowry, M.D.
Assistant Professor of Radiology, Vanderbilt University School of Medicine, Nashville, Tennessee

James O. McNamara, M.D.
Assistant Professor of Neurology, Duke University School of Medicine, Durham, North Carolina

William F. Meacham, M.D.
Clinical Professor and Chairman, Department of Neurosurgery, Vanderbilt University School of Medicine, Nashville, Tennessee

Lilli Musella, Ph.D.
Assistant Professor of Psychiatry, Duke University School of Medicine, Durham, North Carolina

George W. Paulson, M.D.
Clinical Professor of Neurology, Ohio State University College of Medicine, Columbus, Ohio

Raymond P. Roos, M.D.
Instructor in Neurology, Johns Hopkins University School of Medicine, Baltimore, Maryland

M. J. Short, M.D.
Former Assistant Professor of Psychiatry, Duke University School of Medicine; Currently, private practice in Psychiatry, Greenville, South Carolina

Bernard E. Tomlinson, M.D.
Honorary Professor of Pathology, University of Newcastle upon Tyne, Consultant Neuropathologist, Newcastle General Hospital, Newcastle, England

H. Shan Wang, M.B.
Professor of Psychiatry, Duke University School of Medicine; Senior Fellow, Center for the Study of Aging and Human Development, Duke University Medical Center, Durham, North Carolina

Charles E. Wells, M.D.
Professor of Psychiatry and Neurology and Vice-Chairman, Department of Psychiatry, Vanderbilt University School of Medicine Nashville, Tennessee

William P. Wilson, M.D.
Professor of Psychiatry, Duke University School of Medicine, Durham, North Carolina

Contents

CHAPTER 1

Dementia: Definition and Description

Charles E. Wells, M.D.

PROBLEMS OF DEFINITION

Dementia is a word that has successfully defied attempts to limit its meaning and to fix its definition. Each author would like to define his use of the word clearly and precisely (i.e., to make it mean exactly what he wants it to mean); yet most of the semantic difficulties emerge from attempts to assign more precise qualities to the term "dementia" than usage will support.

Part of the problem arises because the same word is used in both lay and medical communication. *Webster's Third New International Dictionary* defines dementia [from the Latin *dement-, demens* (mad) + *ia* (pathological consideration)] as "a condition of deteriorated mentality that is characterized by marked decline from the individual's former intellectual level and often by emotional apathy," whereas the twenty-fifth edition of *Dorland's Illustrated Medical Dictionary* defines it as "a general designation for mental deterioration." Neither definition is sufficiently specific to explain the continued use of the term, but this is an example of codified definition lagging behind accepted usage.

In medicine today, dementia refers only to deterioration of mental function due to organic disease of the cerebral hemispheres. Further, the term serves best for those clinical states resulting from diffuse or disseminated disease of the cerebral hemispheres. In general, the patterns of clinical dysfunction resulting from focal disease are recognizably distinct and separable from those of of diffuse disease. The words (such as, aphasia or agnosia) that designate the clinical syndromes resulting from focal lesions carry precise meanings, and their communicative utility is enormous. Although the aphasic patient suffers a form of dementia, to describe his problem as "dementia" instead of "aphasia" lessens the information transmitted.

On the other hand, patterns of clinical dysfunction resulting from global disease of the hemispheres are neither distinct nor predictable, and the words (such as, delirium and dementia) designating these syndromes of clinical dysfunction fail to transmit an exact clinical picture.Thus their communicative utility is limited. Most of the semantic problems have arisen in this group of diffuse cerebral disorders. This is partly because delirium and dementia are not fixed states but evolving processes, but even their recognition as evolving processes would not resolve problems entirely. The semantic problems also result from the sheer complexity

1

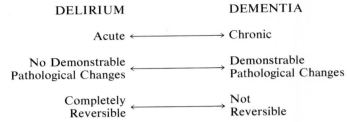

DELIRIUM		DEMENTIA
Acute	⟷	Chronic
No Demonstrable Pathological Changes	⟷	Demonstrable Pathological Changes
Completely Reversible	⟷	Not Reversible

Figure 1. Spectrum of delirium and dementia.

of the symptomatology which has been emphasized anew in recent factor analytical studies.[12, 15] Moreover, the clinical picture resulting from diffuse hemispheric dysfunction depends on a number of relatively independent variables, and the words commonly used to transmit these images (chiefly, "delirium" and "dementia") cannot convey all the pertinent facts about these variables.

The words delirium and dementia are best considered as general terms identifying sectors of a broad clinical spectrum resulting from global brain dysfunction (Fig. 1). Delirium might better be termed "acute exogenous metabolic encephalopathy" as suggested by Posner,[22] and dementia "chronic diffuse cerebral hemispheric degeneration," but both of these terms are too unwieldy. The limitations in our terminology have been examined at length by Lipowski[18] who has suggested a further diagnostic term, "subacute amnestic-confusional state," for a portion of the spectrum between delirium and dementia. The addition of yet another imprecise term to the lexicon would probably complicate our terminology further without significantly increasing its precision. The complexity of the variables plainly does not allow adoption of a terse and unambiguous definition. This volume is entitled *Dementia* because of the term's general utility, not because of its finely honed meaning.

By definition, dementia reflects a change (or deterioration) in mental functions. As such, the patient's symptoms and manifestations of dysfunction can only be judged in comparison with what is known or can be learned about previous function. A thorough evaluation of the patient's normal or usual mentative capacities is therefore a prerequisite for accurate assessment of functional deterioration.

This volume deals largely with clinical disorders that are chronic and irreversible and are attended by pathological alterations that diffusely involve the two hemispheres. Nevertheless, the definition of dementia may be stretched to include other processes. Thus the patient with cerebral damage due to carbon monoxide poisoning is considered to suffer from dementia, although the onset is acute and the course nonprogressive. Further, the patient with cerebral dysfunction due to hypothyroidism is appropriately diagnosed as having dementia, even though the dysfunction may be reversible and pathological alterations are lacking. Clearly, irreversibility will not be considered the *sine qua non* for the diagnosis of dementia here, since a major thrust of this volume is the detection and identification of treatable causes of dementia (the disorders which Roth[24] has termed "secondary dementias").

CLINICAL PRESENTATION

Defects in orientation, memory, intellectual function, judgment, and affectivity are stressed in the usual account of the symptomatology of dementia. These classic features may indeed dominate the clinical picture, but to focus on them exclusively is to emphasize the advanced stages of the dementing process. Such an orientation neglects the richness of the clinical picture to be observed at its inception and in earlier stages of the disease state before such gross malfunction is evident.

In most accounts of dementia, memory loss is emphasized as the earliest and most persistent symptom. There is no question that when a patient presents himself to the physician complaining chiefly of impaired memory, the first diagnostic consideration is likely to be structural brain disease. It is virtually axiomatic, however, that the patient who complains persistently of memory loss is unlikely to have serious memory loss secondary to organic cerebral disease. Indeed, Kahn and associates[16] have shown (in a population of patients over 50 years of age) that complaints of memory loss correlate well with depression and poorly with evidence of brain damage. Even among their patients with organic dysfunction, the severity of the complaint about memory loss was more closely related to the severity of depression than to the extent of organic impairment. It is a common clinical experience to hear patients with depression, anxiety, hysterical features, and schizophrenia complain of memory loss; it is rare in the patient with verified dementia. In fact, memory impairment is usually minimized by patients with significant dementia; it is emphasized only by family and other observers who are likely to perceive the dysfunction with much greater clarity than does the patient. This lack of awareness and concern for memory loss in most patients with significant dementia attests to the effectiveness of the defense mechanisms of denial.

Early in the process of dementia a variety of other symptoms may present and may capture the attention of the patient, his family, and his physician. Many of these early symptoms of dementia differ little either qualitatively or quantitatively from those that occur in normal, healthy individuals who are exhausted, anxious, or subject to severe environmental pressures. These initial symptoms are particularly likely to involve impairment of those qualities that we believe are the result of whole brain function, of those qualities that we consider peculiarly human, perhaps of those qualities that we observe to be quite specific to the individual himself. Thus an early and frequent complaint is that the patient is "not himself," meaning that the patient and his companions have noted the onset of illness in terms of change in functions that are quite specific to the particular person, whether described in terms of alteration of drives, mood, enthusiasms, capacity to give and receive affection, creativity, or other features. Often the patient's attention centers on various somatic complaints, previously present or arising *de novo,* for which no adequate organic cause can be found and for which the usual remedies provide no relief. Here only the physician's acumen prompts him to search beneath the facade of somatic symptoms for the nidus of the problem.

Because these most complex of human brain functions are often first affected in the dementing process, one might guess that usually the onset is readily discernible to the patient and to those about him, but this often is not the case. The onset is often dated in retrospect and with imprecision, the informant being aware that things are seriously amiss at present but unaware just when things began to move in this direction.

In perhaps the finest firsthand description of the onset and progression of the dementing process yet published, one observer wrote:[3]

> Over the period that we worked together, . . . I became gradually aware
> that the fine edge of his intellect was becoming dulled. He was less clear in

discussion and less quick to make the jump from a new piece of evidence to its possible significance. He spent more time over his work and achieved less; and he found it increasingly difficult to get his results ready for publication. He tended also to become portentious and solemn about his subject, as though one small corner of knowledge nearly filled his world, and the wider horizons were narrowing in. The change was so slow as to be barely perceptible, and the signs vanished when I tried to pin them down: they were like those faint stars which are seen more easily when they are not in the direct line of vision. I was left with a feeling of uneasiness which I could not justify.

. . . , after a period of absence, I looked forward with special pleasure to my homecoming, but when we met I knew with immediate certainty that I had lost the companion of my earlier years. The change was as yet mainly a loss of intellectual clarity and he remained himself, but a self that was subtly devitalised. To me it was as though a light had gone out, but no-one else seemed to notice anything amiss. . . .

By this time he was worried about his general health and attended a doctor from time to time with rather vague symptoms. For several years he had been said to have low blood-pressure, but nothing was found wrong apart from this, and he was reassured.

The quotation above emphasizes not only the subtlety of presenting signs and symptoms but how easily they may be overlooked even by a concerned and qualified observer. Paulson[21] calls attention to the retention of social skills by many patients with significantly advanced dementia so that evidence of dementia may be concealed in ordinary encounters and on superficial inquiry. Arie[4] describes how rarely primary physicians are aware of dementia in their elderly patients. Symptoms are likely to be overlooked by the physician because they do not clearly bespeak dementia; they are often overlooked by the family even when they clearly do. Hollender[13] suggests several behavioral observations which should alert the examiner to the possibility of dementia: the patient who expresses too much satisfaction from trivial accomplishments; the patient who struggles too hard to turn out performances which earlier would have required little effort; the patient who refers to notes, guides, calendars too freely; the patient who expresses disinterest in a topic, allowing that his sons or daughters keep up with that sort of thing; the patient who says he will come back to that question later but neglects to do so. Kiloh[17] observes that "any suggestion that the illness is of short duration virtually eliminates the possibility of dementia; exceptions to this rule are rare." Coblentz and coworkers[7] highlight the long delay between the time when symptoms of dementia are first observed by family members and the time when a definitive medical opinion is sought. They suggest that this reflects the family's stereotyped perception that such disorders are untreatable and thus do not demand or profit from early medical attention.

Even the patient so perceptively described above was not taken for specialized medical care until a crisis occurred. It is often the appearance of a crisis rather than the appearance of symptoms which precipitates the call for medical assistance. Arie[4] describes several situations that may result in a crisis calling for immediate medical intervention:

1. Something new has happened to the patient, such as a patient not previously incapacitated by his dementia becoming severely incapacitated by it during an episode of infection.

2. Something has happened in the social milieu, such as the death of the spouse, thus removing a vital environmental support.

3. The crisis is a manipulation of the caring system, as for example, "Enough is enough." Nothing new has happened, but the caretaking person can tolerate the pressure of looking after the demented person no longer.

From a diagnostic and therapeutic standpoint the patient should ideally present himself to the physician so early in the course of dementia that certain identification of the disease process is difficult if not impossible. Sadly enough the patient is much more likely to be presented to the physician so late that no doubt as to diagnosis can arise and irreversible brain damage has already occurred.

CLINICAL COURSE

The American Psychiatric Association's *Diagnostic and Statistical Manual of Mental Disorders*[2] states that the organic brain syndromes (i.e., dementias) are manifested by the following clinical features: impairment of orientation; impairment of memory; impairment of all intellectual functions such as comprehension, calculation, knowledge, and learning; impairment of judgment; and lability and shallowness of affect. These are the criteria by which an unequivocal diagnosis may be established, but they by no means dominate each segment of the clinical course.

Wolff and Chapman[6, 32] have studied extensively the changes in highest integrative functions which result from progressively larger focal lesions of the cerebral hemispheres in man. Although they did not study, serially, changes in function in patients suffering from progressive diffuse cerebral degenerative processes, it appears likely that the deterioration of function which they described with increasingly large focal hemispheric lesions reflects with fair accuracy the progressive dysfunction in the patient suffering from a diffuse cerebral deteriorative disorder.

Chapman and Wolff[6] delineated four categories of functions that are impaired in diseases of the cerebral hemispheres: (1) the capacity to express appropriate feelings and drives; (2) the capacity to employ mental mechanisms (learning, memory, etc) effectively for goal achievements; (3) the capacity to maintain appropriate thresholds and tolerance for frustration and failure and to recover appropriately from them; (4) the capacity to employ effective and modulated defense reactions.

In the incipient phases of cerebral degeneration the individual experiences diminished energy and enthusiasm. He has less interest and concern for vocational, family, and social activities. Lability of affect is common often with considerable increase in the overall anxiety level, particularly as the individual becomes aware of his failing powers. He has less interest in goals and achievements, diminished creativity, less incentive to stick to a task, trouble concentrating, and difficulty screening out disturbing environmental stimuli. Failures, frustrations, changes, postponements, and troublesome decisions produce more annoyance and internal upheaval than usual, and it is harder to recover equilibrium after such disturbances. The individual's characteristic defense mechanisms are utilized more frequently and more blatantly, often with less than normal effectiveness.

As the disease progresses, the achievement of personal ambitions and fulfillment of social responsibilities become less important. The individual becomes increasingly absorbed with himself and his own problems and less concerned with

5

the feelings and reactions of others. His anxiety increases, and marked irritability with outbursts of anger may ensue. Depression often intensifies as he becomes increasingly aware of his diminished abilities. It is during this early phase of illness accompanied by depression that the patient often complains conspicuously of memory loss. Despite the complaint, memory loss may be difficult to demonstrate by available testing techniques. It is almost routine for the patient to complain specifically of loss of memory for recent events, often coupled with an avowal that memories for past events remain crystal clear. It has long been accepted that in organic cerebral disease, recent memories are lost first and remote memories preserved, a manifestation of Ribot's law of regression. Although the principle has not been specifically tested in a sizable cohort of patients with dementia, recent studies in normal aged subjects,[27] depressed aged subjects,[16] and patients with amnestic syndromes[26, 29] fail to substantiate the principle of preservation of memory for remote events when memory for recent events is demonstrably impaired. Kahn and associates[16] suggest that the complaint that recent memory is specifically lost is closely tied to feelings of depression and the cognitive set of depression in which everything current is denigrated. During this phase of the disorder, the individual has trouble making plans, dealing with new situations, and initiating activity. He avoids choices and decisions. Delayed recall and unreliability in calculations may be troublesome, as are slowed speech and understanding. Judgment suffers. Frustration tolerance is usually even further reduced. The person's characteristic defense reactions are utilized excessively in dealing with his environment, but they are less well regulated and less effective.

With worsening of the condition, drives and feelings diminish. The drive for achievement vanishes, and the patient may even lose interest in others' opinions of him. Appropriate dress and personal cleanliness may be ignored. There is usually a diminution of anxiety with progressive flattening of affect. Personal warmth and concern for others often disappear. Now the defects of function enumerated in the *Diagnostic and Statistical Manual*[2] become readily apparent. Defective memory, particularly for recent events, is blatant. Time and space orientation are faulty; the patient is easily lost. Learning ability is markedly impaired. He is unable to function in complex situations, has trouble understanding and following directions, and often loses the train of thought. Some patients are restless and overactive; others, lethargic and lacking in energy. Failure may now be ignored. With diminished drives and appetites, frustrations are not so likely to arise. The patient's characteristic premorbid defense mechanisms are now obvious, and reliance upon them may be damaging rather than protective.

It is usually in this phase of disease that the motor and sensory neurological signs of brain dysfunction begin to appear. The appearance of specific neurological abnormalities does not depend so much upon duration of the disease process as upon the rapidity of the degenerative process and the extent and site of brain damage. Thus in rapidly progressive global diseases, signs of motor and sensory dysfunction may quickly assume prominence, whereas with more slowly progressive and more restricted diseases, the traditional neurological examination may remain normal for long periods before definite abnormalities supervene.

As damage proceeds, drive and ambition disappear. The patient becomes apathetic. The human substance of the personality is lost. There is blunting of all feelings. Danger, loss, pain — even impending death — may rouse only the feeblest and briefest of responses. The patient now requires close care; he is grossly disoriented to place and time. Recent and remote memory are defective. Calculations are impossible save for a few sums long committed to memory. The patient is indifferent or unaware of people and situations. Perceptions are blurred and distorted. Frustrations may be hardly noted or not perceived, and defense mechanisms are dissolved. Survival provides opportunity for the appearance of paralysis, mutism, incontinence, stupor, and coma. Changes in level of consciousness are seldom conspicuous, however, until advanced stages of degeneration are reached, further contrasting the loss of highest-level functions with the preservation of lower-level functions. Neurological dysfunction is always impressive, however, in the terminal stages of hemispheric atrophy.

Thus early in the dementing process, the signs and symptoms of dementia are most related to the sphere of psychological dysfunction, and diagnosis can best be made on the basis of the psychiatric examination and psychological testing. With progression, the psychological functions further decline, but to them are added the neurological signs and symptoms of diffuse disease of the cerebral hemispheres. The division into psychological and neurological phases is perhaps theoretically inadmissible, but it serves to emphasize the utility of different diagnostic measures at different stages of the disease. No one with a modicum of medical and psychological knowledge fails to recognize the symptoms and signs of late-stage dementia; the symptoms and signs of early-stage dementia are, however, far from precise and predictive. The physician in such instances must be particularly alert and perhaps particularly suspicious of organic brain disease if he is to avoid errors in diagnosis and therapy.

DIFFERENTIAL DIAGNOSIS

Whenever the physician encounters a patient whose history, symptomatology, or clinical behavior reveals a disorder of the highest integrative functions, the first differential diagnostic question must be, "Is the disorder functional (i.e., non-organic) or organic?" Although this is the first and basic choice, the answer may not come easily.

Functional Disorders

Regrettably, even to use the word functional is to invite dissent. Some argue that the functional-organic dichotomy should be discarded, for all disorders of perception, cognition, affect, and behavior must be mediated through brain cellular mechanisms (and thus be organic). Such an approach fails to help the physician who assumes responsibility for patient care. A recent suggestion is that "a behavior disorder is 'functional' if it is learning that has modified the brain by normal physiological mechanisms."[11] Such a proposal helps the physician even less, substituting as it does unacceptable speculation for acknowledged ignorance. At our present level of knowledge, functional cannot be defined in terms of what it is but only in terms of what it is not. A "functional disorder" here refers to one in which no cerebral abnormality can be demonstrated by presently available pathological or physicochemical methods.

From a differential diagnostic standpoint, dementia may be confused with a variety of functional disorders. Early in its course, the clinical picture of dementia may specifically suggest neurosis; later, psychosis.

The patient with mild to moderate brain disease often displays symptoms that suggest an anxiety neurosis or a depressive neurosis. Differentiation is usually possible on clinical grounds alone, though one may have to accept a sense of what is going wrong rather than obtain absolute proof early in the course of the disease.

7

Thus before impairment of orientation, memory, and intellectual functions can be demonstrated with certainty, the examiner may respond to a vagueness in the presenting story, an imprecision in detail, or a lack of orderly thought processes that does not fit well with the patient's background and previous performance, bringing to mind the possibility of dementia. Other features are more specific. The neurotic patient almost never has impairment of orientation. Though he often complains of poor memory, its intactness can usually be demonstrated satisfactorily by persistent questioning. Similarly, though the neurotic patient often complains of impaired intellectual functions in general, when his cooperation is achieved for testing, this dysfunction can rarely be substantiated. Disorders of judgment and affectivity are conspicuous in both neurosis and dementia, though a different aura of dysfunction is noted in the two disorders. In neurosis, one senses usually that poor judgment is secondary to inner conflicts and emotions (particularly feelings such as anger and fear) that so preoccupy the individual and distort his perceptions that he is incapable of making logical dispassionate judgments. In dementia, poor judgment usually results from the individual's inability to attend to details and to assimilate the multiple factors that are usually weighed in decision-making, so that choice is directed on the basis of one particular bit of information with disregard for multiple other factors.

The nature of the affective change is also often a distinguishing feature. In neurosis, a pervasive feeling, such as anxiety or depression or anger, is likely to dominate the clinical picture, whereas in dementia the lability of affect is more striking. Thus, the demented patient appears in turn, and often with great rapidity, fearful then sad then angry, and in each situation the affectual response may be appropriate though excessive for the situation. This lability may not, however, be prominent early, when a pervasive feeling of sadness or fearfulness is more common. Indeed, depression has been observed so frequently as an early feature of dementia that it was once thought that in the elderly depression usually progressed to dementia. Alexander[1] among others has emphasized the error of this idea and has stressed the importance of recognition of depressive illness *per se* in the elderly. Nunn and coworkers[20] have shown that the prevalence of neurosis in the elderly is negatively correlated with height of scores on the Wechsler Adult Intelligence Scale, a situation which may compound diagnostic difficulties.

With more severe dysfunction, dementia may be confused with functional psychoses, especially with depression and schizophrenia. The differentiation of dementia from depressive psychosis, particularly in the aged patient, is often challenging. With a depressive illness, the history is often more precise and the date of onset more certain than is usual with dementing illnesses. A history of recent onset with rapid progression is far more characteristic of depression than of dementia. Further, even though cooperation is hard to obtain and responses come with ponderous slowness, the examiner is usually able to demonstrate preservation of orientation, memory, and other intellectual functions in depressive illness — though their demonstration may demand unusual tenacity of the examiner. Certain biological features — such as anorexia, weight loss, constipation, early waking — are more typical of depression than of dementia. Again the mood in affective disorders is much more pervasive and less labile than in dementia. Although alteration in mood is common with dementia, differentiation from a primary disorder of mood is usually possible by clinical examination.

Kiloh[17] has emphasized the extent to which depression can mimic dementia and has called it "pseudo-dementia." He described in these depressed patients an apparent failure of recent memory, inaccurate orientation and a poor knowledge of current events. The impression of dementia may be strengthened by some carelessness in personal habits and neglect of the person; and a poor appetite, weight loss and autonomic changes may combine to produce the appearance of increasing decrepitude. The gait may become slow and shuffling due to psychomotor retardation, adding further to the illusion of involvement of the central nervous system. So often the patient emphasizes the physical components of his illness and fails to mention the mood change. Even if the presence of depression is appreciated, it may well be regarded as a secondary feature, whilst suicidal ideas and attempts may be accepted as evidence of retained insight into the failing intellectual powers.

He further emphasized the dangers of relying on psychological testing for diagnosis in these patients. Some of his patients on psychometric examination showed alterations typical of organic deterioration with restitution to normal after treatment for depression.

Sternberg and Jarvik[28] have studied learning and memory in depressed patients; they demonstrated marked impairment in short-term memory for newly learned materials in these patients with a change toward normal with lifting of the depression. Kiloh[17] suggested that the patient who appears demented clinically but has a history of recent onset plus a normal electroencephalogram should particularly be suspected of pseudo-dementia. Duckworth and Ross[9] have shown that in a population of elderly patients, dementia is diagnosed more often and depression less often in the United States than in either Canada or England. This observation raised the possibility that in the United States, elderly patients with a depressive psychosis have often been misdiagnosed as demented and thus been deprived of effective therapy.

Although disorders of thought are prominent with dementia, it can usually be differentiated clinically from a primary disorder of thought, i.e., schizophrenia. When the cooperation of the schizophrenic patient can be obtained, preservation of orientation, memory, and intellectual functions is demonstrated in all save the most deteriorated. Further, the disorder of thought seen in schizophrenia usually possesses a different texture from that seen in dementia. In schizophrenia one is struck by the sudden and inexplicable twists in the subject's thought content, the tolerance for conflicts, and the conclusions reached on logically unacceptable bases. In dementia, the thoughts expressed take more of a meandering course—one can follow the progression of thoughts but they appear to lead nowhere. A lack of identifiable objective and an inattention to detail are more apparent than are sudden switches in subject. Abnormalities of mood are, of course, also prominent in schizophrenia in which one usually sees a flatness or inappropriateness of affect in contrast to the labile, perhaps poorly regulated but nevertheless appropriate, affective responses of dementia.

Rarely, other functional disorders simulate dementia. Manic psychosis, particularly if it appears for the first time in an older patient, may be confused with dementia,[17, 19, 30] as on rare occasions may hysterical disorders.[17, 30]

Organic Disorders

If in response to the question, "Is the disorder functional or organic?" the disorder is identified as organic, differentiation as to whether the clinical presentation results from diffuse or focal dysfunction of the cerebral hemispheres must first be made. The above account of the clinical patterns observed in dementia (diffuse dysfunction) stressed the variety and diversity of the clinical manifestations. Usually malfunction in varied spheres can be demonstrated by the time the patient with diffuse brain disease first seeks medical assistance. A mosaic of defects, formed from bits of dysfunction in multiple mentative capacities, is typical for the patient suffering from diffuse brain disease. In other patients, however, defects are limited to certain specific memory, language, recognition, or performance functions, with relative preservation of the spectrum of other mentative capacities. Such dense dysfunction in one area with good function in others is typically found in the patient with focal and circumscribed brain disease.

Initially the clinician must ask himself if the patient's observed mentative incapacity might be attributed to an amnestic, agnosic, apractic, aphasic, or other specific defect alone. Horenstein[14] dealt with this subject in detail in the first edition of this book. The clinician might ask if a patient's apparent disorientation, poor memory, loss of previously acquired skills (as a typist, for example), anxiety, depression, and hyperactivity could all result from a defect in language function. If so, this would strongly suggest a lesion primarily involving the left hemisphere which additional testing might further specify. Or the clinician might inquire if a patient's withdrawal, irritability, depression, anergy, clumsiness, and loss of previous skills (as a carpenter, for example) might be explained as resulting from constructional apraxia? If so, this would suggest a focal lesion, possibly in the right parietal lobe. Again, once a dense, limited defect is identified, further testing may aid in the fuller definition of the dysfunction and perhaps its localization. Except for aphasia, circumscribed defects usually lack absolute predictability as to site or even lateralization of lesion, but they do demand a search for the site. Whenever one limited specific mentative defect alone is highlighted through careful and complete clinical evaluation, the likelihood that the clinical syndrome results from a single focal lesion is markedly increased. Of course certain defects, such as a profound aphasia, make appraisal of other mental functions difficult if not impossible, thus clouding the underlying cause.

If the disorder be identified as organic and due to diffuse brain dysfunction, then the clinical differentiation lies between delirium and dementia. Delirium can usually be distinguished from the chronic dementing diseases on the basis of both history and examination. The history is usually one of abrupt and precise onset in delirium, whereas a stuttering or gradual course of uncertain onset is typical of dementia. Alterations in consciousness and physiological functions that are commonly present in delirium may allow an easy differentiation. Changes in level of consciousness are a hallmark of delirium; they are uncommon until the terminal phases of dementia. Depression of consciousness in delirium varies from an inattentive, dazed, dreamy state to stupor. Physiological alterations are both common and prominent in delirium: restlessness, tremor, slurred speech, insomnia, anorexia, nausea, vomiting, constipation, diarrhea, sweating, pallor, flushing, tachycardia, fever. While these may be seen individually in dementia, they are seldom prominent and seldom dominate the clinical picture as they commonly do in delirium. The extreme variability of the clinical appearance, from moment to moment and hour to hour, should be emphasized in delirium—indeed, variability has been called the dominant feature of delirium—whereas a more level plane of dysfunction typifies dementia.

10

DISCUSSION

Dementia is considered here as a spectrum of mental states resulting from disease of the cerebral hemispheres in adult life. The inclusiveness of this definition is emphasized in order (1) to stress the absence of a single condition called dementia and (2) to emphasize the concept of dementia as a broad continuum of dysfunction, ranging from a barely discernible deviation from normal to virtual cerebral death. The condition that we call dementia in any single patient at any one point in time is thus comparable to a single frame in a movie; it may catch the moment quite accurately and with good definition, but it gives only hints of what precedes and what follows. This very changing nature of the manifestations of diffuse and progressive brain disease makes it difficult for us to sculpture from the mass of our materials a form easily recognizable as "dementia."

Other than its changing appearance and character, there are multiple factors that make it difficult to crystalize a concept of the demented state. With focal lesions of the cerebral hemispheres, particularly those that involve primarily the motor and sensory pathways, we are often able to predict quite accurately the clinical state of the patient. Thus one can predict that a lesion properly situated within the left occipital pole will result in a right homonymous hemianopsia or that a lesion appropriately situated in the right internal capsule will result in a left hemiparesis and left hemisensory defect. With focal lesions located outside the primary motor and sensory regions, prediction of the resulting clinical state is much more difficult; with diffuse lesions such prediction of the resulting clinical state is virtually impossible, save with the most gross and totally destructive of lesions.

Dementia is difficult to approach clinically not only because of its panoramic nature and the lack of predictability in its symptoms and signs but because there is ample evidence that the severity of clinical dysfunction sometimes correlates poorly with the severity of the disease process as manifested pathologically. Although several studies[8, 23, 31] have indicated a fair degree of correlation between the severity of intellectual and functional deterioration and the severity of brain degeneration as demonstrated pathologically or by air contrast radiographic studies, there are still notable and intriguing exceptions. In one type of exception, the patient demonstrates profound dementia clinically, yet by conventional radiologic and pathological investigation, only a moderate degree of brain atrophy. This may be explained by supposing that dysfunction secondary to organic factors precedes the actual brain atrophy by a predictable period—that is, it may simply take a while for atrophy to be manifest. Thus more sensitive methods of examination (electron microscopy or perhaps special staining techniques for specific enzymes) might reveal structural defects; air contrast radiographic studies later might reveal progressive cortical atrophy; or longer survival might permit the occurrence of atrophy that might then be revealed by conventional pathological methods.

The more intriguing exception is the individual who appears to be functioning well mentally up until death but whose brain reveals severe atrophy on postmortem examination. Detailed premorbid studies of these individuals, who are usually remarked on only in passing in the literature or with incredulity at the postmortem examination, are lacking. Such studies might be of great value in providing clues as to what protects the individual with severe brain atrophy from the profound functional deterioration that we might expect to be its accompaniment.

11

Generally, the ability of the individual to maintain socially acceptable function despite progressive brain degeneration has been attributed by various authors to the intellectual, social, vocational, and emotional resources prevailing before the onset of illness. This general thesis was promoted most persuasively by Rothschild[25] some years ago. He related the clinical dysfunction resulting from brain tissue loss to the individual's underlying "ability to compensate." He suggested, therefore, that the person whose life had been marked by adaptability to changing events and circumstances would likely prove clinically resistant to the ravages of brain-cell death. This thesis has, unfortunately, never been thoroughly tested, though it has been echoed by Fisch and his associates[10] in a study of "chronic brain syndrome" in the aged population of the community. They found a few individuals with psychological evidence of rather severe brain damage who were able to live alone and still function in the community. They suggested that these individuals were able to do so "because of their superficial, strongly independent type of personality, their desire for autonomy, and their inability to tolerate caretaking persons or concepts of regimentation within an institution." Busse[5] has particularly stressed the relationship between socioeconomic status and the appearance of symptoms due to degenerative brain disease. Others[6, 32] have observed the functional deficit to be greater with rapidly progressive lesions than with slowly developing lesions of the same size. Thus we might guess that the clinical dysfunction from brain atrophy would be much greater should the final stage be reached over a period of several months than should the process have required several or many years. Despite these studies, we still do not understand why some persons continue to function seemingly well despite considerable brain atrophy, whereas others manifest severe mental deterioration with apparently equivalent brain damage.

Another difficulty presents itself, perhaps particularly to the neurologist, in the conceptualization of the demented states. The neurologist is trained to deal with the brain as a complex of systems, and the conventional neurological examination is largely designed to evaluate specific systemic functions, often teasing out with great subtlety dysfunction confined to one particular area of the nervous system or to a particular neural network. While certain particular forms of dementia (Korsakoff's psychosis, for example) result from well-localized or well-systematized lesions of the nervous system, much, and perhaps most, dementia reflects dysfunction of the brain as a whole. It is this concept — that of function and dysfunction of the brain as an entity — that often causes us the greatest difficulty. We must regard the brain as an organ if we are properly to evaluate its function, just as the cardiologist studies cardiac function as a whole and the nephrologist studies renal function as a whole. This does not imply that we must neglect study of component functions, for just as the cardiologist investigates vascular dynamics and muscular contractility, we may investigate modalities such as visual function and memory with great profit. This does imply, however, that the function of the brain as an organ is infinitely richer than what might be suspected from an investigation of its component systems individually. Thus both the conventional neurological approach to brain function (as a combination of sensory, motor, reflex, and symbol-manipulative functions) and the conventional psychiatric approach to brain function (as a combination of affectual, intellectual, and symbolic functions) are equally limiting.

If we regard the peculiarly complex and creative activity of the human brain as the result of the workings of the highly developed cerebral hemispheres as an organ, whose function depends upon multiple morbid and premorbid characteristics, it follows that we must consider dementia as a peculiarly human disorder and that we can find no acceptable counterpart in nature for laboratory investigation. It is thus in these particularly human functions, which might truly be called the highest integrative functions, such as the capacity to think creatively, to deal effectively with new and complex problems, and to love and care for others, that the symptoms and behavioral manifestations of dementia may be most striking. The centrality of these functions for the human being makes dementia a worthy subject for our studies.

REFERENCES

1. ALEXANDER, D. A.: *"Senile Dementia:"* A changing perspective. Br. J. Psychiatry 121:207, 1972.
2. AMERICAN PSYCHIATRIC ASSOCIATION: *Diagnostic and Statistical Manual of Mental Disorders,* ed. 2. American Psychiatric Association, Washington, D.C., 1968.
3. ANONYMOUS AUTHOR: *Death of a mind: A study in disintegration.* Lancet 1:1012, 1950.
4. ARIE, T.: *Dementia in the elderly: diagnosis and assessement.* Br. Med. J. 4:540, 1973.
5. BUSSE, E. W.: Brain syndromes associated with disturbances in metabolism, growth, and nutrition, in Freedman, A. M., and Kaplan, H. J. (eds.): *Comprehensive Textbook of Psychiatry.* The Williams & Wilkins Co., Baltimore, 1967, p. 726.
6. CHAPMAN, L. F., AND WOLFF, H. G.: *The cerebral hemispheres and the highest integrative functions of man.* Arch. Neurol. 1:357, 1959.
7. COBLENTZ, J. M.; MATTIS, S.; ZINGESSER, L. H.; KASOFF, S. S.; WISNIEWSKI, H. M.; AND KATZMAN, R.: *Presenile dementia. Clinical aspects and evaluation of cerebrospinal fluid dynamics.* Arch. Neurol. 29:299, 1973.
8. CORSELLIS, J. A. N.: *Mental Illness and the Ageing Brain.* Maudsley Monograph #9, Oxford University Press, Inc. London, 1962.
9. DUCKWORTH, G. S., AND ROSS, H.: *Diagnostic differences in psychogeriatric patients in Toronto, New York, and London.* Can. Med. Assoc. J. 112:847, 1975.
10. FISCH, M.; GOLDFARB, A. I.; SHAHINIAN, S. P.; AND TURNER, H.: *Chronic brain syndrome in the community aged.* Arch. Gen. Psychiatry 18:739, 1968.
11. GESCHWIND, N.: The borderland of neurology and psychiatry: Some common misconceptions, in Benson, D. F., and Blumer, D. (eds.): *Psychiatric Aspects of Neurological Disease.* Grune and Stratton, New York, 1975, p. 1.
12. GUSTAFSON, L.: *Dementia with onset in the presenile period. A cross-sectional study. Part I. Psychiatric symptoms in dementia with onset in the presenile period.* Acta Psychiatr. Scand. [Suppl.] 257:7, 1975.
13. HOLLENDER, M. H.: Personal communication.
14. HORENSTEIN, S.: Amnestic, agnosic, apractic, and aphasic features in dementing illness, in Wells, C. E. (ed.): *Dementia.* F. A. Davis Co., Philadelphia, 1971.
15. JONSSON, C. O.; WALDTON, S.; AND MÄLHAMMAR, G.: *The psychiatric symptomatology in senile dementia assessed by means of an interview.* Acta Psychiatr. Scand. 48:103, 1972.
16. KAHN, R. L.; ZARIT, S. H.; HILBERT, N. M., AND NIEDEREHE, G.: *Memory complaint and impairment in the aged. The effect of depression and altered brain function.* Arch Gen. Psychiatry 32:1569, 1975.
17. KILOH, L. G.: *Pseudo-dementia.* Acta Psychiatr. Scand. 37:336, 1961.
18. LIPOWSKI, Z. J.: Organic brain syndromes: overview and classification, in Benson, D. F., and Blumer, D. (eds.): *Psychiatric Aspects of Neurological Disease.* Grune and Stratton, New York, 1975, p. 11.
19. MARSDEN, C. D., AND HARRISON, M. J. G.: *Outcome of investigation of patients with presenile dementia.* Br. Med. J. 2:249, 1972.
20. NUNN, C.; BERGMANN, K.; BRITTON, P. G.; FOSTER, E. M.; HALL, E. H.; AND KAY, D. W. K.: *Intelligence and neurosis in old age.* Br. J. Psychiatry 124:446, 1974.

21. PAULSON, G. W.: The neurological examination in dementia, in Wells, C. E. (ed.): *Dementia, ed.* 2. F. A. Davis Co., Philadelphia, 1977.

22. POSNER, J. B.: Delirium and exogenous metabolic brain disease, in Beeson, P. B., and McDermott, W. (eds.): *Textbook of Medicine,* ed. 14. W. B. Saunders Company, Philadelphia, 1975, Vol. I, p. 544.

23. ROTH, M.; TOMLINSON, B. E.; AND BLESSED, G.: *Correlation between scores for dementia and counts of "senile plaques" in cerebral grey matter of elderly subjects.* Nature (Lond.) 209:109, 1966.

24. ROTH, M.: *Mental disorders of the aged: diagnosis and treatment.* Med. World News p. 35 (Oct. 27) 1975.

25. ROTHSCHILD, D.: *Pathologic changes in senile psychoses and their psychobiologic significance.* Am. J. Psychiatry 93:757, 1937.

26. SANDERS, H. I ., AND WARRINGTON, E. K.: *Memory for remote events in amnesic patients.* Brain 94:661, 1971.

27. SQUIRE, L. R.: *Remote memory as affected by aging.* Neuropsychologia 12:429, 1974.

28. STERNBERG, D. E., AND JARVIK, M. E.: *Memory function in depression. Improvement with antidepressant medication.* Arch. Gen. Pschiatry 33:219, 1976.

29. WARRINGTON, E. K.: *Neurological disorders of memory.* Br. Med. Bull. 27:243, 1971.

30. WELLS, C. E.: Personal observations.

31. WILLANGER, R.; THYGESEN, P.; NIELSEN, R.; AND PETERSEN, O.: *Intellectual impairment and cerebral atrophy: A psychological, neurological and radiological investigation.* Dan. Med. Bull. 15:65, 1968.

32. WOLFF, H. G.: Dementia, in Beeson, P. B., and McDermott, W. (eds.): *Textbook of Medicine,* ed. 11. W. B. Saunders Company, Philadelphia, 1963, p. 1569.

14

CHAPTER 2

Dementia in Old Age

H. Shan Wang, M.B.

Dementia is one of the most common clinical syndromes among aged persons, although its exact prevalence has not been established. The medical literature includes approximately 15 reports concerning the prevalence of dementia (or organic brain syndrome, senility, senile psychoses) in the aged; almost all were done outside the United States. The findings of these reports, which have been reviewed in several recent articles,[2, 5, 29, 37] indicate that "severe" dementia may be present in 1.0 to 9.1 percent of the elderly population and "mild" dementia may be present in another 2.6 to 15.4 percent.

In the United States, the most systematic and extensive statistical data in this regard were those reported by the National Institute of Mental Health and by the National Center for Health Statistics. Based on these data approximately 63 percent of the elderly persons who are institutionalized in all public and private psychiatric hospitals, nursing homes, and personal-care homes in the United States are estimated to have dementia.[51] In other words, 2.3 percent of the population aged 65 or over may be considered to have dementia of such severity that institutional care is necessary. Many demented elderly persons contine to live in the community. Using a mental status questionnaire, Pfeiffer[38] found that of a randomized representative sample of residents aged 65 and over from a county in the southeastern United States, about 4 percent showed moderate to severe mental impairment.

The wide variation in the dementia prevalence rate reported by different investigators can be attributed to different methodological factors, such as age limits and surveying and sampling methods. One important factor is the set of criteria used to define dementia, or, more specifically, the set of criteria used to differentiate a pathological disorder of cognitive impairment (or dementia) from what is considered to be the "normal" aging decline of cognitive functioning.

Using the median prevalence rate of 5 percent, it is estimated that in 1970 a minimum of more than one million elderly persons in the United States had significant dementia. The care of these patients is obviously a tremendous burden to families, health professionals, and society as a whole. Assuming no diminution in the prevalence rate, this burden will become heavier as the elderly population continues to increase. It is projected that by the year 2000 the elderly population in the United States will increase 43 percent[42] and patients with dementia will total at least 1.43 million. The problem of caring for these patients is further compounded by two interrelated factors. The first is the scarcity of mental health professionals with a special interest and competence in caring for older people. In 1965, for example, in a survey of more than 16,000 psychiatrists, not one identified geriatric psychiatry as his primary subspeciality.[50] The second factor is the fatalistic attitude that prevails among both families and professionals who provide care for elderly patients with dementia. To a great extent, this attitude can be attributed to our stereotyped views that cognitive decline is inevitable in old age, that decline is due primarily to cerebral pathology, and that since cerebral pathology is irreversible, dementia has a very poor prognosis.

The effect of aging on intellectual function has long been recognized. In fact it is so well recognized that most measures for the assessment of intellectual function are constructed with a correction factor for age. Younger persons are given an age debit; older ones, an age credit. Take, for example, the Wechsler Adult Intelligence Scale (WAIS) — the most widely used psychological measure of intellectual function. A 25-year-old person has to obtain a verbal score of 60 or a performance of 50 in order to be classified as having an I.Q. of 100, the mean value of U.S. population. In contrast, the corresponding values are, respectively, 56 and 37 for a person 60 years old, 44 and 25 for a person over 74 years old. In other words, an average old person is expected to have a verbal ability 7 to 27 percent below and a performance ability 26 to 50 percent below that of an average adult. Wechsler[58] summarized: "Every human capacity after initial growth attains a maximum and then begins to decline. This decline is at first very slow but after a while increases perceptibly. The age at which the maximum is attained varies from ability to ability but seldom occurs beyond 30 and in most cases somewhere in the mid-20's. Once the decline begins, it progresses uninterruptedly. Between the ages of 30 and 60 it is more or less linear."

AGE TREND OF INTELLECTUAL DETERIORATION

There are some questions about the validity and, particularly, the implication of these generalizations concerning the intellectual decline in old age. One common criticism is that these generalizations are derived mainly from cross-sectional studies that probably have exaggerated the pattern of decline in old age.[17] Cross-sectional studies reveal only differences between age groups that could well result from a difference in education and sociocultural background between generations. Using a battery of neuropsychological tests that is independent of education, Halstead[19] has shown that 78 percent of a group of high-level executives, averaging 50 years in age, could perform as well as a group of medical students of much younger ages. Longitudinal studies, on the other hand, can demonstrate more clearly the changes with age, but so far there have been only a few such reports on elderly persons.[3, 17, 23, 39] According to these studies, the intellectual function of healthy elderly persons shows no significant decline over a period of 1 to 3 years. For a longer interval such as 5 to 8 years, the intellectual decline for a group of elderly persons becomes more obvious. Nevertheless, there are considerable individual variations within the group. Birren[3] reported that among 29 healthy elderly persons retested after 5 years, 5 or 17 percent showed slight gain or no change in their WAIS performance. This is confirmed by another longitudinal study.[53] Among 32 community volunteers who had 12 or more years of education and whose good health was maintained for at least 3 to 4 years, 53 percent showed either an increase or no change in their WAIS verbal scores. The corresponding

16

figure for performance was 41 percent. Although the absence of decline on repeated psychological assessment may be attributable in part to a practice or learning effect, these findings nevertheless indicate that intellectual deterioration does not occur in every old person and that it is not a gradual or linear process correlated with age.

From recent findings, particularly those from longitudinal studies, one may conclude that the overall intellectual function of many elderly persons remains unchanged for some time during senescence and then declines more perceptibly, most likely in association with declining health or impending death. This phenomenon, often referred to as "terminal drop," has been extensively reviewed by Siegler.[43]

The intellectual decline in old age usually follows a certain pattern.[6, 24] As a rule, verbal ability, recollection of stored information from the past, and recognition are better preserved than perceptual-integrative ability, recollection of what is recently experienced or learned, and psychomotor skills, especially those involving speed. The memory impairment may result from a disorder of storage rather than a deficit of retrieval.[15] The correlation between age and decline in performance abilities is usually greater than that between age and decline in verbal abilities. Consequently, with advancing age there is also an increasing discrepancy between verbal and performance abilities which has often been used as an indicator of dementia.

ROLE OF THE BRAIN IN DEMENTIA

Why do some old persons become demented and others, though of comparable age, remain intellectually almost intact? If intellectual activities are the behavorial expression of brain activities, a close relationship should be expected to exist between the degree of dementia and the degree of brain impairment. Data so far available in this regard are contradictory, although a review of the literature[55] indicates that more often than not such a relationship can be demonstrated. Thus elderly persons with dementia generally manifest slowing of the electro-encephalogram (EEG); they tend to show a greater reduction in their cerebral oxygen consumption and cerebral blood flow than the elderly whose mental abilities are preserved; and they have more senile plaque formation and more cerebral atrophy at postmortem examination.

EEG studies reveal considerable change with increasing age; even among elderly subjects in apparently good health, EEG abnormalities are common.[52] The characteristic abnormalities of the EEGs of senescent subjects are slowing of the dominant frequency and the appearance of focal defects, particularly over the left anterior temporal region. The slowing of the dominant rhythm is probably a reflection of depression of cerebral metabolism (see below). The significance of the focal defects is unclear, but they are frequent, beginning to appear even in middle age.

EEGs and WAIS scores were obtained on 27 elderly subjects living in the community with two examinations carried out 3.5 years apart.[53] Although there was considerable individual variation, no statistically significant change in verbal or performance scores was demonstrated between the two evaluations, nor was there a significant decrease in the frequency of the occipital alpha rhythm. When the data were evaluated for the individual subjects, however, there was a significant association between slower occipital EEG frequencies and lower verbal and performance scores on the WAIS. Slower frequencies on initial examination were also associated with a greater decline in both verbal and performance scores on the second examination. The frequency and prominence of EEG abnormalities in patients with known dementing illness is well established (see Chapter 10).

Reduction of both cerebral oxygen consumption and cerebral blood flow are common in old persons with or without *apparent* dementia[10, 18, 21, 22, 31, 33, 35, 44, 46, 53] but not in those who are demonstrated to be in excellent mental and physical health.[14] These reductions are, therefore, related not to chronological aging but to brain pathology. In the majority of elderly persons, both reductions reflect a depressed metabolic status of the brain secondary either to primary neuronal degeneration or to brain damage (such as multiple infarctions) caused by disorders outside of the brain tissue. As a rule, the magnitude of these reductions parallels the severity of dementia.[10, 31, 35, 53] It is unclear, however, whether these reductions are greater with primary neuronal degeneration or with multiple infarctions.[18, 22, 33, 44] A correlation between cerebral blood flow and performance ability on WAIS has also been observed in a group of relatively healthy aged persons leading an active life in the community.[53]

The number of senile plaques found in the brain at postmortem examination generally increases with age.[1, 47] Tomlinson, Blessed, and Roth[48] have demonstrated the presence of brain alterations usually seen in senile dementia (senile plaques, Alzheimer's neurofibrillary changes, granulovacuolar degeneration) in the brains of nondemented old people. The mere presence of these changes does not imply the presence of dementia; further studies,[4] however, in which the factor of age was controlled, have demonstrated "a very highly significant association between the average number of plaques in cerebral grey matter and measures of intellectual and personality functioning in old age. . . ." Other studies also confirm the relationship between the degree of brain atrophy (and pathological alterations) and the severity of intellectual and social disintegration.[13, 59]

OUTCOME OF DEMENTIA

Elderly persons with severe dementia have many difficulties leading an independent life in the community; their management in an average family situation likewise is not easy. The result is the large number of elderly persons with dementia admitted for institutional care each year. It is estimated that about 36,000 elderly persons age 65 or over, who had no previous psychiatric hospitalization, were admitted for the first time to a public or private mental hospital during the year of 1966.[51] Dementia accounted for about 78 percent of all these first admissions during that year. As a rule, those patients admitted to a mental hospital who had clinical evidence of dementia or EEG evidence of brain impairment either had a high mortality or required long periods of institutionalization.[54] For example, in a study of a group of elderly patients 2 years after admission, Trier[49] found that 33 percent of those diagnosed as having dementia were still in the hospital and 57 percent had died. Long term hospitalization and death were much higher in this group than in a corresponding group having only psychogenic disorders. Only 9 percent of patients with dementia were discharged from the hospital and could remain in the community at the end of the 2-year period.

In contrast to these generally gloomy predictions, the findings from a longitudinal project at the Duke Center for the Study of Aging and Human Development support the notion that at least some aged persons with dementia can remain in the community and lead a relatively active life. Indicators of brain impairment (EEG abnormalities, cognitive deficits, neurological signs of brain disorder), alone or together, account for only a small proportion of the variance in longevity although they are statistically correlated with longevity.[56] Physical functioning capacity, happiness, and work satisfaction also play an important role in longevity.

Two factors contribute significantly to the poor prognosis or high mortality rate among patients with dementia. First, dementia in aged persons usually has a late onset (except for Alzheimer's disease). Patients who develop such a disorder are therefore expected to have a shorter survival.[54] When the ages of subjects are controlled, the difference in longevity between those with and those without brain impairment becomes less conspicuous.[56] Secondly, patients with significant dementia are frequently institutionalized in public mental hospitals, nursing homes, or personal-care homes. The quality of medical and nursing care in many of these facilities is clearly inadequate and may contribute to the high mortality rate among patients with dementia who also have many other physical illnesses. That inadequacy or lack of care and treatment is a contributing factor to the high mortality rate is strongly supported by a cross-national study between the United States and the United Kingdom.[12] The findings suggest that when elderly patients with affective disorders are labeled as having organic brain syndromes or dementia, they follow a prognostic course with as high a mortality rate as those who really have dementia.

OTHER CONTRIBUTORY OR COMPLICATING FACTORS IN DEMENTIA

The relationship between dementia and brain status has not been consistently observed, and even in those studies demonstrating such a relationship discrepancies still occur in about one-quarter of cases. In Corsellis'[13] study, 20 percent of patients diagnosed as having senile psychosis showed no or little senile plaque formation on postmortem histopathological examination, while moderate to severe senile plaque formation was present in 9 percent of patients having so-called functional psychosis. Discrepancies between senile plaque frequency and intellectual and social deterioration have also been observed by Blessed, Tomlinson, and Roth.[4] Willanger and coworkers[59] did not find significant evidence of dementia in 22 percent of their subjects showing marked cerebral atrophy on pneumoencephalography. Although they encountered no patient with severe intellectual impairment without cerebral atrophy, the degree of atrophy was sometimes much less than would be anticipated from the results of psychological testing. Obrist and Henry[36] also noted that about one-third of their patients diagnosed as having presenile or senile dementia had a cerebral blood flow within the normal range of healthy young adults. It is not uncommon for demented patients to have normal EEGs while psychologically well-preserved patients may have gross EEG abnormalities.[8, 36]

The reliability and sensitivity of the methods employed in these studies unquestionably account for some of the discrepancies observed. It is well known that intellectual function and particularly its assessment, by clinical examination or by psychological test, are susceptible to the influence of many factors.[6] Few studies on dementia have paid attention to the sociocultural background of the subjects, although these sociocultural factors are known to influence intellectual function as well as certain brain variables such as the EEG.[52] Considerable evidence indicates that many somatic, psychological, and social factors participate in the development, manifestation, and outcome of dementia.

Somatic Factors

About three of every four persons 65 years old or over have at least one disabling chronic condition. Furthermore, each illness, once developed, usually lasts longer in elderly persons than in young adults.[11] There is also a close relationship between dementia and physical illness.[25, 28, 45] Many diseases commonly associated with senescence are known to affect the brain adversely.[20, 26] Elderly persons with cardiovascular disease, lung disease, or severe hypertension, for example, have a high incidence of EEG abnormality,[34, 57] and many of them show a great decline in intellectual function.[16, 57] Physical illness can directly impair brain tissue on which the intellectual activities depend. Willanger and his coworkers[59] noted that, with a given degree of cerebral atrophy, older persons showed greater intellectual impairment than younger ones. This finding suggests that the compensatory capacity of the remaining uninvolved brain tissue may be different in the two groups, a difference possibly attributable to a difference in physical health. Social inactivity or isolation, a common sequel to most chronic illnesses, frequently leads to psychological regression and depression, which contribute to and complicate the intellectual deterioration in old age.

Psychological Factors

Among the many psychological factors that are believed to bear on the intellectual deterioration of senescence, premorbid personality and depression are perhaps the two most important.

Premorbid Personality

In discussing his negative result on the relationship between clinical manifestations and pathological findings of the brain, Rothschild[41] considered the discrepancy between these two variables to be the result of a difference in mental compensatory mechanism. Kiev and his coworkers[30] found that patients who demonstrated a high order of adaptive versatility before their illness had less intellectual impairment in relation to loss of brain tissue than those who had for some time exhibited difficulties in overall adaptation with much anxiety. This is consistent with the observation that there seems to be a positive association between compulsive traits and dementia.[32] A compulsive person generally has a high expectation of himself and a strong need to control his relationship with others and with his environment. He generally reacts with excessive anxiety when his ability to control is threatened or jeopardized, as by a decline in his memory or other intellectual functions.

Anxiety of varying severity occurs in most elderly persons when they first become aware of their intellectual impairment. When under stress, these elderly persons may show the same type of psychic responses as do younger patients with brain damage.[27] Some may try to deny the defect; others avoid facing tasks or situations that provoke anxiety, or seek a substitute task or situation with which they believe they can cope; yet others become more rigid and compulsively orderly.

20

The mechanisms preferred by each individual are frequently those most familiar to the individual and hence usually related closely to his premorbid personality.

When an aged person fails to relieve or alleviate the anxiety arising from interactions with his environment he tends to give up or avoid anxiety-provoking activities. Occasionally an aged person may become very aggressive in an attempt to control or manipulate his environment. This approach, however, frequently leads to his further alienation. As the elderly individual becomes more and more withdrawn or disengaged from society, the opportunity for his emotional needs to be gratified also gradually and increasingly diminishes. Under such emotional deprivation, especially if prolonged, many elderly become preoccupied with suspicions, imaginations, or fantasies, while others act out their needs impulsively or in a perverted manner. The ultimate outcome is either severe depression or disintegration of the personality with the emergence of psychotic symptoms such as delusions and hallucinations. This explains why the clinical manifestation of dementia sometimes can be severe in the presence of only mild to moderate structural brain impairment. These psychiatric disorders may also aggravate the already declining physical health and hence lead to a vicious cycle of progressive deterioration.

Depression

Depression is common among the aged, the most common underlying psychogenic factor being a lowering of self-esteem. It may result from declining health; from social isolation and lack of emotional gratification; or from loss of prestige, social position, and economic status following involuntary retirement. The emphasis on the value of productiveness and the general attitude toward old persons in our society undoubtedly add further insult to the already lowered self-esteem of old persons.

The differential diagnosis between affective disorder and dementia has long been emphasized because the former generally is more amenable to treatment. Nonetheless, depression in senescence is frequently overlooked, largely because it does not always follow the same clinical picture as depression in younger patients. In the depression of later life, the manifestations of depressive mood such as sad or guilty feelings, self-deprecatory thoughts, and crying spells are frequently inconspicuous, while psychomotor retardation, impairment of attention and memory, somatic symptoms, and loss of libido and initiative are more prominent. Many of these manifestations can easily be mistakenly attributed to an organic origin. Occasionally, the psychomotor retardation and regression are so severe that of themselves they may simulate dementia. More often, however, dementia and depression occur simultaneously in the same individual. The differentiation of the two components is difficult, if not impossible, and at times only a therapeutic trial with antidepressant or electroconvulsive treatment clarifies the situation. With treatment a patient may improve enough to make a reasonably good adjustment in the community in spite of the persistence of dementia or brain impairment.

Social Factors

Mental disorders in aged persons, like those in the general population, relate to many social factors. It is unclear, however, how directly these factors contribute to the development of dementia in old age since many are likely the outcome rather than the cause. They are important, nonetheless, since their presence often complicates and aggravates the clinical picture or the natural course of dementia, and some of them are readily prevented or corrected.

Social factors or conditions that have been considered as significantly associated with mental disorders of old age include: sex, cultural background, marital status, education, employment, income, family organization, living arrangements, condition and location of dwelling, type of household, and social outlets.[7, 40] The common denominator for most of these social variables is the socioeconomic status of the elderly. For almost all elderly, aging means, sooner or later, loss of employment, spouse, relatives, and friends as well as decline in physical health, mental ability, income, prestige, and standard of living. All these may lead to a lowering of self-esteem and morale. Old persons of low socioeconomic status have more physical illness than those with high status. This is, to a great extent, the outcome of inadequate housing, nutrition, and medical care—all commonly associated with poverty. The elderly individual of low socioeconomic status has less contact with relatives or friends and is less active in various social or organizational activities than elderly individuals of high socioeconomic status. Kay and associates reported that poverty and isolation played a contributory role in mental deterioration.[28] Their findings, however, were not confirmed by another study.[45] The latter study suggested that isolation may be a consequence rather than a cause of most organic mental illness in old age. A study of a group of community volunteers by Busse and Wang[9] revealed that dementia in the elderly is related to the type and amount of activities rather than to social contacts. Inactivity, particularly of intellectual function, is one common characteristic of old age. It may be dependent on the individual's preexisting personality or socioeconomic or educational background, or it may be secondary to physical illness, emotional disorders, or institutionalization. The last two factors—emotional disorders and institutionalization—are probably of the greatest clinical significance, since they are often amenable to treatment or prevention. The outcome of social isolation and inactivity regardless of their origin is usually emotional deprivation and an increase in the decline of physical health and self-esteem.

Another important factor is environmental stress. The ability of an individual to cope with such stress is usually reduced in old age, particularly when there is significant psychomotor retardation and impairment of memory. Because of their difficulties in understanding and remembering new experiences, elderly persons are extremely sensitive to change in their environment. Not infrequently a minor change in the household or in family relationships may precipitate a severe psychological reaction.

DEMENTIA AS A SOCIOPSYCHOSOMATIC DISORDER

Old age is associated with many changes. There is usually a decline in physical health and such intellectual abilities as memory, learning, and perception. There is very often also a loss of prestige, income, and social status. How well a person can adjust in his old age in a given environment depends to a great extent on how successfully he can cope with these changes as well as with various stresses from his environment.

The intellectual deterioration commonly seen among aged persons undoubtedly is closely related to the structural and functional impairment of the brain, which

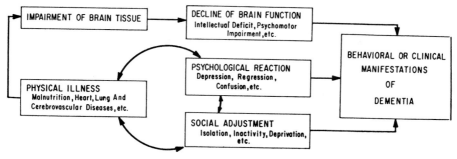

Figure 1

may or may not be recognized by the clinical and laboratory methods currently available. With a given brain impairment some individuals follow a pattern of simple and gradual intellectual deterioration and are without any significant complication. They are able to maintain a relatively active life and make a reasonably good adjustment in the community. In contrast, many others deteriorate rapidly and present a variety of complications—depression, regression, agitation, paranoid symptoms. The differences between these two groups are very likely the result of the differences in their physical health, socioeconomic status, environment, and personality—that is, their emotional needs, self-expectations, and defense mechanisms.

Dementia as a clinical syndrome can therefore be viewed as a sociopsychosomatic disorder (Fig. 1). Although brain impairment is the obligatory factor in most, if not all, cases of intellectual deterioration, many sociopsychological factors also play an important contributory or complicating role. These sociopsychological factors may aggravate the behavioral manifestations of intellectual deterioration. They may also accelerate the decline of physical health, which, in turn, may affect the brain as well as the sociopsychological condition of the individual. Frequently, all these factors interact with each other and form a vicious cycle that leads to further deterioration. Since little can be done about brain tissue that has lost its functional capacity, the interaction of these social, psychological, and somatic factors often becomes the most important determinant of the course and outcome of patients with dementia. Early recognition and correction of these factors may help prevent the development of complications and slow the progression of deterioration.

REFERENCES

1. ARAB, A.: *Plaques séniles et artériosclerose cérébrale.* Rev. Neurol. 91:22, 1954.

2. BERGMANN, K.: *The epidemiology of senile dementia.* Br. J. Psychiatry (Spec. Publ.) 9:100, 1975.

3. BIRREN, J. E.: Increments and decrements in the intellectual status of the aged, in Simon, A., and Epstein, L. J. (eds.): *Aging in Modern Society: Psychiatric Research Report 23.* American Psychiatric Association, Washington, D.C., 1968, p. 207.

4. BLESSED, G., TOMLINSON, B. E., AND ROTH, M.: *The association between quantitative measures of dementia and of senile change in the cerebral grey matter of elderly subjects.* Br. J. Psychiatry 114:797, 1968.

5. BOLLERUP, T. R.: *Prevalence of mental illness among 70-year-olds domiciled in nine Copenhagen suburbs.* Acta Psychiatr. Scand. 51:327, 1975.

6. BOTWINICK, J.: *Cognitive Processes in Maturity and Old Age.* Springer Publishing Co., Inc., New York, 1967.

7. BUSSE, E. W.: Brain syndromes associated with disturbances in metabolism, growth, and nutrition, in Freedman, A. M., and Kaplan, H. I. (eds.): *Comprehensive Textbook of Psychiatry*. The Williams & Wilkins Co., Baltimore, 1967, p. 726.

8. BUSSE, E. W., AND WANG, H. S.: *The value of electroencephalography in geriatrics*, Geriatrics 20:906, 1965.

9. BUSSE, E. W., AND WANG, H. S.: The multiple factors contributing to dementia in old age, in *Excerpta Medica International Congress* Series No. 274. Excerpta Medica, Amsterdam, 1974, p. 818.

10. BUTLER, R. N.; DASTUR, D. K.; AND PERLIN, S.: *Relationship of senile manifestations and chronic brain syndromes to cerebral circulation and metabolism*. J. Psychiat. Res. 3:229, 1965.

11. CONFREY, E. A., AND GOLDSTEIN, M. S.: The health status of aging people, in Tibbitts, C. (ed.): *Handbook of Social Gerontology*. University of Chicago Press, Chicago, 1960, p. 165.

12. COPELAND, J. R. M.; KELLEHER, M. J.; KELLETT, J. M.; GOURLAY, A. J.; COWAN, D. W.; BARRON, G.; AND DE GRUCHY, J.: *Cross-national study of diagnosis of the mental disorders — a comparison of the diagnoses of elderly psychiatric patients admitted to mental hospitals serving Queens County, New York and the former Borough of Camberwell, London*. Br. J. Psychiatry 126:11, 1975.

13. CORSELLIS, J. A. N.: *Mental Illness and the Ageing Brain*. Oxford University Press, London, 1962.

14. DASTUR, D. K.; LANE, M. H.; HANSEN, D. B.; KETY, S. S.; PERLIN, S.; BUTLER, R. N.; AND SOKOLOFF, L.: Effects of aging on cerebral circulation and metabolism in man, in Birren, J. E.; Butler, R. N.; Greenhouse, S. W.; Sokoloff, L.; and Yarrow, M. R. (eds): *Human Aging: A Biological Behavioral Study*. U.S. Government Printing Office, Washington, D.C., 1963, p. 59.

15. DRACHMAN, D. A., AND LEAVITT, J.: *Memory impairment in the aged, storage versus retrieval deficit*. J. Exp. Psychol. 93:302, 1972.

16. EISDORFER, C.: *Psychologic reaction to cardiovascular change in the aged*. Mayo Clin. Proc. 42:620, 1967.

17. EISDORFER, C.: *The WAIS performance of the aged: A retest evaluation*. J. Gerontol. 18:169, 1963.

18. HACHINSKI, V. C.; ILIFF, L. D.; ZIHKA, E.; DU BOULAY, G. H.; MCALLISTER, V. L.; MARSHALL, J.; RUSSELL, R.; AND SYMON, L.: *Cerebral blood flow in dementia*. Arch. Neurol. 32:632, 1975.

19. HALSTEAD, W. C.: Biological intelligence and differential aging, in Weber, I. L. (ed.): *Aging: A Current Appraisal*. University of Florida Press, Gainesville, 1956, p. 63.

20. HARRIS, R.: The relationship between organic brain disease and physical status, in Gaitz, C. M. (ed): *Aging and the Brain*. Plenum Press, New York, 1972, p. 163.

21. HEDLUND, S.; KOHLER, V.; NYLIN, G.; OLSSON, R.; REGNSTROM, O.; ROTHSTROM, E.; AND ASTROM, K. E.: *Cerebral blood circulation in dementia*. Acta Psychiatr. Scand. 40:77, 1964.

22. INGVAR, D. H., AND GUSTAFSON, L.: *Regional cerebral blood flow in organic dementia with early onset*. Acta Neurol. Scand. (Suppl.) 43, 46:42, 1970.

23. JARVIK, L. F.; KALLMAN, F. J.; AND FALEK, A.: *Intellectual changes in aged twins*. J. Gerontol. 17:289, 1962.

24. JARVIK, L. F.; EISDORFER, C.; AND BLUM, J. E. (eds): *Intellectual Functioning in Adults*. Springer Publ. Co., Inc., New York, 1973.

25. KAHN, R. L.; POLLACK, M.; GOLDFARB, A. I.: Factors related to individual differences in mental status of institutionalized aged, in Hoch, P. H., and Zubin, J. (eds.): *Psychopathology of Aging*. Grune and Stratton, New York, 1961, p.104.

26. KARP, H. R.: *Dementia in cerebrovascular disease and other systemic illness*. Curr. Concepts of Cerebrovascular Dis. vii:11, 1972.

27. KATZ, L.; NEAL, M. W.; AND SIMON, A.: Observations on psychic mechanisms in organic psychoses of the aged, in Hock, P. H., and Zubin, J. (eds.): *Psychopathology of Aging*. Grune & Stratton, Inc., New York, 1961, p.160.

28. KAY, D. W. K.; BEAMISH, P.; AND ROTH, M.: *Old age mental disorders in Newcastle upon Tyne, Part II: A study of possible social and medical causes*. Br. J. Psychiatry 110:668, 1964.

29. KAY, D. W. K.: Epidemiological aspects of organic brain disease in the aged, in Gaitz, C. M. (ed): *Aging and the Brain*. Plenum Press, New York, 1972, p.15.

24

30. KIEV, A.; CHAPMAN, L. F.; GUTHRIE, T. C., AND WOLFF, H. G.: The highest integrative functions and diffuse cerebral atrophy. Neurology (Minneap.) 12:385, 1962.

31. LASSEN, N. A.; MUNCK, O.; AND TOTEY, E. R.: *Mental function and cerebral oxygen consumption in organic dementia.* Arch. Neurol., 77:126, 1957.

32. OAKLEY, D. P.: *Senile dementia, some aetiological factors.* Br. J. Psychiatry 111:414, 1965.

33. O'BRIEN, M. D., AND MALLETT, B.: *Cerebral cortex perfusion rates in dementia.* J. Neurol. Neurosurg. Psychiatry 33:497, 1970.

34. OBRIST, W. D., AND BISSELL, L. F.: *The electroencephalogram of aged patients with cardiac and cerebral vascular disease.* J. Gerontol. 10:315, 1955.

35. OBRIST, W. D.; CHIVIAN, E.; CRONQVIST, S.; AND INGVAR, D. H.: *Regional cerebral blood flow in senile and presenile dementia.* Neurology (Minneap.) 20:315, 1970.

36. OBRIST, W. D.; AND HENRY, C. E.: *Electroencephalographic findings in aged psychiatric patients.* J. Nerv. Ment. Dis. 126:254, 1958.

37. PEARCE, J., AND MILLER, E.: *Clinical Aspects of Dementia.* The Williams & Wilkins Co., Baltimore, 1973.

38. PFEIFFER, E.: *A short portable mental status questionnaire for the assessment of organic brain deficit in elderly patients.* J. Am. Geriatr. Soc. 23:433, 1975.

39. PIERCE, R. C.; AND BERKMAN, P. L.: Change in intellectual functioning, in Lowenthal, M. F.; Berkman, P. L.; and associates (eds.): *Aging and Mental Disorder in San Francisco.* Jossey-Bass, Inc., Publishers, San Francisco, 1967, p.177.

40. RILEY, M. W., AND FONER, A.: *Aging and Society. I. An Inventory of Research Findings.* Russell Sage Foundation, New York, 1968.

41. ROTHSCHILD, D.: *Pathologic changes in senile psychoses and their psychobiologic significance.* Am. J. Psychiatry 93:757, 1937.

42. SIEGEL, J. S.: Some demographic aspects of aging in the United States, in Ostfeld, A. M., and Gibson, D. C. (eds.): *Epidemiology of Aging.* U. S. Government Printing Office, Washington, D. C., 1975, p.17.

43. SIEGLER, I. C.: *The terminal drop hypothesis, fact or artifact.* Exp. Aging Res. 1:169, 1975.

44. SIMARD, D.; OLESEN, J.; PAULSON, O. B.; LASSEN, N. A.; AND SKINHOJ, E.: *Regional cerebral blood flow and its regulation in dementia.* Brain 94:273, 1971.

45. SIMON, A.; LOWENTHAL, M. F.; AND EPSTEIN, L.: *Crisis and Intervention.* Jossey-Bass, Inc., San Francisco, 1970.

46. SOKOLOFF, L.: Circulation and metabolism of brain in relation to the process of aging, in Birren, J. E.; Imus, H. A.; and Windle, W. F. (eds.): *The Process of Aging in the Nervous System.* Charles C Thomas, Publisher, Springfield, Ill., 1959, p. 113.

47. TOMLINSON, B. E.: Personal communication, 1966. Quoted in Blessed, Tomlinson, and Roth. See 4, above.

48. TOMLINSON, B. E.: Blessed, G.; and Roth, M.: *Observations on the brain of non-demented old people.* J. Neurol. Sci. 7:331, 1968.

49. TRIER, T. R.: *Characteristics of mentally ill aged: A comparison of patients with psychogenic disorders and patients with organic brain syndromes.* J. Gerontol. 21:354, 1966.

50. U. S. NATIONAL INSTITUTE OF MENTAL HEALTH: *The Nation's Psychiatrists.* U. S. Government Printing Office, Washington, D. C., 1969.

51. WANG, H. S.: Organic brain syndromes, in Busse, E. W., and Pfeiffer, E. (eds.): *Behavior and Adaptation in Late Life.* Little, Brown, and Company, Boston, 1969, p.263.

52. WANG, H. S., AND BUSSE, E. W.: *EEG of healthy old persons, a longitudinal study. I. Dominant background activity and occipital rhythm.* J. Gerontol. 24:419, 1969.

53. WANG, H. S.; OBRIST, W. D.; AND BUSSE, E. W.: *Neurophysiological correlates of the intellectual function of elderly persons living in the community.* Am. J. Psychiatry 126:1205, 1970.

54. WANG, H. S., AND WHANGER, A.: Brain impairment and Longevity, in Palmore, E., and Jeffers, F. (eds.): *Prediction of Life Span-Recent Findings.* D. C. Heath Co., Lexington, Mass., 1971, p.95.

55. WANG, H. S.: Cerebral correlates of intellectual function in senescence, in Jarvik, L. F.; Eisdorfer, C.; and Blum, J. E. (eds.): *Intellectual Functioning in Adults.* Springer Publ. Co., Inc., New York, 1973, p.95.

56. WANG, H. S., AND BUSSE, E. W.: Brain impairment and longevity in community aged persons, in Palmore, E. (ed): *Normal Aging II*. Duke University Press, Durham, 1974, p.263.

57. WANG, H. S., AND BUSSE, E. W.: Heart disease and brain impairment among aged persons, in Palmore, E. (ed): *Normal Aging II*. Duke University Press, 1974, p.160.

58. WECHSLER, D.: *The Measurement and Appraisal of Adult Intelligence,* ed. 4. The Williams & Wilkins Co., Baltimore, 1958.

59. WILLANGER, R.; THYGESEN, P.; NIELSEN, R.; AND PETERSEN, O.: *Intellectual impairment and cerebral atrophy — a psychological, neurological and radiological investigation.* Dan. Med. Bull. 15:65, 1968.

CHAPTER 3

Diseases Presenting as Dementia

Gunter R. Haase, M.D.

INTRODUCTION

Progressive reduction of intellectual function accompanies many diseases. Dementia is the chief clinical feature in some disorders, while in others it may be only a part of the constellation of signs indicating disease of the nervous system or other organs. Differently expressed, dementia may result from degenerative processes primarily involving the brain parenchyma, or it may result from neoplastic or infectious processes affecting the central nervous system, from alterations in intracranial pressure relationships, from reduction of the supply of oxygen or other nutrients to the nervous system, from trauma, or from exogenous or endogenous substances. The clinical form of the emerging dementia will only rarely permit a diagnostic conclusion concerning the causative factors, and a detailed inquiry regarding the patient's personal, family, and medical history is mandatory as well as the assistance of various laboratory studies. Care must be taken not to overlook psychological factors, since severe depression is at times difficult to differentiate from true dementia.[174]

Despite assiduous investigation, a definite diagnosis can be reached only in about half of all demented patients.[174] Even pathological study does not always permit a definite identification of the condition as one of the entities within the classification presently accepted.[133] The purpose of all diagnostic inquiry is to identify the approximately 10 to 15 percent of patients with dementia in whom the disease process may be reversed or halted by appropriate treatment.[174]

In the following discussion, only those conditions producing dementia in adults will be considered (Table 1).

Table 1. Diseases causing dementia

Diffuse Parenchymatous Diseases of the Central Nervous System
  So-called presenile dementias
    Alzheimer's disease
    Pick's disease
    Kraepelin's disease
    Parkinsonism-dementia complex of Guam
    Huntington's chorea
  Senile dementia
  Other degenerative diseases
    Hallervorden-Spatz disease

Table 1. Diseases causing dementia *(Continued)*

    Spinocerebellar degenerations
    Progressive myoclonus epilepsy
    Progressive supranuclear palsy
    Parkinson's disease

Metabolic Disorders
  Myxedema
  Disorders of the parathyroid glands
  Wilson's disease
  Liver disease
  Hypoglycemia
  Remote effects of carcinoma
  Cushing's syndrome
  Hypopituitarism
  Uremia
  Dialysis dementia
  Metachromatic leukodystrophy

Vascular Disorders
  Arteriosclerosis
  Inflammatory disease of blood vessels
    Disseminated lupus erythematosus
    Thromboangiitis obliterans
  Aortic arch syndrome
  Binswanger's disease
  Arteriovenous malformations

Hypoxia and Anoxia

Normal Pressure Hydrocephalus

Deficiency Diseases
  Wernicke-Korsakoff syndrome
  Pellagra
  Marchiafava-Bignami disease
  Vitamin B_{12} and folate deficiency

Toxins and Drugs
  Metals
  Organic compounds
  Carbon monoxide
  Drugs

Brain Tumors

Trauma
  Open and closed head injuries
  Punch-drunk syndrome
  Subdural hematoma
  Heat stroke

Infections
  Brain abscess
  Bacterial meningitis
  Fungal meningitis
  Encephalitis
  Subacute sclerosing panencephalitis
  Progressive multifocal leukoencephalopathy
  Creutzfeldt-Jakob disease
  Kuru
  Behçet's syndrome
  Lues

Other Diseases
  Multiple sclerosis
  Muscular dystrophy
  Whipple's disease
  Concentration-camp syndrome
  Kufs' disease
  Familial calcification of basal ganglia

DIFFUSE PARENCHYMATOUS DISEASES
OF THE CENTRAL NERVOUS SYSTEM

So-called Presenile Dementias

Alzheimer's Disease and Pick's Disease

Alzheimer's disease and Pick's disease, while pathologically distinct, resemble each other so closely in their clinical manifestations that their discussion under a common heading appears justified. Criteria to separate these diseases on clinical grounds[245, 248, 260, 311] are not universally accepted, and the possibility of a separation on the basis of clinical or neuroradiological features is denied or described as extremely difficult by some writers on the subject.[12, 183, 196]

Both diseases usually begin between the ages of 45 and 60. Instances with onset in early adult life have been recorded, and at the upper age range the delimitation from so-called senile dementia is blurred. Patients with Down's syndrome appear to have a high incidence of Alzheimer's disease, particularly those surviving beyond age 40.[74]

The preceding history, both with regard to physical and emotional health, is usually unremarkable in the persons afflicted. The sexes are approximately equally affected, although in some reports females are said to be more susceptible to both disorders.[104, 182, 292] Familial occurrence has been described in both diseases. In a few families with Alzheimer's disease, inheritance as a dominant trait has been suggested,[78, 124, 220] while in other instances a multi-factorial inheritance has been considered more likely.[248] The disease has been observed to occur in only one of monozygotic twins. In Pick's disease, familial instances suggest a dominant autosomal mode of inheritance.[220, 248]

The incidence of Alzheimer's disease reported in most studies is considerably greater than that of Pick's disease, although in Sjögren's study,[248] both occurred with the same frequency.

While loss of intellectual functions is the hallmark of both disorders, the initial symptoms may suggest a psychogenic illness by such features as anxiety, depression, restlessness, or sleep disorder, or, less commonly, by hallucinations, particularly of a visual nature. Pronounced jealousy was the first evidence of the disease in Alzheimer's original patient,[14] and paranoid traits have been prominent in other instances. Disturbances of memory may soon follow these initial deviations or may be the first manifestation of disorder. In either case, impairment of intellectual function soon dominates the clinical picture and may be accompanied by loss of spontaneity and indolence or by purposeless overactivity. Facetiousness ("moria") is seen frequently, as is a disturbance in the formation of moral and ethical judgments. The patients commit professional and social indiscretions; they may prove themselves incapable of handling their business and financial affairs and may run afoul of the law. Their insight is impaired, and their foresight untempered by reality.

The evolution of both disorders is marked by the steadily progressing attrition of mental capacities. While in the early stages, the gravest defect concerns memory, particularly of recent events, eventually all intellectual functions will be affected. The rate of progression varies considerably; some patients reach social incapacity in a few months, while in others this stage may be reached only after several years.

As intellectual deterioration progresses, focal manifestations of neurological disease will frequently supervene. Disorientation in space may result in the patient's becoming lost in familiar surroundings, even in his own home. Disorders of symbol utilization, such as dysphasia, dyslexia, dysgraphia, and dyspraxia, are common though not usually isolated phenomena and may be coupled with repetitive utterances (logoclonia) or repetitive actions. Other focal signs, such as convulsions or central facial paralysis, are common enough to be considered part of the clinical picture, while evidence of a disorder of the upper motor neuron type is usually, but not always,[124] lacking. Various parts of the Klüver-Bucy syndrome are frequently observed.

As the disorder develops, there may be occasional bursts of excitement, but the characteristic course is one of increasing apathy and indolence. The patients show severe dementia, failure to comprehend and communicate with their environment, and eventually incontinence. Forced grasping and groping, suck and snout reflexes, if not present since earlier stages of the disease, appear. Some patients show voracious hunger, in spite of which physical emaciation will progress. Death usually occurs from 5 to 10 years after the diagnosis of the disease, and respiratory infections are the most common cause of death.

As these two disorders have been described thus far, no notice has been taken of the alleged differences between Alzheimer's and Pick's disease. There is an extensive body of literature dealing with semiological characteristics of either disorder. Many of these claims are based on small series of cases and have been subsequently disputed by other writers. Other claims are of a statistical nature, asserting, for instance, that convulsions occur more often in Alzheimer's disease, or that localizing signs are "not very evident" in Alzheimer's disease and "more evident" in Pick's disease.[311]

The clinician confronted with a patient with dementia in middle life will not receive much assistance from such indicators. Perhaps more serious consideration must be given to the claim[248] that patients with Alzheimer's disease will, either early or in the later stages of their illness, show a "rigidity of extrapyramidal type" with cogwheel phenomenon. Coupled with this is said to be a syndrome of "direct forward staring." This syndrome, observed in one series [248] in 14 of 23 patients with Alzheimer's disease, consists of a failure to move the eyes in either plane ("the gaze is as if it were locked in a fixed forward stare"). Spatial disorientation may be one of the chief symptoms of Alzheimer's disease.[69]

The increase in muscle tone, referred to above, was found in one study in 14 of 18 patients with Alzheimer's disease[248] and was not accompanied by tremor. Myoclonic jerks have, however, been encountered in some cases.[78, 124] Sjögren[248] observed the frequent occurrence of a disorder of gait in patients with Alzheimer's disease. He described the difficulty experienced by patients in earlier stages of this disease as one in "realizing the rhythm and coordinating of the movements necessary for normal gait . . . the gait is slow, unsteady, clumsy, but without pulsion phenomenon." Sjögren, Sjögren, and Lindgren[248] believed the disturbance resembled apraxia of gait, and suggested that this disorder of gait may be ascribed to lesions in the prefrontal regions. At a later time in the evolution of the disorder, some patients may demonstrate "marche à petits pas."

The disturbance of gait observed in patients with Alzheimer's disease was not seen in any of the patients with Pick's disease. The incidence of changes of muscular tone was also significantly greater in the group of patients with Alzheimer's disease than in that with Pick's disease, being present in 14 patients with Alzheimer's disease and in 1 case with Pick's disease.

The occurrence of convulsive seizures has been deemed another feature enabling the clinician to differentiate Alzheimer's disease from Pick's disease. In Sögren's study, convulsions occurred in 4 out of 18 patients with histologically proved Alzheimer's disease and in 1 of 18 patients with histologically proved Pick's disease. Sourander[252] reported epileptic seizures in 75 percent of 68 histopathologically verified cases of Alzheimer's disease. In 44 percent of the cases with seizures, they were characterized as generalized (grand mal) and in 64 percent as minor spells such as "drop fits—hypokinetic fits" and masticatory seizures, with rhythmic chewing, smacking, or lip smacking associated with loss of consciousness.

A number of other features asserted to be of distinguishing value, such as the presence or absence of motor excitement or apathy, occurred with sufficient frequency in both groups to put their differential-diagnostic value into question.

In summary, it is very difficult to attempt a differentiation of Alzheimer's disease from Pick's disease on clinical grounds alone. At present, judgment must be reserved about the significance given the presence of extrapyramidal features and the gait disturbance described above in the diagnosis of Alzheimer's disease.

The EEG does not show specific abnormalities relating to the subgroups of dementia, but the incidence of abnormalities is reported to be greater and more consistent in Alzheimer's disease than in any of the other entities.[106, 157, 159] Absence or reduction of alpha activity is particularly striking in patients with Alzheimer's disease and may progress to the emergence of patterns in the theta and delta range, at times occurring in bursts. In Pick's disease, the EEG may be normal.[106, 273] The degree of EEG abnormality does not appear to be related to the degree of cerebral atrophy or the duration of the illness. It has been asserted that in Alzheimer's disease the severe degrees of EEG abnormality tend to be correlated with severe degrees of dementia.[106]

The cerebrospinal fluid in both conditions is usually normal.

Pneumoencephalographic investigation will usually demonstrate cerebral atrophy by increase in the width of the sulcal markings and by ventricular enlargement, particularly of the anterior and temporal horns, but will not assist in the differential diagnosis between Pick's and Alzheimer's disease. Similar information can now be gained with greater ease by computerized axial tomography.

Other laboratory studies are of little value in differential diagnosis, except for their use in excluding other diseases, such as syphilis of the central nervous system.

It is sometimes possible to establish the diagnosis during life by cortical biopsy.[108] More commonly, autopsy findings provide the conclusive evidence. In both disorders, specific pathological changes are restricted to the brain and will impress, on gross inspection, by the evidence of cortical atrophy, combined with ventricular enlargement. The brain weight is reduced, often below 1000 gm. In Alzheimer's disease, the atrophy is diffuse over the cortical mantle but most striking in the frontal and occipital lobes. In Pick's disease, the atrophy is most impressive in the frontal and temporal lobes. In the temporal lobes, the atrophy usually involves the middle and inferior temporal gyri, and characteristically, the superior temporal gyrus is involved only in its anterior third. The subcortical white matter participates in the shrinkage of the affected areas and this has led to the term *lobar sclerosis*. Subcortical gray structures may also participate in the atrophy.[182, 312] An increase in frequency of the haptoglobin Hpl in patients with Alzheimer's disease has been observed[204] and has been interpreted as indicating a decreased efficiency in immune responsiveness. Studies on the spinal fluid of patients with Alzheimer's disease have shown an impaired metabolism of dopamine and 5-hydroxytrypta-mine, as well as increases of lactate and lactate/pyruvate ratio, indicating the possibility of cellular hypoxia in this disease.[107]

Histologically, Alzheimer's disease is characterized by neurofibrillary degenerative changes in the neurons and by the presence of argyrophilic plaques, primarily in the cerebral cortex and less consistently in the basal ganglia. These findings are accompanied by a loss of nerve cells. In Pick's disease, the prominent histological abnormality is a cell loss in the affected areas, associated with extensive gliosis. The cell loss is most impressive in the outer layers of the cortex. The remaining nerve cells may show swelling and argyrophilic inclusions ("Pick cells").[313] Cases showing histological features of both Alzheimer's and Pick's disease have been described.[27]

Electron microscopic studies[150, 166, 274, 280] have shown the neurofibrillary alteration to consist of hollow fibrils which displace the normal organelles of the cells. The plaques have a core of amyloid fibrils surrounded by abnormal dendrites and axons.

Kraepelin's Disease

Another form of dementia, characterized by catatonia, was described by Kraepelin in 1910. McMenemey[182] states that 17 cases have been reported. Other features included anxiety, depression, restlessness, and speech defects. The usual duration of the illness was 1 to 2 years. Pathological changes included destruction of the Nissl substance in the neurons, particularly in the frontal and central areas and in Ammon's horn, and eventual loss of ganglion cells. Schaumburg and Suzuki,[238] describing a form of presenile dementia in six members of a family, observed pathological changes similar to those described in Kraepelin's disease, including atrophy of all lobes of the brain, with diffuse loss of neurons in all layers, only slight glial proliferation, and diffuse demyelination in the white matter. No specific changes, such as neurofibrillary degeneration or senile plaques, were observed. Schaumburg and Suzuki[238] felt that in the majority of cases reported as Kraepelin's disease, other plausible causes could explain the pathological changes, and they agreed with McMenemey[182] that the existence of Kraepelin's disease as a pathological entity is doubtful. Disregarding arguments about nomenclature, their paper brings to attention other, nonspecific types of dementia in adult life. The pedigree presented by Schaumburg and Suzuki suggests a dominant pattern of inheritance.

Parkinsonism-Dementia Complex of Guam

Among the indigenous Chamorro population of Guam and neighboring islands, a high incidence of neurological disease has been found.[72, 73, 127, 128, 129, 223] While a syndrome resembling amyotrophic lateral sclerosis (ALS) is the most common neurological illness, accounting for approximately 10 percent of all deaths in Guam, frequent instances were observed of a disorder combining progressive dementia with features of Parkinson's disease and at times with features of amyotrophic lateral sclerosis.[127, 128] Subsequent studies suggest that in the Mariana and Caroline Islands persons of ethnic background other than the Chamorros may also fall victim to this disorder.[72]

A reevaluation of these disorders in 1966[72] concerned 176 patients, of whom

32

104 presented clinically as ALS, while 72 presented with the parkinsonism-dementia complex. Half of 22 additional patients, initially observed to be suffering from Parkinson's disease without dementia, developed features of dementia within a year of onset of the illness.

Those individuals presenting with ALS were usually between 40 and 50 years old (range of 20 to 67 years), while the patients first afflicted with the parkinsonism-dementia complex were usually in their 50's. Of the 104 ALS patients, 5 developed the parkinsonism-dementia syndrome (on the average 5 years after onset of the ALS): 5 patients developed Parkinson's disease without dementia; and 2 patients, an "organic mental syndrome" without parkinsonian features. Of the original 72 parkinsonism-dementia patients, 27 developed ALS.

The presenting signs of the dementia were usually memory deficits and disorientation for time, place, and person, associated with or followed by changes in personality or behavior patterns, which progressed to increasing confusion and apathy. Bradykinesia, rigidity, and tremor completed the picture in the typical case.

Neuropathological studies showed that all 48 ALS patients examined histologically had, in addition to the characteristics of ALS, the features of parkinsonism-dementia, and of 45 patients with parkinsonism-dementia, 17 had the histological features of ALS.

The pathological characteristics of the parkinsonism-dementia complex were diffuse cerebral atrophy, particularly of the frontal and temporal lobes, with ventricular enlargement ranging from minimal to severe. The globus pallidus and substantia nigra were atrophied, and in the latter area there was loss of the normal pigment. Widespread neurofibrillary changes were seen in the cortex and subcortical nuclei, while senile (argyrophilic) plaques and Lewy bodies were rarely encountered.[128]

The presence of similar neuropathological changes in the Guam cases of ALS, as well as the clinical association of ALS and parkinsonism-dementia complex, may be considered evidence that these cases share a common etiological factor, the nature of which has remained elusive thus far. The evidence is not sufficiently strong to point to a genetically determined basis, and the geographical grouping of cases still leaves open the possibility of environmental factors.[223]

Huntington's Chorea

George Huntington[135] described in 1872 a disorder affecting a mother and daughter characterized by choreiform movements and progressive mental deterioration. Similar patients had been described earlier,[220] and subsequent reports indicated the disease occurred in almost all races. The sexes are equally affected.

Various genetic studies[220] agree on the dominant inheritance of the disease. Based on the observed differences in the age of onset of the disorder, the hypothesis has been advanced that there may be two genetically heterogeneic forms of Huntington's chorea.[28, 300] If the disease presents before the age of 20, it has probably been transmitted by the father.[35] More commonly, clinical manifestations do not become apparent until the fourth or fifth decade of life. Frequently, the exact onset is difficult to determine since observers may report that the afflicted person appeared "nervous," "fidgety," or "mentally unstable" for many years. Before the appearance of clinical signs there is no definite means of identifying persons destined to develop this disease, except perhaps for the EEG,[154, 211] which is reported to "possibly become abnormal a few years before clinical signs are present," and psychological tests.[105] The provocation of chorea in persons at risk by the administration of L-Dopa is beset with practical and ethical problems and cannot be recommended.[67]

Usually the disease becomes manifest by the appearance of the choreic movements which affect facial expression or the muscles of the trunk or extremities. While at first the afflicted person may be able to incorporate the involuntary movements into purposeful actions, he gradually loses this measure of control; his voluntary activities and even his repose become disrupted by continual movements. They may interfere with his ability to fall asleep, although, once he is asleep, they will cease. Respiration and speech, as well as gait and stance, are affected by the movements.

Usually, mental alterations will become evident after the appearance of involuntary movements, while in other instances, they will develop simultaneously or even precede the movement disorder. They may become apparent as neurotic manifestations, such as anxiety states, irritability, or depression, or as simple deterioration of intellectual capacities, such as memory loss, impairment of abstract reasoning, or failure to grasp simple concepts. Some patients show faulty judgments in professional or financial matters or become offensive because of moral or ethical lapses. At times, paranoid or delusional features suggesting a "functional" psychosis may predominate. The incidence of suicide is high in families with Huntington's chorea.[183]

Some afflicted members of a family may show only the choreic features or only the dementia. In some cases, particularly those with early onset, hypokinesia and rigidity may be prominent features.[29, 44, 141] In a few instances, convulsive seizures have been observed.

Laboratory studies usually yield normal values, although at times the protein level of the cerebrospinal fluid is raised. The pneumoencephalogram may show enlargement of the ventricles, with loss of convexity of the caudate nucleus and evidence of cortical atrophy, but the severity of atrophy does not closely parallel the clinical manifestations.[31]

A high incidence of diabetes in patients with Huntington's chorea has been reported, as well as disturbances of liver function.[34, 218]

Claims that the intracellular level of magnesium and calcium is elevated in Huntington's chorea were not confirmed in later studies.

The progression of the disorder is slow and the average survival after onset is approximately 15 years, respiratory infections being the most common cause of death.

Pathological alterations specific for the disease are restricted to the nervous system and consist of loss of nerve cells in the caudate nucleus and putamen and in the deeper layers of the cortex, particularly in the frontal lobes. Slight to marked glial proliferation may be observed in the affected areas of the basal ganglia.[182]

Senile Dementia

The clinical picture of senile dementia is similar to that of Alzheimer's disease, although, by definition, the onset is later in life and the progression is slower. Defects of memory are usually observed early, followed by confusion as to space and time, inconsistency in work habits, reduction of attention and interest, and deterioration in personal habits. The patients may misplace objects and then accuse others of theft. They frequently will roam at night, wander away from home, or, in the hospital, enter other patients' rooms. They may become incontinent or satisfy their toilet needs in inappropriate places. At times, the onset of the illness is related by family members to an acute emotional or physical stress, such as an infection or operation. Characteristics already discernible in the premorbid personality may become accentuated, while in other instances, witnesses assert that the changes in the patient bear no relation to his previous personality.

The following subtypes have been described[68] although the lines of distinction are rarely sharply drawn in the individual patient: (1) simple deterioration, (2) depressed and agitated type, (3) delirious and confused type, (4) hyperactive type with motor restlessness and loquaciousness, (5) paranoid type.

Focal neurological signs are not part of the picture, although muscular rigidity, gait disturbances, and tremor may be observed.

Physicians with appropriate experience will recognize a certain arbitrariness in the classification described, since individual patients may not only show the features of more than one type but may also be classified differently at different points in the evolution of their disorder. The most constant feature is the progressive attrition of memory and other intellectual capacities, although not only the age of onset but also the rate of progression may vary greatly. While the disease is not fatal in itself, it will at times be responsible for accidents or exposure and in other instances indirectly result in bedsores or systemic infection. Benefits from L-Dopa therapy have been both claimed and disclaimed.[63, 207]

Close relatives of patients with senile dementia have a risk four times that of the general population of developing the disease, and either a multifactorial or a dominant mode of inheritance is likely.[220]

The pathological substrate in senile dementia, in particular its relation to the changes of Alzheimer's disease, has been a matter of controversy and has been summarized by McMenemey.[182]

The brains of most patients with senile dementia show diffuse atrophy, argyrophilic plaques, and Alzheimer's neurofibrillary changes. "If one accepts them, in spite of their late age of onset, as instances of Alzheimer's disease, then few cases remain to be labelled senile dementia."[182] Neumann and Cohn[196] and Raskin and Ehrenberg[222] also believe that no sound argument can be advanced for separating the cases of presenile dementia of Alzheimer type from cases of identical clinical and pathological features but a later onset. A direct relationship between the number of plaques in cerebral gray matter and the degree of dementia has been observed.[30]

There remain a number of instances of senile brain disease in which neither significant Alzheimer changes nor evidence of other disease, such as arteriosclerosis or infectious processes, are observed.[8, 179] For these, the term *simple senile atrophy* (atrophia senilis simplex) has been recommended.[182]

Other Degenerative Diseases

Hallervorden-Spatz Disease

Hallervorden and Spatz[116] described in 1922 a family in which 5 out of 9 siblings suffered from a disorder characterized by progressive dementia, spastic paralysis, and athetosis. The disease usually began late in the first decade of life and progressed to death in the second or third decade. Approximately 30 verified cases have been recorded[186] although other cases in the literature may well belong to this group.[58] Other clinical features, less constant, include foot deformities, chorea or athetosis, optic atrophy, retinitis pigmentosa, ocular palsies, dysarthria, and convulsions. Familial occurrence has been observed in some of the recorded cases.[220]

On pathological examination, rust-brown coloring has been observed in the globus pallidus and substantia nigra due to the presence of iron-containing pigment. Associated with this have been variable degrees of cellular loss and glial proliferation and inconstant histological changes in other parts of the brain and spinal cord.

Spinocerebellar Degenerations

Loss of intellectual functions is observed at times in the spinocerebellar degenerations. Greenfield[109] quotes Bell and Carmichael as having found "mental deficiency" in 23 percent of 242 families with Friedreich's ataxia. In 76 families with spastic paraplegia, the incidence was 27.5 percent. In some instances, the intellectual changes affected only nonataxic members. Sjögren[247] observed oligophrenia in 15 of 84 cases of Friedreich's ataxia and progressive dementia in 58 percent. Mental changes, with varying degrees of prominence, have been noted in many of the subforms of spinocerebellar degenerations.[6, 47, 98, 149, 170, 210]

Progressive Myoclonus Epilepsy

The familial occurrence of a disorder combining myoclonic jerking and generalized convulsions was first described by Unverricht[288] in 1891. In 1895, he described another family with a similar disorder.[289] In both families, the affected members developed myoclonic muscle contractions in late childhood or early adolescence. The progressive severity of the myoclonic contractions eventually interfered with ordinary activities, but dementia was not part of the clinical picture nor was it evident in the cases of Lundborg.[165] In 1911, Lafora and Glueck[152] described the postmortem findings in a 17-year-old boy who, in addition to myoclonus and generalized convulsions, had suffered from a rapidly progressing dementia. They found concentric inclusions in the neurons of cerebral cortex, basal ganglia, brainstem, and spinal cord. Similar inclusions have been found in the heart, liver, and skeletal muscles of other patients.[119, 241] Despite similar clinical features, Lafora bodies have not been found at autopsy in all instances, and the following types of myoclonus epilepsy are now recognized:[117, 119]

1. Lafora body disease, with onset usually in the second decade of life progressing to death in a few years, and accompanied by dementia.[119, 138, 241] There is also on record a case of presenile dementia with "Lafora-like" intraneuronal inclusions but without seizures or myoclonus.[272]

2. Myoclonus epilepsy in lipidosis (familial amaurotic idiocy). The onset is usually earlier, progression may be more rapid or more protracted, dementia is less consistently present and may be accompanied by retinitis pigmentosa or macular degeneration.[117, 230, 303]

3. Myoclonus epilepsy in diseases with system degeneration, i.e., spinocerebellar degenerations with onset in the second decade or later. There is slow progression, usually without significant dementia, but with occasional presence of foot deformity, kyphoscoliosis, or ataxia in patients or their close relatives.[117, 200]

Progressive Supranuclear Palsy

A group of patients was described in 1964[258, 259] with a syndrome combining supranuclear paralysis of extraocular movements, particularly in the vertical plane, with dementia, dysarthria, pseudobulbar palsy, and dystonic rigidity of the neck and truck. Signs of cerebellar and pyramidal dysfunction were less constant. The disorder affecting mainly males usually began in the sixth decade and progressed to death in a few years.

Pathological changes included cell loss, neurofibrillary alterations, gliosis, and demyelination in various regions of the basal ganglia, brainstem, and cerebellum, while the cortex was usually normal.[278]

Subsequent reports have pointed out the occurrence of involuntary movements and involvement of the brainstem nuclei.[32, 54] A degenerative or viral etiology was considered possible by Steele and coworkers,[259] but attempts to transmit the disease to primates have been unsuccessful.[258]

The view has been advanced that the dementia shown by patients with this disease has specific features indicating subcortical involvement of the nervous system.[7] It is marked by forgetfulness, slowness of thought processes, apathy which may be interrupted by outbursts of rage, inappropriate laughing and crying, and impaired ability to manipulate acquired knowledge. "Underlying these clinical abnormalities seems to be an excessive time delay in the carrying out of intellectual functions."[7]

Parkinson's Disease

In his original description of the disease bearing his name, Parkinson stated that "the senses and intellect" remained unaffected.[208] Subsequently, instances of mental changes accompanying the various forms of Parkinson's disease have been recorded.[175] Pollock and Hornabrook[219] observed variable degrees of dementia in all forms of Parkinson's disease but "predominantly in those with associated arteriosclerosis." Intellectual impairment was also found in patients with idiopathic parkinsonism in the study by Loranger and coworkers,[162] who used the Wechsler Adult Intelligence Scale. Upon retesting after 5 to 13 months of treatment with L-Dopa, about half of the patients improved "the equivalent of 10 I.Q. points or more." This beneficial effect was not maintained when the patients were retested after an average of 30 months of L-Dopa therapy, and almost all patients had reverted to the pretreatment level of intellectual functioning.[163]

Permanent dementia has been described as a possible adverse effect of L-Dopa therapy.[314]

METABOLIC DISORDERS

Myxedema

Psychological alterations are common in patients with myxedema. These range from apathy, depression, and stupor to delusional psychosis and dementia.[139, 198, 236] Since other clinical signs of myxedema need not accompany the psychological and mental alterations, evaluation of thyroid function is important in the study of patients with progressive dementia. Unless treatment is instituted early, some degree of mental impairment may remain permanently.

37

Disorders of the Parathyroid Glands

In hyperparathyroidism, neurological changes are uncommon, although lethargy and confusional states may accompany hypercalcemia from any cause.[21, 155] In one series of 33 cases of hyperparathyroidism, 4 patients had psychiatric manifestations.[143] Dementia, while rare, has been observed.

Neurological abnormalities are more commonly seen in patients with hypoparathyroidism and include convulsions, papilledema, paresthesia, hyperreflexia, tetany, weakness, and EEG abnormalities. Psychiatric alterations include toxic-delirious states, irritability, and psychosis. Instances of dementia have been encountered.[75, 132, 232] Mental dullness," often present since birth,[246, 271] is also observed in cases of pseudohypoparathyroidism.[86]

Wilson's Disease (Hepatolenticular Degeneration)

In 1912, Wilson described the clinical entity named after him.[310] Its clinical features are protean and are referable to the damage of the liver or central nervous system. They include evidence of liver failure, such as jaundice of ascites, and neurological symptoms or signs, such as rigidity, tremor, dystonic movements and postures, disturbances of speech and swallowing, and, infrequently, convulsions, transient coma, and "mental changes."[311] The latter at times may resemble schizophrenia[4, 25] and in other instances may present as variable degrees of dementia, especially in the final stages.[59, 60, 110, 269] Improvement of mental functioning has been observed after treatment with penicillamine.

Wilson commented that the loss of intellectual functions may be more apparent than real, suggested by the "idiotic appearance" of the patients to which may be added the interference with communication resulting from the dysarthria. He remarks that, "facility, docility, childishness, and emotional overaction form the chief features of the more chronic cases, together with a narrowing of the mental horizon."[311] In a psychological study[146] employing a battery of tests, 7 patients with Wilson's disease all showed some "loss in the capacity for conceptual thinking" which was greatest in those patients with the longest duration of illness.

Wilson's disease is inherited as an autosomal recessive trait, and consanguinity is common in the ancestry of afflicted persons.[25]

Liver Disease

A permanent and progressive neurological disorder may be observed in persons suffering from chronic hepatic insufficiency.[294, 299] In addition to evidence of dementia, clinical features include tremor, asterixis, ataxia, and speech disorder. Athetosis, chorea, and "action myoclonus" are encountered at times. The mental alteration is of variable degree and is characterized by defects in memory, abstracting ability, attentiveness, and concentration, accompanied by indolence and apathy.

The hepatic insufficiency may be due to cirrhosis, inflammatory disease, or surgical portacaval shunts. Victor, Adams, and Cole[294] found in all patients an elevation of the blood ammonia level or an abnormality on testing of the ammonium tolerance. While hepatic coma had occurred on one or more occasions in the majority of these patients, the relationship of the coma to the encephalopathy was variable. Coma preceded the evolution of the encephalopathy in some instances, while it occurred only after onset of the neurological disorder in other cases. Treatment with levodopa produces little change in the intellectual deficits.[71]

The significant neuropathological changes are a patchy necrosis at the junction of cerebral cortex and white matter and in the striatum, degeneration of neurons in cortex, cerebellum, and lentiform nuclei, and an increase in the size and number of protoplasmic astrocytes.

Hypoglycemia

Survivors of hypoglycemic attacks, regardless of cause (endogenous or exogenous insulin, functional hypoglycemia), may suffer permanent neurological damage, such as hemiplegia, aphasia, tremor and other extrapyramidal manifestations, and especially dementia and significant personality changes.[94, 229] The pathological alterations in the brain resemble those produced by anoxia.

Remote Effects of Carcinoma

Dementia has been observed as part of the neurological syndrome associated with carcinoma.[36, 180] In one series of 42 patients, progressive dementia accompanied other neurological disorders in 14 instances.[36] Mental alteration occurred with particular frequency in patients with cortical-cerebellar degeneration but was also encountered in some patients with peripheral neuropathy and other neuromuscular disorders. The progression of the dementia was variable.

In the majority of instances, pathological examination failed to show abnormalities capable of explaining the mental picture. Inflammatory changes were encountered in some cases, particularly in the subthalamic nuclei and in the nuclei of the brainstem.

The primary neoplasms were located in the lungs in the great majority of cases. The ovaries, prostate, rectum, and breasts were infrequently the site of the primary tumor.

Cushing's Syndrome

Psychiatric disturbances are common in Cushing's syndrome,[254, 285] and range from fatigability and irritability to psychotic degrees of derangement, in particular, severe depressions. Mental dullness is observed at times and may be coupled with some memory impairment. Substantial improvement may follow appropriate treatment, although progressive dementia following radiation therapy of the pituitary region has been reported.[254] Hypopituitarism (Sheehan's syndrome) has also been associated with dementia.[118]

Uremia

Renal failure is frequently accompanied by neurological features, including myoclonus and fasciculations, tremor, asterixis, convulsions, muscular alterations, and evidence of peripheral neuropathy.[161, 286] Emotional lability, irritability, and confusional states are common and may at times progress to impairment of memory, both for remote and recent events, failure to assimilate new material, and disturbance of comprehension, abstraction, and orientation. Korsakoff's psychosis and Wernicke's encephalopathy may be encountered, particularly in instances with superimposed nutritional deficiency. In cases amenable to therapy, reversal of the neurological and mental disturbances is the usual consequence.

Dialysis Dementia

In occasional patients on a long term hemodialysis program, a progressive and irreversible neurological syndrome has been observed.[40, 168] These patients usually had been undergoing dialysis for several years when subtle personality changes were noted during each dialysis, reversing several hours after cessation of the procedure. Gradually, speech disorders, myoclonus, asterixis, and seizures followed, and the syndrome became persistent with progressive deterioration of mental capabilities. The EEG showed marked abnormality with high voltage slowing and paroxysmal or slow wave discharges.

Laboratory studies did not indicate the presence of the disequilibrium syndrome, and no consistent neuropathological abnormalities were found in those patients who died. Trace metal analyses of the brains showed high concentrations of tin and decreased levels of rubidium. The etiology of this syndrome has not yet been established.

Adult Metachromatic Leukodystrophy

Metachromatic leukodystrophy is a medically determined disorder of myelin metabolism in which there is selective destruction of myelin in the nervous system due to an inborn error of cerebroside-sulfate metabolism. This progressive disorder usually manifests itself in early childhood, but there are families in which the disease becomes apparent clinically during adult life.[130, 193] The pattern of inheritance for both the infantile and adult forms appears to be autosomal-recessive.

Progressive dementia is a prominent and early feature in most cases of the adult form, to which are added incoordination, visual disturbance, tremor, rigidity, and sphincter dysfunction. This disorder is fatal after variable periods of time.

VASCULAR DISORDERS

Arteriosclerosis

The diagnosis of "arteriosclerotic dementia" is frequently made in instances of gradual reduction of intellectual capacities, particularly if evidence of systemic or retinal arteriosclerosis is available. There is good evidence that this diagnosis is not justified by the facts in a large percentage of cases.

The degree of correlation between systemic, retinal, and cerebral arteriosclerosis has been reported to be of a low order.[13] Equally, the correlation of the degree of cerebrovascular arteriosclerosis and dementia is limited. In one study,[221] no difference was found in the character, location, and degree of arteriosclerotic changes between demented and nondemented elderly persons. The high incidence of senile plaques and neurofibrillary changes in elderly demented persons[81, 222, 282] suggests that many of these persons are suffering from a parenchymatous degenerative disorder, i.e., Alzheimer's disease.

Using a different approach combining psychiatric techniques and cerebral blood flow studies, Butler[42] also concluded that factors other than arteriosclerosis have to be advanced to explain the organic brain syndrome of many elderly persons.

The view that brain parenchyma undergoes progressive attrition due to chronic hypoxia resulting from cerebral arteriosclerosis is not tenable. Instead, the evidence indicates that repeated infarction of brain tissue may lead to dementia ("multi-infarct dementia").[114] Fisher states, in discussing lacunar infarcts, "There is no doubt that as the number of lacunes increases producing the lacunar state (or état lacunaire), mental deterioration occurs."[81] These multiple infarcts are usually due to thromboembolic disease of the extracranial vessels or the heart and are only infrequently due to atheromatous disease of intracranial vessels.

Dementia is observed in instances of carotid artery occlusive disease[49, 64, 83, 212, 213, 244] with a reported frequency as high as 29 percent in bilateral disease. Surgical treatment, i.e., endarterectomy, has been reported beneficial in some cases.[64, 213, 308]

These vascular events account for a relatively small percentage of demented patients. In Sourander and Sjögren's study[252] of 258 women with dementia, 132 belonged to the group of Alzheimer's disease and related conditions, 54 had other organic encephalopathies, and 72 made up the cerebrovascular group. In the study by Marsden and Harrison, [174] only 8 of 84 cases of dementia were of vascular origin.

An unusual cause of dementia was described by Torvik and coworkers[284] who in three elderly patients found widespread thromboses of small arteries and veins throughout the body but particularly in the brain. The main symptom had been progressive dementia, but cortical blindness and peripheral vascular disease also was observed. There was no evidence of increased blood coagulability, and the cause of this disorder was unknown.

A different set of events has been described in a single case as "hyperlipidemic dementia."[122] This patient, a diabetic with very high serum triglycerides, had originally been diagnosed as having arteriosclerotic dementia. On a low calorie, low cholesterol diet, her mental status improved. She later relapsed at which time her triglyceride level was again found to be elevated. With appropriate treatment, her mental state again improved dramatically.

Inflammatory Disease of Blood Vessels

DISSEMINATED LUPUS ERYTHEMATOSUS. Both neurological and psychiatric dysfunction are common in disseminated lupus.[99] The neurological manifestations include convulsions, hemiplegia, aphasia, and disorders of cranial and peripheral nerves. In the psychiatric sphere, depression and schizophreniform psychoses are encountered, but the most common finding is an "organic mental syndrome," characterized by confusion, disorientation, memory deficits, and visual and auditory hallucinations.[201, 262] The development of these mental changes is not related to the administration of steroids or the presence of uremia.

THROMBOANGIITIS OBLITERANS. Thromboangiitis obliterans or Buerger's disease is a disputed entity. It is said to involve cerebral vessels in up to 20 percent of cases.[99] Clinically, episodes of transient focal dysfunction may gradually lead to diffuse reduction of intellectual function.

Aortic Arch Syndrome ("Pulseless Disease")

Aortic arch syndrome is a broad term designating obliteration of the arteries arising from the convexity of the aorta. The causes include arteriosclerosis, syphilitic aortitis, and an inflammatory arteritis, known also as *Takayasu's arteritis*. The neurological features are manifold[53, 265] and include pulse irregularities or pulselessness, convulsions, visual disturbances, focal cerebral infarctions, memory impairment, and dementia.[4]

Binswanger's Disease ("Subcortical Arteriosclerotic Encephalopathy")

Binswanger's disease is the term assigned to the pathological finding of severe atrophy of the cerebral white matter affecting one or many convolutions of the hemispheres. The clinical features of the 8 cases forming the basis of Binswanger's presentation were progressive dementia, beginning between 50 and 65 years of age, coupled with signs of focal cerebral disease. These included hemiparesis, hemianesthesia, hemianopsia, or aphasia. The focal disturbances presented in an apoplectiform manner and included convulsive episodes. The progression of the disease was slow extending usually over more than 10 years. Binswanger described only the macroscopic changes in his cases. Most of the small number of patients reported subsequently had arteriosclerosis with prominent involvement of the small arteries supplying the white matter and accompanied by areas of demyelination.[57, 203] The coexistence of arteriosclerosis and a demyelinating process has been considered coincidental by some who view the process as related to other demyelinating diseases.[195] Because of this confusion, it has been suggested that "obscure cases of subcortical demyelination which are not clearly related to arteriosclerotic changes should not be associated with the name of Binswanger" and that, moreover, the term *subcortical arteriosclerotic encephalopathy* should be adopted.[203]

Arteriovenous Malformations

Psychiatric alterations, in particular reduction of intellectual capacities, have been observed in 50 percent or more of patients with arteriovenous malformations.[202, 283] The aberration is variable and extends from mild derangements to severe dementia. Progressive brain atrophy due to shunting of blood through the arteriovenous malformation is believed to be responsible for the mental alterations,[202] but destruction of brain tissue by hemorrhage and blocking of the CSF-pathways due to adhesive arachnoiditis following subarachnoid hemorrhage may well be contributing factors.

HYPOXIA AND ANOXIA

Reduction of oxygen supply to the central nervous system leads to neuronal dysfunction and, eventually, to death of nerve cells. Different types of anoxia may be classified according to the mechanism responsible:

1. Anemic or ischemic anoxia occurs mainly after cardiac arrest and complete circulatory arrest, such as strangulation, and in severe anemia or hemorrhage.

2. Anoxic anoxia is the result of decreased oxygen tension in circulating blood. Its causes include reduction of respiratory capacity (central or neuropathic respiratory failure, occlusion of airways by mechanical factor or disease processes, asthma), reduction of oxygen tension in the inspired air (resulting from high altitude, anesthesia, or exposure to poisonous fumes), or impaired oxygen saturation of blood due to cardiovascular anomalies.

3. Stagnant anoxia results from reduced oxygen delivery to the brain be-

cause of slowing of the circulation in such conditions as cardiac failure and polycythemia.

4. In histotoxic anoxia the cells cannot utilize the available oxygen because of interference by toxic substances (such as, cyanide, alcohol) or lack of substrate (such as in hypoglycemia.)

The gray matter of the brain is more severely affected by oxygen lack than the white matter, and preferential destruction of nerve cells is observed in the globus pallidus, corpus Luysi, striatum, visual cortex, and Ammon's horn. The location and nature of neuronal destruction vary considerably and depend at least in some measure on the type of anoxia, its severity, and its duration. Complete oxygen deprivation in vulnerable areas of the brain for more than 4 to 5 minutes leads to cell death,[257] but even lesser periods of oxygen lack may lead to neuronal changes.[185] Recovery from an anoxic episode, regardless of cause, may be complete or partial. Residual neurological features include a variety of focal neurological signs, such as hemiparesis, athetosis, parkinsonism, aphasia, apraxia, and agnosia. Varying degrees of dementia are encountered.[216, 229] Neurological deterioration is at times observed following a period of recovery and beginning 7 to 21 days after the acute anoxic episode or exposure to carbon monoxide.[217, 229] While this event has been most commonly observed after carbon monoxide poisoning, it has also been encountered after anesthesia, cardiac arrest, and hypoglycemia.

Pathologically, the brain in such patients shows diffuse hemispheric demyelination with sparing of the subcortical connecting fibers and most of the neuronal mantle which remains remarkably unscathed. There is a high mortality in such delayed reactions, and the majority of the survivors suffer a moderate to severe dementia.[217]

NORMAL PRESSURE HYDROCEPHALUS

Progressive dementia accompanying communicating hydrocephalus with a normal or nearly normal pressure of the cerebrospinal fluid has been recognized as a potentially treatable condition in recent years.[2, 85, 115, 125, 184] In addition to the slowly progressive dementia, gait disturbances — ataxic or apractic in nature — and incontinence have been observed in many of the reported cases. The condition may develop without recognizable preceding events or may follow subarachnoid hemorrhage, trauma, or chronic meningitis or may accompany neoplasms.

Pneumoencephalographic examination demonstrates dilatation of the ventricular system without evidence of obstruction but with little or no air over the convexity of the hemispheres. The diagnosis is confirmed by isotope-encephalography.[160] which demonstrates isotope concentration in the ventricular system. In instances of ventricular dilatation secondary to cerebral atrophy, the isotope is usually not concentrated in the ventricles in a similar manner.

Some patients with this condition may improve temporarily after lumbar puncture or pneumoencephalography, while abrupt worsening following these procedures has been encountered in other instances.

Shunt procedures (lumboperitoneal or ventriculoatrial) have benefited a significant proportion of the reported patients, the degree of improvement ranging from a resumption of self-care to a return to the premorbid occupation. Some measure of improvement has also been reported to follow shunt procedures in parenchymatous degenerative brain disease.[15] The pathophysiology of the condition is yet unclear. It has been hypothesized that, in the presence of enlargement of the ventricular system, the total force exerted on the ventricular walls will be increased even in the face of "normal" spinal fluid pressure since the force acting upon the ventricular wall is the product of pressure times surface area. If this "hydraulic press effect" exceeds the elasticity of the brain tissue, enlargement of the ventricles will ensue. The validity of this concept has been contested,[95] since it fails to take into consideration the structural properties of the ventricular walls.

DEFICIENCY DISEASES

Wernicke-Korsakoff Syndrome

Mental disturbance is almost ubiquitous in the Wernicke syndrome and was absent in only 10 percent of the patients of a large series.[295] Several different types of mental abnormalities were observed:
1. Delirium tremens.
2. Korsakoff's psychosis.
3. A state of indifference and apathy with limited attention span and inability to concentrate, disorientation in place and time, and impairment of memory and judgment. Treatment with thiamine may improve the patient's alertness and attentiveness, and the features of Korsakoff's psychosis may become more apparent.

The memory defect is the most prominent feature of Korsakoff's psychosis and expresses itself as an inability to incorporate new information into the store of knowledge. In addition, there is difficulty in proper sequential ordering of past events;[296] the patient can no longer differentiate temporal foreground and background, resulting in confabulation, the juxtaposition of temporally unrelated events. Beyond the impairment of memory formation, disturbances in cognitive functions and concept formation have been demonstrated in patients with Korsakoff's psychosis.[274, 275] Treatment with thiamine results in variable degrees of recovery, ranging from complete restoration of intellectual functions to socially incapacitating degrees of mental impairment.

Pellagra

Nicotinic acid deficiency in its full-blown form produces the clinical triad of pellagra, including dermatitis, diarrhea, and mental changes. It is probable that the deficiency of other vitamins plays a role in the clinical manifestations of the disease. The mental abnormalities cover a wide range and include depression, apathy, irritability, confusional and delirious states, and dementia. Other neurological manifestations include spasticity, ataxia, hyperreflexia, visual disturbances, and peripheral neuropathy.[253]

Marchiafava-Bignami Disease

Marchiafava-Bignami disease is a rare disorder characterized pathologically by necrosis of the central portions of the corpus callosum. The process mainly affects the rostral part of the corpus callosum, but degeneration of the anterior and posterior commissures, the centrum semiovale, and the middle cerebellar peduncles has also been observed.[183]

Since it was first reported in 1903, less than 100 cases have been reported in the literature. The majority have been males of Italian stock, but persons of other ethnic backgrounds and a few women have also been afflicted.[136] Excessive alcoholic intake, particularly of red wine, has been recorded in most instances, and an etiological relationship to this beverage has been suspected. This supposition cannot be upheld, however, since the disease has been observed in persons consuming other types of alcoholic beverages as well as persons without any history of alcoholic abuse.[136] The disease is probably directly or indirectly due to a nutritional imbalance or avitaminosis, but the exact pathogenesis is unclear.

The clinical manifestations may begin suddenly or insidiously and may be precipitated by a bout of drinking or an infection. Bilateral stiff-legged gait disturbances may usher in the disease, or the patient may fall without recognizable reason. In other instances, mental alterations, such as delirium, stupor, agitation, or progressive dementia, may mark the onset of the disorder and may be followed by focal or generalized convulsions, aphasia, apraxia, muscular rigidity, tremors, or hemiparesis. The illness lasts from a few days to several months. The clinical picture is usually progressive and is not usually influenced by any therapeutic measures, although recovery with vitamin B therapy has been reported in one case.[158] The correct diagnosis is usually made only at the time of postmortem examination.

Vitamin B_{12} and Folate Deficiency

Mild mental changes are commonly observed in vitamin B_{12} deficiency[87, 249] and may be present before any abnormalities can be observed in blood or bone marrow.[266] The mental alterations include confusion, depression, irritability, and forgetfulness; and paranoid features are stressed by some authors. Progressive failure of all intellectual functions is encountered at times. The psychiatric changes may develop independently from other neurological manifestations of the disease but are accompanied by EEG changes. Significant improvement or complete restoration of function can be expected with vitamin B_{12} therapy. Folate deficiency has been found to be associated with a high incidence of organic mental syndromes which may be reversed by folic acid therapy.[226]

TOXINS AND DRUGS

A large number of drugs and exogenous toxins affect the central nervous system. Frequently, contact with these agents produces an "acute brain syndrome" characterized by disturbances of mentation, alterations of perception and behavior, and emotional instability. In some instances, a chronic illness may develop, usually characterized by impairment of orientation, memory, and general intellectual performance.

Metals

Lead intoxication, in the adult usually the result of industrial exposure or the use of illicit alcohol ("moonshine"), produces an encephalopathy characterized by irritability, memory impairment, disorientation, and drowsiness. Convulsions are commonly observed, and coma may supervene.[16, 185, 311]

Mental alterations occur also in mercury intoxication, particularly after exposure to organic mercury compounds.[151] The epidemic occurrence of a neurological disorder in Minamata Bay, Japan, is thought to be due to an organic mercury compound. Clinical symptoms and signs in afflicted persons include incoordination, involuntary movements, signs of corticospinal tract dysfunction, and variable degrees of emotional and intellectual disorders.[151]

Manganese poisoning, occurring mainly in miners, produces features of a disorder of the extrapyramidal system, with severe tremors, muscular rigidity, and a disturbance of gait.[1] Psychosis has been observed as well as severe mental deterioration.[185]

Organic Compounds

The majority of organic compounds capable of affecting the nervous system produce an acute toxic picture, frequently resulting in death. Prolonged effects, with mental deterioration, follow exposure to nitrobenzenes, aniline compounds, bromine hydrocarbons, and tri-ortho-cresyl-phosphate,[18] and prolonged exposure to carbon disulfide and carbon tetrachloride.[263]

Carbon Monoxide

Recovery from the acute stage of carbon monoxide poisoning may be followed, at times after a period of relative well-being lasting 7 to 21 days, by progressive deterioration of neurological functions with dementia, Korsakoff's psychosis, manic or depressive states, and features resembling Parkinson's disease.[217, 242] Gradual recovery, complete or partial, may take place. Mental dullness, depression, and memory deficits may also result from chronic exposure to small concentrations of carbon monoxide.[97, 311]

Drugs

Reduction of mental functions, sufficient to suggest chronic brain disease, follows the prolonged and excessive use of bromides,[46] paraldehyde, or barbiturates. Other signs suggesting drug intoxication, such as drowsiness, ataxia, slurring of speech, or hallucinations, may assist in the diagnosis but at times may be lacking. Marked reduction of psychomotor activity and retardation of thought processes may also accrue from the use of the tranquilizing drugs.

It has been suggested that the major anticonvulsive drugs, diphenylhydantoin (Dilantin), primidone (Mysoline), as well as phenobarbital, are capable of producing various neurological alterations, including dementia, by their interference with the metabolism of folic acid and vitamin B_{12}.[225] In a series of 8 patients with analgesic nephropathy, 4 had definite and 2 had possible evidence of dementia.[194] The brains of 9 other patients with analgesic abuse were examined, and neurofibrillary changes were found in 4; senile plaques were found in 6 of the seven phenacetin abusers. In those patients who had used aspirin only, no abnormalities were detected. Prolonged use of phenacetin may lead, therefore, to both clinical and pathological features of Alzheimer's disease.

BRAIN TUMORS

The great frequency of mental and emotional disorders in patients with cerebral neoplasms has been reported in many studies.[22, 41, 113, 120, 123, 144, 189, 192, 239, 251, 301] A detailed review of the available material is not intended here. There is seen throughout the literature a continuing thread of argument concerning the specificity, or lack of specificity, of the psychiatric derangement according to the tumor location, extent, or histological characteristics. The problem is compounded by

46

several difficulties, not the least of which results from the lack of sharp semantic definitions. The term *dementia* may well at times be too inclusive, for instance, in cases showing a specific memory deficit akin to the Korsakoff syndrome. In other instances, faulty responses on the part of the patient may be the result of apathy and a reduced level of alertness rather than an expression of specific conceptual difficulties.

In addition, the extent of the neoplasm and its effect on adjacent and remote parts of the brain is usually hard to determine. Edema, compression of neighboring structures, interference with cerebral blood flow, and the effect of increased intracranial pressure on the entire central nervous system contribute to the emerging clinical picture. Moreover, the cerebral localization of intellectual functions is still poorly understood,[215] and the study of brain tumors is not particularly suitable to enlarging the available body of information concerning this aspect. Wilson[311] went so far as to say that, "Most analyses and allocations of mental syndromes accompanying cerebral tumors are worthless."

Mental or behavioral alterations in general occur in 50 to 70 percent of all brain tumors.[239, 251, 298, 301] Dementia or memory loss has been reported in instances of neoplasms involving, in particular, the frontal lobes[12, 88, 192] but also in tumors of the third ventricle and hypothalamus,[231, 256, 309] thalamus,[5, 250] occipital lobes,[9, 89, 239] parietal lobes,[239] temporal lobes,[148] and corpus callosum.[11, 19, 190] Many of these reports seek to relate a specific mental disorder with the involved area.

An opposing view is held by Walther-Büel,[301] who based his conclusions on 600 cases of brain tumors, 60 of which he examined personally. He found it possible to divide the mental disorders encountered into two broad categories:

1. "Chronic organic psychosyndromes," with prominent memory disturbance, little or no disturbance of attentiveness, affective lability, and a high degree of fatigability in all mental performances.

2. Disturbances of consciousness with prominent reduction of attentiveness, inability to concentrate, and incoherence of thought, eventually progressing to torpor and stupor.

Both symptom constellations were encountered with equal frequency in the patient population studied and did not appear to be related to the location of the tumors in the brain. The organic psychosyndrome was infrequently encountered in children and young adults, but its incidence, as well as its severity, increased in the higher age groups. Disturbances of consciousness, on the other hand, were observed in all age groups, regardless of the location of the neoplasm.

Although specific changes in mentation cannot be correlated with brain tumors in various locations, dementia of recent onset must always alert the physician to the possibility of primary or secondary cerebral neoplasia and prompt complete evaluation to diagnose or exclude brain tumor.

TRAUMA

Open and Closed Head Injuries

Severe reduction of intellectual function is not a common result of head injuries.[112] Miller and Stern[188] reexamined 92 survivors of severe head injuries from 3 to 40 years after the initial insult. Some degree of dementia was present in 10 patients, but these authors concluded that, "major cerebral trauma is clearly statistically insignificant as a cause of dementia severe enough to demand long-term hospital care." In a Finnish study[126] of 3552 war injured followed for 22 to 26 years, Korsakoff's syndrome was observed in 23 survivors and grave dementia in 11. In a Japanese study,[205] disorders of intellectual function were observed in 22 instances of 1168 cases of closed head injuries. Even after prolonged post-traumatic unconsciousness (in excess of 3 weeks), a socially disabling reduction of intellectual function is not the common end result, although some degree of intellectual deficit was observed in the majority of survivors.[291]

Disruption of nerve fibers by shearing forces has been postulated as a mechanism producing dementia in survivors of head injuries.[268]

Progressive dementia, as an expression of Alzheimer's disease, Pick's disease, or Creutzfeldt-Jakob disease, following head injury has been recorded.[50, 268]

The Punch-Drunk Syndrome

An insidiously progressive cerebral disorder may develop in former boxers years after their career in the ring has ended.[52, 176, 255] The number of fights, in particular the number of head blows and knockouts, appears to bear a relation to the syndrome which is characterized by dementia ("dementia pugilistica") and cerebellar and extrapyramidal dysfunction. Convulsions occur in some affected persons. Pneumoencephalographic studies show cerebral atrophy, and abnormalities of the septum pellucidum have been seen in a high percentage of cases.[66, 176] The neuropathological alterations are those of multiple cortical infarcts or of Alzheimer's disease.[268]

Subdural Hematoma

The gradual accumulation of blood in the subdural space may be accompanied by a reduction of intellectual functions similar to that observed in patients with brain tumors. Particularly in the elderly, the clinical course of subdural hematoma may resemble parenchymatous degenerative disease.[214, 270] A demented state may also be the end result in operated cases of subdural hematoma.[55] In elderly patients with a recent onset of progressive dementia, subdural hematoma should always be considered as a potential cause.

Heat Stroke

The acute hyperpyrexia of heat stroke may lead to severe neurological damage. Dementia is said to result in about 10 percent of survivors of heat stroke.[311]

INFECTIONS

Brain Abscess

The psychiatric features of brain abscess may resemble those of brain tumors. Reduction of intellectual abilities may persist after surgical treatment.[276]

Bacterial Meningitis

Only rarely does acute bacterial meningitis in the adult leave significant residual intellectual impairment.[77] In one report concerning 99 patients with bacterial meningitis, permanent mental defects were seen in only 3 cases, all children.[61]

48

More severe neurological sequelae have been found after tuberculous meningitis, affecting 23 of 100 children surviving this disease.[164] Six of these children were profoundly mentally retarded, all showing other major neurological deficits as well. In adults, 11 of 178 patients surviving tuberculous meningitis for at least 1 year after start of treatment had "marked impairment of intellect, judgment, and skills."[76]

Fungal Meningitis

Acute or subacute mental disorders are commonly among the early signs of fungal meningitis, and in one study they occurred in 3 of 7 patients with histoplasma meningitis and in 26 patients with cryptococcal meningitis.[290] The mental features observed probably did not suggest dementia in the cases of histoplasma meningitis,[287] but confusion, personality changes, and memory defects were present in a small percentage of the cases of cryptococcal meningitis.[43]

Encephalitis

In most of the forms of viral encephalitis occurring in the Western world, serious effects on mental function in adults are usually transient while persistent neurological and intellectual deficits may occur in children.[183] These sequelae are seen with greater frequency and are more severe in the Eastern equine form than in the St. Louis type or Western equine encephalitis.

Mental deterioration was found in 4 of 56 former U.S. servicemen who had survived an attack of Japanese B encephalitis.[111]

In contrast, severe mental disorders are frequently the end result in survivors of herpes simplex encephalitis and other forms of inclusion body encephalitis.[93, 100, 183] A progressive dementia has been observed in patients suffering from a subacute form of encephalitis affecting the limbic area.[37] Inclusion bodies were not seen in the histological material from these cases and only rarely in cases of chronic encephalitis with focal seizures and intellectual deterioration.[3]

Subacute Sclerosing Panencephalitis (SSPE)

Subacute sclerosing panencephalitis (SSPE), a chronic disorder of the nervous system related to the measles virus, produces a progressive picture of mental deterioration associated with myoclonic jerks and periodic complexes in the EEG. The spinal fluid colloidal gold curve is abnormal, and measles antibodies in the CSF are elevated. The disorder, which usually affects children, may run a very protracted or relapsing course and may occasionally present in adult life.[45, 62]

Progressive Multifocal Leukoencephalopathy

A demyelinating disorder accompanying Hodgkin's disease and chronic lymphocytic leukemia was first recognized in 1958.[17] The term "progressive multifocal leukoencephalopathy" was used to describe this disorder. By 1970, Richardson[228] was able to review 83 cases, and others have been added to the literature since.[56]

The disorder has been found not only in association with leukemia and lymphoma but also with polycythemia vera, sarcoidosis, tuberculosis, Whipple's disease, carcinomatosis, and immunodeficiency states.[147] It is progressive and leads to death in a few weeks to months, although successful treatment with cytarabine has been reported.[24]

The clinical features include evidence of disseminated nervous system lesions manifested by variable neurological signs such as ataxia, dysarthria, paresis, visual field defects or blindness, confusional states, seizures, progressive dementia, and coma. The cerebrospinal fluid is usually normal while the EEG commonly shows nonspecific abnormalities.

The pathological changes consist of multiple areas of demyelination with relative sparing of neuron and axis cylinders, alterations of oligodendrocytes, bizarre giant astrocytes, and destruction of the granule cells of the cerebellar cortex. Virus particles have been demonstrated in a number of cases,[316] and at least two types of papova virus (SV40 and JC) have been identified.[304, 305]

Creutzfeldt-Jakob Disease

Creutzfeldt-Jakob disease is a diffuse disorder of the nervous system, marked by neuronal degeneration, glial proliferation, and, frequently, status spongiosus.

Not only the nomenclature but also the clinical range of its manifestations have been matters of dispute. Although a term such as *subacute presenile polioencephalopathy*[38] may be a more adequate description of the entity, the eponymic term is sufficiently honored by usage to make its displacement unlikely.

The first report, published by Creutzfeldt in 1920,[51] concerned a 23-year-old woman who died after a neurological illness of 2½ years' duration. Pathological examination of the brain disclosed diffuse alterations in the gray matter of the cerebral cortex and of subcortical gray structures. In the following year, Jakob reported three similar cases, to which he added two more instances in his monograph[137] on the extrapyramidal disorders published in 1923.

Over 200 cases have been reported up to the present, the majority having been confirmed by histological study (biopsy or postmortem examination).[145, 177] Familial occurrence has been noted in several instances with dominant autosomal transmission the apparent mode of inheritance.[178] In one instance, husband and wife were afflicted simultaneously by the same disorder, surviving respectively 2 and 4 months.[140] A relatively high incidence in Libyan Jews has been reported.[101]

The disease usually becomes apparent between the ages of 40 and 60, and the sexes are equally affected. While some afflicted persons have lived for several years after the diagnosis, the usual duration is measured in months. About half of all patients survived less than 9 months.

In the early stages, neurotic manifestations, such as anxiety, nervousness, excessive startle reaction, fatigability, depression, and loss of appetite may predominate; while in other instances, loss of memory, euphoria, confusion, lability in the affective sphere, hallucinations, delusions, or behavioral changes suggest a functional psychotic disorder. In still other patients, the illness may declare itself from the outset as a neurological disorder by disturbances of speech or coordination or by paresthesiae, visual disturbances, involuntary movements, or episodic loss of consciousness. Transient remission of symptoms for weeks or months may occur, but in most instances, the range of symptoms increases and definite signs of neurological disease appear, often asymmetrically. Most consistently, these indicate involvement of the upper motor neuron with appearance of suck and snout responses, forced grasping, plantar extensor responses, and spasticity, or manifestations of extrapyramidal disease, including tremors, choreiform or athetoid movements, myoclonic discharges, dystonia, or muscular rigidity.

Signs indicating disorder of the lower motor neuron, such as muscular wasting and fasciculations, and signs of brainstem involvement, such as diplopia, anisocoria, or nystagmus, appear with less regularity. Cerebellar dysfunction may be the initial manifestation or may appear at a later stage in the course of the disease.[38] An exaggerated startle response is a common observation,[80] and convulsive seizures have been observed.

As the illness progresses, the patient may become mute and assume decorticate or decerebrate postures. Some patients lapse into an akinetic mute state or coma, which usually is fatally terminated by a respiratory infection.

In the majority of instances, examination of the spinal fluid will yield normal results,[243] although increase of the protein content, usually of a mild degree, has been reported in about 10 percent of cases.

The pneumoencephalogram usually shows evidence of mild to moderate ventricular enlargement and cortical atrophy, particularly over the frontal portions of the brain. Abnormalities of the EEG have been reported in more than 90 percent of the patients.[39, 177] In the early stages, diffuse or focal slowing may be observed. As the disorder progresses, periodic biphasic or triphasic discharges may be superimposed on a slow, low-voltage background activity. These slow bursts may be accompanied by myoclonic jerking. Considered pathognomonic by some, this pattern has also been found in instances of subacute inclusion body encephalitis[156] and has not been invariably present in the reported cases of Creutzfeldt-Jakob disease.

On pathological examination, mild to moderate atrophic changes are observed in the cortex, at times predominantly in the frontal, parietal, or temporal areas. With less consistency, pathological alterations are seen in the basal ganglia, corticospinal tracts, motor neurons, thalamus, and cerebellum.

Histologically, diffuse ganglion cell loss is observed in the affected areas, while the remaining cells may be swollen with lipochrome. Status spongiosus, particularly of the deeper cortical layers, is a common finding as is astrocytic proliferation. Electron microscopic studies[103, 172] have shown the "status spongiosus" to be due to dilatation of cellular processes involving astrocytes and neurons.

The etiology of the condition remains unclear. The possibility of a relationship to pellagra of the central nervous system has been commented upon,[182] and both astrocytes and neurons have been considered to be the cellular elements primarily affected by the disorder. Experimental transmission of the disease by intracerebral or peripheral inoculation of suspensions of brain material from affected patients into chimpanzees and New World monkeys has been accomplished in a number of instances.[233] Chimpanzees so inoculated have developed a disease marked by myoclonus, paresis, somnolence, visual disturbances, and fasciculations after 11 to 16 months, while in New World monkeys the incubation period averaged 23 to 29 months. Neuropathological findings in diseased primates included astrocytosis, neuronal degeneration, and status spongiosus. It is remarkable that successful transmission was accomplished in two familial cases;[233] these may represent instances of genetically defined susceptibility to a viral agent or vertical transmission of the agent. On the other hand, in a number of instances of the disease as defined on histological grounds, transmission experiments have been unfruitful.

Possible person-to-person transmission of Creutzfeldt-Jakob disease has been

51

reported in one instance.[65] A 55-year-old man died of pneumonia after an illness of 2 months marked by incoordination, memory deficit, involuntary movements, and myoclonia. At autopsy, the characteristic findings of Creutzfeldt-Jakob disease were found. The cornea was transplanted from him to a 55-year-old woman who 18 months later developed a neurological disease marked by difficult swallowing, mutism, and myoclonus. She died after a decorticate state had developed. The autopsy in this case also showed Creutzfeldt-Jakob disease, and it is probable that the disease was transmitted by the corneal transplantation.

Although virus-like particles have been found in brain biopsies of patients with Creutzfeldt-Jakob disease,[293] the agent has otherwise not been characterized by any immune response or by any effect in tissue cultures. Ultrastructural and microchemical observations in this disease suggest a cellular permeability defect resulting from a membrane alteration and leading to intracytoplasmic fluid accumulation.[23]

Treatment with Idoxyuridine has been unsuccessful, but the antiviral agent, Amantadine, has been used in a few cases with reported success.[24] One patient so treated showed "remarkable initial improvement" for 2 months and then deteriorated and died; another patient was considered cured 30 months after the start of treatment.

The protean clinical and pathological manifestations of this disorder have resulted in considerable controversy, and it has been suggested that the cases falling into this group may be heterogeneous. This has resulted in attempts to classify subtypes or to separate altogether groups of patients on the basis of clinical or pathological characteristics.[177] Although, at present, judgment must be reserved about the validity of establishing subtypes, certain groups of cases are sufficiently different from the majority to warrant consideration:

1. Nevin and associates[197] presented 8 patients with clinical features similar to the ones described above. These authors felt, however, that the pathological features of their cases, and of 15 others collected from the literature, differed from the "classical" Creutzfeldt-Jakob disease insofar as status spongiosus was a more common feature of an entity they termed *subacute spongiform encephalopathy* (SSE) with a predilection for the occipital cortex, little or no degeneration of the motor nuclei in brainstem and spinal cord, or degeneration of myelinated tracts. The type of cell shrinkage as well as the behavior of astrocytes also were, in their opinion, different from the findings in Creutzfeldt-Jakob disease.

Nevin and his group[197] included under the heading of SSE 2 of the patients originally described by Heidenhain.[121] To these cases, and 1 of their own, Meyer, Leigh, and Bagg[187] attached the designation of *Heidenhain's syndrome*. Clinically, these cases were characterized by cortical blindness and dementia, and pathologically by involvement of the occipital cortex. Nevin's group believed that vascular impairment was the most likely cause of SSE. The validity of separating these cases has been contested.[243]

2. Patients with prominent thalamic involvement were reported by Stern,[261] Schulman,[240] and Garcin, Brion, and Khochnevis.[92]

3. An ataxic form, with prominent involvement of the granular layer of the cerebellum, has been recorded by Brownell and Oppenheimer,[38] who, in addition to 4 cases of their own, collected 6 similar instances from the literature. Others have been added since.[102]

McMenemey[182] suggests that at the present time it appears most reasonable to consider these conditions as constituting "a group of disorders of like character," without necessarily implying the same etiology for all cases.

52

Kuru

A peculiar neurological disease among the Fore tribesmen of New Guinea was first recognized in 1957 by Gajdusek and Zigas.[90] The disease, which affects primarily adult females and children of both sexes, begins with disturbances of locomotion and shaking of the head and extremities. In the further evolution of the disorder, chorea or athetosis, lability of emotional expression, disturbances of extraocular movements, and progressive signs of cerebellar involvement appear. The total duration of the illness is less than 2 years, and dementia develops frequently in the late stages.[131]

Gajdusek, Gibbs, and Alpers[91] were able to produce experimentally a disease resembling kuru clinically and pathologically in chimpanzees inoculated with brain tissue derived from kuru patients and to repeat the process by second and third passages. There is strong evidence that kuru may be the clinical result of infection with a slow-growing virus, possibly transmitted by the tribal custom of cannibalism.[142]

Behçet's Syndrome

Behçet's syndrome is a rare entity, possibly of viral origin. Its main clinical characteristics include ulcerations of the mouth and genitalia, and iritis. Other frequent manifestations are erythema nodosum, thrombophlebitis, a nonspecific skin sensitivity, and neurological involvement, which occurs in about 25 percent of cases. The illness affects preferentially young males and tends to run a protracted, remitting course, although slow progression may also be observed.

The neurological features include headaches, pleocytosis, signs of involvement of the brainstem, spasticity, and parkinsonism.[297] Intellectual deterioration is encountered at times. Claims for a viral etiology of this disorder are yet unconfirmed.[183, 297]

Lues

Dementia paralytica, or general paresis, is due to direct invasion of the brain by Treponema pallidum, which leads to cortical atrophy with thickening of the leptomeninges. Once one of the leading causes for admission to mental institutions, fresh instances of the disease are now infrequently encountered.

Men are affected more frequently than women, and the disease usually declares itself 10 to 20 years after the initial luetic infection. In the period before modern treatment of syphilitic infections, it was estimated that approximately 5 percent of persons with untreated syphilis would develop dementia paralytica.[311]

The onset is usually gradual, although it may be marked in a more dramatic manner by convulsions or a stroke-like event. Minor alterations in conduct, errors in judgment, carelessness in personal appearance, instability, mood swings, depressive or hypomanic features mark the initial deviation from the previous state of health. The disease process may travel along several different roads, and a number of clinical subtypes have been enumerated.[311] The common denominator, however, is the attrition of intellectual, social, and moral capacities. Other features such as euphoria, megalomania, depression, agitation, and apathy are only variations on the basic theme. Signs of neurological disease, such as tremors, dysarthria, pupillary changes, or ataxia, may accompany the personality disintegration but may be absent or provide only a dim background to the central events.

53

The serological test for syphilis in blood and spinal fluid are nearly always positive, although seronegative cases have been reported[48] and serve to set this disease apart from other dementing processes. Treatment of general paresis with penicillin cures the disease and often has some beneficial effect on the dementia.

OTHER DISEASES

Multiple Sclerosis

Significant intellectual deterioration is uncommon in the early stages of multiple sclerosis, but features of organic brain disease emerge frequently as the disease progresses.[20, 235] On psychological tests, the loss of abstracting ability has been found to approximate the extent of neurological damage.[209] In the majority of instances, alterations in the affective sphere are more prominent than intellectual deterioration. Rarely, a marked progressive dementia has been recorded.[26, 311]

Muscular Dystrophy

Among patients with progressive muscular dystrophy, mental deficiency is encountered with greater frequency than in other disabling disorders.[8, 199, 234, 302, 315] It is probable that this mental defect is nonprogressive in contrast to that encountered in myotonic muscular dystrophy. Intellectual deterioration and social descent are observed in this disorder with considerable frequency.[167] Thomasen[281] found mental defects dating back to early childhood in many of his myotonic cases. Moreover, he observed progressive intellectual deterioration in one third of his patients, particularly those in whom the clinical manifestations of the disease became first apparent in childhood. The cause of this deterioration is not yet understood, but pneumoencephalographic evidence of ventricular enlargement has been presented.[224]

Whipple's Disease

Whipple's disease is an uncommon disorder, characterized clinically by weakness, weight loss, steatorrhea, and polyarthritis and pathologically by the accumulation of PAS-positive material in the macrophages of the intestinal mucosa and in the mesenteric lymph nodes.

The disease affects mainly middle-aged males. Neurological manifestations have been reported, including dysarthria, ophthalmoplegia, ataxia, myoclonus, and dementia.[153, 264] The neuropathological findings were those of a nodular encephalitis with accumulation of PAS-positive material. Progressive multifocal leukoencephalopathy has also been reported in association with Whipple's disease.[228]

Concentration-Camp Syndrome

In a number of survivors of severe nutritional deprivation in European concentration camps, progressive mental changes were observed. These presented originally as neurotic manifestations, with signs of organic brain disease later supervening. The pneumoencephalogram showed evidence of cerebral atrophy.[70, 307]

54

Kufs' Disease (Neuronal Ceroid-Lipofuscinosis)[33]

This disorder, also called "adult amaurotic idiocy," is very rare; it is transmitted as a Mendelian recessive. It produces various kinds of motor disorders, ataxia, myoclonus, and dementia, beginning in adult life and ending in death after many years. At autopsy, neurons and astrocytes show accumulation of lipopigments.

Familial Calcification of Basal Ganglia

Calcification of the basal ganglia occurs most commonly in hypoparathyroidism. Mental and other neurological abnormalities are well recognized both in calcification of the basal ganglia and in hypoparathyroidism. There are, however, families on record with several members showing basal ganglionic calcification but without evidence of parathyroid disorder.[191] Inheritance by both the dominant and recessive route has been described in involved families. Members of families with this disorder may show pyramidal signs as well as extrapyramidal dysfunction, seizures, incoordination, and dementia. In still other families, mental retardation may be an associated finding.

GENETIC ASPECTS OF DEMENTIA

Several of the diseases producing dementia appear — at least in some cases — to be determined by genetic factors. The evidence for genetic transmission is strong

Table 2. Genetic aspects of dementia

Disease	Mode of Transmission	References	Remarks
Alzheimer's	Dominant or multifactorial	78, 124, 220, 248	Genetic factors apparent in only a limited number of instances.
Pick's	Dominant-autosomal	220, 248, 292	Genetic factors apparent in only a limited number of instances.
Creutzfeldt-Jakob	Dominant-autosomal	147, 178	Only few familial instances.
Huntington's chorea	Dominant-autosomal	220	
Senile dementia	Dominant or multifactorial	220	Risk of relative of propositus is four times the risk of general population.
Hallervorden-Spatz	Undetermined		Only few instances of familial occurrence recorded.
Spinocerebellar degenerations	Variable	6, 47, 109, 149, 170, 210, 220	
Myoclonus epilepsy (Lafora-type)	Autosomal recessive	117, 119	
Wilson's	Autosomal recessive	220	

in some diseases but is much more tentative in relatively rare conditions. In still other diseases, the principle of "genetic heterogeneity" appears to operate, which states that phenotypic similarity may be produced by genotypically different conditions.

For detailed evaluation of the available evidence, reference is made to the monograph *The Genetics of Neurological Disorders,* by R. T. C. Pratt.[220]

REFERENCES

1. ABD EL NABY, S., AND HASSANEIN, M.: *Neuropsychiatric manifestations of chronic manganese poisoning.* J. Neurol. Neurosurg. Psychiatry 28:282, 1965.
2. ADAMS, R. D.; FISHER, C. M.; HAKIM, S.; OJEMANN, R. G.; AND SWEET, W. H.: *Symptomatic occult hydrocephalus with "normal" cerebrospinal fluid pressure.* New Engl. J. Med. 273:117, 1965.
3. AGUILAR, M. J., AND RASMUSSEN, T.: *Role of encephalitis in pathogenesis of epilepsy.* Arch. Neurol. 2:663, 1960.
4. AITA, J. A.: *Neurologic Manifestations of General Diseases.* Charles C Thomas, Publisher, Springfield, Ill., 1964.
5. AJURIAGUERRA, J. DE; HÉCAEN, H.; AND SADOUN, R.: *Les troubles mentaux au cours des tumeurs de la région méso-diencéphalique.* L'Encéphale 43:406, 1954.
6. AKELAITIS, A. J.: *Hereditary form of primary parenchymatous atrophy of cerebellar cortex associated with mental deterioration.* Am. J. Psychiatry 94:1115, 1938.
7. ALBERT, M. L.; FELDMAN, R. G.; AND WILLIS, A. L.: *The "subcortical dementia" of progressive supranuclear palsy.* J. Neurol. Neurosurg. Psychiatry 37:121, 1974.
8. ALEXANDER, D. A.: *"Senile dementia": A changing perspective.* Br. J. Psychiatry 121:207, 1972.
9. ALLEN, I. M.: *A clinical study of tumours involving the occipital lobe.* Brain 53:194, 1930.
10. ALLEN, T. D., AND RODGIN, D. W.: *Mental retardation in association with progressive muscular dystrophy.* Am. J. Dis. Child. 100:208, 1960.
11. ALPERS, B. J.: *A note on the mental syndrome of corpus callosum tumors.* J. Nerv. Ment. Dis. 84:621, 1936.
12. ALPERS, B. J., AND MANCALL, E. L.: *Clinical Neurology,* ed. 6. F. A. Davis Co., Philadelphia, 1971.
13. ALPERS, B. J.; FORSTER, F. M.; AND HERBERT, P. A.: *Retinal, cerebral and systemic arteriosclerosis. A histopathologic study.* Arch. Neurol. Psychiat. 60:440, 1948.
14. ALZHEIMER, A.: *Über eine eigenartige Erkrankung der Hirnrinde.* Centralblatt Nervenheilk. Psychiat. 18:177, 1907.
15. APPENZELLER, O., AND SALMON, J. H.: *Treatment of parenchymatous degeneration of the brain by ventriculo-atrial shunting of the cerebrospinal fluid.* J. Neurosurg. 26:478, 1967.
16. ARING, C. D., AND TRUFANT, S. A.: *Effects of heavy metals on the central nervous system.* Proc. Assn. Res. Nerv. Ment. Dis. 32:463, 1953.
17. ASTRÖM, K. E.; MANCALL, E. L.; AND RICHARDSON, E. P., JR.: *Progressive multifocal leukoencephalopathy; a hitherto unrecognized complication of chronic lymphocytic leukaemia and Hodgkin's disease.* Brain 81:93, 1958.
18. BAKER, A. B., AND TICHY, F. Y.: *The effects of the organic solvents and industrial poisonings on the central nervous system.* Proc. Assn. Res. Nerv. Ment. Dis. 32:475, 1953.
19. BALDUZZI, O.: *Die tumoren des corpus callosum.* Arch. Psychiatr. Nervenkr. 79:1, 1927.
20. BALDWIN, M. V.: *A clinico-experimental investigation into the psychologic aspects of multiple sclerosis.* J. Nerv. Ment. Dis. 115:299, 1952.
21. BARTTER, F. C.: *The parathyroid gland and its relationship to diseases of the nervous system.* Proc. Assn. Res. Nerv. Ment. Dis. 32:1, 1953.
22. BARUK, H.: *Les troubles mentaux dans les tumeurs cérébrales.* Thèse, G. Doin et Cie, édit., Paris, 1926.
23. BASS, N. H.; HESS, H. H.; AND POPE, A.: *Altered cell membranes in Creutzfeldt-Jakob disease.* Arch. Neurol. 31:174, 1974.

24. BAUER, W. R.; TUREL, A. P.; AND JOHNSON, K. P.: *Progressive multifocal leukoencephalopathy and Cytarabine: Remission with treatment.* J.A.M.A. 226:174, 1973.

25. BEARN, A. G.: Wilson's Disease, in Stanbury, J. B., Wyngaarden, J. B., and Fredrickson, D. S. (eds.): *The Metabolic Basis of Inherited Disease,* ed. 3. McGraw-Hill Book Co., New York, 1972.

26. BERGIN, J. D.: *Rapidly progressing dementia in disseminated sclerosis.* J. Neurol. Neurosurg. Psychiatry 20:285, 1957.

27. BERLIN, L.: *Presenile sclerosis (Alzheimer's disease) with features resembling Pick's disease.* Arch. Neurol. Psychiat. 61:369, 1949.

28. BIRD, E. D.; CARO, A. J.; AND PILLING, J. B.: *Sex-related factor in inheritance of Huntingtons' chorea.* Ann. Hum. Genet. 37:255, 1974.

29. BITTENBENDER, J. B., AND QUADFASEL, F. A.: *Rigid and akinetic forms of Huntington's chorea.* Arch. Neurol. 7:275, 1962.

30. BLESSED, G.; TOMLINSON, B. E.; AND ROTH, M.: *The association between quantitative measures of dementia and of senile change in the cerebral grey matter of elderly subjects.* Br. J. Psychiatry 114:797, 1968.

31. BLINDERMAN, E. E.; WEIDNER, W.; AND MARKHAM, C. H.: *The pneumoencephalogram in Huntington's chorea.* Neurology (Minneap.) 14:601, 1964.

32. BLUMENTHAL, H., AND MILLER, C.: *Motor nuclear involvement in progressive supranuclear palsy.* Arch. Neurol. 20:362, 1969.

33. BOEHME, D. H.; COTTRELL, J. C.; LEONBERG, S. C.; AND ZEMAN, W.: *A dominant form of neuronal ceroid-lipofuscinosis.* Brain 94:745, 1971.

34. BOLT, J. M., AND LEWIS, G. P.: *Huntington's chorea.* Q. J. Med. 42:151, 1973.

35. BRACKENRIDGE, C. J.: *Relation of type of initial symptoms and line of transmission to ages at onset and death in Huntington's chorea.* Clin. Genet. 2:287, 1971.

36. BRAIN, R., AND HENSON, R. A.: *Neurological syndromes associated with carcinoma.* Lancet 2: 971, 1958.

37. BRIERLEY, J. B.; CORSELLIS, J. A. N.; HIERONS, R.; AND NEVIN, S.: *Subacute encephalitis of later adult life. Mainly affecting the limbic areas.* Brain 83:357, 1960.

38. BROWNELL, B., AND OPPENHEIMER, D. R.: *An ataxic form of subacute presenile polioencephalopathy (Creutzfeldt-Jakob disease).* J. Neurol. Neurosurg. Psychiatry 28:350, 1965.

39. BURGER, L. J.; ROWAN, A. J.; AND GOLDENSOHN, E. S.: *Creutzfeldt-Jakob disease. An electroencephalographic study.* Arch. Neurol. 26:428, 1972.

40. BURKS, J.; HUDDLESTONE, J.; LEWIN, E.; ALFREY, A., AND RUDOLPH, H.: *A progressive encephalopathy in chronic dialysis patients* (abstract). Neurology (Minneap.) 24:359, 1974.

41. BUSCH, E.: *Psychical symptoms in neurosurgical disease.* Acta Psychiatr. Neurol. Scand. 15: 257, 1940.

42. BUTLER, R. N.: *Psychiatric aspects of cerebrovascular disease in the aged.* Proc. Assn. Res. Nerv. Ment. Dis. 41: 255, 1961.

43. BUTLER, W. R.; ALLING, D. W.; SPICKARD, A.; AND UTZ, J. P.: *Diagnostic and prognostic value of clinical and laboratory findings in cryptococcal meningitis.* New Engl. J. Med. 270:59, 1964.

44. BYERS, R. K.; GILLES, F. H.; AND FUNG, C.: *Huntington's disease in children: Neuropathological study of four cases.* Neurology (Minneap.) 23:561, 1973.

45. CAPE, C. A.; MARTINEZ, A. J.; ROBERTSON, J. T.; HAMILTON, R.; AND JABBOUR, J. T.: *Adult onset of subacute sclerosing panencephalitis.* Arch. Neurol. 28:124, 1973.

46. CARNEY, M. W. P.: *Five cases of bromism.* Lancet 2:523, 1971.

47. CARTER, H. G., AND SUKAVAJANA, C.: *Familial cerebello-olivary degeneration with late development of rigidity and dementia.* Neurology (Minneap.) 6:976, 1956.

48. CH'IEN, L.; HATHAWAY, M.; AND ISRAEL, C. W.: *Seronegative dementia paralytica.* J. Neurol. Neurosurg. Psychiatry 33:376, 1970.

49. CLARKE, E., AND HARRISON, C. V.: *Bilateral carotid artery obstruction.* Neurology 6:705, 1956.

50. CORSELLIS, J. A. N., AND BRIERLEY, J. B.: *Observations on the pathology of insidious dementia following head injury.* Br. J. Psychiatry 105:714, 1959.

51. CREUTZFELDT, H. G.: *Über eine eigenartige herdförmige Erkrankung des Zentralnervensystems.* Z. ges. Neurol. Psychiat. 57:1, 1920.

52. CRITCHLEY, M.: *Medical aspects of boxing, particularly from a neurological viewpoint.* Br. Med. J. 1:357, 1957.

53. CURRIER, R. D.; DEJONG, R. N.; AND BOLE, G. G.: *Pulseless disease: Central nervous system manifestations.* Neurology (Minneap.) 4:818, 1954.

54. DAVID, N. J.; MACKEY, E. A., AND SMITH, J. L.: *Further observations in progressive supranuclear palsy.* Neurology (Minneap.) 18:349, 1968.

55. DAVIES, F. L.: *Mental abnormalities following subdural hematoma.* Lancet 1:1369, 1960.

56. DAVIES, J. A.; HUGHES, J. T.; AND OPPENHEIMER, D. R.: *Richardson's disease (progressive multifocal leukoencephalopathy).* Q. J. Med. 42:481, 1973.

57. DAVISON, C.: *Progressive subcortical encephalopathy. (Binswanger's disease).* J. Neuropathol. Exp. Neurol. 1:42, 1948.

58. DEMYER, W.; HARTER, D. H.; AND ZEMAN, W.: *Familial spasticity, hyperkinesia and dementia.* Acta Neuropathol. (Berl.) 4:28, 1964.

59. DENNY-BROWN, D.: *Abnormal copper metabolism and hepatolenticular degeneration.* Proc. Assn. Res. Nerv. Ment. Dis. 32:190, 1952.

60. DENNY-BROWN, D., AND PORTER, H.: *The effect of BAL (2, 3-dimercaptopropanol) on hepatolenticular degeneration (Wilson's disease).* New Engl. J. Med. 245:917, 1951.

61. DODGE, P. R., AND SWARTZ, M. N.: *Bacterial meningitis—a review of selected aspects. II. Special neurologic problems, postmeningitis complications and clinicopathological correlations.* New Engl. J. Med. 272:1003, 1965.

62. DONNER, M.; WALTIMO, O.; PORRAS, J.; FORSIUS, H.; AND SAUKKONEN, P. L.: *Subacute sclerosing panencephalitis as a cause of chronic dementia and relapsing brain disorder.* J. Neurol. Neurosurg. Psychiatry 35:180, 1972.

63. DRACHMAN, D. A., AND STAHL, S.: *Extrapyramidal dementia and levodopa.* Lancet 1:809, 1975.

64. DRAKE, E. W., JR.; BAKER, M.; BLUMENKRANTZ, J.; AND DAHLGREN, H.: *The quality and duration of survival in bilateral carotid occlusive disease. A preliminary survey of the effect of thromboendarterectomy.* Transactions Sixth Conference on Cerebral Vascular Diseases. Grune & Stratton, Inc., New York, 1968.

65. DUFFY, P.; WOLF, J.; COLLINS, G.; DEVOE, A. G.; STREETEN, G.; AND COWAN, D.: *Possible person-to-person transmission of Creutzfeldt-Jakob disease.* New Engl. J. Med. 290:692, 1974.

66. Editorial: *Boxing brains.* Lancet 2:1064, 1973.

67. Editorial: *Presymptomatic detection of Huntington's chorea.* Br. Med. J. 3:540, 1972.

68. EHRENTHEIL, O.: *Differential diagnosis of organic dementias and affective disorders in aged persons.* Geriatrics 12:426, 1957.

69. EIDEN, H. F., AND LECHNER, H.: *Über psychotische Zustandsbilder bei der Pickschen und Alzheimerschen Krankheit.* Arch. Psychiatr. Nervenkr. 184:393, 1950. (Quoted by Sjögren et al. See Reference 248).

70. EITINGER, L.: *Concentration Camp Survivors in Norway and Israel.* Universitetsforlaget, Oslo, and Allen and Unwin, London, 1964.

71. ELITHORN, A.; LUNZER, M.; AND WEINMAN, J.: *Cognitive deficits associated with chronic hepatic encephalopathy and their response to levodopa.* J. Neurol. Neurosurg. Psychiatry 38:794, 1975.

72. ELIZAN, T. S.; CHEN, K.; MATHAI, K. V.; DUNN, D.; AND KURLAND, L. T.: *Amyotrophic lateral sclerosis and parkinsonism-dementia complex.* Arch. Neurol. 14:347, 1966.

73. ELIZAN, T. S.; HIRANO, A.; ABRAMS, B. M.; NEED, R. L.; VANKUIS, C.; AND KURLAND, L. T.: *Amyotrophic lateral sclerosis and parkinsonism-dementia complex of Guam.* Arch. Neurol. 14:356, 1966.

74. ELLIS, W. G.; MCCULLOCH, J. R.; AND CORLEY, C. L.: *Presenile dementia in Down's syndrome.* Neurology (Minneap.) 24:101, 1974.

75. ERAUT, D.: *Idiopathic hypoparathyroidism presenting as dementia.* Br. Med. J. 1:429, 1974.

76. FALK, A.: *Tuberculous meningitis in adults, with special reference to survival, neurologic residuals and work status.* Am. Rev. Respir. Dis. 91:823, 1965.

77. FARMER, T. W.: *Neurologic complications during meningococcic meningitis treated with sulfonamide drugs.* Arch. Intern. Med. 76:201, 1945.

78. FELDMAN, R. G.; CHANDLER, K. A.; LEVY, L. L.; AND GLASER, G. H.: *Familial Alzheimer's disease.* Neurology (Minneap.) 13:811, 1963.

79. FIELDS, W. S.; EDWARDS, W. H.; AND CRAWFORD, E. S.: *Bilateral carotid artery thrombosis.* Arch. Neurol. 4:369, 1961.

80. FISHER, C. M.: *The clinical picture in Creutzfeldt-Jakob disease.* Trans. Am. Neurol. Assn. 85: 147, 1960.

81. FISHER, C. M.: *Dementia in cerebral vascular diseases.* Transactions Sixth Conference on Cerebral Vascular Diseases, Grune & Stratton, Inc., New York, 1968.

82. FISHER, M.: *Senile-dementia—a new explanation of its causation.* Can. Med. Assoc. J. 65:1, 1951.

83. FISHER, M.: *Occlusion of the carotid arteries.* Arch. Neurol. Psychiat. 72:187, 1954.

84. FOLEY, J. M., AND DENNY-BROWN, D.: *Subacute progressive bulbar myoclonus.* J. Neuropath. Exp. Neurol. 16:133, 1957.

85. FOLTZ, E. I., AND WARD, A. A.: *Communicating hydrocephalus from subarachnoid hemorrhage.* J. Neurosurg. 13:546, 1956.

86. FRAME, B., AND CARTER, S.: *Pseudohypoparathyroidism.* Neurology (Minneap.) 5:297, 1955.

87. FRASER, T. N.: *Cerebral manifestations of Addisonian pernicious anemia.* Lancet 2:458, 1960.

88. FRAZIER, C. H.: *Tumor involving the frontal lobe alone.* Arch. Neurol. Psychiat. 35:525, 1936.

89. FRAZIER, C. H., AND WAGGONER, R. W.: *Tumors of the occipital lobe.* Arch. Neurol. Psychiat. 22:1086, 1929.

90. GAJDUSEK, D. C., AND ZIGAS, V.: *Kuru: Clinical, pathological and epidemiological study of an acute progressive degenerative disease of the central nervous system among natives of the Eastern Highland of New Guinea.* Am. J. Med. 26:442, 1959.

91. GAJDUSEK, D. C.; GIBBS, C. J., JR.; AND ALPERS, M.: *Transmission and passage of experimental "kuru" to chimpanzees.* Science 155:212, 1967.

92. GARCIN, R.; BRION, S.; AND KHOCHNEVIS, A.: *Le syndrome de Creutzfeldt-Jakob et les syndromes cortico-striés du presenium.* Rev. Neurol. 106:506, 1962.

93. GASCON, G., AND GILLES, F.: *Limbic dementia.* J. Neurol. Neurosurg. Psychiatry 36:421, 1973.

94. GAUTIER-SMITH, P. C.: Clinical aspects of hypoglycaemia, in Cumings, J. N., and Kremer, M. (eds.): *Biochemical Aspects of Neurological Disorders.* (Second Series) J. B. Lippincott Company (Blackwell Scientific Publications), Philadelphia, 1965.

95. GESCHWIND, N.: *The mechanism of normal pressure hydrocephalus.* J. Neurol. Sci. 7:481, 1968.

96. GIBBS, C. J.; GAJDUSEK, D. C.; ASHER, D. M.; ALPERS, M. P.; BECK, E.; DANIEL, P. M.; AND MATTHEWS, W. B.: *Creutzfeldt-Jakob disease (spongiform encephalopathy): Transmission to the chimpanzee.* Science 161:388, 1968.

97. GILBERT, G. J.; AND GLASER, G. H.: *Neurologic manifestations of chronic carbon monoxide poisoning.* New Engl. J. Med. 261:1217, 1959.

98. GILMAN, S., AND HORENSTEIN, S.: *Familial amyotrophic dystonic paraplegia.* Brain 87:51, 1964.

99. GLASER, G. H.: Neurologic complications of internal disease, in Baker, A. B. (ed.): *Clinical Neurology.* Hoeber-Harper, New York, 1962, Chap 46.

100. GLASER, G. H; SOLITAIRE, G. B.; AND MANUELIDIS, E. E.: *Acute and subacute inclusion encephalitis.* Res. Publ. Assn. Res. Nerv. Ment. Dis. 44:178, 1964.

101. GOLDHAMMER, Y.; BUBIS, J. J.; SAROVAPINHAS, I.; AND GRAHAM, J.: *Subacute spongiform encephalopathy and its relation to Jakob-Creutzfeldt disease.* J. Neurol. Neurosurg. Psychiatry 35:1, 1972.

102. GOMORI, A. J.; PARTNOW, M. J.; HOROUPIAN, D. S.; AND HIRANO, A.: *Ataxic form of Creutzfeldt-Jakob disease.* Arch. Neurol. 29:318, 1973.

103. GONATAS, N. K.; TERRY, R. D.; AND WEISS, M.: *Ultrastructural studies in Jakob-Creutzfeldt disease.* Trans. Am. Neurol. Assoc. 89:13, 1964.

104. GOODMAN, L.: *Alzheimer's disease.* J. Nerv. Ment. Dis. 117:97, 1953.

105. GOODMAN, R. M.; HALL, C. L., JR.; TERANCO, L.; PERRINE, G. A., JR.; AND ROBERTS, P. L.: *Huntington's chorea.* Arch. Neurol. 15:345, 1966.

106. GORDON, E. B., AND SIM, M.: *The EEG in presenile dementia.* J. Neurol. Neurosurg. Psychiatry 30:285, 1967.

107. GOTTFRIES, C. G.; KJÄLLQUIST, A.; PONTÉN, U.; ROOS, B. E.; AND SUNDBÄRG, G.: *Cerebrospinal fluid pH and monoamine and glycolytic metabolites in Alzheimer's disease.* Br. J. Psychiatry 124:280, 1974.

108. GREEN, M. A., STEVENSON, L. D., FONSECA, J. E., AND WORTIS, S. B.: *Cerebral biopsy in patients with presenile dementia.* Dis. Nerv. Svst. 13:303, 1952.

109. GREENFIELD, J. G.: *The Spino-Cerebellar Degenerations.* Charles C Thomas, Publisher, Springfield, Ill., 1954.

110. GREENFIELD, J. G.: Hepatolenticular degeneration (Wilson's disease), in Blackwood, W., et al. (ed.): *Greenfield's Neuropathology,* ed. 2. The Williams & Wilkins Co., Baltimore, 1966.

111. GROSSBERG, S.; HEYMAN, A.; AND KEEHN, R. J.: *Neurologic sequelae of Japanese encephalitis.* Trans. Am. Neurol. Assoc. 87:114, 1962.

112. GURDJIAN, E. S., AND WEBSTER, J. E.: *Head Injuries.* Little, Brown and Company, Boston, 1958.

113. GUVENER, A.; BAGCHI, B. K.; KOOI, K. A.; AND CALHOUN, H. D.: *Mental and seizure manifestations in relation to brain tumors.* Epilepsia 5:166, 1964.

114. HACHINSKI, V. C.; LASSEN, N. A.; AND MARSHALL, J.: *Multi-infarct dementia.* Lancet 2:207, 1974.

115. HAKIM, S., AND ADAMS, R. D.: *The special clinical problems of symptomatic hydrocephalus with normal cerebrospinal fluid pressure. Observations on cerebrospinal fluid hydrodynamics.* J. Neurol. Sci. 2:307, 1965.

116. HALLERVORDEN, J., AND SPATZ, H.: *Eigenartige Erkrankung im extrapyramidalen System mit besonderer Beteiligung des Globus pallidus und der Substantia nigra.* Z. ges. Neurol. Psychiat. 79:254, 1922.

117. HALLIDAY, A. M.: The clinical incidence of myoclonus, in Williams, D. (ed.): *Modern Trends in Neurology,* ed. 4. Appleton-Century-Crofts, New York, 1967.

118. HANNA, S. M.: *Hypopituitarism (Sheehan's syndrome) presenting with organic dementia.* J. Neurol. Neurosurg. Psychiatry 33:192, 1970.

119. HARRIMAN, D. G. F., AND MILLAR, J. H. D.: *Progressive familial myoclonic epilepsy in three families: Its clinical features and pathological basis.* Brain 78:325, 1955.

120. HÉCAEN, H.: AND AJURIAGUERRA, J. DE: *Troubles mentaux au cours des tumeurs intracraniennes.* Masson et Cie, Paris, 1956.

121. HEIDENHAIN, A.: *Klinische und anatomische Untersuchungen über eine eigenartige organische Erkrankung des Zentralnervensystems im Praesenium.* Z. ges. Neurol. Psychiat. 118:49, 1928.

122. HEILMAN, K. M., AND FISHER, W. R.: *Hyperlipidemic dementia.* Arch. Neurol. 31:67, 1974.

123. HENRY, G. W.: *Mental phenomena observed in cases of brain tumor.* Am. J. Psychiat. 12:415, 1932.

124. HESTON, L. L.; LOWTHER, D. L. W.; AND LEVENTHAL, C. M.: *Alzheimer's disease.* Arch. Neurol. 15:225, 1966.

125. HILL, M. E.; HOUGHEED, W. M.; AND BARNETT, H. J. M.: *A treatable form of dementia due to normal-pressure, communicating hydrocephalus.* Can. Med. Assoc. J. 97:1309, 1967.

126. HILLBOM, E., AND CARHO, L.: Posttraumatic Korsakoff syndrome, in Walker, A. E.; Caveness, W. F.; and Critchley, M. (eds.): *The Late Effects of Head Injury.* Charles C Thomas, Publisher, Springfield, Ill., 1969.

127. HIRANO, A.; KURLAND, L. T.; KROOTH, R. S.; AND LESSELL, S.: *Parkinsonism-dementia complex, an endemic disease on the island of Guam: I. Clinical features.* Brain 84:642, 1961.

128. HIRANO, A.; MALAMUD, N., ELIZAN, T. S.; AND KURLAND, L. T.: *Amyotrophic lateral sclerosis and parkinsonism-dementia complex on Guam.* Arch. Neurol. 15:35, 1966.

129. HIRANO, A.; MALAMUD, N.; AND KURLAND, L. T.: *Parkinsonism-dementia complex, an endemic disease on the island of Guam: II. Pathological features.* Brain 84:662, 1961.

130. HIROSE, G., AND BASS, N. H.: *Metachromatic leukodystrophy in the adult.* Neurology (Minneap.) 22:312, 1972.

131. HORNABROOK, R. W.: *Kuru—a subacute cerebellar degeneration. The natural history and clinical features.* Brain 91:53, 1968.

60

132. HOSSAIN, M.: *Neurologic and psychiatric manifestations in idiopathic hypoparathyroidism: Response to treatment.* J. Neurol. Neurosurg. Psychiatry 33:153, 1970.

133. HUGHES, C. P.; MYERS, F. K.; SMITH, K.; AND TORACK, R. M.: *Nosologic problems in dementia: A clinical and pathologic study of 11 cases.* Neurology (Minneap.) 23:344, 1973.

134. HUNTER, R.; DAYAN, A. D.; AND WILSON, J.: *Alzheimer's disease in one monozygotic twin.* J. Neurol. Neurosurg. Psychiatry 35:707, 1972.

135. HUNTINGTON, G.: *On chorea.* Med. and Surg. Reporter, Phila. 26:317, 1872.

136. IRONSIDE, R.; BOSANQUET, F. D.; AND MCMENEMEY, W. H.: *Central demyelination of the corpus callosum (Marchiafava-Bignami disease).* Brain 84:212, 1961.

137. JAKOB, A.: *Die extrapyramidalen Erkrankungen.* Springer, Berlin, 1923.

138. JANEWAY, R.; RAVENS, J. R.; PEARCE, L. A.; ODOR, D. L.; AND SUZUKI, K.: *Progressive myoclonus epilepsy with Lafora inclusion bodies. I. Clinical, genetic, histopathologic and biochemical aspects.* Arch. Neurol. 16:565, 1967.

139. JELLINEK, E. H.: *Fits, faints, coma and dementia in myxedema.* Lancet 2:1010, 1962.

140. JELLINGER, K.; SEITELBERGER, F.; HEISS, W. D.; AND HOLCZABEK, W.: *Conjugal form of subacute spongiform encephalopathy (Creutzfeldt-Jakob disease).* Wien. Klin. Wochenschr. 84:245, 1972. Abstracted in DeJong, R. N., and Sugar, O. (eds.): *Yearbook of Neurology and Neurosurgery.* Yearbook Medical Publisher, Chicago, 1973.

141. JERVIS, C. A.: *Huntington's chorea in childhood.* Arch. Neurol. 9:244, 1963.

142. JOHNSON, R. T., AND JOHNSON, K. P.: Slow chronic virus infections of the nervous system, in Plum, F. (ed.): *Recent Advances in Neurology.* F. A. Davis Co., Philadelphia, 1969.

143. KARPATI, G., AND FRAME, B.: *Neuropsychiatric disorders in primary hyperparathyroidism.* Arch. Neurol. 10:387, 1964.

144. KESCHNER, M.; BENDER, M. B.; AND STRAUSS, I.: *Mental symptoms associated with brain tumor. Study of 530 verified cases.* J.A.M.A. 110:714, 1938.

145. KIRSCHBAUM, W. R.: *Jakob-Creutzfeldt disease.* American Elsevier Publishing Co., New York, 1968.

146. KNEHR, C. A., AND BEARN, A. G.: *Psychological impairment in Wilson's disease.* J. Nerv. Ment. Dis. 124:251, 1956.

147. KNIGHT, A.; O'BRIEN, P.; AND OSOBA, D.: *"Spontaneous" progressive multifocal leukoencephalopathy: Immunologic aspects.* Ann. Intern. Med. 77:229, 1972.

148. KOLODNY, A.: *The symptomatology of tumours of the temporal lobe.* Brain 51:385, 1928.

149. KONIGSMARK, B. W.; AND WEINER, L. P.: *The olivopontocerebellar atrophies: A review.* Medicine 49:227, 1970.

150. KRIGMAN, M. R.; FELDMAN, R. G.; AND BENSCH. K.: *Alzheimer's presenile dementia.* Lab. Invest. 14:381, 1965.

151. KURLAND, L. T.; FARO, S. N., AND SIEDLER, H.: *Minamata disease.* World Neurol. 1:370, 1960.

152. LAFORA, G., AND GLUECK, B.: *Beitrag zur Histopathologie der myoklonischen Epilepsie.* Z. ges. Neur. Psychiat. 6:1, 1911.

153. LAMPERT, P.; TOM, M. I.; AND CUMINGS, J. N.: *Encephalopathy in Whipple's disease.* Neurology (Minneap.) 12:65, 1962.

154. LEESE, S. M.; POND, D. A.; SHIELDS, J.; AND RACE, R. R.: *A pedigree of Huntington's chorea, with a note on linkage data.* Ann. Eugen. 17:92, 1952.

155. LEHRER, G. M.: *Neuropsychiatric manifestations of hypercalcemia.* Arch. Neurol. Psychiat. 81:709, 1959.

156. LESSE, S.; HOEFER, P. F. A.; AND AUSTIN, J. H.: *The electroencephalogram in diffuse encephalopathies.* Arch. Neurol. Psychiat. 79:359, 1958.

157. LETEMENDIA, F., AND PAMPIGLIONE, G.: *Clinical and electroencephalographic observations in Alzheimer's disease.* J. Neurol. Neurosurg. Psychiatry 21:167, 1958.

158. LEVENTHAL, C. M.; BARINGER, J. R.; ARNASON, B. G.; AND FISHER, C. M.: *A case of Marchiafava-Bignami disease with clinical recovery.* Trans. Am. Neurol. Assoc. 90:87, 1965.

159. LIDDELL, D. W.: *Investigations of EEG findings in presenile dementia.* J. Neurol. Neurosurg. Psychiatry 21:173, 1958.

160. LIN, J. P.; GOODKIN, R.; TONG, E. C. K.; EPSTEIN, F. J. AND VINCIGUERRA, E.: *Radioiodinated serum albumin (RISA) cisternography in the diagnosis of incisural block and occult hydrocephalus.* Radiology 90:36, 1968.

161. LOCKE, S.; MERRILL, J. P.; AND TYLER, H. R.: *Neurological complications of uremia.* Arch. Intern. Med. 108:519, 1961.

162. LORANGER, A. W.; GOODELL, H.; McDOWELL, F. H.; LEE, J. E.; AND SWEET, R. D.: *Intellectual impairment in Parkinson's syndrome.* Brain 95:405, 1972.

163. LORANGER, A. W.; GOODELL, H.; McDOWELL, F. H.; LEE, J. E.; AND SWEET, R. D.: *Parkinsonism, L-dopa, and intelligence.* Am. J. Psychiatry 130:1386, 1973.

164. LORBER, J.: *Long-term follow-up of 100 children who recovered from tuberculous meningitis.* Pediatrics 28:778, 1961.

165. LUNDBORG, H.: *Der Erbgang der progressiven Myoclonus-Epilepsie.* Z. ges. Neur. Psychiat. 9: 353, 1912.

166. LUSE, S. A., AND SMITH, J. R.: *The ultrastructure of senile plaques.* Am. J. Pathol. 44:553, 1964.

167. MAAS, O., AND PATERSON, A. S.: *Genetic and familial aspects of dystrophia myotonica.* Brain 66:55, 1943.

168. MAHURKAR, S.; DHAR, S.; SALTA, R.; MEYERS, L., JR.; SMITH, E. C.; AND DUNEA, C.: *Dialysis dementia.* Lancet 1:1412, 1973.

169. MAJTÉNY, K.: *Beiträge zur Pathologie der subakuten spongiösen Enzephalopathie.* Acta Neuropathol. 4:491, 1965.

170. MALAMUD, N., AND COHEN, P.: *Unusual form of cerebellar ataxia with sex-linked inheritance.* Neurology (Minneap.) 8:261, 1958.

171. MALAMUD, N.; HIRANO, A.; AND KURLAND, L. T.: *Pathoanatomic changes in amyotrophic lateral sclerosis on Guam—special reference to occurrence of neurofibrillary changes.* Arch. Neurol. 5:401, 1961.

172. MARIN, O.; AND VIAL, J. D.: *Neuropathological and ultrastructural findings in two cases of subacute spongiform encephalopathy.* Acta Neuropathol. 4:218, 1964.

173. MARKHAM, C. H., AND KNOX, J. W.: *Observations on Huntington's chorea in childhood.* J. Pediatr. 67:46, 1965.

174. MARSDEN, C. D., AND HARRISON, M. J. G.: *Outcome of investigation of patients with presenile dementia.* Br. Med. J. 2:249, 1972.

175. MARTIN, W. E.; LOEWENSON, R. B.; RESCH, J. A.; AND BAKER, A. B.: *Parkinson's disease: clinical analysis of 100 patients.* Neurology (Minneap.) 23:783, 1973.

176. MAWDSLEY, C., AND FERGUSON, F. R.: *Neurological disease in boxers.* Lancet 2:795, 1963.

177. MAY, W. W.: *Creutzfeldt-Jakob disease, I. Survey of the literature and clinical diagnosis.* Acta Neurol. Scand. 44:1, 1968.

178. MAY, W. W.; ITABASHI, H. H.; AND DEJONG, R. N.: *Creutzfeldt-Jakob disease. II. Clinical, pathologic and genetic study of a family.* Arch. Neurol. 19:137, 1968.

179. McDONALD, C.: *Clinical heterogeneity in senile dementia.* Br. J. Psychiatry 115:267, 1969.

180. McGOVERN, G. P.; MILLER, D. H.; AND ROBERTSON, E.: *A mental syndrome associated with lung carcinoma.* Arch. Neurol. Psychiat. 81:341, 1959.

181. McMENEMEY, W. H.: *Alzheimer's disease: problems concerning its concept and nature.* Acta Neurol. Scand. 39:369, 1963.

182. McMENEMEY, W. H.: The dementias and progressive diseases of the basal ganglia, in Blackwood, W., et al. (eds.): *Greenfield's Neuropathology,* ed. 2. The Williams & Wilkins Co., Baltimore, 1966.

183. MERRITT, H. H.: *A Textbook of Neurology,* ed. 5. Lea & Febiger, Philadelphia, 1973.

184. MESSERT, B., AND BAKER, N. H.: *Syndrome of progressive spastic ataxia and apraxia associated with occult hydrocephalus.* Neurology 16:440, 1966.

185. MEYER, A.: Intoxications, in Blackwood, W., et al. (eds.): *Greenfield's Neuropathology,* ed. 2. The Williams & Wilkins Co., Baltimore, 1966. Chap. 4.

186. MEYER, A.: The Hallervorden-Spatz syndrome, in Blackwood, W., et al. (eds.): *Greenfield's Neuropathology,* ed. 2. The Williams & Wilkins Co., Baltimore, 1966.

187. MEYER, A., LEIGH, D., AND BAGG, C. E.: *A rare presenile dementia associated with cortical blindness (Heidenhain's syndrome).* J. Neurol. Neurosurg. Psychiatry 17:129, 1954.

188. MILLER, H., AND STERN, G.: *The long-term prognosis of severe head injury.* Lancet 1:225, 1965.

189. MOERSCH, F. P.: *Psychic manifestations in brain tumors.* Am. J. Psychiatry 4:705, 1925.

190. MONIZ, E.: *Les tumeurs du corps calleux.* L'Encéphale 22:514, 1927.

191. MOSKOWITZ, M. A.; WINICKOFF, R. N.; AND HEINZ, E. R.: *Familial calcification of the basal ganglia.* New Engl. J. Med. 285:72, 1971.

192. MULDER, D. W.: Psychoses with brain tumors and other chronic neurologic disorders, in Arieti, S. (ed.): *American Handbook of Psychiatry.* Basic Books. New York, 1959, Chap. 55.

193. MÜLLER, D.; PILZ, H.; AND TERMEULEN, V.: *Studies on adult metachromatic leukodystrophy, Part 1 (Clinical, morphological and histochemical observations in two cases).* J. Neurol. Sci. 9: 567, 1969.

194. MURRAY, R. M.; GREENE, J. G.; AND ADAMS, J. H.: *Analgesic abuse and dementia.* Lancet 2: 242, 1971.

195. NEUMANN, M. A.: *Chronic progressive subcortical encephalopathy — report of a case.* J. Gerontol. 2:57, 1947.

196. NEUMANN, M. A., AND COHN, R.: *Incidence of Alzheimer's disease in a larger mental hospital.* Arch. Neurol. Psychiat. 69:615, 1953.

197. NEVIN, S.; MCMENEMEY, W. H.; BEHRMAN, S.; AND JONES, D. P.: *Subacute spongiform encephalopathy — A subacute form of encephalopathy attributable to vascular dysfunction (spongiform cerebral atrophy).* Brain 83:519, 1960.

198. NICKEL, S. N., AND FRAME, B.: *Neurologic manifestations of myxedema.* Neurology (Minneap.) 8:54, 1958.

199. NIEDERMEYER, E.; ZELLWEGER, H.; AND ALEXANDER, T.: *Central nervous system manifestations in myopathics.* Proceedings 8th International Congress of Neurology, Vienna, vol. 2, p. 293, 1965.

200. NOAD, K. B., AND LANCE, J. W.: *Familial myoclonic epilepsy and its association with cerebellar disturbance.* Brain 83:618, 1960.

201. O'CONNOR, J. F., AND MUSHER, D. M.: *Central nervous system involvement in systemic lupus erythematosus.* Arch. Neurol. 14:157, 1966.

202. OLIVECRONA, H., AND RIIVES, J.: *Arteriovenous aneurysms of the brain; their diagnosis and treatment.* Arch. Neurol. Psychiat. 59:567, 1948.

203. OLSZEWSKI, J.: *Subcortical arteriosclerotic encephalopathy.* World Neurol. 3:359, 1962.

204. OPDENVELDE, W., AND STAM, F. C.: *Haptoglobin types in Alzheimer's disease and senile dementia.* Br. J. Psychiatry 122:331, 1973.

205. OTO, Y.: Psychiatric studies on civilian head injuries, in Walker, A. E.; Caveness, W. F.; and Critchley, M. (eds.): *The Late Effects of Head Injury.* Charles C Thomas, Publisher, Springfield, Ill., 1969.

206. PALLIS, C. A., AND SPILLANE, J. D.: *A subacute progressive encephalopathy with mutism, hypokinesia, rigidity and myoclonus.* Q. J. Med. 26:349, 1957.

207. PARKES, J. D.; MARSDEN, C. D.; REES, J. D.; CURZON, G.; KANTAMANENI, B. D.; KNILL-JONES, R.; AKBAR, A.; DAS, S.; AND KATARIA, M.: *Parkinson's disease, cerebral arteriosclerosis and senile dementia.* Q. J. Med. 43:49, 1974.

208. PARKINSON, J.: *An essay on the shaking palsy.* (Reprinted.) Arch. Neurol. 20:441, 1969.

209. PARSONS, O. A.; STEWART, K. D.; AND ARENBERG, D.: *Impairment of abstracting ability in multiple sclerosis.* J. Nerv. Ment. Dis. 125:221, 1957.

210. PASKIND, H. A., AND STONE, T. T.: *Familial spastic paralysis.* Arch. Neurol. Psychiat. 30:481, 1933.

211. PATTERSON, R. M., BAGCHI, B. K., AND TEST, A.: *The prediction of Huntington's chorea, an electroencephalographic and genetic study.* Am. J. Psychiatry 104:786, 1948.

212. PAULSON, G. W., AND PERRINE, G., JR.: *Cerebral vascular disease in mental hospitals.* Transactions Sixth Conference on Cerebral Vascular Diseases. Grune & Stratton, New York, 1968.

213. PAULSON, G. W.; KAPP. J.; AND COOK, W.: *Dementia associated with bilateral carotid artery disease.* Geriatrics 21:159, 1966.

214. PERLMUTTER, I.: *Subdural hematoma in older persons.* J.A.M.A. 176:212, 1961.

215. PIERCY, M.: Studies of the neurological basis of intellectual function, in Williams, D. (ed.): *Modern Trends in Neurology*. Appleton-Century-Crofts, New York, 1967.

216. PLUM, F., AND POSNER, J. B.: *Diagnosis of Stupor and Coma*, ed. 2. F. A. Davis Co., Philadelphia, 1972.

217. PLUM, F.; POSNER, J. B.; AND HAIN, R. F.: *Delayed neurological deterioration after anoxia*. Arch. Intern. Med. 110:18, 1962.

218. POLDOLSKY, S.; LEOPOLD, N. A.; AND SAX, D. S.: *Increased frequency of diabetes mellitus in patients with Huntington's chorea*. Lancet 1:1356, 1972.

219. POLLOCK, M., AND HORNABROOK, R. W.: *The prevalence, natural history and dementia of Parkinson's disease*. Brain 89:429, 1966.

220. PRATT, R. T. C.: *The Genetics of Neurological Disorders*. Oxford monographs on medical genetics, Oxford University Press, New York, 1967.

221. RASKIN, N., AND EHRENBERG, R.: *Cerebral arteriosclerosis*. Am. Pract. Digest Treatment 7: 1095, 1956.

222. RASKIN, N., AND EHRENBERG, R.: *Senescence, senility and Alzheimer's disease*. Am. J. Psychiatry 113:133, 1956.

223. REED, D.; PLATO, C.; ELIZAN, T.; AND KURLAND, L. T.: *The ALS-Parkinsonism-dementia complex: A ten-year-follow-up on Guam*. Am. J. Epidemiol. 83:54, 1966.

224. REFSUM, S.; ENGESET, A.; AND LÖNNUM, A.: *Pneumoencephalographic changes in dystrophia myotonica*, Acta Psychiat. Neurol. Scand. (Suppl.) 137:98, 1959.

225. REYNOLDS, E. H.: *Mental effects of anticonvulsants and folic acid metabolism*. Brain 91:197, 1968.

226. REYNOLDS, E. H.; ROTHFELD, P.; AND PINCUS, J. H.: *Neurological disease associated with folate deficiency*. Br. Med. J. 2:398, 1973.

227. RICHARDSON, E. P., JR.: Progressive multifocal leukoencephalopathy, in Brain, R. L., and Norris, F. H., Jr. (eds.): *Remote Effects of Cancer on the Nervous System*. Contemporary Neurology Symposia, Vol. I., Grune & Stratton, New York, 1965.

228. RICHARDSON, E. P., JR.: Progressive multifocal leukoencephalopathy, in Vinken, P. J., and Bruyn, G. W. (eds.): *Handbook of Clinical Neurology*, Vol. 9, Chap. 18. North-Holland Publishing Company, Amsterdam, 1970.

229. RICHARDSON, J. C.; CHAMBERS, R. A.; AND HEYWOOD, P. M.: *Encephalopathies of anoxia and hypoglycemia*. Arch. Neurol. 1:178, 1959.

230. RICHARDSON, M. E., AND BORNHOFEN, J. H.: *Early childhood cerebral lipidosis with prominent myoclonus*. Arch. Neurol. 18:34, 1968.

231. RIDDOCH, G.: *Progressive dementia, without headache or changes in the optic discs, due to tumours of the third ventricle*. Brain 59:225, 1936.

232. ROBINSON, K. C.; KALLBERG, M. H.; AND CROWLEY, M. F.: *Idiopathic hypoparathyroidism presenting as dementia*. Br. Med. J. 2:1203, 1954.

233. ROOS, R.; GAJDUSEK, D. C.; AND GIBBS, C. J., JR.: *The clinical characteristics of transmissible Creutzfeldt-Jakob disease*. Brain 96:1, 1973.

234. ROSMAN, N. P.; AND KAKULAS, B. A.: *Mental deficiency associated with muscular dystrophy. A neuropathological study*. Brain 89:769, 1966.

235. ROSS, A. T., AND REITAN, R. M.: *Intellectual and affective functions in multiple sclerosis*. Arch. Neurol. Psychiat. 13:663, 1955.

236. SANDERS, V.: *Neurologic manifestations of myxedema*. New Engl. J. Med. 266:547 and 599, 1962.

237. SANDERS, W. L., AND DUNN, T. L.: *Creutzfeldt-Jakob disease treated with Amantadine*. J. Neurol. Neurosurg. Psychiatry 36:581, 1973.

238. SCHAUMBURG, H. H., AND SUZUKI, K. L.: *Non-specific familial presenile dementia*. J. Neurol. Neurosurg. Psychiatry 31:479, 1968.

239. SCHLESINGER, B.: *Mental changes in intracranial tumors and related problems*. Conf. Neurol. 10:225, 322, 1950.

240. SCHULMAN, S.: *Bilateral symmetrical degeneration of the thalamus*. J. Neuropath. Exp. Neurol. 15:208, 1956.

241. SCHWARZ, G. A., AND YANOFF, M.: *Lafora's disease — a distinct genetically determined form of Unverricht's syndrome*. Arch. Neurol. 12:172, 1965.

242. SCHWEDENBERG, T. H.: *Leukoencephalopathy following carbon monoxide asphyxia*. J. Neuropathol. Exp. Neurol. 18:597, 1959.
243. SIEDLER, H., AND MALAMUD, N.: *Creutzfeldt-Jakob's disease*. J. Neuropathol. Exp. Neurol. 22: 381, 1963.
244. SILVERSTEIN, A.: *Occlusive disease of the carotid arteries*. Circulation 20:4, 1959.
245. SIM, M., AND SUSSMAN, I.: *Alzheimer's disease: Its natural history and differential diagnosis*. J. Nerv. Ment. Dis. 135:489, 1962.
246. SIMPSON, J. A.: *The neurological manifestations of idiopathic hypoparathyroidism*. Brain 75:76, 1952.
247. SJÖGREN, T.: *Klinische und erbbiologische Untersuchungen über die Heredoataxien*. Acta Psychiat. Kbh. Suppl. 27, 1943; quoted from Wilson, S. A. K.[311]
248. SJÖGREN, T.; SJÖGREN, H.; AND LINDGREN, A. G. H.: *Morbus Alzheimer and Morbus Pick. A genetic, clinical and pathoanatomical study*. Acta Psychiat. Neurol. Scand. (Suppl.) 82:1, 1952.
249. SMITH, A. D.: *Megaloblastic madness*. Br. Med. J. 2:1840, 1960.
250. SMYTH, G. E., AND STERN, K.: *Tumours of the thalamus — clinico-pathological study*. Brain 61: 339, 1938.
251. SONIAT, T. L. L.: *Psychiatric symptoms associated with intracranial neoplasms*. Am. J. Psychiatry 108:19, 1951.
252. SOURANDER, P., AND SJÖGREN, H.: The concept of Alzheimer's disease and its clinical implications, in Wolstenholme, G. E. W., and O'Connor, M. (eds.): *Alzheimer's Disease and Related Conditions*. J. & A. Churchill, London, 1970.
253. SPILLANE, J. D.: *Nutritional Disorders of the Nervous System*. Livingstone, Edinburgh, 1947.
254. SPILLANE, J. D.: *Nervous and mental disorders in Cushing's syndrome*. Brain 74:72, 1951.
255. SPILLANE, J. D.: *Five boxers*. Br. Med. J. 2:1205, 1962.
256. SPROFKIN, B. E., AND SCIARRA, D.: *Korsakoff psychosis associated with cerebral tumors*. Neurology (Minneap.) 2:427, 1952.
257. STEEGMAN, A. T.: *Anoxic encephalopathy and the cerebral circulation with reference to cardiovascular and respiratory disease*. Reports VII International Congress of Neurology, Rome, p.197, 1961.
258. STEELE, J. C.: *Progressive supranuclear palsy*. Brain 95:693, 1972.
259. STEELE, J. C.; RICHARDSON, J. C.; AND OLSZEWSKI, J.: *Progressive supranuclear palsy*. Arch. Neurol. 10:333, 1964.
260. STENGEL, E.: *A study of the symptomatology and differential diagnosis of Alzheimer's disease and Pick's disease*. J. Ment. Sci. 89:1, 1943.
261. STERN, K.: *Severe dementia associated with bilateral symmetrical degeneration of the thalamus*. Brain 62:157, 1939.
262. STERN, M., AND ROBBINS, E. S.: *Psychoses in systemic lupus erythematosus*. Arch. Gen. Psychiatry 3:205, 1960.
263. STEVENS, H., AND FORSTER, F. M.: *Effect of carbon tetrachloride on the nervous system*. Arch. Neurol. Psychiat. 70:635, 1953.
264. STOUPEL, N.; MONSEU, G.; PARDOE, A.; HEIMANN, R.; AND MARTIN, J. J.: *Encephalitis with myoclonus in Whipple's disease*. J. Neurol. Neurosurg. Psychiatry 32:338, 1969.
265. STRACHAN, R. W.: *The natural history of Takayasu's arteriopathy*. Q. J. Med. 33:57, 1964.
266. STRACHAN, R. W., AND HENDERSON, J. G.: *Psychiatric syndromes due to avitaminosis B_{12} with normal blood and bone marrow*. Q. J. Med. 34:303, 1965.
267. STRACHAN, R. W., AND HENDERSON, J. G.: *Dementia and folate deficiency*. Q. J. Med. 60:189, 1967.
268. STRICH, S. J.: The pathology of brain damage due to blunt head injuries, in Walker, A. E.; Caveness, W. F.; and Critchley, M. (eds.): *The Late Effects of Head Injury*. Charles C Thomas, Publisher, Springfield, Ill., 1969.
269. STRICKLAND, G. T., AND LEUK, M. L.: *Wilson's disease*. Medicine 54:113, 1975.
270. STUTEVILLE, P., AND WELCH, K.: *Subdural hematoma in the elderly person*. J.A.M.A. 168: 1445, 1958.
271. SUGAR, O.: *Central neurological complications of hypoparathyroidism*. Arch. Neurol. Psychiat. 70:86, 1953.

272. SUZUKI, K.; DAVID, E.; AND KUTSCHMAN, B.: *Presenile dementia with "lafora-like" intraneuronal inclusions.* Arch. Neurol. 25:69, 1971.

273. SWAIN, J. M.: *Electroencephalographic abnormalities in presenile atrophy.* Neurology (Minneap.) 9:722, 1959.

274. TALLAND, G. A.: *Psychological studies of Korsakoff's psychosis. II. Perceptual functions.* J. Nerv. Ment. Dis. 127:197, 1958.

275. TALLAND, G. A.: *Psychological studies of Korsakoff's psychosis. III. Concept formation.* J. Nerv. Ment. Dis. 128:214, 1969.

276. TARKKANEN, J. V.: *Otogenic brain abscess.* Acta Otolaryngol. (Suppl.) 185, 1963.

277. TAVERAS, J. M., AND WOOD, E. H.: *Diagnostic Neuroradiology,* ed. 2. The Williams & Wilkins Co., Baltimore, 1976.

278. TELLEZ-NAGEL, I., AND WISNIEWSKI, H. M.: *Ultrastructure of neurofibrillar tangles in Steele-Richardson-Olszewski syndrome.* Arch. Neurol. 29:324, 1973.

279. TERRY, R. D.: *The fine structure of neurofibrillary tangles in Alzheimer's disease.* J. Neuropathol. Exp. Neurol. 22:629, 1963.

280. TERRY, R. D.; GONATAS, N. K.; AND WEISS, M.: *Ultrastructural studies in Alzheimer's presenile dementia.* Am. J. Pathol. 44:269, 1964.

281. THOMASEN, E.: *Myotonia.* Ejnar Munksgaard, Copenhagen, 1948.

282. TOMLINSON, B. E.; BLESSED, G.; AND ROTH, M.: *Observations on the brains of demented old people.* J. Neurol. Sci. 11:205, 1970.

283. TÖNNIS, W.; SCHIEFER, W.; AND WALTER, W.: *Signs and symptoms of supratentorial arteriovenous aneurysms.* J. Neurosurg. 15:471, 1958.

284. TORVIK, A.; ENDRESEN, G. K. M.; ABRAHAMSEN, A. F., AND GODAL, H. C.: *Progressive dementia caused by an unusual type of generalized small vessel thrombosis.* Acta Neurol. Scand. 47:137, 1971.

285. TRETHOWAN, W. H., AND COBB, S.: *Neuropsychiatric aspects of Cushing's syndrome.* Arch. Neurol. Psychiat. 67:283, 1952.

286. TYLER, H. R.: *Neurologic disorders in renal failure.* Am. J. Med. 44:734, 1969.

287. TYNES, B. S.; CRUTCHER, J. C.; AND UTZ, J. P.: *Histoplasma meningitis.* Ann. Intern. Med. 59:615, 1973.

288. UNVERRICHT, H.: *Die Myoclonie.* Franz Deuticke, Leipzig, 1891.

289. UNVERRICHT, H.: *Über familiäre Myoclonie.* Deut. Z. Nervenheilk. 7:32, 1895.

290. UTZ, J. P.: *Histoplasma and cryptococcus meningitis.* Res. Publ. Assn. Res. Nerv. Ment. Dis. 44:378, 1964.

291. VAN DER ZWAN, A.: Late results from prolonged traumatic unconsciousness, in Walker, A. E.; Caveness, W. F.; and Critchley, M. (eds.): *The Late Effects of Head Injury.* Charles C Thomas, Publisher, Springfield, Ill., 1969.

292. VAN MANSFELT, J.: *Pick's Disease. A Syndrome of Lobar Cerebral Atrophy.* Enschede, 1954.

293. VERNON, M. L.; PUCILLO, D. A.; AND HAMILTON, R.: *Jacob-Creutzfeldt disease: Virus-like particles in two brain biopsies.* Fed. Proc. 29:286, 1970.

294. VICTOR, M.; ADAMS, R. D.; AND COLE, M.: *The acquired (non-Wilsonian) type of chronic hepatocerebral degeneration.* Medicine 44:345, 1965.

295. VICTOR, M.; ADAMS, R. D.; AND COLLINS, G. H.: *The Wernicke-Korsakoff Syndrome.* F. A. Davis Co., Philadelphia, 1971.

296. VICTOR, M.; TALLAND, G. A.; AND ADAMS, R. D.: *Psychological studies of Korsakoff's psychosis: I. General intellectual functions.* J. Nerv. Ment. Dis. 128:528, 1959.

297. WADIA, N., AND WILLIAMS, E.: *Behçet's syndrome with neurological complications.* Brain 80: 59, 1957.

298. WAGGONER, R. W.: Brain syndromes associated with intracranial neoplasm, in Freedman, A. M., and Kaplan, H. I. (eds.): *Comprehensive Textbook of Psychiatry.* The Williams & Wilkins Co., Baltimore, 1967. Chap. 20.4.

299. WAGGONER, R. W., AND MALAMUD, N.: *Wilson's disease in the light of cerebral changes following ordinary acquired liver disorders.* J. Nerv. Ment. Dis. 96:410, 1942.

300. WALLACE, D. C., AND HALL, A. C.: *Evidence of genetic heterogeneity in Huntington's chorea.* J. Neurol. Neurosurg. Psychiatry 35:789, 1972.

301. WALTHER-BÜEL, H.: *Die Psychiatrie der Hirngeschwülste.* Acta Neurochir. (Suppl. 2), 1961.

302. WALTON, J. N.: *Disorders of Voluntary Muscles,* ed. 3. Churchill Livingstone, London, 1974.

303. WATSON, C. W., AND DENNY-BROWN, D.: *Myoclonus epilepsy as a symptom of diffuse neuronal disease.* Arch. Neurol. Psychiatry 70:151, 1953.

304. WEINER, L. P.; HERNDON, R. M.; NARAYAN, O.; JOHNSON, R. T.; SHAH, K.; RUBENSTEIN, L. J.; PREZIOSI, T. J.; AND CONLEY, F. K.: *Isolation of virus related to SV40 from patients with progressive multifocal leukoencephalopathy.* New Engl. J. Med. 286:385, 1972.

305. WEINER, L. P.; NARAYAN, O.; PENNEY, J. B.; HERNDON, R. M.; FERINGA, E. R.; TOURTEL-LOTTE, W. W.; AND JOHNSON, R. T.: *Papovavirus of JC type in progressive multifocal leukoencephalopathy: rapid identification and subsequent isolation.* Arch. Neurol. 29:1, 1973.

306. WHITFIELD, C. L.; CH'IEN, L. T.; AND WHITEHEAD, J. D.: *Lead encephalopathy in adults.* Am. J. Med. 52:289, 1972.

307. WILLANGER, R.; THYGESEN, P.; NIELSEN, R.; AND PETERSON, O.: *Intellectual impairment and cerebral atrophy.* Danish Med. Bull. 15:65, 1968.

308. WILLIAMS, M., AND MCGEE, T. E.: *Psychological study of carotid occlusion and endarterectomy.* Arch. Neurol. 10:293, 1964.

309. WILLIAMS, M., AND PENNYBACKER, J.: *Memory disturbances in third ventricle tumors.* J. Neurol. Neurosurg. Psychiatry 17:115, 1954.

310. WILSON, S. A. K.: *Progressive lenticular degeneration: A familial nervous disease associated with cirrhosis of the liver.* Brain 34:295, 1912.

311. WILSON, S. A. K.: *Neurology,* ed. 2. Butterworth and Co., Ltd., London, 1954.

312. WINKELMAN, N., AND BOOK, M. H.: *Asymptomatic extrapyramidal involvement in Pick's disease.* J. Neuropathol. Exp. Neurol. 8:30, 1949.

313. WISNIEWSKI, H. M.; COBLENTZ, J. M.; AND TERRY, R. D.: *Pick's disease.* Arch. Neurol. 26:97, 1972.

314. WOLF, S. M., AND DAVIS, R. L.: *Permanent dementia in idiopathic Parkinsonism treated with Levodopa.* Arch. Neurol. 29:276, 1973.

315. WORDEN, D. K., AND VIGNOS, P. J.: *Intellectual function in childhood progressive muscular dystrophy.* Pediatrics 29:968, 1962.

316. ZU RHEIN, G. M., AND CHOU, S. M.: *Papova virus in progressive multifocal leukoencephalopathy.* Proc. Assn. Res. Nerv. Ment. Dis. 44:307, 1968.

CHAPTER 4

Normal Pressure Hydrocephalus

Robert Katzman, M.D.

The description of the syndrome of normal pressure hydrocephalus by Hakim and Adams[55] and Adams and coworkers[3] had a major impact upon neurology during the past decade. In its most common form, a communicating hydrocephalus develops producing a distinctive triad of clinical manifestations: gait disturbance (often the first and most disturbing symptom), progressive dementia, and, usually at a somewhat later state, urinary incontinence. Insertion of a shunt to relieve the hydrocephalus may produce dramatic alleviation of these symptoms. Two groups of patients have been identified. In one group, the disorder is *secondary* to previous head trauma, subarachnoid hemorrhage, or meningitis; whereas in the other group, often designated *idiopathic* normal pressure hydrocephalus, the cause is not apparent, the onset is often insidious, and the course is progressive. Occasionally, patients with internal obstructive hydrocephalus present this clinical syndrome, although frequently such patients present signs of increased intracranial pressure. In a review of the literature through 1970, Katzman and Pappius[78] found reported cases of 191 adult patients with normal pressure hydrocephalus, 47 of which were the idiopathic form. By the end of 1975, it was possible to compile reports of 914 cases in adults, 314 of which were the idiopathic form (Table 1).

Despite advances in diagnostic methods and accumulating clinical experience, the clinician concerned with an individual patient may face a dilemma, for the diagnostic criteria continue to be imprecise and the postoperative morbidity high. Yet, no physician wants to deny a patient with progressive dementia or gait disturbance an opportunity for recovery.

How then is the physician to reconcile his desire to reverse the symptoms in patients with progressive dementias and gait disturbances with his desire to "do no harm?" Adams and his colleagues[2, 109, 110] have suggested that the best results will be obtained if patients with the most typical clinical syndromes and the most typical laboratory findings are selected for shunt therapy. Although there is substantial evidence, which we will consider below, that these criteria are far from perfect, they are, nevertheless, the best available. Therefore, we will discuss in this chapter the most typical and atypical features in the clinical presentation and results of diagnostic tests to provide some basis for judgment by the individual physician. We will attempt to point out those features which lead the physician not to pursue the diagnosis. At the same time, however, we must recognize that our understanding of these disorders is fragmentary, and that the physician's ap-

Table 1. Etiology of hydrocephalus as reported in 914 adult patients[a]

Subarachnoid hemorrhage		315
Head injury		102
Aqueductal stenosis		34
Meningitis		34
Post-craniotomy		43
Obstructive lesions, fourth ventricle		21
Tumors, third ventricle		26
Basilar artery ectasia or aneurysm		11
Tumors, other locations including pituitary adenomas		7
Basilar impression, with or without Paget's disease		4
Syringomyelia		1
"Encephalopathy," "encephalitis"		2
Idiopathic or unknown		314
associated with: Parkinson's disease	15	
Alzheimer's disease	7	
Cerebrovascular disease	4	
Huntington's chorea	2	
Chronic epilepsy	2	

[a]This is a compilation of 191 cases analyzed by Katzman and Pappius (1973) plus the addition of 690 cases reported since 1968 and listed in the references.

proach may be markedly altered as our knowledge of the pathological and pathophysiological aspects of these disorders advances.

Prevalence and Age of Incidence

There are no accurate surveys on which to base an estimate of the prevalence of normal pressure hydrocephalus. Despite the large and expanding number of case reports, it has become abundantly clear that few of the demented patients in chronic hospitals or nursing homes will be found to have this condition or to respond to shunt therapy.[24] It is of interest, however, to attempt an educated guess as to the frequency of this syndrome. In a survey of patients admitted to the National Hospital, Queen Square, for the investigation of dementia, Marsden and Harrison[91] reported that idiopathic normal pressure hydrocephalus was diagnosed in 5 of 86 patients with dementia, a frequency of approximately 6 percent. Our own experience in a recent 1 year survey of patients admitted for investigation of dementia to a New York City municipal hospital is that this diagnosis was made in 3 of 56 patients; again, a frequency of about 5 percent. In both series, the patients were less than 70 years old. Looking at the age of incidence of idiopathic normal pressure hydrocephalus (Fig. 1), it is evident that this diagnosis is usually made in the presenium, with a peak in the late 50s. Assuming that idiopathic normal pressure hydrocephalus is usually a disease of the presenium, and assuming that only 5 to 10 percent of all persons with dementia are under 65 (an estimate based upon extrapolation of the age prevalence data on all forms of dementia in the Gruenberg[53] and Nielsen[105] surveys), the total number of cases of normal pressure hydrocephalus in the population of the United States would be between 2,000 and 12,000 (see Katzman and Karasu,[77] dependent upon estimate of patients with dementia or organic mental syndromes used in the United States). These figures would be in serious error if the age incidence of normal pressure hydrocephalus shown in Figure 1 were an artifact produced by the reluctance of the physician to

70

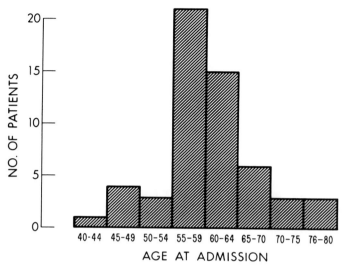

"IDIOPATHIC NORMAL-PRESSURE" HYDROCEPHALUS

Figure 1. Age at admission of patients with diagnosis of idiopathic normal pressure hydrocephalus compiled from published list. From Katzman.[75]

perform contrast studies in older patients. Presumably, with the increasing use of computerized axial tomography, it will be possible to resolve this question.

Normal CSF Pressure: Some Preliminary Pathophysiological Considerations

An important aspect of this syndrome is the presence of normal cerebrospinal fluid (CSF) pressure. Although there were early case reports of patients with communicating hydrocephalus and normal CSF pressure,[42] increased intracranial pressure had been considered one of the major manifestations of hydrocephalus. Thus the recognition that adults with hydrocephalus often have normal CSF pressure was a signal contribution of Hakim and Adams.[55] However, it has been difficult to understand the mechanisms underlying this fact. Hakim and Adams suggested that the increase in ventricular size was initially due to an increase in intraventricular pressure, but as ventricular surface area increased, the ventricle acted like an elastic balloon with the pressure decreasing in proportion to the surface area increase in the presence of a constant force that was assumed to be exerted. Unfortunately, this ingenious hypothesis does not appear to hold up upon critical analysis.[46] Rather, experimental studies suggest the CSF pressure returns to normal as a consequence of the development of alternate routes of CSF absorption.

Current understanding of hydrocephalus still depends upon the concept of CSF circulation developed by the neurosurgeon Dandy.[29, 32] Circulation of CSF begins with the elaboration of fluid in the ventricles and is aided by arterial pulsations of the choroid plexuses. Fluid circulates from the lateral ventricles into the third ventricle and then into the fourth ventricle. If obstructions are placed at the foramen between these ventricles, the ventricle upstream from the obstruction markedly enlarges producing an *internal* or *obstructive* hydrocephalus. The fluid passes from the fourth ventricle to the cisterna magna and then circulates into the cerebral and spinal subarachnoid spaces. The absorption of CSF occurs at arachnoid villi present near sagittal and other venous sinuses and along nerve roots and sheaths. Whether there is some CSF absorption from the subarachnoid space over the cerebral convexities into either pial blood vessels or into Virchow-Robin spaces in the cerebral cortex has not been resolved. A *communicating* hydrocephalus may develop if the flow of CSF to the cerebral subarachnoid space is impeded (as by meningeal fibrosis) as a consequence of pathological changes in the villi themselves or as a result of sinus thrombosis.

In man, CSF is formed at a rate of about 0.35 ml./min. This rate does not change appreciably either as CSF pressure changes or as a result of hydrocephalus.[28, 86, 88, 119] The pressure independence of CSF formation reflects the fact that CSF is formed by a secretory process. This pressure independence has been confirmed by most investigators,[16, 23, 28, 58, 69, 126] although one group reported a decrease in formation rate as intraventricular pressure increased.[60, 61] In contrast, CSF is absorbed by a pressure-dependent mechanism acting as a one-way valve thought to reside in the arachnoid villi,[32, 78, 145, 146] but the ultrastructural basis of this action is not understood.[5, 125, 141, 142]

Following obstruction of CSF pathways, alternate routes of absorption must quickly develop. The rate of formation of CSF is such that if no CSF were absorbed, the volume of the ventricular and subarachnoid spaces would increase four to six-fold in one day, a situation not compatible with life. In fact, the development of alternate routes of absorption can be demonstrated;[41, 61, 69, 100, 101, 121, 133-135, 147] in experimental animals, for example, using dyes and radioactive tracers, it can be shown that there is movement of large molecules across the ependymal surface.

Electron microscopic studies show that as hydrocephalus develops the ependyma becomes stretched and flattened. There is gross extracellular edema and destruction of fibers and cellular elements. As the process continues, the white matter becomes atrophic and spongy. Chemical studies show loss of tissue solids and an increase in water. Tissue profiles of isotopically labeled tracers indicate both increased extracellular space and bulk flow of CSF into the periventricular white matter. Presumably, this fluid is then absorbed into adjacent brain capillaries; no doubt the increase in ventricular surface area provides access to a greater number of capillaries.

In chronic hydrocephalus in experimental animals, these absorptive processes may become sufficient to remove CSF at the same rate that it is secreted, and CSF pressure becomes normal.[16, 71] However, despite the normal CSF pressure, the system is drastically changed. Periventricular atrophy, demyelination, and edema interfere with normal function of cells and fiber systems. Early the process may be reversible, but if frank necrosis supervenes, complete recovery will not be possible. In addition, the mechanism of CSF absorption will have been altered. In particular, the pressure dependence of CSF absorption may be partially lost. This has been described both in calves with communicating hydrocephalus due to vitamin A deficiency and in patients with normal pressure hydrocephalus.[23, 86-88] The development of the infusion manometric test described below was based upon these observations.

CLINICAL PRESENTATION

The Triad: Gait Disturbance, Dementia, Incontinence

GAIT. A most prominent feature of this syndrome is gait disturbance. Adams[2] has stated that each of the 50 patients diagnosed as normal pressure hydrocephalus at the Massachusetts General Hospital over a ten-year period had unsteadiness of gait associated with deterioration of mental functioning. Although there are some patients without gait disturbance who have responded to shunting,[68, 132] there is little doubt that gait impairment is a hallmark of the typical syndrome and that patients with gait disturbance are likely to be the best candidates for shunts.[14, 68, 74, 98]

The gait disturbance may take many forms. Often, there is an element of spasticity with increase in deep tendon reflexes in the lower extremities and bilateral Babinski's reflexes. Many years ago, Yakovlev[152] described a progressive spastic paraparesis with increased deep tendon reflexes and extensor plantar responses as characteristic of children with progressive hydrocephalus. He called attention to the greater involvement of the legs as compared to the hands with usual sparing of the face. He suggested that this paraplegia of hydrocephalus was due to the distention of the long, descending paracentral fibers which course from the frontal cortex to the lower extremities. In contrast, the descending fibers involved in face and arm movements, separated from the ventricle and protected by the body of the caudate, are thus relatively spared the stretching by the hydrocephalic dilatation of the lateral ventricles. Unsteadiness which is made worse on attempts at tandem walking occurs about as frequently as spasticity. Messert and Baker[97] pointed out the frequency of a combined spastic ataxic gait in hydrocephalus. The spasticity is not usually associated with weakness on muscle testing nor is the ataxia associated with evidence of cerebellar disturbance if the legs are tested individually.

In addition to the spastic ataxia, the patient may often show difficulty in initiating walking or movement of his foot. This is often referred to as a gait apraxia, although purists may object to this term. Sometimes, the feet appear "glued" to the floor as if held by a "magnet" (see especially Messert and Baker[97]). Botez and coworkers[19] found that one of the early signs in normal pressure hydrocephalus is a tonic pressor and grasp reflex of the foot which may be related to the appearance of the "magnet" gait. Again, these elements have been attributed to frontal lobe disturbances secondary to ventricular dilatation.[97] In some patients, the difficulty in initiating gait may closely resemble the bradykinesia of parkinsonism, and numerous instances are cited in the literature in which patients have initially been diagnosed as having Parkinson's disease.

DEMENTIA. The dementia of normal pressure hydrocephalus is often described as mild and of insidious onset. Terms such as "slowing up of mental process," "decrease in spontaneity," "apathy," and "inattention" have been used. Benson and coworkers[14] noted, "In the early stages, apathy is more striking than depression of cognitive ability." Even the reduction in performance I.Q. observed early in this disorder may be secondary to slowness on timed tasks rather than true cognitive, perceptual, or constructional dysfunction and in this regard be similar to other "subcortical" dementias. In the ordinary progression of the disorder, memory impairment and disorientation may develop later in the disease, but aphasia and other specific cortical defects are not ordinarily encountered.

INCONTINENCE. Urinary incontinence is reported as a frequent occurrence late in this disorder. Rarely, fecal incontinence may occur. Adams has suggested that patients actually suffer from an "anosognosia of micturition," being unaware of their incontinence. This symptom may not be helpful in differentiating patients with normal pressure hydrocephalus from those with Alzheimer's or other progressive presenile or senile dementias, because urinary incontinence is a frequent accompaniment of these disorders also.

Other Clinical Features

Disturbances of Consciousness; Akinetic Mutism

An alteration in the state of consciousness is more often seen as a feature of hydrocephalus with increased intracranial pressure than in "normal pressure" hydrocephalus. Nevertheless, some patients with a communicating hydrocephalus secondary to intracranial bleeding or trauma and a normal CSF pressure may present with mental obtundation, lethargy, akinetic mutism, or coma. In patients with idiopathic normal pressure hydrocephalus, akinetic mutism has occurred as a complication of pneumoencephalography.

Behavioral Disturbances

The typical patient with normal pressure hydrocephalus is quiet, withdrawn, and slow, but occasionally patients are irrational, paranoid, and aggressive.[26, 117] Rice and Gendelman[117] suggested that symptoms such as anxiety, delusional thinking, ideas of reference, hallucinations, and mood and personality changes may represent the emergence of pathological and emotional conflicts following weakening of defensive structures by the hydrocephalic process. Thus, such symptoms would be related to prior emotional problems and are not specific for hydrocephalus *per se*. In contrast, depression is reported frequently to accompany normal pressure hydrocephalus. In some cases, there may in fact be a "pseudo-depression," with the slowing of psychological processes misinterpreted as a depression. In other instances, however, patients have expressed depressive thoughts which have sometimes persisted following surgical shunt.[2] There is the possibility that in some patients, shunting may ameliorate a depression, leading to a therapeutic response unrelated to the basic underlying pathology. In particular, this possibility must be considered in some patients with Alzheimer's disease and enlarged ventricles in whom transient improvement following shunting has been observed.

Additional Neurological Findings

Although a gait disturbance associated with increased deep tendon reflexes in the lower extremities and bilateral Babinski's signs is the most common observation, some patients show other abnormal reflexes such as Hoffmann's, grasp, and snout reflexes. It is not difficult to imagine these as late sequelae of hydrocephalus with further stretching of long tracts. More difficult to understand are reports of other inconstant features such as nystagmus and disturbances of extraocular motility.

The gait dyspraxia often seen in patients with normal pressure hydrocephalus may resemble the gait of Parkinson's disease. However, a number of patients have been reported who, in addition, show other parkinsonian signs such as tremor, masked facies, cogwheel rigidity, hypophonia, and bradykinesia.[68, 85] In these patients, gait and mentation improved after shunt therapy, but the other parkinsonian features did not. L-Dopa did prove beneficial, thus normal pressure hydrocephalus and Parkinson's disease may have coexisted. In contrast were the observations of Sypert and coworkers[136] who studied 3 patients with clear-cut parkinsonian features associated with dementia and hydrocephalus in whom parkinsonian symptoms such as tremor, plastic rigidity and cogwheeling in upper extremities, and masked facies were relieved by shunt procedures. On postmortem examination, one patient was found to have a dense adhesive arachnoiditis obliterating the basilar cisterns and a chronic granular ependymitis resulting in a secondary aqueductal stenosis, both associated with a left anterior cerebral artery aneurysm which had been clipped during life. There were no changes in substantia nigra or basal ganglia that would suggest a true Parkinson's disease.

DIAGNOSTIC PROCEDURES

Pneumoencephalography

Because the pneumoencephalogram outlines both the ventricular and subarachnoid spaces, it has been the most important procedure in the diagnosis of communicating hydrocephalus. The current use of the pneumoencephalogram in the differential diagnosis of dementia is described in detail in Chapter 11. In patients with recent subarachnoid hemorrhage, cerebral contusion, or meningitis, demonstration of an enlarging ventricular system may be sufficient for diagnosis. In others, especially those in whom an idiopathic form of normal pressure hydrocephalus is suspected, the problem is the differentiation of communicating hydrocephalus from ventricular enlargement secondary to parenchymal degeneration (hydrocephalus *ex vacuo*). LeMay and New[82] and Benson and coworkers,[14] reviewing the pneumoencephalograms in 41 patients who had undergone ventricular shunts, established precise pneumoencephalographic criteria for the diagnosis of obstructive or communicating hydrocephalus. The characteristics in communicating hydrocephalus included enlargement of the anterior portion of the lateral ventricles with their height over 40 mm., corpus callosal angle of 120° or less on an AP film with the patient supine, widened basilar cistern with an abrupt cutoff, and absence of air in the cerebral subarachnoid space. These findings are consistent with observations made both in patients and in experimental animals that the hydrocephalic process does not affect the ventricular system evenly, but that the frontal and temporal horns enlarge before the rest of the ventricular system. It has been found, however, that these characteristics are not pathognomonic, because they may also occur in some patients with proven Alzheimer's disease.[25] Moreover, in the original report of LeMay and New,[82] these pneumoencephalographic findings did not differentiate between patients who responded to shunt and those who did not. For example, although 19 patients with an excellent response to shunt had a corpus callosal angle of less than 120°, 14 of the 21 patients with a poor response also had an angle less than 120°; ventricular height was greater than 40 mm. in 9 of 16 with excellent response, and in 8 of 20 with poor response; obstruction of the basilar cisterns was present in 3 with excellent response, in 4 with poor response; and gas was found over the cortical convexities in 7 with excellent response and 13 with poor response. Similar findings have been reported by Wood and coworkers,[151] Shenkin and coworkers,[128] Greitz and Grepe,[49] and Stein and Langfitt.[132] An additional criterion said to be helpful is enlargement of the temporal horn,[130] but again this is not pathognomonic.[49, 113]

Some patients who later respond to shunt show clinical deterioration, sometimes quite serious, after pneumoencephalography.[10] Whether this is due to increased intracranial pressure following pneumoencephalography (as performed by the fractional installation method in which air is injected prior to removal of fluid) is not certain, but this complication is said to appear less often if an adequate amount of fluid is removed.[47]

Angiography

Enlarged lateral ventricles are easily detected on angiography by elevation and straightening of pericallosal artery, separation of thalamostriate vein from the midline on AP venous views, and changes in curvature of large Sylvian vessels. Angiography thus provides an alternative method for determining ventricular enlargement in patients with communicating hydrocephalus.[14, 18, 90, 112] Other angiographic features may suggest aqueductal stenosis, third ventricle tumor, or a posterior fossa mass.[18, 112] It can be argued that angiographic changes depend on secondary displacement of vessels or altered curvature, whereas the pneumoencephalogram directly demonstrates ventricular enlargement. However, the angiogram may be used in the diagnosis of hydrocephalus, especially when it may provide additional useful information as, for example, in patients with subarachnoid hemorrhage in whom a repeat angiogram gives vital data about the aneurysm or A-V malformation as well as about ventricular size. Another instance is in the patient in whom cerebral blood flow is being measured by the intracarotid technique.

Isotope Cisternography

The development of radioiodinated serum albumin (RISA) cisternography by Di Chiro[35] and its subsequent widespread use have been important consequences of the interest in diagnosis of normal pressure hydrocephalus. RISA cisternography is a relatively safe procedure, there being only three reports in the literature[34, 36, 106] of aseptic meningitis secondary to intrathecal RISA. Other isotopes (such as indium, technetium), easily conjugated to protein, are also available. The details of cisternographic findings are described in detail in Chapter 11. For normal pressure hydrocephalus, the most characteristic finding is ventricular stasis—accumulation of the isotope in the ventricular system and its persistence there for 24 to 48 hours or more. Ventricular stasis has been found useful in detecting the development of communicating hydrocephalus following trauma or subarachnoid hemorrhage.[92, 120, 148] Many authors accept ventricular filling and stasis as a *sine qua non* for the diagnosis of normal pressure hydrocephalus, and, in fact, there appears to be a high correlation between positive cisternograms and the other evidence suggesting the presence of a communicating hydrocephalus.[14, 57, 82, 95, 109, 113, 148] Nevertheless, substantial data exist demonstrating that many patients with ventricular stasis do not improve with shunts, and in some series this test has differentiated poorly between shunt responders and nonresponders.[90, 116, 127, 138, 150, 151] Stasis occurs in some patients who have proven

Alzheimer's disease with very large ventricles[25] and rarely in asymptomatic individuals.[80] Ventricular stasis is, no doubt, at least partially correlated with the absolute size of the ventricles, but this may not be the only factor.[12] James and coworkers[71] investigated six patients with enlarging ventricles following documented meningitis, acute subdural hematoma, or subarachnoid hemorrhage, and these findings combined with the results of RISA cisternography in experimental animals led to the conclusion that ventricular stasis does not occur during the early development of hydrocephalus but is an end-state phenomenon.

TRANSFER OF ISOTOPE TO BLOOD. If the level of isotope in the plasma is monitored during cisternography, in patients with ventricular stasis the plasma level is lower than in patients with normal CSF dynamics.[1, 13, 89] Similar findings are observed in animals with experimental communicating hydrocephalus produced by the injection of silicone into the basilar cisterns.[133, 135] This finding has been used as semiquantitative confirmation that the isotope is pooled in the ventricle but can be absorbed into the blood stream from the ventricle without passing over the cerebral convexities or entering the venous sinuses. This may also be used as an additional confirmatory test for communicating hydrocephalus. Whether it can differentiate patients with large ventricles secondary to an atrophic process from patients with a true communicating hydrocephalus is uncertain.

Computerized Axial Tomography

Since computerized axial tomography demonstrates the size of the ventricular system and subarachnoid spaces and since it is a noninvasive procedure, it almost immediately became the diagnostic procedure of choice in patients in whom normal pressure hydrocephalus is suspected.

The depiction of the ventricular and subarachnoid spaces shown by computerized axial tomography is not necessarily identical to that seen on pneumoencephalography. In one series, enlarged cerebral subarachnoid spaces were noted on computerized axial tomography in patients in whom no air had passed into these spaces on pneumoencephalography.[67] Such a finding is compatible with a subarachnoid block between the basilar cisterns and the cerebral convexities but could also suggest an underlying atrophic process. Also, ventricles may be smaller on computerized axial tomography than on pneumoencephalography. It is known that ventricular dilatation may occur after introduction of air, presumably due to some distending property of the introduced gas.[118] This is thought to be an unusual event occurring in patients with hydrocephalus due to parenchymal degeneration, but perhaps some distention of the ventricles occurs routinely when gas or air is introduced into the cerebrospinal fluid spaces.

Infusion Manometric Test

A characteristic of communicating hydrocephalus in animals with normal or slightly elevated CSF pressure is that although CSF absorption must equal CSF production for the pressure to be normal or only slightly elevated, the normal ability of the CSF system to increase fluid absorption as a function of pressure is lost.[23] This concept is theoretically compelling, since pressure-dependent CSF fluid absorption is consistent with the valvular absorption mechanism, the arachnoid villi presumably acting as these valves.[32, 146] Therefore, impairment of access to the arachnoid villi ought to produce at least a substantial alteration in the rate of CSF absorption as a function of CSF pressure. Indeed, utilizing the technique of ventriculo-lumbar perfusion at the time of shunting in a small group of patients with normal pressure hydrocephalus, Lorenzo and associates[86-88] found that CSF absorptive capacity was limited, the intracranial pressure rising sharply as the rate of perfusion of artificial CSF was increased above a threshold value which varied from patient to patient.

We introduced the infusion manometric test to provide a means of estimating CSF absorptive capacity during lumbar puncture.[76] Sterile saline or artificial CSF was infused into the lumbar subarachnoid space at a rate of 0.7 ml./min., about twice the rate of formation of CSF. In normal individuals, such infusions led to elevation of CSF pressure which then plateaued below 300 mm. H_2O. This infusion load led to a greater increase in pressure in patients with relatively acute communicating hydrocephalus produced by meningeal carcinomatosis, recent subarachnoid hemorrhage, or meningitis.[62, 76] However, in patients with idiopathic normal pressure hydrocephalus or chronic communicating hydrocephalus, more variable results have been obtained. Some investigators have reported good to excellent correlation with therapeutic response or other evidence of active hydrocephalus,[90, 143] while others have reported false negatives or poor correlation with therapeutic response.[93, 110, 132, 150] In some patients with partially compensated communicating hydrocephalus, the infusion load presented may be inadequate to demonstrate an absorption block, a finding consistent with those of Lorenzo and his associates.[86-88] Nelson and Goodman[104] have reported better results by carrying out the test at higher infusion speeds. A group of French investigators[72, 73] has described a variation of this test, measuring the pressure change with infusion at 0.75 and 2 ml./min. and using the ratio of the difference in pressures of the two plateaus to the difference in rate of infusion to calculate a "resistance" to absorption. In a series of patients with normal pressure hydrocephalus, they reported an almost perfect correlation between shunt response and an abnormal resistance value. Thus, their results (which require confirmation) are consistent with the presence of a communicating hydrocephalus in these patients. It is also probable in some instances that patients diagnosed as having "normal pressure hydrocephalus" do not, in fact, have a true communicating hydrocephalus.

Electroencephalography

Diverse experiences with the electroencephalogram have been reported. According to one recent report,[68] 21 of 25 patients with idiopathic normal pressure hydrocephalus showed generalized slowing. More typical are the observations of Brown and Goldensohn[22] who found in 11 patients with idiopathic normal pressure hydrocephalus that the electroencephalogram was normal in 6 of the group and showed normal background rhythms on which were imposed focal or generalized slowing in the remainder. These findings become useful in differentiating normal pressure hydrocephalus from Alzheimer's disease, since in patients with Alzheimer's disease with moderate to severe dementia, a disappearance of normal alpha rhythms together with a large increase in 4 to 6/second and sometimes slower frequencies are seen. Hence, in a patient with a moderate to severe dementia, normal background activity on electroencephalography may suggest normal pressure hydrocephalus.

Cerebral Blood Flow

The finding of reduced regional cerebral blood flow with preserved vascular reactivity in patients with presenile and senile dementia has been a consistent one.[25, 64, 65, 94, 103, 108] Greitz[48] reported that 26 patients with clinical, pneumoencephalographic, and angiographic evidence of hydrocephalus, with both normal and elevated CSF pressure, had significant impairment of cerebral blood flow. Moreover, Greitz and coworkers[51] found that cerebral blood flow increased following an atrioventricular shunt, the degree of increase correlating with clinical improvement. Greitz postulated that the circulatory disturbance might be responsible for "serious, but reversible, symptoms." Similar findings were reported by Salmon and Timperman[124] in patients with hydrocephalus following head trauma.

Of particular interest is the recent observation (made by two separate groups, Mathew and coworkers[94] and Raichle and coworkers[114]) that an increase in cerebral blood flow following removal of CSF is a highly reliable predictor of a positive response to shunt therapy. Cerebral blood flow was measured after removal of enough CSF to lower the CSF pressure by 50 percent. Patients with normal pressure hydrocephalus in whom cerebral blood flow increased by over 15 percent showed the best response to shunting. In sharp contrast, patients with cerebral atrophy secondary to Alzheimer's disease or vascular disease showed no increase in cerebral blood flow following removal of CSF. Cerebral blood flow is normally independent of changes in arterial or CSF pressures and is controlled by the metabolic need of the tissue, a phenomenon termed autoregulation. It has been suggested that in normal pressure hydrocephalus there is a defect in autoregulation such that cerebral blood flow is reduced below the metabolic need of the brain. The implications of this most interesting finding both for diagnosis and for understanding the pathophysiology of normal pressure hydrocephalus are apparent, but until these observations are replicated, it is probably best to be cautious.

ETIOLOGY

Subarachnoid Hemorrhage

Subarachnoid hemorrhage is the most frequent cause of hydrocephalus in adults, accounting for approximately 35 percent of the patients with adult hydrocephalus (Table 1). An acute communicating hydrocephalus occurs in about 10 percent of patients with bleeding aneurysms at the time of hospital admission.[115] In these patients, it is often difficult to distinguish between symptoms ascribable to acute hydrocephalus and symptoms secondary to subarachnoid hemorrhage. Thus, the presence of a decreased level of consciousness, convulsions, agitation, pyramidal signs, and paralysis of ocular motor nerves in these patients[115] is not qualitatively different from the constellation of symptoms observed in others with subarachnoid hemorrhage without communicating hydrocephalus. Recognition of the hydrocephalus is important, however, because in some cases shunting will relieve herniation and may decrease the possibility of chronic hydrocephalus.

The acute hydrocephalus occurring with subarachnoid hemorrhage is presumably due to the physical interference with CSF absorption by red cells.[20, 45, 96, 149]

Subsequently, however, one can demonstrate both in animal models and in autopsy studies that meningeal thickening occurs at the base of the brain as a result of subarachnoid blood together with a variable fibrosis of the arachnoid over the cortex.[8, 9, 56, 79, 129] Study of serial angiograms suggests the incidence of hydrocephalus in patients with subarachnoid hemorrhage to be about one-third,[15, 44, 52] but the incidence of symptomatic hydrocephalus persisting after the bleed is about 10 percent. Yasargil and coworkers[153] reported 28 cases out of 250 aneurysms, and Theander and Granholm[139] reported 5 among 56 survivors in a long-term follow-up of spontaneous subarachnoid hemorrhage.

In the more typical instance, communicating hydrocephalus is recognized when, after some improvement in the patient's condition following either the initial bleed or a reparative operative procedure, the patient's condition deteriorates, often with headache, nausea, vomiting, mental obtundation, and disorientation.[42, 79, 129] The diagnosis is usually made angiographically, since the possibility of a re-bleed is also considered. Although in the majority of cases there is intracranial hypertension, rarely the CSF pressure is found to be normal (e.g., Foltz and Ward[42]). In others, however, there may be a significant delay between the ictus and the onset of hydrocephalic symptoms; these patients may present as more typical examples of the clinical syndrome of normal pressure hydrocephalus.

Theander and Granholm[139] reported on an interesting group of 5 patients with hydrocephalus persisting a year or more after subarachnoid hemorrhage. The clinical symptomatology in 4 was that of a Korsakoff's syndrome; that is, the patients appeared to have a specific memory defect with other intellectual and cognitive functions more nearly normal. Whether this was a result of the hydrocephalus or of the location of the original bleed is uncertain.

Many American neurosurgeons and neurologists have been reluctant to carry out serial angiography following subarachnoid hemorrhage to determine whether or not communicating hydrocephalus has developed. The advent of computerized axial tomography makes it possible to determine changes in ventricular size with a noninvasive procedure. With the high incidence of symptomatic hydrocephalus following subarachnoid hemorrhage, it may be used to determine routinely whether ventricular enlargement is present, perhaps at three weeks and three months after subarachnoid hemorrhage. Ventricular enlargement *per se* without symptoms would not necessarily lead one to shunt therapy, since the hydrocephalus might be spontaneously arrested; but if ventricular enlargement were present, more frequent follow-ups to determine whether the process is progressing or receding would be warranted. With such management, it may be possible to treat developing hydrocephalus early so that the incidence of symptomatic "normal pressure hydrocephalus" due to this cause will decrease.

Head Trauma

Of the 3 patients initially reported by Hakim in his thesis[54] 2 were patients in whom neurological dysfunction occurring after head trauma was found to be due to communicating hydrocephalus with reversal of symptoms after shunting. The neurological symptoms in these patients were more flagrant than those with "idiopathic" normal pressure hydrocephalus and included akinetic mute states and tetraparesis. The significant advance made in identifying these patients was the realization that the CSF pressure could be normal in hydrocephalus. In the series of

Ojemann,[109] head trauma is as frequent a cause of "normal pressure hydrocephalus" as subarachnoid hemorrhage. The mechanism by which head trauma produces communicating hydrocephalus may involve subarachnoid hemorrhage at the time of injury in at least some patients.[42, 59] In those in whom the post-traumatic symptomatology and the symptomatology due to the hydrocephalus merge, the diagnosis is usually suspected when the patient has shown some recovery and then deteriorates. There may be a significant interval, however, between the trauma and the clinical syndrome of hydrocephalus. For example, patient number 9 of Foltz and Ward[42] was a 64-year-old male who had fallen off a truck 11 years prior to admission at which time he was unconscious and his spinal fluid was "very bloody." One year later, a gait disturbance along with mental deterioration occurred and was slowly progressive for 10 years. When examined, he had easy distractibility, poor memory, weakness and spasticity of the lower extremities (with ataxia, bilateral ankle clonus, and bilateral Babinski's signs), and a positive snout reflex. His gait was "slow, shuffling and propulsive." Spinal fluid presssure was 100 mm. A pneumoencephalogram showed advanced communicating hydrocephalus. Unfortunately, a shunt did not help, perhaps because of the long time interval.

The frequency of communicating hydrocephalus after head trauma is probably low considering the high incidence of head trauma and the limited number of cases of communicating hydrocephalus reported. Of cases of hydrocephalus in adults culled from the literature (Table 1), only 1 percent were reportedly due to head trauma. When the head trauma is severe and probable or verified hydrocephalus identified, the clinician has a basis on which to associate the two conditions. Because of the high incidence of mild to moderate head trauma in the population, however, it is impossible to ascertain whether a previous mild head trauma is related to a patient's normal pressure hydrocephalus.

Obstructive or Noncommunicating Hydrocephalus

In some patients, symptoms of internal or obstructive hydrocephalus may be indistinguishable from those common in patients with communicating hydrocephalus. Of the 6 patients reported by Messert and Baker[97] with the syndrome of progressive spastic ataxia and apraxia associated with occult hydrocephalus, 4 had an obstructive hydrocephalus, and 2 of 10 patients with secondary hydrocephalus reported by Oiemann and coworkers[110] had an obstructive hydrocephalus. The most common causes of obstruction are aqueductal stenosis, cholesteatoma, colloid cysts of the third ventricle, and metastatic carcinoma of the third or fourth ventricle. Cerebellar infarction may also produce a picture of hydrocephalus. The dementia sometimes associated with Paget's disease of the skull may, in some cases, be due to obstructive hydrocephalus produced by basilar invagination.[27] An unusual patient with pituitary adenoma presenting as dementia without visual or endocrine difficulties was reported by Aleksic and George.[4] The adenoma in its extracellular extension had compressed the foramen of Monro on one side, producing a hydrocephalic involvement of the lateral ventricle. At operation, the pressure in the involved ventricle was only 85 mm./H_2O, thus being by definition a low-pressure hydrocephalus. Although obstructive lesions only account for 9 percent of the cases reported in Table 1, most such cases are probably accepted as straightforward and reports are not published. In an earlier compilation,[78] obstructive lesions accounted for 20 percent of the cases of hydrocephalus in adults. In such cases, the lesion can be readily identified with proper radiographic procedures, and although the offending mass can only rarely be removed surgically, the indications for shunting are straightforward.

Ectasia of the Basilar Artery

Atherosclerosis of the basilar artery with dilatation sometimes to the point of formation of a saccular aneurysm is not an uncommon finding at autopsy in older hypertensive patients. A group in Stockholm has reported 7 patients[39, 40, 50] with symptomatic hydrocephalus produced by basilar ectasia or saccular aneurysm of the basilar artery. All the patients were hypertensive and presented with a spastic ataxic gait or apraxia of gait and a presenile dementia. In addition, several had increased intracranial pressure as manifested by papilledema, headaches, nausea, and vomiting or increased spinal fluid pressure, and thereby differed from patients with the true "normal pressure hydrocephalus." Pneumoencephalography or ventriculography showed a clear-cut deformity of the third ventricle produced by the abnormal basilar artery. In addition, there was an apparent communicating hydrocephalus with air accumulating in the basilar cisterns but not over the convexities. These findings are significant since a number of patients reported to have normal pressure hydrocephalus are hypertensive and might have enlarged basilar arteries. The specific pneumoencephalographic deformity of the third ventricle as reported by the Swedish workers has apparently not been observed in other centers as a cause of occult hydrocephalus (see, for example, Adams,[2] Heinz and coworkers,[57] Hill and coworkers,[59] Ojemann[109]).

PATHOLOGY OF IDIOPATHIC NORMAL PRESSURE HYDROCEPHALUS

In a recent review, Adams[2] suggested that "a low-grade asymptomatic meningeal disease, possibly inflammation of undetermined etiology has occurred." Indeed, meningeal fibrosis, especially involving the arachnoid coverings of the convexities, has been found in several autopsy and biopsy studies. DeLand and coworkers[33] and Vessal and coworkers[144] reported patchy to dense proliferation of the arachnoid in 5 autopsied cases of normal pressure hydrocephalus. Four of these patients, however, had severe cerebrovascular disease in addition.

We have reported 1 patient with a typical syndrome of normal pressure hydrocephalus and marked arachnoid thickening in the presence of normal cortical architecture on biopsy;[75] however, in another patient there was only mild meningeal thickening on biopsy.[25, 77] In contrast to these results, Stein and Langfitt[132] reported 3 patients who had positive response to shunting as well as clinical and laboratory presentations consistent with normal pressure hydrocephalus; 2 of the biopsies were normal, and the third showed microvascular changes of hypertension. In addition, these authors reported on 12 biopsies in patients who did not respond to shunt: 6 showed changes of Alzheimer's disease; 3 showed nonspecific cortical atrophy; and 3 were normal. The presence of Alzheimer's disease among the nonresponders and the presence of microvascular disease among the responders represent two special problems to be dealt with below. Normal or nonspecific biopsies in both responders and non-responders raise the question of whether these patients had localized arachnoid thickening in an area removed from the biopsy or a subcortical disease process not apparent in the tissue removed (e.g., a lacunar state involving white matter). Thus, there are at least 3 pathologies in patients in whom the diagnosis of normal pressure hydrocephalus is made: meningeal thickening presumably due to a prior subclinical infectious process, trauma, or hemorrhage; Alzheimer's disease; or cerebrovascular disease. Let us consider the problems of the latter two diagnoses.

Alzheimer's Disease and Normal Pressure Hydrocephalus

Ventricular enlargement occurs secondary to atrophy of cerebral white matter or periventricular nuclear masses, a process termed hydrocephalus *ex vacuo* or *central* atrophy. Ventricular enlargement is seen at autopsy in a small percentage of individuals presumably asymptomatic during life.[99] In patients with unequivocal senile dementia predominantly of the Alzheimer type histologically, 5 of 50 brains showed severe ventricular dilatation.[140] Marked ventricular dilatation was found by Coblentz and coworkers[25] on penumoencephalography in 5 of 10 patients who had histologically verified Alzheimer's disease. Several of these patients also showed abnormalities on isotope cisternography including ventricular stasis. One patient with histologically verified Alzheimer's disease not only had these laboratory changes characteristic of normal pressure hydrocephalus but also gait disturbance, urinary incontinence, and progressive dementia. In another patient in this group, the infusion manometric test, pneumoencephalogram, and isotope cisternogram were characteristic of a communicating hydrocephalus.

Are the disturbed CSF dynamics in such patients simply due to a severe hydrocephalus *ex vacuo* or does a communicating hydrocephalus coexist with the Alzheimer's disease? Sohn and coworkers[131] reported on a patient in whom normal pressure hydrocephalus had been diagnosed during life and who was found at autopsy to have both Alzheimer's disease and arachnoid thickening. These authors postulated the coexistence of these two processes, perhaps with meningeal thickening occurring as part of the Alzheimer process. But in the 5 patients with positive laboratory findings reported by Coblentz and associates,[23] arachnoid thickening was not observed on biopsy nor on postmortem examination in 1. Recent experimental data suggest that features thought to be characteristic of communicating hydrocephalus, such as ventricular stasis on isotope cisternography, are more a feature of marked ventricular enlargement than of the obstructive process *per se*.[69]

Although it has been suggested that some patients with Alzheimer's disease might be improved by shunting,[122, 123, 127] this is not the usual experience. Occasionally, a patient may show a functional improvement for a few months, but the Alzheimer disease process will overtake this.[84] Whether such improvement is due to the stress of the neurosurgical treatment alleviating an unrecognized depression resembling a dementia or to some other unknown therapeutic action of the shunt is conjectural. It is evident nevertheless that the vast majority of patients with Alzheimer's disease do poorly after shunting.[2, 25, 93, 109, 132] Therefore, one of the problems facing the clinician, is identification of those patients with Alzheimer's disease and a pseudocommunicating hydrocephalus, patients who ought *not* to have an operation. At present, this identification can be made with certainty only by cerebral biopsy; laboratory examinations, by definition, not helping in this differentiation. The clinical presentation becomes very important. Gait impairment early in Alzheimer's is rare; therefore, patients with the classical triad in whom gait disturbance precedes dementia or is accompanied by very mild dementia are unlikely to have Alzheimer's disease. Indeed, the most successful treatment of idiopathic normal pressure hydrocephalus has been by physicians who insisted on these criteria.[2, 68, 109]

Hypertensive Vascular Disease and Normal Pressure Hydrocephalus

A surprising finding has been the high incidence of hypertensive cerebrovascular disease found at autopsy in patients whose conditions had been diagnosed in life as normal pressure hydrocephalus, including patients who had unequivocal improvement after shunting. Of 5 autopsy patients reported on by Vessal and coworkers,[144] 4 had significant cerebrovascular disease in addition to arachnoid fibrosis. The cerebrovascular changes included an organized thrombus in the left anterior cerebral artery with a corresponding cystic infarct in the medial portion of the left anterior frontal lobe, an intracerebral hematoma with herniation and dural sinus thrombosis, and 2 instances of multiple lacunar infarcts. In 1 of the latter cases, the arachnoid thickening was patchy and did not obliterate the subarachnoid space.

Earnest and coworkers[38] reported on 2 patients with hypertensive vascular disease and multiple, deep cerebral infarcts but with normal leptomeninges and arachnoid villi. In both cases, clinical and radiological criteria characteristic of idiopathic normal pressure hydrocephalus were fulfilled. We[81] studied a patient admitted because of gait disturbance and very mild dementia whose pneumoencephalogram, RISA cisternogram, and computerized axial tomogram were characteristic of communicating hydrocephalus and who showed dramatic improvement after shunting. The patient's symptoms and neurological examination were considered so characteristic of normal pressure hydrocephalus that his findings, recorded on videotape, had been used for demonstrations and cited in the literature.[75] He deteriorated neurologically 7 months after shunting although his shunt was functioning, and died after a pulmonary embolism. On postmortem examination multiple old and new lacunar infarcts were found without evidence of disease of the meninges or the arachnoid villi. The patient on his initial admission had been known to be hypertensive and at postmortem had cardiomegaly consistent with hypertensive cardiovascular disease. One of the patients of Earnest and coworkers[38] also showed improvement after shunting.

That lacunar infarcts, affecting the same long tracts as true hydrocephalus, can produce gait disturbance, mild dementia, and urinary incontinence is not surprising. What is difficult to explain is the marked improvement with shunting. Were these simply coincidences, the patient recovering from recent infarcts at the time of surgery? Could a hydrocephalus *ex vacuo* lead to stasis of cerebrospinal fluid with accumulations of toxic metabolities which are removed by shunting? Could the alteration in structure of the periventricular tissue by the microinfarcts lead to a distention of the ventricles on a mechanical basis which is relieved by shunt?[38] Could part of normal CSF absorption occur via parenchymal blood vessels, the vascular pathology interfering with this absorption?[75] Could hypertensive vascular disease lead to a loss of autoregulation, a reduction in CSF pressure then leading to increased cerebral blood flow?[81] Sufficient evidence to permit a choice of these explanations is not yet available.

RESPONSE TO THERAPY

The percentage of patients in whom neurosurgical shunt procedures lead to clear-cut improvement in daily functioning varies tremendously from series to series, from a high of 43 positive responders among 50 patients[109] to lows of 0 out of 8[10] and 1 out of 12 responders.[116] Nevertheless, in the literature some averages appear that fit many series. As shown in Table 2, the overall incidence of positive responders after shunting in 351 adult patients is 55 percent. The percentage of positive responders is much higher in the secondary forms of normal pressure hydrocephalus (64.7 percent) than in the idiopathic form (40.9 percent). To be weighed against this is a mortality rate following shunt of 6 to 9 percent as reported in 2 large series involving 156 patients,[63, 151] the occurrence of epidural and subdural hematomas in over 5 percent,[37] and other shunt-related complications in over 40 percent.

Table 2. Positive[a] response to shunts reported in 351 adult patients[b] with normal pressure hydrocephalus

	Positive Responders	Patients Operated	% Positive Response
"Idiopathic"	59	144	40.9
"Secondary"	134	207	64.7
Total	193	351	55.5

[a]"Positive response" equivalent to "responder;" "moderate," "marked," "complete," or nonspecified "improvement;" "fair," "good," "excellent" result. Other non-positive response patients were described as "minimal," "no response," "worsened," death.
[b]Compilation of data reported in the references.

The question of whether adults with communicating hydrocephalus should be treated by a shunt inserted into a ventricle or into the spinal subarachnoid space (e.g., a lumbar-peritoneal shunt) is not resolved. In favor of a trial of the lumbar-peritoneal shunt is the high incidence of subdural and intracerebral hematomas that occur with ventricular placement in older individuals, but the patency of the spinal subarachnoid space must be demonstrated.

One would assume that improvement is due to relief of the communicating hydrocephalus. This is undoubtedly true in those patients in whom hydrocephalus develops after subarachnoid hemorrhage or other overt meningeal process. In some patients with presumed idiopathic hydrocephalus, however, no change in ventricular size occurs after treatment even though the shunt appears to be working and even though the patient shows clinical improvement.[67, 128] One explanation might be that a very chronic hydrocephalic process had produced irreversible destruction of tissue, functional recovery occurring in other areas only partially affected; but alternative explanations exist, including the probability that some of these patients have an underlying atrophic process.

CONCLUSION

It has become evident that separate consideration of secondary and idiopathic normal pressure hydrocephalus is useful. It has long been accepted that patients with symptomatic internal or obstructive hydrocephalus (due, for example, to aqueductal stenosis or third ventricle tumor) should be treated with a ventricular shunt if the primary lesion cannot be removed. Similarly, accumulated experience leads one to recommend shunt therapy in patients who develop a symptomatic communicating hydrocephalus following subarachnoid hemorrhage, head trauma, or meningitis. In such instances, radiographic evidence of the internal or subarachnoid obstructive process and of enlarging (as on serial studies) or markedly enlarged ventricules is of especial importance in establishing the diagnosis. The significant contribution to our understanding is the recognition that lumbar and ventricular fluid pressure may be normal.

The clinical dilemma then is posed by the syndrome of idiopathic normal pressure hydrocephalus. In view of the significant morbidity and mortality that may occur with ventricular shunts in adults, the 40 percent response rate is somewhat discouraging. The variability in success rate with shunts partly reflects the fact that some patients with the diagnosis of idiopathic normal pressure hydrocephalus may have Alzheimer's disease and cerebrovascular (especially hypertensive small vessel) disease. The group of patients with Alzheimer's disease includes those in whom ventricular dilatation is so pronounced that pneumoencephalograms and isotope cisternograms appear to demonstrate a communicating hydrocephalus. Short of cortical biopsy, the key to the differential diagnosis may be the clinical presentation; those patients in whom gait disturbance is predominant and dementia mild are least likely to have Alzheimer's disease. Even though there are instances in which patients with severe dementia have improved after shunting, the clinician must approach such patients cautiously. Indeed, in considering patients with ventricular enlargement of unknown etiology, the therapeutic success rate in patients without a gait disturbance will be low, in fact probably less than the rate of serious complications of surgery. The converse of this is that patients with the classic syndrome, including primary gait disturbance, mild dementia, more or less characteristic radiographic findings, with or without urinary incontinence, should be offered shunt therapy, because the therapeutic response rate becomes reasonable.[2, 14, 68, 98, 109, 110] Hypertensive vascular disease is not a contraindication to shunt therapy, if the patient is well compensated medically. It should be emphasized, however, that the number of patients with idiopathic normal pressure hydrocephalus who meet such criteria and respond to therapy is small and that most neurological centers only encounter 1 or 2 in a year.

REFERENCES

1. ABBOTT, M., AND ALKSNE, J.F.: *Transport of intrathecal I*^{125} *RISA to circulating plasma.* Neurology (Minneap.) 18:870, 1968.

2. ADAMS, R. D.: *Recent observations on normal pressure hydrocephalus.* Schweiz. Arch. Neurol. Neurochir. Psychiatr. 116:7, 1975.

3. ADAMS, R. D.; FISHER, C. M.; HAKIM, S.; OJEMANN, R.G.; AND SWEET, W. H.: *Symptomatic occult hydrocephalus with "normal" cerebrospinal-fluid pressure.* New Engl. J. Med. 273:117, 1965.

4. ALEKSIC, S. N., AND GEORGE, A. E.: *Dementia and low-pressure hydrocephalus in a patient with pituitary adenoma.* J. Neurol. Sci. 19:341, 1973.

5. ALKSNE, J. F., AND WHITE, L. E.: *Electron-microscope study of the effect of increased intracranial pressure on the arachnoid villus.* J. Neurosurg. 22:481, 1965.

6. AMUNDSEN, P.; KRISTIANSEN, K.; AND PRESTHUS, J.: *Clinical encephalographic and isotope investigations of hydrocephalus in adults.* Acta Radiol. [Diagn.] (Stockh.) 13:492, 1972.

7. AVANT, W. S., JR., AND TOOLE, J. F.: *Diagnostic guidelines in hydrocephalic dementia.* N.C. Med. J. 33:120, 1972.

8. BAGLEY, C., JR.: *Blood in the cerebrospinal fluid. Resultant functional and organic alterations in the central nervous system. A. Experimental data.* Arch. Surg. 17:18, 1928.

9. BAGLEY, C., JR.: *Blood in the cerebrospinal fluid. Resultant functional and organic alterations in the central nervous system. B. Clinical data.* Arch. Surg. 17:39, 1928.

10. BANNISTER, C. M.: *Report of 8 patients with low-pressure hydrocephalus treated by CSF diversion with disappointing results.* Acta Neurochir. 27:1, 1972.

11. BANNISTER, R.; GILFORD, E.; AND KOCEN, R.: *Isotope encephalography in the diagnosis of dementia due to communicating hydrocephalus.* Lancet 2:1014, 1967.

12. BARTELT, D.; JORDAN, C. E.; STRECKER, E.-P.; AND JAMES, A. E.: *Comparison of ventricular enlargement and radiopharmaceutical retention: A cisternographic-pneumoencephalographic comparison.* Radiology, 116:111, 1975.

13. BEHRMAN, S.; CAST, I.; AND O'GORMAN, P.: *Two types of curves for transfer of RIHSA from cerebrospinal fluid to plasma in patients with normal pressure hydorcephalus.* Neurosurg. 35: 677, 1971.

14. BENSON, D. F.; LeMAY, M.; PATTEN, D. H.; AND RUBENS, A. B.: *Diagnosis of normal- pressure hydrocephalus.* New Engl. J. Med. 283:609, 1970.

15. BERGVALL, U., AND GALERA, R.: *Time relationship between subarachnoid haemorrhage, arterial spasm, changes in cerebral circulation and posthaemorrhagic hydrocephalus.* Acta Radiol. [Diagn.] (Stockh.) 9:229, 1969.

16. BERING, E. A., JR., AND SATO, O.: *Hydrocephalus: Changes in formation and absorption of cerebrospinal fluid within the cerebral ventricles.* J. Neurosurg. 20:1050, 1963.

17. BLIEK, A. J., AND MILLER, J. D. R.: *RISA cisternography—A review of 29 cases.* J. Can. Assoc. Radiol. 22:215, 1971.

18. BOLLER, F.; LeMAY, M.; AND WRIGHT, R. L.: *Diagnosis and differentiation of various types of hydrocephalus in adults by angiograph.* Br. J. Radiol. 43:384, 1970.

19. BOTEZ, M. I.; LEVEILLE, J.; BERUBE, L., AND BOTEZ-MARQUARD, T.: *Occult disorders of the cerebrospinal fluid dynamics. Early diagnosis criteria.* Eur. Neurol. 13:203, 1975.

20. BRADFORD, F. K., AND SHARKEY, P. C.: *Physiologic effects from the introduction of blood and other substances into the subarachnoid space of dogs.* J. Neurosurg. 19:1017, 1962.

21. BREIG, A.; EKBOM, K.; GREITZ, T.; AND KUGELBERG, E.: *Hydrocephalus due to elongated basilar artery. A new clinicoradiological syndrome.* Lancet 1:874, 1967.

22. BROWN, D. G., AND GOLDENSOHN, E. S.: *The electroencephalogram in normal pressure hydrocephalus.* Arch. Neurol. 29:70, 1973.

23. CALHOUN, M. C.; HURT, H. D.; EATON, H. D.; ROUSSEAU, J. E., JR.; AND HALL, R. C., JR.: *Rates of formation and absorption of cerebrospinal fluid in bovine hypovitaminosis A.* J. Dairy Sci. 50:1486, 1967.

24. CHANDRASEKARAN, S., AND REYNOLDS, R. E.: *Occult hydrocephalus in the elderly.* J. Am. Geriatric. Soc. 18:481, 1970.

25. COBLENTZ, J. M.; MATTIS, S.; ZINGESSER, L. H.; KASOFF, S. S.; WISNIEWSKI, H. M.; AND KATZMAN, R.: *Presenile dementia. Clinical aspects and evaluation of cerebrospinal fluid dynamics.* Arch. Neurol. 29:299, 1973.

26. CROWELL, R. M.; TEW, J. M., JR., AND MARK, V. H.: *Aggressive dementia associated with normal pressure hydrocephalus. Report of two unusual cases.* Neurology (Minneap.) 23:461, 1973.

27. CULEBRAS, A.; FELDMAN, R. G.; AND FAGER, C. A.: *Hydrocephalus and dementia in Paget's disease of the skull.* J. Neurol. Sci. 23:307, 1974.

28. CUTLER, R. W. P.; PAGE, L.; GALICICH, J.; AND WATTERS, G. V.: *Formation and absorption of cerebrospinal fluid in man.* Brain 91:707, 1968.

29. DANDY, W. E.: *Experimental hydrocephalus.* Ann. Surg. 70:129, 1919.

30. DANDY, W. E., AND BLACKFAN, K. D.: *An experimental and clinical study of internal hydrocephalus.* J.A.M.A. 61:2216, 1913.

31. DANDY, W. E., AND BLACKFAN, K. D.: *Internal hydrocephalus.* Am. J. Dis. Child. 14:424, 1917.

32. DAVSON, H.; DOMER, F. R.; AND HOLLINGS, J. R.: *Mechanism of drainage of cerebrospinal fluid.* Brain, 96:329, 1973.

33. DeLand, F. H.; James, A. E., Jr.; Ladd, D. J.; and Konigsmark, B. W.: *Normal pressure hydrocephalus: A histologic study.* Am. J. Clin. Pathol. 58:58, 1972.
34. Detmer, D., and Blacker, A. M.: *A case of aseptic meningitis secondary to intrathecal injection of I 131 human serum albumin.* Neurology (Minneap.) 17:642, 1965.
35. Di Chiro, G.; Reames, P. M.; and Matthews, W. B., Jr.: *RISA-ventriculography and RISA-cisternography.* Neurology (Minneap.) 14:185, 1964.
36. Dramov, B., and Dubou, R.: *Aseptic meningitis following intrathecal radioiodinated serum albumin.* Calif. Med. 115:64, 1971.
37. Driesen, W. and Elies, W.: *Epidural and subdural haematomas as a complication of internal drainage of cerebrospinal fluid in hydrocephalus.* Acta Neurochir. 30:85, 1974.
38. Earnest, M. P.; Fahn, S.; Karp, J. H.; and Rowland, L. P.: *Normal pressure hydrocephalus and hypertensive cerebrovascular disease.* Arch. Neurol. 31:262, 1974.
39. Ekbom, K., and Greitz, T.: *Syndrome of hydrocephalus caused by saccular aneurysm of the basilar artery.* Acta Neurochir. 24:71, 1971.
40. Ekbom, K.; Greitz, T.; and Kugelberg, E.: *Hydrocephalus due to ectasia of the basilar artery.* J. Neurol. Sci. 8:465, 1969.
41. Fishman, R. A., and Greer, M.: *Experimental obstructive hydrocephalus.* Arch. Neurol. 8:156, 1963.
42. Foltz, E. L.; and Ward, A. A., Jr.: *Communicating hydrocephalus from subarachnoid bleeding.* J. Neurosurg. 13:546, 1956.
43. Forslo, H.; Forssman, B.; Jarpe, S.; and Radberg, C.: *RISA cisternography in possible hydrocephalus.* Acta Radiol. [Diag.] (Stockh.) 13:531, 1972.
44. Galera, R., and Greitz, T.: *Hydrocephalus in the adult secondary to the rupture of intracranial arterial aneurysms.* J. Neurosurg. 32:634, 1970.
45. Gardner, W. J.; Spitler, D. K.; and Whitten, C.: *Increased intracranial pressure caused by increased protein content in the cerebrospinal fluid: An explanation of papilledema in certain cases of small intracranial and intraspinal tumors, and in the Guillian-Barre syndrome.* New Engl. J. Med. 250:932, 1954.
46. Geschwind, N.: *The mechanism of normal pressure hydrocephalus.* J. Neurol. Sci. 7:481, 1968.
47. Gilbert, G. J.: *Correspondence: Pneumoencephalography in normal-pressure hydrocephalus.* New Engl. J. Med. 285:177, 1971.
48. Greitz, T.: *Effect of brain distension on cerebral circulation.* Lancet 1:863, 1969.
49. Greitz, T.; and Grepe, A.: *Encephalography in the diagnosis of convexity block hydrocephalus.* Acta Radiol. [Diag.] (Stockh.) 11:232, 1971.
50. Greitz, T.; Ekbom, K.; Kugelberg, E.; and Breig, A.: *Occult hydrocephalus due to ectasia of the basilar artery.* Acta Radiol. [Diag.] (Stockh.) 9:310, 1969.
51. Greitz, T.; Grepe, A.; Kalmer, M.; and Lopez, J.: *Pre- and postoperative evaluation of cerebral blood flow in low-pressure hydrocephalus.* J. Neurosurg. 31:644, 1969.
52. Griffith, H. B.; Cummins, B. H.; and Thomson, J. L. G.: *Cerebral arterial spasm and hydrocephalus in leaking arterial aneurysms.* Neuroradiology 4:212, 1972.
53. Gruenberg, E. M. L.: *A mental health survey of older persons,* in Hoch, P. H., and Zubin, J. (eds.): *Comparative Epidemiology of the Mental Disorders.* Grune & Stratton, New York, 1961.
54. Hakim, S.: *Some observations on C.S.F. pressure. Hydrocephalic syndrome in adults with "normal" C.S.F. pressure. (Recognition of a new syndrome.)* Thesis, Javeriana University School of Medicine, Bogota, Columbia, 1964.
55. Hakim, S., and Adams, R. D.: *The special clinical problem of symptomatic hydrocephalus with normal cerebrospinal fluid pressure. Observations on cerebrospinal fluid hydrodynamics.* J. Neurol. Sci. 2:307, 1965.
56. Hammes, E. J., Jr.: *Reaction of meninges to blood.* Arch. Neurol. Psychiat. 52:505, 1944.
57. Heinz, E. R.; Davis, D. O.; Karp, H. R.: *Abnormal isotope cisternography in symptomatic occult hydrocephalus. A correlative isotopic-neuroradiological study in 130 subjects.* Radiology 95:109, 1970.
58. Heisey, S. R.; Held, D.; and Pappenheimer, J. R.: *Bulk flow and diffusion in the cerebrospinal fluid system of the goat.* Am. J. Physiol. 203:775, 1962.

88

59. HILL, M. E.; LOUGHEED, W. M.; AND BARNETT, H. J. M.: *A treatable form of dementia due to normal pressure, communicating hydrocephalus.* Can. Med. Assoc. J. 97:1309, 1967.

60. HOCHWALD, G. M., AND SAHAR, A.: *Effect of spinal fluid pressure on cerebrospinal fluid formation.* Exp. Neurol. 32:30, 1971.

61. HOCHWALD, G. M.; SAHAR, A.; SADIK, A. R.; AND RANSOHOFF, J.: *Cerebrospinal fluid production and histological observations in animals with experimental obstructive hydrocephalus.* Exp. Neurol. 25:190, 1969.

62. HUSSEY, R.; SCHANZER, B.; AND KATZMAN, R.: *A simple constant-infusion manometric test for measurement of CSF absorption. II. Clinical studies.* Neurology (Minneap.) 20:665, 1970.

63. ILLINGWORTH, R. D.; LOGUE, V.; SYMON, L.; AND UEMURA, K.: *The ventriculocaval shunt in the treatment of adult hydrocephalus. Results and complications in 101 patients.* J. Neurosurg. 35:681, 1971.

64. INGVAR, D. H., AND GUSTAFSON, L.: *Regional cerebral blood flow in organic dementia with early onset.* Acta Neurol. Scand. [Suppl.] 43:42, 1970.

65. INGVAR, D. H., AND SCHWARTZ, M. S.: The cerebral blood flow in low pressure hydrocephalus, in Lundberg, N.; Pontén, U.; and Brock, M. (eds.): *Intracranial Pressure II. Proceedings of the Second International Symposium on Intracranial Pressure.* Springer-Verlag, New York, 1975, p. 153.

66. JACOB, H.; IIZUKA, R.; AND LUTCHKE, A.: *Prasenile leukencephalopathische hydrocephalie. Zur differentialdiagnose hirnorganischer psycho syndrome mit neurologischer hydrocephalus-symptomatik im hoheren lebensalter.* Z. Neurol. 202:64, 1972.

67. JACOBS, L., AND KINKEL, W.: *Computerized axial transverse tomography in normal pressure hydrocephalus.* Neurology (Minneap.) 26:501, 1976.

68. JACOBS, L.; CONTI, D.; KINKEL, W. R.; AND MANNING, E. J.: *"Normal pressure" hydrocephalus.* J.A.M.A. 235:510, 1976.

69. JAMES, A. E., JR.; BURNS, B.; HOR, W. F.; STRECKER, E.-P.; MERZ, T.; BUSH, M.; AND PRICE, D. L.: *Pathophysiology of chronic communicating hydrocephalus in dogs (Canis familiaris). Experimental studies.* J. Neurol. Sci. 24:151, 1975.

70. JAMES, A. E., JR.; SPERBER, E.; STRECKER, E.-P.; DIGEL, C.; NOVAK, G.; AND BUSH, M.: *Use of serial cisternograms to document dynamic changes in the development of communicating hydrocephalus: A clinical and experimental study.* Acta Neurol. Scand. 50:153, 1974.

71. JAMES, A. E.; STRECKER, E.-P.; NOVAK, G. R.; AND BURNS, B.: *Correlation of serial cisternograms and cerebrospinal fluid pressure measurements in experimental communicating hydrocephalus.* Neurology (Minneap.) 23:1226, 1973.

72. JANNY, P.; FLORI, B.; GEORGET, A. M.; AND VEYRE, A.: *La résistance à l'écoulement du liquide céphalo-rachidien dans l'hydrocéphalie à pression normale.* Rev. Neurol. (Paris) 131:211, 1975.

73. JANNY, P.; GODENÈCHE, P.; FLORI, B.; AND RAYNAUD, E.-J.: *La résistance à l'écoulement du liquide céphalo-rachidien. Méthode de mesure et application clinique.* Rev. Neurol. (Paris) 128:161, 1973.

74. KATZMAN, R.: *A reversible form of dementia?* Medical World News Rev. 1:65, 1974.

75. KATZMAN, R.: Cerebrospinal fluid physiology and normal pressure hydrocephalus, in Gershon, S., and Terry, R. (eds.): *The Neurobiology of Aging.* Raven Press. In press, 1976.

76. KATZMAN, R., AND HUSSEY, F.: *A simple constant-infusion manometric test for measurement of CSF absorption: I. Rationale and method.* Neurology (Minneap.) 20:534, 1970.

77. KATZMAN, R., AND KARASU, T. B.: Differential diagnosis of dementia, in Fields, W. S., (ed.): *Neurological and Sensory Disorders in the Elderly.* Symposia Specialists, Miami, 1975, p. 103.

78. KATZMAN, R., AND PAPPIUS, H. M.: *Brain Electrolytes and Fluid Metabolism.* The Williams & Wilkins Co., Baltimore, 1973.

79. KIBLER, R. F.; COUCH, R. S. C.; AND CROMPTON, M. R.: *Hydrocephalus in the adult following spontaneous subarachnoid haemorrhage.* Brain 84:45, 1961.

80. KIEFFER, S. A.; WOLFF, J. M.; AND WESTREICH, G.: *The borderline scinticisternogram.* Radiology 106:133, 1973.

81. KOTO, A.; ROSENBERG, G.; ZINGESSER, L. H.; HOROUPIAN, D.; AND KATZMAN, R.: Unpublished observations.

82. LeMay, A., and New, P. F. J.: *Radiological diagnosis of occult normal pressure hydrocephalus.* Radiology 96:347, 1970.

83. Lethlean, K., and Gye, R.: *Dementia in the adult due to occult hydocephalus.* Proc. Aust. Assoc. Neurol., 6:13, 1969.

84. Lijtmaer, H.; Fuld, P.; and Katzman, R.: Letter to Editor. Arch. Neurol. 33:304, 1976.

85. Lin, J. P.-T.; Goodkin, R.; Tong, E. C. K.; Epstein, F. J.; and Vinciguerra, E.: *Radioiodinated serum ablumin (RISA) cisternography in the diagnosis of incisural block and occult hydrocephalus.* Radiology 90:36, 1968.

86. Lorenzo, A. V., and Bresnan, M. J.: *Deficit in cerebrospinal fluid absorption in patients with symptoms of normal pressure hydrocephalus.* Dev. Med. Child. Neurol. 15:34, 1973.

87. Lorenzo, A. V.; Bresnan, M. J.; and Barlow, C. F.: *Cerebrospinal fluid absorption deficit in normal pressure hydrocephalus.* Arch Neurol. 30:387, 1974.

88. Lorenzo, A. V.; Page, L. K.; and Watters, G. V.: *Relationship between cerebrospinal fluid formation, absorption and pressure in human hydrocephalus.* Brain 93:679, 1970.

89. Mahaley, M. S., Jr.; Wilkinson, R. H., Jr.; Sivalingham, S.; Friedman, H.; Tyson, W.; and Goodrich, J. K.: *Radionuclide blood levels during Alzheimer's disease.* J. Neurosurg. 41: 471, 1974.

90. Maira, G.; Bareggi, S. R.; Di Rocco, C.; Calderini, G.; and Morselli, P. L.: *Monoamine acid metabolites and cerebrospinal fluid dynamics in normal pressure hydrocephalus: Preliminary results.* J. Neurol. Neurosurg. Psychiatry 38:123, 1975.

91. Marsden, C. D., and Harrison, M. J. G.: *Correspondence: Presenile dementia.* Br. Med. J. 3: 50, 1972.

92. Martini, T., and Oberson, R.: *Cisternographie radio-isotopique chez les hydrocéphales post-tramatiques.* Acta Radiol. [Diagn.[(Stockh.) 9:635, 1969.

93. Mathew, N. T.; Hartmann, A.; and Meyer, J. S.: *Diagnostic evaluation of normal pressure hydrocephalus.* Trans. Am. Neurol. Assoc. 99:227, 1974.

94. Mathew, N. T.; Meyer, J. S.; Bell, R. L.; Johnson, P. C.; and Neblett, C. R.: *Regional cerebral blood flow and blood volume measured with the gamma camera.* Neuroradiology 4:133, 1972.

95. McCullough, D. C.; Harbert, J. C.; Di Chiro, G.; and Ommaya, A. K.: *Prognostic criteria for cerebrospinal fluid shunting from isotope cisternography in communicating hydrocephalus.* Neurology (Minneap.) 20:594, 1970.

96. McQueen, J. D., and Jelsma, L. F.: *Intracranial hypertension: Cerebrospinal fluid pressure rises following intracisternal infusions of blood components in dogs.* Arch. Neurol. 16:501, 1967.

97. Messert, B., and Baker, N. H.: *Syndrome of progressive spastic ataxia and apraxia associated with occult hydrocephalus.* Neurology (Minneap.) 16:440, 1966.

98. Messert, B., and Wannamaker, B. B.: *Reappraisal of the adult occult hydocephalus syndrome.* Neurology (Minneap.) 24:224, 1974.

99. Messert, B.; Wannamaker, B.; and Dudley, A.: *Reevaluation of the size of the lateral ventricles of the brain.* Neurology (Minneap.) 22:941, 1972.

100. Milhorat, T. H.; Clark, R. G.; and Hammock, M. K.: *Experimental hydrocephalus. Part 2: Gross pathological findings in acute and subacute obstructive hydrocephalus in the dog and monkey.* J. Neurosurg. 32:390, 1970.

101. Milhorat, T. H.; Clark, R. G.; Hammock, M. K., and McGrath, P. P.: *Structural, ultrastructural, and permeability changes in the ependyma and surrounding brain favoring equilibration in progressive hydrocephalus.* Arch. Neurol. 22:397, 1970.

102. Moody, D. M., and Potts, D. G.: *Pneumoencephalographic evidence of increased transventricular absorption of cerebrospinal fluid.* Radiology 104:601, 1972.

103. Munck, O.; Barenholdt, O.; and Busch, H.: *Cerebral blood flow in organic dementia measured with the Xenon-133 desaturation method.* Scand. J. Clin. Lab. Invest. Suppl. 102, p.XII: A, 1968.

104. Nelson, J. R., and Goodman, S. J.: *An evaluation of the cerebrospinal fluid infusion test for hydrocephalus.* Neurology (Minneap.) 21:1037, 1971.

105. Nielsen, J.: *Geronto-psychiatric period-prevalence investigation in a geographically delimited population.* Acta Psychiatr. Scand. 38:307, 1963.

90

106. NICOL, C. F.: *A second case of aseptic meningitis following isotope cisternography using I* [131] *human serum albumin.* Neurology (Minneap.) 17:199, 1967.

107. NORNES, H.; ROOTWELT, K.; AND SJAASTAD, O.: *Normal pressure hydrocephalus. Long-term intracranial pressure recording.* Eur. Neurol. 9:261, 1973.

108. OBRIST, W. D.; CHIVIEN, E.; CRONQUIST, S.; AND INGVAR, D. H.: *Regional cerebral blood flow in senile and presenile dementia.* Neurology (Minneap.) 20:315, 1970.

109. OJEMANN, R. G.: *Normal pressure hydrocephalus.* Clin. Neurosurg. 18:337, 1971.

110. OJEMANN, R. G.; FISHER, C. M.; ADAMS, R. D.; SWEET, W. H.; AND NEW, P. F. J.: *Further experience with the syndrome of "normal" pressure hydrocephalus.* J. Neurosurg. 31:279, 1969.

111. OTTO, H.; ULLERICH, D.; AND LOHR, E.: *Syringomyelie und normal pressure hydrocephalus.* J. Neurol. 208:299, 1975.

112. PETROV, J.: *Détermination angiographique du degré de la dilatation acquise des ventricules cérébraux latéraux.* Acta Radiol. [Diagn.] (Stockh.) 9:420, 1969.

113. PHILIPPON, J.; RICOU, P.; AND ANCRE, D.: *Résultats de la dérivation du liquide céphalo-rachidien dans l'hydrocéphalie à pression normale de l'adulte.* Rev. Neurol. (Paris) 130:333, 1974.

114. RAICHLE, M. E.; EICHLING, J. O.; H.-GADO, R. L.; GRUBB, R. L., JR.; AND TERPOGOSSIAN, M. M.: *Cerebral blood volume in dementia,* in Lundberg, N.; Ponten, U.; and Brock, M. (eds.): *Intracranial Pressure II. Proceedings of the Second International Symposium on Intracranial Pressure.* Springer-Verlag, New York, 1975, p. 150.

115. RAIMONDI, A. J., AND TORRES, H.: *Acute hydrocephalus as a complication of subarachnoid hemorrhage.* Surg. Neurol. 1:23, 1973.

116. RAU, H.; FÄS, A.; HORST, W., AND BAUMGARTEN, G.: *Hydrocephalus communicans.* J. Neurol. 207:279, 1974.

117. RICE, E., AND GENDELMAN, S.: *Psychiatric aspects of normal pressure hydrocephalus.* J.A.M.A. 223:409, 1973.

118. ROVIT, R. L.; SCHECHTER, M. M.; ORTEGA, B.; AND BRINKER, R. A.: *Progressive ventricular dilatation following pneumoencephalography.* J. Neurosurg. 36:50, 1972.

119. RUBIN, R. C.; HENDERSON, E. S.; OMMAYA, A. K.; WALKER, M. D.; AND RALL, D. P.: *The production of cerebrospinal fluid in man and its modification by acetazolamide.* J. Neurosurg. 25:430, 1966.

120. RUDD, T. G.; O'NEAL, J. T.; AND NELP, W. B.: *Cerebrospinal fluid circulation following subarachnoid hemorrhage.* J. Nucl. Med. 12:61, 1971.

121. SAHAR, A.; HOCHWALD, G. M.; AND RANSOHOFF, J.: *Alternate pathway for cerebrospinal fluid absorption in animals with experimental obstructive hydrocephalus.* Exp. Neurol. 25:200, 1969.

122. SALMON, J. H.: *Senile and presenile dementia. Ventriculo-atrial shunt for symptomatic treatment.* Geriatrics 24:67, 1969.

123. SALMON, J. H.: *Adult hydrocephalus. Evaluation of shunt therapy in 80 patients.* J. Neurosurg. 37:423, 1972.

124. SALMON, J. H., AND TIMPERMAN, A. L.: *Cerebral blood flow in posttraumatic encephalopathy.* Neurology (Minneap.) 21:33, 1971.

125. SHABO, A. L., AND MAXWELL, D. S.: *The morphology of the arachnoid villi: A light and electron microscopic study in the monkey.* J. Neurosurg. 29:451, 1968.

126. SHAYWITZ, B. A.; KATZMAN, R.; AND ESCRIVA, A.: *CSF formation and* [24]*Na clearance in normal and hydrocephalic kittens during ventriculocisternal perfusion.* Neurology (Minneap.) 19:159, 1969.

127. SHENKIN, H. A.; GREENBERG, J.; BOUZARTH, W. F.; GUTTERMAN, P.; AND MORALES, J.O.: *Ventricular shunting for relief of senile symptoms.* J.A.M.A. 225:1486, 1973.

128. SHENKIN, H. A.; GREENBERG, J. O.; AND GROSSMAN, C. B.: *Ventricular size after shunting for idiopathic normal pressure hydrocephalus.* J. Neurol. Neurosurg. Psychiatry 38:833, 1975.

129. SHULMAN, K.; MARTIN, B. F.; POPOFF, N.; AND RANSOHOFF, J.: *Recognition and treatment of hydrocephalus following spontaneous subarachnoid hemorrhage.* J. Neurosurg. 20:1040, 1963.

130. SJAASTAD, O.; SKALPE, I., AND ENGESET, A.: *The width of the temporal horn in the differential diagnosis between pressure hydrocephalus and hydrocephalus ex vacuo.* Neurology (Minneap.) 19:1087, 1969.

131. SOHN, R. S.; SIEGEL, B. A.; GADO, M.; AND TORACK, R. M.: *Alzheimer's disease with abnormal cerebrospinal fluid flow.* Neurology (Minneap.) 23:1058, 1973.

132. STEIN, S. C., AND LANGFITT, T. W.: *Normal-pressure hydrocephalus. Predicting the results of cerebrospinal fluid shunting.* J. Neurosurg. 41:463, 1974.

133. STRECKER, E. -P., AND JAMES, A. E., JR.: *The evaluation of cerebrospinal fluid flow and absorption: Clinical and experimental studies.* Neuroradiology 6:200, 1973.

134. STRECKER, E. -P.; KELLEY, J. E. T.; MERZ, T.; AND JAMES, A. E., JR.: *Transventricular albumin absorption in communicating hydrocephalus. Semiquantitative analysis of periventricular extracellular space utilizing autoradiography.* Arch. Psychiatr. Nervenkr. 218:369, 1974.

135. STRECKER, E. -P.; SCHEFFEL, U.; KELLEY, J. E. T.; AND JAMES, A. E., JR.: *Cerebrospinal fluid absorption in communicating hydrocephalus. Evaluation of transfer of radioactive albumin from subarachnoid space to plasma.* Neurology (Minneap.) 23:854, 1973.

136. SYPERT, G. E.; LEFFMAN, H.; AND OJEMANN, G. A.: *Occult normal pressure hydrocephalus manifested by parkinsonism-dementia complex.* Neurology (Minneap.) 23:234, 1973.

137. TANG, B. -H.; LIEBERMAN, A.; AND ROVIT, R.: *Huntington's chorea associated with normal pressure hydrocephalus.* Eur. Neurol. 13:189, 1975.

138. TATOR, C. H., AND MURRAY, S.: *A clinical, pneumoencephalographic and radioisotopic study of normal-pressure communicating hydrocephalus.* Can. Med. Assoc. J. 105:573, 1971.

139. THEANDER, S., AND GRANHOLM, L.: *Sequelae after spontaneous subarachnoid haemorrhage, with special reference to hydrocephalus and Korsakoff's syndrome.* Acta Neurol. Scand. 43:479, 1967.

140. TOMLINSON, B. E.; BLESSED, G.; AND ROTH, M.: *Observations on the brains of demented old people.* J. Neurol. Sci. 11:205, 1970.

141. TRIPATHI, B. J., AND TRIPATHI, R. C.: *Vacuolar transcellular channels as a drainage pathway for cerebrospinal fluid.* J. Physiol. (Lond.) 239:195, 1974.

142. TRIPATHI, R.: *Tracing the bulk outflow route of cerebrospinal fluid by transmission and scanning electron microscopy.* Brain Res. 80:503, 1974.

143. TROTTER, J. L.; LUZECKY, M.; SIEGEL, B. A.; AND GADO, M.: *Cerebrospinal fluid infusion test. Identification of artifacts and correlation with cisternography and pneumoencephalography.* Neurology (Minneap.) 24:181, 1974.

144. VESSAL, K.; SPERBER, E. E.; AND JAMES, A. E., JR.: *Chronic communicating hydrocephalus with normal CSF pressures: A cisternographic-pathologic correlation.* Ann. Radiol. (Paris) 17:785, 1974.

145. WEED, L. H.: *Studies on cerebro-spinal fluid. III. The pathways of escape from the subarachnoid spaces with particular reference to the arachnoid villi.* J. Med. Res. 31:51, 1914.

146. WELCH, K., AND FRIEDMAN, V.: *The cerebrospinal fluid valves.* Brain 83:454, 1960.

147. WELLER, R. O., AND WISNIEWSKI, H.: *Histological and ultrastructural changes with experimental hydrocephalus in adult rabbits.* Brain 92:819, 1969.

148. WILLIAMS, J. P.; PRIBRAM, H. F. W.; LYNDE, R. H.; AND SHARPE, A. R.: *Isotope cisternography in the evaluation of patients with subarachnoid hemorrhage.* J. Nucl. Med. 11:592, 1970.

149. WOLFSON, L. I.; KATZMAN, R.; AND ESCRIVA, A.: *Clearance of amine metabolites from the cerebrospinal fluid: The brain as a "sink."* Neurology (Minneap.) 24:772, 1974.

150. WOLINSKY, J. S.; BARNES, B. D.; AND MARGOLIS, M. T.: *Diagnostic tests in normal pressure hydrocephalus.* Neurology (Minneap.) 23:706, 1973.

151. WOOD, J. H.; BARTLET, D.; JAMES, A. E., JR., AND UDVARHELYI, G. B.: *Normal-pressure hydrocephalus: Diagnosis and patient selection for shunt surgery.* Neurology (Minneap.) 24:517, 1974.

152. YAKOVLEV, P. I.: *Paraplegias of hydrocephalics. (A clinical note and interpretation.)* Am. J. Ment. Defic. 51:561, 1947.

153. YASARGIL, M. G.; YONEKAWA, Y.; ZUMSTEIN, B., AND STAHL, H. -J.: *Hydrocephalus following spontaneous subarachnoid hemorrhage.* J. Neurosurg. 39:474, 1973.

CHAPTER 5

Viruses and Dementia

Raymond P. Roos, M.D., and
Richard T. Johnson, M.D.

Viral infections of the central nervous system cause varied signs and symptoms because of the selective vulnerability of different neural cell populations to different viruses. When the cerebral cortex or cortical-cortical connections are a major site of infection, disorders of consciousness and mentation may be salient findings. If this infection is acute and self-limited, a static intellectual deficit may persist; if the infection is slow or chronic, progressive mental deterioration may be manifest.

Some viruses such as rubella and cytomegaloviruses infect primarily the fetal brain, thereby causing congenital mental dysfunction which may be severe or subtle.[60, 61] Others such as herpes simplex virus and some arboviruses can cause severe, acute, postnatal encephalitis with ensuing dementia. Recently, several slowly evolving infections of the central nervous system have been recognized in which dementia is a major clinical feature. This dementia may result from a chronic inflammatory encephalitis as in subacute sclerosing panencephalitis, progressive rubella panencephalitis, and chronic tick-borne encephalitis; from subcortical demyelination as in progressive multifocal leukoencephalopathy; or from noninflammatory cortical neuronal degeneration as in Creutzfeldt-Jakob disease.

DEMENTIA AS A SEQUELA OF ACUTE INFECTIONS

Viral Meningitis, Encephalitis, and Postinfectious Encephalomyelitis

Many viruses can invade the central nervous system in the course of acute systemic infection. In viral meningitis presumably only meninges are involved, causing fever, headache, meningismus, and a pleocytosis. In encephalitis there are signs of parenchymal involvement such as seizures, increased intracranial pressure, and disorders of consciousness. Postinfectious encephalomyelitis may also cause signs of encephalitis, but this syndrome usually develops relatively late in the course of exanthemata, is characterized pathologically by perivenous inflammation and demyelination, and, like experimental allergic encephalitis, may have an immunopathological basis.

The same spectrum of viruses causes both acute meningitis and encephalitis. Some viruses, such as the enteroviruses and mumps, tend to cause benign meningitis; whereas others, such as arboviruses and herpes simplex virus, tend to cause severe encephalitis with permanent residua.[90] Postinfectious encephalomyelitis, as seen complicating measles infection and Jennerian vaccination, may also lead to permanent sequelae, such as mental retardation.[1, 120, 125]

Even the enteroviruses, however, can cause mild encephalitis; sequelae occasionally are seen in children, particularly in those less than 1 year old. In one series, 3 of 19 cases had sequelae involving speech and language development, and 5 had slight intellectual or behavioral abnormalities.[110] Similarly, in mumps encephalitis sequelae are unusual, although severe residua involving disorders of mentation may rarely be seen.[71, 92]

Nervous system infections with the arthropod-borne encephalitis viruses more frequently lead to severe sequelae. In Eastern, Western, and California virus encephalitides, permanent deficits are common in the very young. In general, Eastern encephalitis has a low rate of subclinical infection, a high rate of mortality, and a very high rate of severe sequelae in survivors. In one series, the majority of survivors under 5 years of age had mental retardation, speech problems, and seizures.[41] Western encephalitis has a much higher rate of inapparent infections and a lower rate of sequelae after clinical disease. Nevertheless, major mental and motor deficits are found in half of the patients who contract the disease under 1 month of age.[43] A delay in the clinical appearance of deficits has suggested that Western encephalitis virus might cause chronic infection in infants; however, Finley's studies suggest that the acute disease affects cerebral ontogenesis and that neurological deficits which become manifest later are not determined by persistent infection. California encephalitis causes inapparent infection in adults but can produce a clinical encephalitis in children with rare sequelae.[6, 21] Venezuelan equine encephalitis, a recently recognized cause of encephalitis in this country, can produce severe sequelae or death in individuals under 15, usually causes subclinical disease or an influenzal syndrome in individuals 15 to 50, and is associated with a self-limited encephalitis with complete recovery in patients over 50.[40] St. Louis encephalitis differs from the other North American arbovirus encephalitides because mortality and morbidity are greater among adults over 40 years of age. In a follow-up of 52 patients, 60 percent of elderly patients had memory deficits 1 year after infection.[119]

In each of these infections, the inflammatory process tends to be diffuse throughout the grey and/or white matter leading to variable clinical manifestations and sequelae. In contrast, herpes simplex virus infects selective areas of the brain, presents more characteristic clinical signs, and leads to a stereotyped residual mental deficit.

Herpes Simplex Virus Encephalitis

In adults, herpetic encephalitis is usually due to type 1 herpes simplex virus and is usually not associated with visceral or cutaneous herpetic disease. The appearance of rather characteristic focal neurological signs amidst a background of encephalitic symptomatology differs from the clinical picture in other encephalitides.[7, 35, 68, 93] Encephalitis may develop abruptly or evolve gradually. When clinical disease evolves insidiously, bizarre behavior, hallucinations, and other manifestations of psychosis may be evident for several days before seizures (focal or generalized) and focal signs, such as hemiparesis or aphasia, develop. Confusion may progress to stupor or coma. The electroencephalogram (EEG) is distinctive with repetitive, periodic sharp and slow wave complexes, usually

94

localized in the frontal or frontotemporal area, against a diffusely slow background activity.[118] Spinal fluid (CSF) pleocytosis and elevated protein are usually found; variable numbers of red cells may or may not be present. Although the encephalitis is usually bilateral, greater involvement of one inferior frontal or temporal lobe may suggest an abscess or tumor. The diagnosis is difficult, because virus is usually not recoverable from spinal fluid and because herpes simplex serum antibody can nonspecifically increase in the course of other infections. Definitive diagnosis can be made by demonstration of antigen or recovery of virus utilizing brain biopsy or autopsy material.[70]

Since diagnosis is often made only at autopsy, the actual morbidity and mortality of herpes simplex virus encephalitis is uncertain. This encephalitis is probably fatal in about half of the patients, however, and severe deficits may occur in a large percentage of survivors. The localization of necrosis to the inferior frontal and temporal lobes frequently leads to a severe amnestic syndrome (Korsakoff's psychosis), although a more global dementia in addition to motor abnormalities and seizures may also be seen.[35]

SLOW VIRUS INFECTIONS CAUSING PROGRESSIVE DEMENTIA

The concept that viruses cause acute, evanescent infections is well known, but only recently have viruses been recognized to cause slowly progressive degenerative neurological diseases. The term "slow virus infections" originated in veterinary literature in reference to sheep diseases such as scrapie and visna.[116] The term is applied to infections with long incubation periods followed by slowly progressive disease leading to death. Slow viral infections can be caused by conventional viruses, such as visna, or by unconventional agents, such as scrapie.

Conventional viruses can cause slow infections because of abnormalities of the virus replicative cycle, as in subacute sclerosing panencephalitis, or because of abnormalities of the host's immune response, as in progressive multifocal leukoencephalopathy. The unconventional agents are responsible for the subacute spongiform viral encephalopathies, which include the human diseases kuru and Creutzfeldt-Jakob. Although these agents can replicate and pass through 220 μ filters, they are unconventional in their physical and chemical properties, their apparent lack of antigenicity, and their failure to form recognizable virion structures as detected by electron microscopy.

Chronic Encephalitis as a Cause of Dementia

Subacute Sclerosing Panencephalitis

CLINICAL FEATURES. The onset of subacute sclerosing panencephalitis (SSPE) is usually between the ages of 2 and 21 with a mean age of onset of 7.2 years;[69] however, cases have been documented in the third decade of life.[18] SSPE is more than 3 times as common in males than females and may be more frequent in rural areas.[12, 29, 66]

Typically, patients have insidious changes in behavior and a subtle decline in intellect usually manifest as a deterioration in school performance.[45] Weeks or months later, myoclonic jerks develop. A characteristic EEG consisting of repetitive discharges of high amplitude slow waves followed by a flat background, the "suppression burst" pattern, is frequently seen.[85] Chorioretinitis, papilledema, and optic atrophy are not infrequent.[44, 95, 107] As dementia and myoclonus progress, corticospinal tract signs, cerebellar signs, rigidity, and dystonia may develop. Eventually, the patient lapses into a mute, stuporous, rigid state with evidence of autonomic instability such as temperature fluctuations and sweating abnormalities.

Most cases have an insidious onset and progress to death in 1 to 3 years. Approximately 10 percent of patients have a fulminant course causing death within 3 months;[55, 65] another 10 percent survive 4 to 10 years, occasionally with transient remissions.[65]

The CSF usually has a normal cell count and normal glucose and protein content. A first-zone colloidal gold curve is typically present, reflecting an elevated concentration of gamma globulin. This increase in gamma globulin is due to oligoclonal IgG which corresponds, in large part, to measles antibody. These elevated levels of measles antibody have been found in the serum and CSF of virtually all cases of SSPE and are crucial in establishing a diagnosis. A reduced serum-to-CSF ratio of measles antibody is found, suggesting intracranial production of antibodies. CSF contains antibodies reacting with multiple antigens of the measles virion, although the predominant reaction is against the internal nucleocapsid antigen.[2, 96]

PATHOLOGY. The histopathological lesions in SSPE are usually most severe in the posterior cerebral hemispheres with lesser involvement of more rostral areas, brainstem, cerebellum, spinal cord, and retina. A panencephalitis is present with perivascular and leptomeningeal mononuclear cell infiltration, neuronophagia, and microglial proliferation.[122] In addition, neuronal loss, gliosis, and

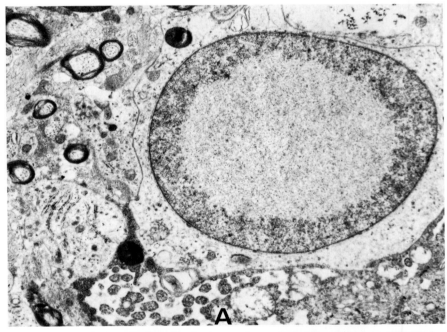

Figure 1A. Electron micrograph of an oligodendrocyte from a brain biopsy of a case of SSPE showing an intranuclear inclusion filled with viral nucleocapsids. (X 9,500)

96

variable degrees of demyelination are observed. Myelin loss may result from oligodendroglial infection or from neuronal infection with axonal degeneration. Inclusions corresponding to the filamentous nucleocapsids of measles virus are found in the nuclei and cytoplasm of neurons and glia (Fig. 1A and B).[62]

ETIOLOGY. In the original descriptions of the inclusions in SSPE by Dawson,[25, 26] the possibility of a viral etiology was suggested. A relationship with measles virus was not suspected until Bouteille and coworkers.[11] described the similarity between the fine structure of the inclusions and the nucleocapsids of paramyxoviruses. In 1967, Connolly and coworkers[22] demonstrated exceptionally high levels of measles antibody in the serum and CSF of 3 patients with SSPE as well as evidence of measles virus antigen in brain tissue by immunofluorescent staining. In 1968, measles virus cytopathic effect was seen in tissue cultures derived from brain of patients with SSPE,[8] and 1 year later using co-cultivation methods, complete, infectious measles virus was isolated.[64, 100]

PATHOGENESIS. The mechanism by which the common virus of measles can lead to persistent infection and chronic disease is unknown. Host immune factors and immaturity may be important for induction of persistent infection, but the status of the virus during the long incubation period is unclear. Defective strains of measles virus appear to be involved during the expression of the disease and in its chronic course.

A standard measles virus, rather than a variant, is probably involved in the orig-

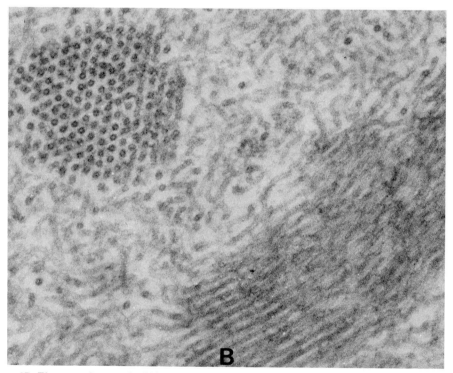

Figure 1B. Electron micrograph of higher magnification from a brain biopsy of a case of SSPE showing the viral nucleocapsids cut in different planes. (X 110,000)

inal infection as suggested by the absence of outbreaks of SSPE and the lack of clusters of cases.[69] The ability of measles infections to alter cell-mediated immunity transiently during both natural[129] and experimental infections[88] may be important in the induction of persistent infection. The immaturity of the host may also be important. SSPE patients frequently have a history of having had clinical measles infection under 2 years of age.[12, 29] Experimental studies have demonstrated that the age of the host may be important in the production of aberrant measles infections due to the presence of maternal antibody, due to age-related differences in the host's immune response, or due to age-related differences in susceptibility of cells of the nervous system. The presence of maternal antibody in suckling hamsters at the time of measles virus inoculation can produce a latent infection.[132] Byington and Johnson[17] inoculated hamsters with the Mantooth strain of SSPE virus and produced a chronic encephalitis with persistent, cell-associated virus in weanlings but found no clinical disease or virus persistence in adults; these differences were attributed to differences between the immune responses of the two age groups. Experiments in mice have emphasized varying age-related susceptibility of the central nervous system cells in the production of defective measles virus infection.[58]

The mechanism for virus persistence remains obscure in SSPE patients, although there is some evidence that measles virus may persist in many, if not all, individuals after the initial, conventional infection. It is possible that the initial interaction of the measles virus with an immature, immunologically disturbed host may somehow favor virus persistence, especially in the central nervous system. During the usual 2 to 10 year incubation period before the onset of SSPE symptoms, a mutant measles virus may be selected, possibly fostered by the presence of elevated measles antibody levels. Presumably, SSPE symptomatology appears when a critical number of cells become dysfunctional because of infection with the defective virus.

Immune factors, although of probable importance in induction of the disease, do not appear to play a critical role in expression of the disease. Blaese[9] failed to reveal any abnormalities of the immune system, except for some suggestion of abnormal lymph node architecture in an extensive *in vitro* and *in vivo* study of 9 patients with SSPE. A blocking factor in sera and CSF of SSPE patients has recently been described.[2] This may represent antigen-antibody complexes known to exist in SSPE[27] which may interfere with certain *in vitro* tests of cell-mediated immunity. The frequency and significance of this factor remain to be determined.

There is convincing evidence of the importance of an incompletely infectious, or defective, virus in the expression of the disease and in its prolonged clinical course. The cell-associated nature of the virus and its defectivity would favor a slowly evolving infection that is not affected by high serum antibody levels. Complete cell-free virus is often impossible to isolate from SSPE cases.[73] Incomplete maturation of virus is seen in the brain[36] and in SSPE virus-infected tissue[37] or organ culture.[103] Immunoperoxidase studies of SSPE virus-infected tissue culture have also suggested incomplete virus particles and altered or absent virus protein(s).[37] Recent biochemical studies reveal significant differences between SSPE virion structural protein and those of measles virus.[91]

The role of measles virus in SSPE seems established, but the pathogenesis of SSPE is still incompletely understood. The dynamic roles played by the immune system of the host and by the changing properties of the measles virus are yet to be defined.

Progressive Rubella Panencephalitis

INTRODUCTION, CLINICAL FEATURES. Progressive rubella panencephalitis is a recently recognized late manifestation of fetal rubella infection. Townsend and coworkers[123] and Weil and coworkers[133] described 4 patients who had presumptive evidence of congenital rubella infection, remained stable neurologically, and then had intellectual deterioration beginning at ages 11 and 12. Seizures, myoclonus, cerebellar ataxia, and corticospinal tract signs followed within a few years. Slowing on EEG was seen in 3 patients and periodic low amplitude polyspike complexes in 1. CSF protein was elevated in each patient, and a slight CSF mononuclear cell pleocytosis was present in 3; raised CSF gamma globulin levels were found in the 3 patients tested. The 3 patients in whom virus serologic studies were performed had elevated levels of rubella antibody in sera and CSF.

Previously, Lebon and Lyon[80] briefly reported a chronic progressive degenerative disease in a 14-year-old boy who had 10 to 30 lymphocytes in the CSF with increased gamma globulin, elevated levels of rubella antibody in the serum and CSF, but no known history of rubella. In retrospect, the neurological disease may have resulted from clinically inapparent congenital rubella.

PATHOLOGY. Histopathology of 3 cases showed a subacute to chronic panencephalitis with meningeal and perivascular lymphocytic and plasma cell infiltration, microglial nodules, gliosis, and mild neuronal loss. Mineralization, similar to that seen in infants dying of congenital rubella infections, was a prominent feature. Two cases had striking cerebellar atrophy. The presence of mineralization and the lack of inclusion bodies are distinguishing histopathological features in differentiating between rubella panencephalitis and subacute sclerosing panencephalitis.

ETIOLOGY. Rubella virus was isolated from the brain biopsy of one case.[133] Presumably the virus caused an intrauterine infection, persisted with no overt clinical progression for 12 years, and then led to a subacute panencephalitis. Although rubella is known to cause persistent, noncytopathic infections, the reason for the delayed expression of this neurological disease is unclear. One wonders whether other agents—presently known or unknown—cause clinical or subclinical infection *"in utero"* followed by a late, progressive neurological disease in survivors.

Other Chronic Encephalitides

In addition to SSPE and rubella, chronic encephalitis has been described as an opportunistic infection of immunosuppressed individuals and as a persistent sequela of tick-borne encephalitis. In children with agammaglobulinemia, enteroviruses such as Poliovirus can persist within the central nervous system producing progressive motor and mental deficits.[24] Although reports are infrequent concerning subacute encephalitis in adults, adenovirus type 32 has been isolated from the brain of an immunosuppressed lymphosarcoma patient with a 4 week history of mental changes and seizures,[108] and cytomegalovirus infections have been associated with confusional states and psychosis in adults receiving immunosuppressive therapy.[34]

A chronic inflammatory encephalitis has been described in the Soviet Union[115] and in North America[104] in patients with epilepsia partialis continua and associated progressive mental and motor deterioration. As many as 83 percent of patients with the Soviet form, Kozhevnikov's epilepsy, have an antecedent history of acute tick-borne encephalitis.[76] Nonspecific febrile illness of some sort precedes the onset of seizures in more than 50 percent of the North American cases.[104] Although no virus has been isolated from the North American cases, tick-borne encephalitis virus has been isolated from blood, spinal fluid, and brain tissue from Kozhevnikov's epilepsy patients.[20,77] Clarification of the mechanism of virus persistence and disease induction may result from recent experiments documenting the delayed production of movement disorders following inoculation of tick-borne encephalitis virus in rhesus monkeys.[4]

Limbic encephalitis associated with carcinoma,[23] Behçet's disease,[19] uveo-meningoencephalitis syndrome,[106] and Vilyuisk's encephalitis of the Soviet Union[101] have also been identified as putative chronic viral encephalitides, although the etiology of these conditions has not been firmly established.

DEMYELINATING DISEASE AS A CAUSE OF DEMENTIA

Progressive Multifocal Leukoencephalopathy

CLINICAL FEATURES. Progressive multifocal leukoencephalopathy (PML) is an opportunistic infection occurring in immunologically compromised individuals. Over one-half of the cases are associated with lymphoproliferative disease; many of the remainder, with sarcoid, tuberculosis, and other neoplasms.[105] Cases have also occurred in patients undergoing vigorous immunosuppression in order to maintain renal allografts[81, 84] or to treat systemic lupus erythematosus.[134] A few well-documented cases have been reported in individuals with no known history or autopsy evidence of an underlying disease.[15]

PML is a world-wide disease with an average age of onset in the 50s; the youngest reported patient was 18 years old.[94] Patients develop progressive multifocal neurological signs such as hemiparesis, aphasia, seizures, intellectual decline, personality change, gait abnormalities, and visual problems.[105] Cerebellar, brainstem, and spinal cord signs are less common. The EEG is typically abnormal, progressing from focal to diffuse delta activity. The CSF is normal except for rare cases with minimal protein elevation. A terminal stage with prominent dementia, motor deficits, and coma ensues. Death usually occurs 3 to 6 months after onset, although cases with courses longer than 10 years and with transient remissions have been reported.[74, 121]

PATHOLOGY. Although, at times, the neuropathological abnormalities in PML are subtle and can be missed, the lesions are usually sufficiently evident to enable a certain diagnosis on gross and microscopic examination of the brain. The primary lesions are foci of demyelination, with relative sparing of axons, most commonly in the white matter directly beneath the cortex. In the demyelinated areas, the astrocytes are large, with bizarre mitotic figures, nuclear forms, and chromatin patterns. Oligodendrocytes are absent within these areas; surrounding oligodendrocytes are enlarged with intranuclear inclusions.[5] In 1965, two groups independently reported electron microscopic demonstration of papovavirus-like particles corresponding to the oligodendroglial inclusion bodies (Fig. 2A and B); the particles were thought to resemble the polyomasimian virus 40 (SV40) group of papovaviruses.[117, 136]

ETIOLOGY. Despite numerous attempts, virus was not isolated from PML until 1971. Padgett and coworkers,[98] using primary cultures of human fetal brain, iso-

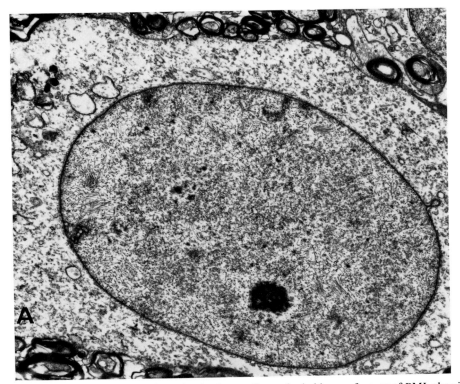

Figure 2A. Electron micrograph of an oligodendrocyte from a brain biopsy of a case of PML showing an intranuclear inclusion filled with viral particles. (X 8,100)

lated a new papovavirus, the JC virus. Weiner and coworkers,[134] working with primary and continuous African green monkey kidney cells isolated two viruses serologically identical to SV40 virus. JC virus has been the virus isolated or identified by immune electron microscopy in all subsequent cases.[94]

In 1971, another new papovavirus, BK virus, was found in the urine of a renal transplant patient who had no neurological disease.[52] This virus has not yet been implicated in PML.

PATHOGENESIS. Serologic studies show that JC and BK viruses commonly infect humans and produce no known clinical disease in immunologically normal individuals.[51, 97, 114] SV40 virus antibodies, however, occur much less commonly.[112] It is assumed that immunosuppression results in activation of a latent papovavirus causing PML; however, an alternative explanation is that an immunosuppressed individual has a primary encounter with a papovavirus leading to PML.

Investigations of PML regarding the incubation period, the route of virus entry, and the extent of extraneural infection have been limited by lack of an experimental model. Inoculation of JC, SV40, or BK viruses in experimental animals produces tumors[39, 113, 130] but not demyelination. The recent finding of naturally occurring spontaneous PML in macaques with underlying systemic diseases, especially lymphoma, will perhaps improve our understanding of the human disease.[57]

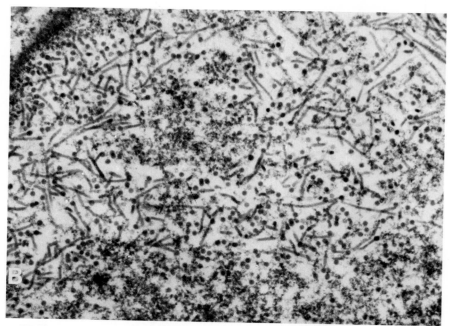

Figure 2B. Electron micrograph of higher magnification from a brain biopsy of a case of PML showing round and elongated papovavirus particles. By immune electron microscopy and tissue culture isolation, the virus was identified as SV40 virus. (X 33,700)

NONINFLAMMATORY DISEASE AS A CAUSE OF DEMENTIA

Creutzfeldt-Jakob Disease

CLINICAL FEATURES. Creutzfeldt-Jakob disease (CJD) is a world-wide disease occurring with an approximate incidence of 1 per million population.[46] A focus among Libyan Jews has been reported by Kahana and associates[72] with an incidence of approximately 30 per million; however, their reported total number affected was 13, only 8 of which had a definite diagnosis. An epidemiological study of the United States and Canada noted a northern preponderance among the 69 cases reported, although this was thought to have resulted from an artifact of the method of case ascertainment.[10] In a study of 46 patients in England and Wales, clusters of 3 cases in one small community and of 5 patients in another area were documented.[87]

CJD begins in the fifth and sixth decades of life in the majority of patients, although patients in their 20s and their 70s have been described.[124] As many as 10 percent of cases may be familial[124] with a distribution most consistent with autosomal dominant inheritance.[42] Affected relatives within the same pedigree have similar clinical and pathological findings.[42] Familial cases tend to have earlier onsets than sporadic cases.[109]

In its most characteristic dramatic presentation and course, CJD is fairly stereotyped; as Denny-Brown[28] described: "Progressive dementia with no imminence of cause . . . and the most fantastic degree of disintegration of the higher functions of the brain occurring with a galaxy of abnormal signs, is a startling syndrome. . . . The picture is so characteristic, once you have seen one or two cases and are aware of the problem, that the disease will seldom be missed."

Mental state abnormalities are usually the first sign of disease. All cases eventually become severely demented, usually to a severe degree in less than 6 months. Myoclonus is commonly present and may be stimulus sensitive. The EEG usually shows diffuse slowing with periodic sharp wave complexes.[16] Along with this basic triad of dementia, myoclonus, and a characteristic EEG, a melange of neurological abnormalities may be seen, including pyramidal, extrapyramidal, cerebellar, sensory, and lower motor neuron signs. The CSF is typically normal, although mildly elevated CSF protein values are occasionally found. Usually in less than a year, the patient dies in a terminal state of mute, akinetic rigidity.[109]

Although the diagnosis of the conventional CJD cases is "seldom missed," the rarer, more atypical clinical presentations are frequently misdiagnosed. For example, patients with the amyotrophic form of CJD may cause confusion since they may have early lower motor neuron signs, late dementia, a prolonged course (over 2 years) and neither myoclonus nor a characteristic EEG.[3]

PATHOLOGY. CJD is a member of the group of "subacute spongiform virus encephalopathies" along with scrapie, kuru, and transmissible mink encephalopathy. The histopathological hallmarks usually found in the subacute spongiform virus encephalopathies are neuronal loss, astrocytosis, and cytoplasmic vacuolation of neurons and astrocytes (status spongiosus) (Fig. 3).[78]

In CJD the neuronal loss can have a predilection for the anterior horn (the

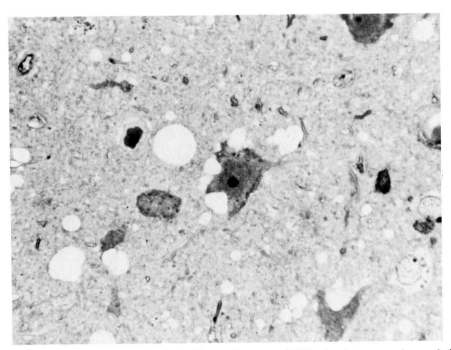

Figure 3. A photomicrograph of a brain biopsy of a case of CJD showing neuronal vacuolation. Toluidine blue stain. (X 250)

amyotrophic form), the cerebellum (the Brownell-Oppenheimer variant,[13] the "ataxic form" of CJD[56]), or the parietal and occipital lobes (Heidenhain's syndrome)[89] leading to appropriate clinical symptomatology. Astrocytosis of the grey matter may be very remarkable, at times suggesting a diagnosis of astrocytoma on brain biopsy.[109] The status spongiosus, of varying severity, corresponds under electron microscopy to vacuolated and swollen neuronal processes and perikaryal cytoplasm; spongiform changes occur less frequently in astrocytic processes.[79] Curled membrane fragments are frequently found at the edges of the vacuoles and occasionally in the lumen.

The apparent specificity of the histopathological abnormalities may be misleading. The neuronal loss and gliosis are not unusual findings in other degenerative diseases. The spongiosus is insignificant or even absent in some cases.

Plaques are found in the cerebellum in over 10 percent of cases of CJD;[46] similar plaques are seen in kuru and scrapie. In the latter disease these plaques have been found identical at an ultrastructural level to the senile plaques of Alzheimer's disease.[135]

ETIOLOGY. The absence of clinical signs of inflammation in CJD, such as fever or CSF pleocytosis, or of histopathological findings of inclusion bodies or inflammatory infiltrates made consideration of a viral etiology unlikely in the past. Van Rossum[127] wrote in 1968, "exogenous factors play no part in its pathogenesis." The transmissibility of CJD was finally determined through studies of kuru and scrapie.

Kuru, a subacute cerebellar disease occurring in the Fore linquistic group and in their immediate neighbors in New Guinea, was described by Gajdusek and Zigas[48] in 1957. The disease as reported primarily affected adult females and young children of both sexes, causing death in less than 1 year. Clues to kuru's etiology were supplied in 1959 by Hadlow,[59] a veterinary neuropathologist, who remarked on the epidemiological, clinical, and pathological similarity between kuru and scrapie, a disease of sheep and goats. Hadlow commented that scrapie was known to be experimentally transmissible to nonaffected sheep and goats with an incubation period of several years, and he postulated that kuru might be a slow virus infection transmissible to subhuman primates.

Gajdusek, Gibbs, and Alpers inoculated 220 μ filtered brain suspensions of kuru-affected brain intracerebrally into a variety of animals including chimpanzees and held them for a prolonged period of observation. Finally, in 1965, 20 and 21 months after inoculation, 2 chimpanzees developed an ataxic disease and died 5 to 9 months later with pathological evidence of subacute spongiform virus encephalopathy.[50] Eleven human cases of kuru have now been proven transmissible with an incubation period of 10 to 82 months in chimpanzees. Secondary as well as primary transmission occurs by intracerebral or peripheral routes of inoculation of brain or pooled viscera. Old World monkeys, New World monkeys, and the mink, in addition to chimpanzees, have proven susceptible.[46, 47]

Klatzo, and coworkers,[75] in an initial description of kuru pathology, remarked on the similarity between kuru and CJD. Attempts at transmission of CJD were soon initiated following the success with kuru. In 1968, a chimpanzee developed ataxia, hemiparesis, and myoclonus 13 months after inoculation with filtered CJD-affected brain suspension, dying 2 months later with pathological signs of subacute spongiform virus encephalopathy.[54]

CJD has now been transmitted from over 51 cases of sporadic CJD and from 5 familial CJD cases from separate pedigrees.[124] In addition to these familial cases, a similar spongiform encephalopathy has been produced in subhuman primates inoculated with 2 cases from 2 separate pedigrees clinically and pathologically diagnosed as Alzheimer's disease.[124] One patient had dementia, seizures, spasticity, and probable myoclonus with autopsy evidence of Alzheimer's disease. Pathology of the other case is unfortunately based on a biopsy specimen; and details regarding the clinical course after the biopsy are not known. It is possible that these 2 patients diagnosed as familial Alzheimer's disease — and conceivably all patients with this diagnosis — have, in fact, a form of CJD with abundant plaques, little spongiosus, and some tangles; this hypothesis is supported by the observation that familial Alzheimer's disease patients frequently have myoclonus in addition to dementia[67] and that the inoculated subhuman primates develop a typical spongiform encephalopathy. Alternatively, these 2 patients may have had both familial Alzheimer's disease and CJD — the latter disease being transmissible. One is reluctant at this time to postulate that Alzheimer's disease, in general, is transmissible since inoculation of subhuman primates with more than 30 specimens from sporadic Alzheimer's disease patients has not yet produced experimental disease.[46]

The incubation period of CJD varies from 11 to over 71 months in the chimpanzee. In addition to the chimpanzee, Old World monkeys, New World monkeys, and the domestic cat have proven susceptible following intracerebral and, in some cases, peripheral inoculation.[46] Transmission of CJD to mice[14] and to guinea pigs[83] has also been reported. Human to human transmission has been suspected in a case involving the development of a rapidly progressive spongiform encephalopathy in a patient 18 months after receiving a corneal transplant from an individual who had died of CJD.[38]

The physical and chemical properties of the transmissible CJD agent appear to be similar to the scrapie agent.[46] Although the scrapie agent is a replicating, filterable particle, its thermostability and its resistance to UV inactivation, nucleases, and formalin set it off from all previously known conventional viruses. The lack of a detectable antibody response to the agent in the natural or experimental disease and of recognizable viral particles by electron microscopy have also contributed to suggestions that the scrapie agent may be an unusual, naked nucleic acid containing structure — such as a viroid[33] — or possibly a new replicating entity without a nucleic acid. Recent experiments, however, have not upheld the theory of the viroid nature of scrapie.[86, 131]

PATHOGENESIS. Despite the successful transmission of CJD, the pathogenesis and mode of natural spread of CJD remain obscure. Horizontal contact spread appears to be very uncommon in CJD. Bobowick and associates[10] found no apparent contact or evidence of possible occupational contamination in a group of 38 CJD patients. In Matthews' epidemiological study[87] 3 cases of CJD were found living within a small area, and the possibility of contact was raised but not established. There are 2 reports of conjugal cases of CJD, although both involve questionable diagnoses.[53, 87] There is only 1 case report of CJD in medical or paramedical personnel.[50]

The extreme scarcity of cases in members of the medical profession and among spouses of affected patients seems surprising considering the successful transmissibility via parenteral inoculation, the apparent susceptibility of most primates (as evidenced by the susceptibility of many species of subhuman primates and of the patient who received the corneal transplant), the hardiness and high infectivity of the transmissible agent, and the agent's presence in non-neural tissue. The rarity of obvious horizontal transmission may possibly be explained by the absence of the CJD agent in body fluids thereby preventing transmission by conventional routes. The agent has not been identified in blood, and other bodily fluids are presently under investigation.[46] This hypothesis is supported by the finding that kuru, similarily believed to be absent from body fluids, has never spread to visitors to the kuru area.[47] Presumably the subacute spongiform virus encephalopathies can be laterally transmitted when there is contamination by gross tissue, as exemplified by presumed transmission of CJD by corneal transplantation, spread of kuru during endocannibalism,[46] possible transmission of scrapie by placental ingestion,[99] and spread of transmissible mink encephalopathy by natural cannibalism of mink.[47]

The successful oral transmission of some subacute spongiform encephalopathies has made the dietary history of CJD patients of interest. The possibility that CJD may be transmitted by ingestion of incompletely cooked scrapie-infected animal material has been raised, but there is little supporting evidence.[46] In an American epidemiological study of CJD patients over one-third of patients had a history of eating hog brains, although this number was not statistically different from that of the control group.[10] It has been speculated that the focus of CJD in Libyan Jews may be related to their practice of eating bovine brain and eyes.[63]

Genetic factors seem to be important in all of the subacute spongiform virus encephalopathies. Kuru was originally thought to be a genetic disease; family studies continue to stress the role of genetic factors.[46] Susceptibility of sheep to scrapie appears to be under genetic control[30, 32] as does the length of the incubation period in different breeds of mice.[31] Without question, genetic factors play an important part in CJD, especially in the cases that appear to be dominantly inherited and transmissible. Hypotheses that have been suggested to explain the transmissibility of an apparently genetic disease include: vertical passage of the agent transplacentally, via infected sperm or egg, or via integration of the viral genome into germ cells; horizontal passage through exposure to other affected family members; genetic susceptibility to a common CJD agent, to a rare CJD agent, or to a second agent that induces latent CJD agent.[42] The question of how an apparently hereditary disease is also transmissible is extraordinarily provocative having implications in studies of other familial neurological diseases.

CONCLUSION

The recognition of viral agents in the causation of dementing diseases has clarified certain confused clinical and pathological disease entities. Not until the measles virus became implicated was it generally accepted that Dawson's "inclusion encephalitis,"[25, 26] Pette and Doring's "panencephalitis,"[102] and van Bogaert's "subacute sclerosing leukoencephalitis"[126] were a single disease, now called SSPE. Over 10 syndromes can be unequivocally considered CJD as a result of transmission studies. It is apparent that greater understanding of etiology can help redefine clinical and pathological definitions of diseases.

The discovery of an infectious etiology for certain forms of dementia provides the hope of therapy for diseases formerly considered idiopathic, inexorable abiotrophies. Unfortunately, at this time, despite numerous therapeutic attempts with both antiviral agents and immunotherapeutic drugs, no satisfactory treatment exists for acute or chronic encephalitis, PML, or CJD. Rational treatment for these diseases must await a better understanding of their pathogenesis. One feature complicating therapeutic considerations is that irreversible cerebral damage probably has occurred by the time the first clinical symptoms appear. For this reason, prophylaxis and vaccination are desirable — especially against agents implicated in not uncommon disease states, such as measles virus in postinfectious encephalomyelitis and SSPE. At present, however, there is uncertainty about the effect of measles vaccine on SSPE. The finding that the average 6-year incubation period between primary measles infection and signs of SSPE is not altered by intervening immunization suggests that vaccination does not precipitate or hasten the development of SSPE;[111] the apparent decline in cases in recent years may indicate a preventive effect.[65]

The implication of viruses in the etiology of chronic neurological diseases has stimulated virological investigations of other neurological degenerative processes. The results of further subhuman primate inoculations with cases of Alzheimer's disease, as well as Pick's disease, are awaited with interest. The recent report of RNA-dependent DNA-polymerase activity in a cytoplasmic particulate fraction of brain tissue from patients with Guamanian amyotrophic lateral sclerosis and the parkinsonism-dementia complex and from some normal Guamanians[128] suggests that an oncornavirus present in Guamanians might interact with other factors in disease production. Virological studies of such diseases as non-Guamanian amyotrophic lateral sclerosis, paralysis agitans, progressive supranuclear palsy, and striatonigral degeneration are also in progress.

Acknowledgments

The authors thank Robert M. Herndon, M.D., Peter Ostrow, M.D., and Maria Mazlo, M.D. of the Johns Hopkins Hospital for providing photomicrographs. We also wish to thank Dr. D. C. Gajdusek for providing unpublished data. Dr. Roos is the recipient of Special Fellowship NS 02256 from the National Institutes of Health.

REFERENCES

1. AARLI, J. A.: *Nervous complications of measles: Clinical manifestations and prognosis.* Eur. Neurol. 12:79, 1974.

2. AHMED, A , ET AL.: *Demonstration of a blocking factor in the plasma and spinal fluid of patients with subacute sclerosing panencephalitis.* J. Exp. Med. 139:902, 1974.

3. ALLEN, I. V., ET AL.: *A study of a patient with the amyotrophic form of Creutzfeldt-Jakob disease.* Brain 94:715, 1971.

4. ASHER, D. M.: Movement disorders in rhesus monkeys after infection with tick-borne encephalitis, in Meldrum, B. S., and Marsden, L. D. (eds.): *Advances in Neurology,* Vol. 10. Raven Press, New York, 1975.

5. ASTROM, K. -E.; MANCALL, E. L.; AND RICHARDSON, E. P., JR.: *Progressive multifocal leukoencephalopathy.* Brain 81:93, 1958.

6. BALFOUR, H. H., ET AL.: *California arbovirus (La Crosse) infections. I. Clinical and laboratory findings in 66 children with meningoencephalitis.* Pediatrics 52:680, 1973.

7. BARINGER, J. R.: Human herpes simplex virus infections, in Thompson, R. A., and Green, J. R. (eds.): *Infectious Diseases of the Central Nervous System.* Raven Press, New York, 1974.

8. BAUBLIS, J. V., AND PAYNE, F. E.: *Measles antigen and syncytium formation in brain cell cultures from subacute sclerosing panencephalitis (SSPE).* Proc. Soc. Exp. Biol. Med. 129:593, 1968.

9. BLAESE, R. M., AND HOFSTRAND, H.: *Immunocompetence of patients with SSPE.* Arch. Neurol. 32:494, 1975.

10. BOBOWICK, A. R., ET AL.: *Creutzfeldt-Jakob Disease: A case-control study.* Am. J. Epidemiol. 98:381, 1973.

11. BOUTEILLE, M., ET AL.: *Sur un cas d'encéphalite subaiguë à inclusions. Etude anatomoclinique et ultrastructurale.* Rev. Neurol. (Paris) 118:454, 1965.

12. BRODY, J. A., AND DETELS, R.: *SSPE: A zoonosis following aberrant measles.* Lancet 2:500, 1970.

13. BROWNELL, B., AND OPPENHEIMER, D. R.: *An ataxic form of subacute presenile polioencephalopathy (Creutzfeldt-Jakob disease).* J. Neurol. Neurosurg. Psychiatry 28:350, 1965.

14. BROWNELL, B., ET AL.: *Experimental transmission of Creutzfeldt-Jakob disease.* Lancet 2:186, 1975.

15. BRUN, A., ET AL.: *Aspects on the variability of progressive multifocal leukoencephalopathy.* Acta Neuropathol. (Berl.) 24:232, 1973.

16. BURGER, L. J.; ROWAN, A. J., AND GOLDENSOHN, E. S.: *Creutzfeldt-Jakob disease: an electroencephalographic study.* Arch. Neurol. 26:428, 1972.

17. BYINGTON, D. P., AND JOHNSON, K. P.: *Experimental subacute sclerosing panencephalitis in the hamster: Correlation of age with chronic inclusion-cell encephalitis.* J. Infect. Dis. 126:18, 1972.

18. CAPE, C. A., ET AL.: *Adult onset of subacute sclerosing panencephalitis.* Arch. Neurol. 28:124, 1973.

19. CHAJEK, T., AND FAINARU, M.: *Behçet's disease: report of 41 cases and a review of the literature.* Medicine 54:179, 1975.

20. CHUMAKOV, M. P.; VOROB'JEVA, N. N.; AND BEL'JAJEVA, A. L.: *Study of the ultra-viral encephalitides. III. Kozhevnikov's epilepsy and tick-borne encephalitis.* Zh. Nevropatol. Psikhiatr. 13:63, 1944.

21. CHUN, R. W. M., ET AL.: *California arbovirus encephalitis in children.* Neurology (Minneap.) 18:369, 1968.

22. CONNOLLY, J. H., ET AL.: *Measles-virus antibody and antigen in subacute sclerosing panencephalitis.* Lancet 1:542, 1967.

23. CORSELLIS, J. A. N.; GOLDBERG, C. J.; AND NORTON, A. R.: *"Limbic encephalitis" and its association with carcinoma.* Brain 91:481, 1968.

24. DAVIS, L. E., ET AL.: *Chronic progressive poliomyelitis.* J. Neuropathol. Exp. Neurol. In press.

25. DAWSON, J. R.: *Cellular inclusions in cerebral lesions of lethargic encephalitis.* Am. J. Pathol. 9: 7, 1933.

26. DAWSON, J. R.: *Cellular inclusions in cerebral lesions of epidemic encephalitis: second report.* Arch. Neurol. 31:685, 1934.

27. DAYAN, A. D., AND STOKES, M. I.: *Immune complexes and visceral deposits of measles antigens in subacute sclerosing panencephalitis.* Br. Med. J. 2:374, 1972.

28. DENNY-BROWN, D.: *Discussion.* Trans. Am. Neurol. Assoc. 85:149, 1960.

29. DETELS, R., ET AL.: *Further epidemiological studies of subacute sclerosing panencephalitis.* Lancet 2:11, 1973.

30. DICKINSON, A. G., ET AL.: *Some factors controlling the incidence of scrapie in Cheviot sheep infected with a Cheviot-passage scrapie agent.* J. Comp. Pathol. 78:313, 1968.

31. DICKINSON, A. G.; MEIKLE, M. H.; AND FRASER, H.: *Identification of a gene which controls the incubation period of some strains of scrapie agent in mice.* J. Comp. Pathol. 78:293, 1968.

32. DICKINSON, A. G.; STAMP, J. T.; AND RENWICK, C. C.: *Maternal and lateral transmission of scrapie in sheep.* J. Comp. Pathol. 84:19, 1974.

33. DIENER, T. O.: *Viroids: the smallest known agents of infectious disease.* Annu. Rev. Microbiol. 28:23, 1974.

34. DORFMAN, L. J.: *Cytomegalovirus encephalitis in adults.* Neurology (Minneap.) 23:136, 1973.

35. DRACHMAN, D. A.; AND ADAMS, R. D.: *Herpes simplex and acute inclusion-body encephalitis.* Arch. Neurol. 7:61, 1962.

36. DUBOIS-DALCQ, M.; COBLENTZ, J. M.; AND PLEET, A. B.: *Subacute sclerosing panencephalitis: unusual nuclear inclusions and lengthy clinical course.* Arch. Neurol. 31:355, 1974.

37. DUBOIS-DALCQ, M., ET AL.: *Comparison between productive and latent subacute sclerosing panencephalitis viral infection in vitro: an electron microscopic and immunoperoxidase study.* Lab. Invest. 30:241, 1974.

108

38. DUFFY, P., ET AL.: *Possible person-to-person transmission of Creutzfeldt-Jakob disease*. N. Engl. J. Med. 290:692, 1974.

39. EDDY, B. E., ET AL.: *Identification of the oncogenic substance in rhesus monkey kidney cell cultures as simian virus 40*. Virology 17:65, 1962.

40. EHRENKRANZ, N. J., AND VENTURA, A. K.: *Venezuelan equine encephalitis virus infection in man*. Annu. Rev. Med. 25:9, 1974.

41. FEEMSTER, R. F.: *Eastern equine encephalitis: sequelae*. Neurology (Minneap.) 8:883, 1958.

42. FERBER, R. A., ET AL.: Familial Creutzfeldt-Jakob disease: transmission of the familial disease to primates, in Subirana, A., and Burrows, J. M. (eds.): *Proceedings of the Xth International Congress of Neurology*. Excerpta Medica International Congress. Series No. 319, Amsterdam, 1974.

43. FINLEY, K. H., ET AL.: *Western encephalitis and cerebral ontogenesis*. Arch. Neurol. 16:140, 1967.

44. FONT, R. L.; JENIS, E. H.; AND TUCK, K. D.: *Measles maculopathy associated with subacute sclerosing panencephalitis*. Arch. Pathol. 96:168, 1973.

45. FREEMAN, J. M.: *The clinical spectrum and early diagnosis of Dawson's encephalitis*. J. Pediatr. 75:590, 1969.

46. GAJDUSEK, D. C., AND GIBBS, C. J., JR.: Slow virus infections of the nervous system and the laboratories of slow, latent, and temperate virus infections, in Tower, D. B. (ed.): *The Nervous System*, Vol. 2. Raven Press, New York, 1975.

47. GAJDUSEK, D. C., AND GIBBS, C. J., JR.: Subacute and chronic diseases caused by atypical infections with unconventional viruses in aberrant hosts, in Pollard, M. (ed.): *Perspectives in Virology*, Vol. 8. Academic Press, New York, 1973.

48. GAJDUSEK, D. C., AND ZIGAS, V.: *Degenerative disease of the central nervous system in New Guinea. The endemic occurrence of "kuru" in the native population*. N. Engl. J. Med. 257:974, 1957.

49. GAJDUSEK, D. C., ET AL.: Transmission of subacute spongiform encephalopathy to the chimpanzee and squirrel monkey from a patient with papulosis atrophicans maligna of Kohlmeier—Degos, in Subirana, A., and Burrows, J. M. (eds.): *Proceedings of the Xth International Congress of Neurology*. Excerpta Medica International Congress Series No. 319, Amsterdam, 1974.

50. GAJDUSEK, D. C.; GIBBS, C. J., JR., AND ALPERS, M.: *Experimental transmission of a kuru-like syndrome to chimpanzees*. Nature (Lond.) 209:794, 1966.

51. GARDNER, S. D.: *Prevalence in England of antibody to human polyomavirus (B. K.)*. Br. Med. J. 1:77, 1973.

52. GARDNER, S. D., ET AL.: *New human papovavirus (B. K.) isolated from urine after renal transplantation*. Lancet 1:1253, 1971.

53. GARZULY, F.; JELLINGER, K., AND PILZ, P.: *Subakute spongiose encephalopathie (Jakob Creutzfeldt Syndrom) Klinische-morphologische Analyse von 9 Fallen*. Arch. Psychiatr. Nervenkr. 214:207, 1971.

54. GIBBS, C. J., JR., ET AL.: *Creutzfeldt-Jakob disease (spongiform encephalopathy): transmission to the chimpanzee*. Science 161:388, 1968.

55. GILDEN, D. H.; RORKE, L. B.; AND TANAKA, R.: *Acute SSPE*. Arch. Neurol. 32:644, 1975.

56. GOMORI, A. J., ET AL.: *The ataxic form of Creutzfeldt-Jakob disease*. Arch. Neurol. 29:318, 1973.

57. GRIBBLE, D. H., ET AL.: *Spontaneous progressive multifocal leukoencephalopathy (PML) in macaques*. Nature (Lond.) 254:602, 1975.

58. GRIFFIN, D. E., ET AL.: *Age dependence of viral expression: comparative pathogenesis of two rodent-adapted strains of measles virus in mice*. Infect. Immun. 9:690, 1974.

59. HADLOW, W. J.: *Scrapie and kuru*. Lancet 2:289, 1959.

60. HANSHAW, J. B., ET AL.: CNS sequelae of congenital cytomegalovirus infection, in Krugman, S., and Gershon, A. A. (eds.): *Progress in Clinical and Biological Research*, Vol. 3. Alan R. Liss, Inc., New York, 1975.

61. HARDY, J. B., ET AL.: *Adverse fetal outcome following maternal rubella after the first trimester of pregnancy*. J.A.M.A. 207:2414, 1969.

62. HERNDON, R. M., AND RUBINSTEIN, L. J.: *Light and electron microscopic observations of the*

development of viral particles in the inclusions of Dawson's encephalitis (subacute sclerosing panencephalitis). Neurology (Minneap.) 18 (Part 2): 8, 1968.

63. HERZBERG, L., ET AL.: *Creutzfeldt-Jakob disease: hypothesis for high incidence in Libyan Jews in Israel.* Science 186:848, 1972.

64. HORTA-BARBOSA, L., ET AL.: *Subacute sclerosing panencephalitis: isolation of measles virus from a brain biopsy.* Nature (Lond.) 221:974, 1969.

65. JABBOUR, J. T.; DUENAS, D. A., AND MODLIN, J.: *SSPE: clinical staging, course, and frequency, 1975.* Arch. Neurol. 32:493, 1975.

66. JABBOUR, J. T., ET AL.: *Epidemiology of subacute sclerosing panencephalitis (SSPE). A report of the SSPE Registry.* J.A.M.A. 220:959, 1972.

67. JAKOB, H.: Muscular twitching in Alzheimer's disease, in Wolstenholme, G. E. W., and O'Connor, M. (eds.): *Alzheimer's Disease and Related Conditions.* Churchill, London, 1970.

68. JOHNSON, K. P.; ROSENTHAL, M. S.; AND LERNER, P. I.: *Herpes simplex encephalitis: The course in five virologically proven cases.* Arch. Neurol. 27:103, 1972.

69. JOHNSON, R. T.: *Subacute sclerosing panencephalitis.* J. Infect. Dis. 121:227, 1970.

70. JOHNSON, R. T.; OLSON, L. C., AND BUESCHER, E. L.: *Herpes simplex virus infections of the nervous system: Problems in laboratory diagnosis.* Arch. Neurol. 18:260, 1968.

71. JOHNSTONE, J. A.; ROSS, C. A. C., AND DUNN, M.: *Meningitis and encephalitis associated with mumps infection: A 10-year survey.* Arch. Dis. Child. 47:647, 1972.

72. KAHANA, E., ET AL.: *Creutzfeldt-Jakob disease: Focus among Libyan Jews in Israel.* Science 183:90, 1973.

73. KATZ, M., AND KOPROWSKI, H.: *The significance of failure to isolate infectious viruses in cases of subacute sclerosing panencephalitis.* Arch. Gesamte Virusforsch. 41:390, 1973.

74. KEPES, J. J.; CHOU, S. M.; AND PRINCE, L. W.: *Progressive multifocal leukoencephalopathy with 10-year survival in a patient with non-tropical sprue: report of a case with unusual light and electron microscopic features.* Neurology (Minneap.) 25:1006, 1975.

75. KLATZO, I., GAJDUSEK, D. C.; AND ZIGAS, V.: *Pathology of kuru.* Lab. Invest. 8:799, 1959.

76. KOMANDENKO, N. I., et al.: *The clinical picture and some problems of the pathogenesis of progressive forms of tick-borne encephalitis.* Zh. Nevropatol. Psikhiatr. 72:1000, 1972.

77. KRAMINSKAJA, N. N.; MEIEROVA, R. A.; AND ZHIVOLJAPINA, R. R.: *Materials for the study of tick-borne encephalitis in the Ekhirit-Belegat region of Irkutsk Oblast'.* Dokl. Irkutskogo Protivochumnogo Instituta 8:189, 1969.

78. LAMPERT, P. W.; GAJDUSEK, D. C.; AND GIBBS, C. J., JR.: Pathology of dendrites in subacute spongiform virus encephalopathies, in Kreutzberg, G. W. (ed.): *Advances in Neurology,* Vol. 12. Raven Press, New York, 1975.

79. LAMPERT, P. W.; GAJDUSEK, D. C.; AND GIBBS, C. J., JR.: *Subacute spongiform virus encephalopathies. Scrapie, kuru and Creutzfeldt-Jakob disease: A review.* Am. J. Pathol. 68:626, 1972.

80. LEBON, P., AND LYON, G.: *Non-congenital rubella encephalitis.* Lancet 2:468, 1974.

81. LEGRAIN, M., ET AL.: *Leuco-encéphalopathie multifocale progressive après transplantation rénale.* J. Neurol. Sci. 23:49, 1974.

82. LINK, H.; PANELIUS, M.; AND SALMI, A. A.: *Immunoglobulins and measles antibodies in subacute sclerosing panencephalitis: demonstration of synthesis of oligoclonal IgG with measles antibody activity within the central nervous system.* Arch. Neurol. 28:23, 1973.

83. MANUELIDIS, E. E.: *Transmission of Creutzfeldt-Jakob disease from man to the guinea pig.* Science 190:571, 1975.

84. MANZ, H. J.: *Progressive multifocal leukoencephalopathy after renal transplantation.* Ann. Intern. Med. 75:77, 1971.

85. MARKAND, O. N.; AND PANSZI, J. G.: *The electroencephalogram in subacute sclerosing panencephalitis.* Arch. Neurol. 32: 719, 1975.

86. MARSH, R. F., ET AL.: *Scrapie and transmissible mink encephalopathy: search for infectious nucleic acid.* J. Virol. 13: 993, 1974.

87. MATTHEWS, W. B.: *Epidemiology of Creutzfeldt-Jakob disease in England and Wales.* J. Neurol. Neurosurg. Psychiatry 38: 210, 1975.

88. MCFARLAND, H. F.: *The effect of measles virus infection on T and B lymphocytes in the mouse. I. Suppression of helper cell activity.* J. Immunol. 113: 1978, 1974.

110

89. MEYER, A.; LEIGH, D.; AND BAGG, C. E.: *A rare presenile dementia associated with cortical blindness (Heidenhain's syndrome).* J. Neurol. Neurosurg. Psychiatry 17: 129, 1954.

90. MEYER, H. M., JR., ET AL.: *Central nervous system syndromes of "viral" etiology. A study of 713 cases.* Am. J. Med. 29:334, 1960.

91. MILLER, C. A., AND FIELDS, B. N.: *Measles and subacute sclerosing panencephalitis (SSPE) viruses: Comparative characterization of purified particles.* J. Neuropathol. Exp. Neurol. In press.

92. MILLER, H. G.; STANTON, J. B.; AND GIBBONS, J. L.: *Parainfectious encephalomyelitis and related syndromes: a critical review of the neurological complications of certain specific fevers.* Q. J. Med. 25:427, 1956.

93. MILLER, J. K.; HESSER, F.; AND TOMPKINS, V. N.: *Herpes simplex encephalitis: Report of 20 cases.* Ann. Intern. Med. 64: 92, 1966.

94. NARAYAN, O., ET AL.: *Etiology of progressive multifocal leukoencephalopathy.* N. Engl. J. Med. 289: 1278, 1973.

95. NELSON, D. A., ET AL.: *Retinal lesions in subacute sclerosing panencephalitis.* Arch. Ophthalmol. 84: 613, 1970.

96. NORRBY, E., ET AL.: *The measles virus antibody response in subacute sclerosing panencephalitis and multiple sclerosis,* in Zeman, W.; Lennette, E. H.; and Brunson, J. G. (eds.): *Slow Virus Diseases.* The Williams & Wilkins Co., Baltimore, 1974.

97. PADGETT, B. L.; AND WALKER, D. L.: *Prevalence of antibodies in human sera against JC virus, an isolate from a case of progressive multifocal leukoencephalopathy.* J. Infect. Dis. 127: 467, 1973.

98. PADGETT, B. L., ET AL.: *Cultivation of papova-like virus from human brain with progressive multifocal leukoencephalopathy.* Lancet 1: 1257, 1971.

99. PATTISON, I. H., ET AL.: *Spread of scrapie to sheep and goats by oral dosing with fetal membranes from scrapie affected sheep.* Vet. Rec. 90: 465, 1972.

100. PAYNE, F. E.; BAUBLIS, J. V.; AND ITABASHI, H. H.: *Isolation of measles virus from cell cultures of brain from a patient with subacute sclerosing panencephalitis.* N. Engl. J. Med. 281: 585, 1969.

101. PETROV, P. A.: *Vilyuisk encephalitis in the Yakut republic (U.S.S.R.).* Am. J. Trop. Med. Hyg. 19: 146, 1970.

102. PETTE, H., AND DORING, G.: *Uber einheimische Panencephalomyelitis vom Charakter der Encephalitis japonica.* Deutsch. Z. Nervenheilk. 149: 7, 1939.

103. RAINE, C. S., ET AL.: *Subacute sclerosing panencephalitis virus: Observations on neuroadapted and non-neuroadapted strain in organotypic central nervous system cultures.* Lab. Invest. 31: 42, 1974.

104. RASMUSSEN, T., AND McCANN, W.: *Clinical studies of patients with focal epilepsy due to "chronic encephalitis."* Trans. Am. Neurol. Assoc. 93: 89, 1968.

105. RICHARDSON, E. P., JR.: *Our evolving understanding of progressive multifocal leukoencephalopathy.* Ann. N.Y. Acad. Sci. 230:358, 1974.

106. RIEHL, J.-L., AND ANDREWS, J. M.: *The uveomeningoencephalitic syndrome.* Neurology (Minneap.) 16:603, 1966.

107. ROBB, R. N., AND WATTERS, G. V.: *Ophthalmic manifestations of subacute sclerosing panencephalitis.* Arch. Ophthalmol. 83:426, 1970.

108. ROOS, R., ET AL.: *Isolation of an adenovirus 32 strain from human brain in a case of subacute encephalitis.* Proc. Soc. Exp. Biol. Med. 139: 636, 1972.

109. ROOS, R.; GAJDUSEK, D. C., AND GIBBS, C. J., JR.: *The clinical characteristics of transmissible Creutzfeldt-Jakob disease.* Brain 96: 1, 1973.

110. SELLS, C. J.; CARPENTER, R. L.; AND RAY, C. G.: *Sequelae of central-nervous-system enterovirus infections.* N. Engl. J. Med. 293: 1, 1975.

111. SEVER, J. L., ET AL.: *Constant incubation period for subacute sclerosing panencephalitis — Effect of measles vaccines.* Neurology (Minneap.) 25:364, 1975.

112. SHAH, K. V.: *Evidence for an SV40-related papovavirus infection of man.* Am. J. Epidemiol. 95: 199, 1972.

113. SHAH, K. V.; DANIEL, R. W.; AND STRANDBERG, J. D.: *Sarcoma in a hamster inoculated with BK virus, a human papovavirus.* J. Natl. Cancer Inst. 54: 945, 1975.

111

114. SHAH, K. V.; DANIEL, R. W.; AND WARSZAWSKI, R. N.: *High prevalence of antibodies to BK virus, an SV40-related papovavirus, in residents of Maryland.* J. Infect. Dis. 128: 784, 1973.

115. SHAPOVAL, A. N.: *Chronic forms of tick-borne encephalitis in the Far East.* Zh. Nevropatol. Psikhiatr. 14 (2): 59, 1945.

116. SIGURDSSON, B.: *Rida, a chronic encephalitis of sheep, with general remarks on infections which develop slowly and some of their special characteristics.* Br. Vet. J. 110: 341, 1954.

117. SILVERMAN, L., AND RUBINSTEIN, L. J.: *Electron microscopic observations on a case of progressive multifocal leukoencephalopathy.* Acta Neuropathol. (Berl.) 5: 215, 1965.

118. SMITH, J. B., ET AL.: *A distinctive clinical EEG profile in herpes simplex encephalitis.* Mayo Clin. Proc. 50: 469, 1975.

119. SMITH, J. E.: *St. Louis encephalitis: Sequelae.* Neurology (Minneap.) 8: 884, 1958.

120. SPILLANE, J. D.; AND WELLS, C. E. C.: *The neurology of Jennerian vaccination.* Brain 87: 1, 1964.

121. STAM, F. C.: *Multifocal leukoencephalopathy with slow progression and very long survival.* Psychiatr. Neurol. Neurochir. 69: 453, 1966.

122. TELLEZ-NAGEL, I., AND HARTER, D. H.: *Subacute sclerosing leukoencephalitis. I. Clinicopathological, electron microscopic, and virologic observations.* J. Neuropathol. Exp. Neurol. 25: 560, 1966.

123. TOWNSEND, J. J., ET AL.: *Progressive rubella panencephalitis: late onset after congenital rubella.* N. Engl. J. Med. 292:990, 1975.

124. TRAUB, R. D.; GAJDUSEK, D. C., AND GIBBS, C. J., JR.: Transmissible virus dementias. The relation of transmissible spongiform encephalopathy to Creutzfeldt-Jakob disease, in Kinsbourne, M., and Smith, L. (eds.): *Aging, Dementia and Cerebral Function.* Spectrum Publishing, Inc., Flushing, New York. In press.

125. TYLER, H. R.: *Neurological complications of rubeola (measles).* Medicine 36: 147, 1957.

126. VAN BOGAERT, L.: *Une leuco-encéphalite sclérosante subaigüe.* J. Neurol. Neurosurg. Psychiatry 8:101, 1945.

127. VAN ROSSUM, A.: Spastic pseudosclerosis (Creutzfeldt-Jakob disease), in Vinken, P. J., and Bruyn, G. W. (eds.): *Handbook of Clinical Neurology,* Vol. 6. North Holland Publishing Co., Amsterdam, 1968.

128. VIOLA, M., ET AL.: *RNA-instructed DNA polymerase activity in a cytoplasmic fraction in brains from Guamanian patients.* J. Exp. Med. 142: 483, 1975.

129. VON PIRQUET, C.: *Das verhalten der kutanen Tuberkulinreaktion während der Masern.* Dtsch. Med. Wochenschr. 34: 1297, 1908.

130. WALKER, D. L., ET AL.: *Human papovavirus (JC): induction of brain tumors in hamsters.* Science 181: 674, 1973.

131. WARD, R. L.; PORTER, D. D.; AND STEVENS, J. G.: *Nature of the scrapie agent; evidence against a viroid.* J. Virol. 14:1099, 1974.

132. WEAR, D. J.; AND RAPP, F.: *Latent measles virus infection of the hamster central nervous system.* J. Immunol. 107: 1593, 1971.

133. WEIL, M. L., ET AL.: *Chronic progressive panencephalitis due to rubella virus simulating subacute sclerosing panencephalitis.* N. Engl. J. Med. 292:994, 1975.

134. WEINER, L. P., ET AL.: *Isolation of virus related to SV40, from patients with progressive multifocal leukoencephalopathy.* N. Engl. J. Med. 286:385, 1972.

135. WÍSNIEWSKI, H. M.; BRUCE M. E.; AND FRASER, H.: *Infectious etiology of neuritic (senile) plaques in mice.* Science 190: 1108, 1975.

136. ZU RHEIN, G. M., AND CHOU, S. M.: *Particles resembling papova viruses in human cerebral demyelinating disease.* Science 148: 1477, 1965.

112

CHAPTER 6

The Pathology of Dementia

Bernard E. Tomlinson, M.D.

Dementia, a disorder which results in deterioration of memory, personality, and social behavior and which commonly terminates in inability to communicate or behave rationally in any way, may result from almost any widespread destructive condition of the brain. A list of conditions leading to this state may be found in Slaby and Wyatt.[169] The subject is also discussed in great breadth by Haase.[74] In this chapter no attempt will be made to describe in detail the morphology of all the numerous conditions which may lead to dementia. The greater part of the chapter deals with the morphological changes and "mechanisms" which lead to dementia in those numerically important states associated with this condition. Explanations of the mechanisms are often incomplete, but much progress has been made in the past decade.

Although, it is usual to make a distinction between so-called presenile and senile dementias, such subheadings will not be used here, since they merely separate the disorders by age of onset—the division usually being at 65 years of age. This division is of little use, and its replacement by a more rational grouping of the disorders producing dementia would clearly be welcome. Such a classification would preferably have an etiological basis.

Many diseases which produce dementia may do so in either middle or old age. Before the age of 65, many conditions produce dementia; some of these may assume more importance as their incidence increases. Some neurological disorders which previously were quickly fatal in most instances are now commonly "cured" in the sense that death early in the course of the illness is rare. Such a condition is tuberculous meningitis. However, it is still not always possible to diagnose tuberculous meningitis early enough to prevent some brain damage with mental deterioration. The likelihood of brain damage increases if treatment has been delayed. The two diseases which produce the majority of cases of dementia in the presenium—Alzheimer's disease and multifocal ischemic lesions (usually referred to as arteriosclerotic or arteriopathic dementia)—are also responsible for the largest number of cases of dementia in old age. On the whole, however, the variety of disorders which produce dementia in middle age is greater than that which occurs in old age.

At present, not all cases of dementia can be explained; occasionally no clue to the origin of the dementia can be obtained from morphological studies alone. There are, therefore, some truly dementing processes, progressive and possibly irreversible, for which the explanation is one of altered cerebral function unaccompanied by recognizable morphological change. Although the number of instances in which no morphological cerebral abnormality is found is small, it is not justifiable to say in every case with morphological abnormality that the morphological abnormality found accounts for the dementia. This is particularly so in old age where senile changes and ischemic softening may be quite prominent in normal, well-preserved old subjects.[188, 192]

In the presenile group, the cause of the dementia is usually obvious morphologically. In the senile group, there is still a difference of opinion as to how justified the morphological diagnosis may be in some instances; this disagreement arises from the already mentioned tendency for morphological changes at both a gross and microscopic level to occur in the brains of normal old people.

Unfortunately, misunderstanding exists about the term "senile dementia." For some it is a general term designating a dementing process commencing in old age irrespective of the type of disease process involved. For others it is synonymous with the predominant dementing clinical picture in old age which is associated with morphological changes similar or identical to those of Alzheimer's disease in the presenile period. Controversy still exists as to whether Alzheimer's disease from the presenium into extreme old age is merely differentiated by age of onset, rapidity of progress, or some variation in symptomatology. Certainly among morphologists there is substantial agreement, much strengthened by electron microscopic evidence accumulated over the past decade, that the diseases of the two age periods are inseparable and that age is perhaps the only, though in some ways an important, separating factor. To avoid confusion, the term Alzheimer's disease and senile dementia of Alzheimer type (SDAT) will be used in this chapter to distinguish the two disorders, although the author shares the majority view that on morphological grounds the disorders are indistinguishable.

Confusion has also arisen over the etiology of some cases of dementia due to the reluctance of many pathologists to perform the investigations necessary to establish the nature of the dementing process and due to differing interpretations of the findings. Insufficient morphological study has lead to the impression that a larger number of cases of dementia cannot be explained morphologically than is actually so and, also, to errors about the size and type of lesions which produce dementia. When one or more small softenings are found in the basal ganglia at autopsy, it is tempting to utilize the explanation that arteriosclerotic ischemic disease has been the basis of the process. Many clinicians will accept this explanation, because the view is still widely held that this is the predominant type of dementia in old age. Many intracranial neoplasms present with personality changes and occasionally as an insidious dementing process. In the great majority of cases, neurological evidences of an intracranial mass develop during life, but occasional cases run the clinical course of a primary dementia until death. Failure to diagnose an irremovable glioma or secondary neoplasm may not be tragic, but the same cannot be said of meningiomas which may also present with personality change[51] or progressive dementia.[61] Recovery from dementia after surgical removal of a meningioma clearly establishes the causal relationship, but when meningiomas are first revealed at autopsy, it should not be assumed that the etiology of the dementia has been unearthed. In my experience, meningiomas are the most frequently found benign intracranial neoplasms in both normal and demented old people. While not denying that a large meningioma may cause or contribute to dementia, it should not be accepted as the only explanation for a chronic dementing process without

114

the usual extensive examination of the brain which would be performed if the brain presented no obvious morphological change. Truly demented old subjects with a meningioma unexpectedly found at autopsy usually, but not always, have senile dementia of Alzheimer type. In a recent case, an 82-year-old woman, fit, active, and a hard-working Councilwoman until a year before her death, suffered a rapidly progressive dementia without the development of localizing neurological signs or evidence of increasing intracranial pressure. She was found at autopsy to have a massive parasagittal meningioma indenting both frontal lobes and producing much distortion of the anterior horns of the lateral ventricles with considerable edema of the white matter in the adjacent compressed and distorted hemispheres. Additionally, microscopic examination revealed extensive subcortical gliosis throughout the rest of the brain and in both temporal lobes and widespread moderately severe astrocytic proliferation within the cortex. The precise nature of this widespread change has not been determined or classified, but it certainly could not be accepted as a known association or consequence of even a massive benign tumor pressing on the hemispheres.

An additional factor confusing the morphological explanations of dementia has been, and probably still is, inaccurate clinical diagnosis. This is seen particularly in older patients presenting with rapid clouding of consciousness or confusion whose primary disorder lies outside the central nervous system and especially in patients whose dominant psychiatric abnormality is severe depression. The diagnosis of dementia is too readily applied to confused or depressed old people and misdiagnosis is not uncommon in younger patients. Of 106 cases referred by neurologists or psychiatrists as presenile dementia to the National Hospital, London, 15 were definitely not demented, and the most common source of error was a depressive illness.[118] Indeed difficulties in distinguishing between organic and functional disturbances in old age is not surprising, since it is less than 25 years since firm evidence of the separation of such disorders was produced.[97, 149, 150] Only in the last 20 years has it become customary for skilled psychometric testing to be used on patients suspected of dementia; and unfortunately in many cases, at least in Britain, such testing is still not performed.

In the past some confusion relating to the nature of the morphological changes associated with dementia, particularly in old age, has unquestionably resulted from clinical inaccuracy. It is justifiable and sometimes necessary for the morphologist to resist the pressures of clinical colleagues for a full pathological investigation of the brain if the clinical records throw doubt on the diagnosis of dementia. The majority of patients dying in acute or chronic confusional states or with severe depression in old age, both of which may be mistaken for dementia, show either no morphological changes at all or only those changes common in intellectually well-preserved old people.[192] The relatively tedious and time-consuming histological investigation needed to establish the precise morphological diagnosis in dementia is only justified if similar care, expertise, and investigation has gone into the clinical assessment of the case.

PATHOLOGICAL PROCESSES WHICH MAY PRODUCE DEMENTIA AND THEIR DISTRIBUTION

Any widely destructive process within the cerebral hemispheres will produce dementia. In some disorders, abnormalities involve all areas of the cerebral cortex but not necessarily to the same extent. In Alzheimer's disease or senile dementia of Alzheimer type it may be impossible to find a single uninvolved microscopic field in any area of cortex. The morphological abnormalities involve the nerve cells and their processes, and striking lesions occur within the perikaryon and at synaptic level within the cortex. It has also been maintained that generalized cortical neuron loss is always present, but this remains to be established quantitatively. It is easy to accept that such widespread cortical lesions, if they mirror abnormal nerve cell and synapse function, are responsible for major cerebral dysfunction which manifests itself as a severe global dementia. In Pick's disease abnormalities of cortical neurons and severe neuron loss are also present, though not so evenly and widely distributed. Atrophy is often severe and generalized in Alzheimer's disease and severe but more localized in Pick's disease. However, atrophy and brain weight are very variable particularly in elderly subjects with dementia, reflecting the changes which occur in many normal old subjects in addition to the the effects and severity of morphological processes producing the dementia. Here then are two diseases which are probably primarily neuronal and which affect wide areas of cortex, with irregular and relatively slight abnormalities of white matter, basal ganglia, and brain stem. In the parkinsonism dementia complex of Guam, extensive cortical neurofibrillary degeneration, identical with that found in Alzheimer's disease, occurs throughout the cortex, but severe similar pathology is present in the basal ganglia, thalamus, hypothalamus, and parts of the brain stem. Other diseases with widespread severe cortical neuron destruction are Creutzfeldt-Jakob disease, general paresis, most instances of post-anoxic dementia, and occasional cases of dementia associated with widespread small vessel disease. In all of these, the severe intellectual, emotional, and personality disturbance which occurs is easy to understand.

Some other diseases affect the cerebral white matter particularly, leaving the cortex for the most part intact. In some instances of multi-infarct dementia the majority of lesions are in in hemispheric white matter, although cortex, basal ganglia, and brain stem rarely, if ever, escape entirely. In these cases, dementia is presumably explained by severance of major cortical connections which may interfere with overall cerebral function as effectively as widespread destruction of nerve cells. White matter pathology with relatively little grey involvement is seen in multiple sclerosis and Schilder's disease, both of which may be associated with dementia. In Schilder's disease severe dementia is seen; in multiple sclerosis it is seen only in the later stages of the disease. Although myelin loss is emphasized as the primary abnormality in both conditions, destruction of axons is often eventually so extensive that functional interference is presumably almost as complete as in white matter infarction of similar extent. Multifocal leukoencephalopathy, a rare disorder almost certainly of viral origin and principally affecting hemispheric white matter, also occasionally produces a global dementia.

Other dementing diseases affect subcortical nuclear masses, classically and apparently primarily. Huntington's chorea produces striking atrophy of the caudate head and putamen as a result of nearly total nerve cell loss and gliosis; however, cortical nerve cell loss is also severe and may be the most significant contributor to dementia in this disorder. The same could be true of the dementia of Wilson's disease, in which the basal ganglia, particularly the putamen and globus pallidus, undergo the most severe changes, but cortical nerve nerve cell loss is also extensive. Other disorders, particularly Wernicke's encephalopathy, primarily a dysmnesic syndrome, produce lesions largely, if not entirely, confined to the tissues around the third ventricles, the aqueduct, and the fourth ventricle. A mantle of brain some 5mm. wide is severely disrupted throughout the whole length and extent of the hypothalamus including the medial thalamic nuclei and anterior fornix. A circle of tissue around the aqueduct is similarly involved. Morphological lesions outside this circumscribed area cannot usually be demonstrated. In progressive supranuclear palsy,[145, 172] nerve cell loss and gliosis, with neurofibrillary tangle formation and granulovacuolar degeneration, are present in the brain stem, basal ganglia, and cerebellum. However, cerebral white matter and cortical lesions are minimal or absent. It is perhaps significant, in view of the latter, that dementia is usually mild in this disorder. In Parkinson's disease, dementia is rarely a prominent or early feature, but mild intellectual deterioration appears to affect many cases in the late stages. The striking lesions in Parkinson's disease are in the substantia nigra. Some cases that develop severe dementia have all the additional features of senile dementia of Alzheimer type, but others do not have cortical evidence of this disorder, and the dementing process, possibly associated with cortical neuron loss, remains unexplained. A rarer dementia associated with basal ganglia disease is that found in bilateral thalamic degeneration[19, 157, 173] in which thalamic neuron loss and gliosis are severe. Of possible significance is a case reported by Stern[173] in which dementia was also severe and dense gliosis was present throughout the white matter of the hemispheres. Evidence that bilateral and relatively restricted ischemic lesions of the thalamus may produce dementia is growing;[160] one would plead that extensive morphological studies be undertaken in any such cases to ensure that no other factor has participated.

Some diseases having memory loss as the dominant feature (which should correctly be designated dysmnestic states) are associated with lesions largely confined to the anterior temporal lobes, particularly the hippocampus and its related structures. Occasionally bilateral vascular lesions destroy these areas, usually along with other vascular territories,[25, 193, 196] and bilateral anterior temporal lobectomy for intractable epilepsy may lead to severe amnesia.[126] The role of the temporal lobes in memory has recently been reviewed.[194] All the anterior temporal structures are heavily involved in Alzheimer's and Pick's disease, although never without other widespread lesions. However, an occasional case with a severe dysmnestic syndrome presents with bilateral gliosis of anterior temporal lobes of uncertain origin. Limbic encephalitis, usually associated with bronchogenic carcinoma but not with cerebral metastases, produces viral-type inflammatory lesions with severe neuronal destruction and gliosis largely confined to the anterior temporal lobes, associated with profound memory loss which results in many subjects being categorized as demented.[46, 81] Some such subjects have viral type lesions extending beyond the temporal lobes. Other non-metastatic carcinomatous effects on the central nervous system, such as cerebellar degeneration, in which the appearance does not suggest a viral disorder, may be associated with dementia.[22, 81] Concrete evidence that the encephalomyelitis associated with carcinoma results from viral invasion has not been produced so far.

Many other disorders which may result in dementia are associated with destructive lesions in various parts of the brain. Of greatest incidence is arteriopathic dementia in which multiple foci of ischemic destruction are usually present in both hemispheres and are commonly present in other brain territories. Vascular lesions, often predominantly basal in the hemispheres, are a significant factor in dementia following meningitis, though necrosis from direct cerebral invasion or toxicity of the infecting organisms and progressive obstructive hydrocephalus from meningeal adhesions are important. The latter condition is particularly important since it is amenable to therapy. That obstructive hydrocephalus may produce, among other symptoms, intellectual deterioration is not surprising. The relief of symptomatology and the recovery from apparently progressive dementia which follow "shunting" in some cases of hydrocephalus with normal cerebrospinal fluid pressure is still unexplained but well authenticated.[4, 11, 75] The numerous failures of "shunting" in cases initially diagnosed as normal pressure hydrocephalus are usually readily explained at autopsy. What morphological changes, if any, exist in those who recover remain to be determined. Widespread ischemic damage almost certainly accounts for the dementia which occasionally follows rupture of an intracranial aneurysm, and infarction often plays some part in dementia following severe brain injury although the direct tearing of fiber tracts and the tissue destruction associated with laceration and hemorrhage all combine to produce devastating brain damage. The unique and curious pathology of the well-known "dementia-pugilistica" is also widespread and strikingly varied.

Most dementing processes present evidence of widespread cerebral hemisphere disease, some of which will now be examined in greater detail. The numerous disorders potentially associated with dementia (including uremia, liver failure, vitamin B_{12} deficiency, hyperparathyroidism, etc.) not only rarely present as dementia but show no consistent or often even significant morphological brain changes. This lack of significant morphological findings even applies to myxedema "dementia" in which the patient presents with severe retardation of intellectual and motor function and the true diagnosis remains undetected. Because only an occasional case of such disorders merits consideration as dementia, they will not be further discussed here. *Brain Dysfunction in Metabolic Disorders*[143] covers this topic extensively, and the psychiatric disturbances in endocrine disorders are ably analyzed by Sachar[154] in that volume.

INCIDENCE OF DISEASES PRODUCING DEMENTIA

Reliable and precise information on the incidence of different diseases producing dementia is difficult to find. Because diagnosis of the dementing process in some reported series may have been made by retrospective case note review,[42] there is the possibility that depressive and confusional states were mistaken for dementia. This is even more likely when one considers that confirmation of the diagnosis in doubtful cases by psychometry and other means with observation of progressive deterioration is rare. Furthermore, hardly any series can avoid bias or selection in some form. A group of patients who were initially sent to a neurologist may contain an unusual number with focal neurological abnormalities and, therefore, may contain an excessively large number of patients with tumors or vascular disease. Series reported from long-stay psychiatric hospitals may contain significant diagnostic errors and are unlikely to include processes such as Creutzfeldt-Jakob disease or gliomas which would normally be screened out on initial examination. The location of a hospital and the nature of the population served may produce an unusual incidence of particular disorders, for instance, alcohol-induced dementia. Also the incidence of dementia from various causes as reported 50 years ago may have materially altered due to refinement of diagnostic criteria, recognition of "new" disorders, and successful therapy of previously important diseases such as syphilis. Unquestionably the age of patients in any group also affects the reported incidence of contributing disorders as does the thoroughness of the final morphological analysis in those cases coming to autopsy.

Despite these difficulties, recent papers make it possible to make some statement about the incidence of different diseases producing dementia, although many local circumstances still affect the results. Marsden and Harrison,[118] reporting on 84 cases of established presenile dementia, arrived at the diagnoses given in Table 1 on clinical grounds. It is significant that of the original 106 cases admitted with the diagnosis of dementia, 15 were definitely not demented (8 were depressed) and 7 were not proven to be demented.

These figures probably reflect the incidence of the more common diseases presenting with dementia in the presenium. What is hidden in the 48 cases of unknown cause is open to conjecture; but the likelihood, as Marsden and Harrison[118] suggest, is that many (probably the great majority) had Alzheimer's disease and that a significant contribution was made by vascular lesions. The precise diagnosis can only be reached in a proportion of such cases by biopsy which may be difficult to justify. Where this has been done in cases presenting with progressive dementia with evidence of cerebral atrophy, a high proportion has been shown to have Alzheimer's disease.[35, 164, 165] Only complete autopsy studies of such a group will determine the precise morphological categories; however, even with exhaustive studies, it will usually not be possible to categorize or classify all cases.[90, 193]

Autopsy studies of demented patients in old age have included quantitative or semiquantitative measurements of senile changes (senile plaques, neurofibrillary tangles, and granulovacuolar degeneration) and of cerebral ischemic destruction.[42, 193, 209] They have shown general agreement that senile dementia of Alzheimer type is the most significant contributor, with cerebral softening (arteriosclerotic, arteriopathic, or multi-infarct dementia) being the second most important. In a considerable number of cases, senile dementia of Alzheimer type and significant softening coexist.[42, 55, 144, 193] Figures for dementia arising from the combined effects of the two disorders vary greatly, particularly when quantitative assessments of the lesions have not been made. Thus, when small basal ganglia and thalamic softenings are given major significance,[36, 153] arteriosclerotic disease may be thought to contribute to 50 percent of cases. If quantitative changes are taken into account, however, softenings may contribute to as few as 15 to 20 percent.[193] These disorders (senile dementia of Alzheimer type, multi-infarct dementia, or a combination) probably account for 75 to 90 percent of cases of dementia

Table 1. Incidence of different diseases producing dementia*

Intracranial space occupying masses		8
Gliomas	3	
Metastases	2	
Benign lesions	3	
Arteriosclerotic dementia		8
Dementia in alcoholics		6
Possible normal pressure communicating hydrocephalus		5
Creutzfeldt-Jakob disease		3
Huntington's chorea		3
Post-traumatic cerebral atrophy		1
Post-subarachnoid hemorrhage		1
Limbic encephalitis		1
Cerebral atrophy of unknown cause		48

*Compiled data of Marsden and Harrison.[118]

above the age of 65,[42, 193] and in old females, senile dementia of Alzheimer type may account for 80 percent or more. Some authors consider that SDAT accounts for approximately 80 percent of all dementia in old age.[58] The remaining cases result from almost as many causes as are seen in the presenile period, though Creutzfeldt-Jakob disease, Pick's disease, and Huntington's chorea rarely present over 65 years, and chronic subdural hematoma, myxedema, and cerebral atrophy of unknown cause may account for proportionately more cases.

PATHOLOGY OF THE IMPORTANT DEMENTING DISEASES

Alzheimer's Disease and Senile Dementia of Alzheimer Type

The pathology of these two disorders will be discussed together because on the basis of both light and electron microscopic studies there seems no justification for attempting to distinguish between them. There is no doubt that the morphological changes tend to be more severe and less variable in the presenile form. But aside from this, present evidence strongly favors the proposition that the diseases are fundamentally the same and largely distinguished only by age of onset.

Gross Observations

Alzheimer's presenile dementia has been morphologically a well-defined entity for many years.[8, 105, 124, 140] The brain at autopsy is usually, though not invariably, shrunken, often weighing below 1,060gm. and not uncommonly below 1,000gm.. Occasionally severe and characteristic histological changes are present in brains of normal weight and appearance. Cortical atrophy is prominent and usually widespread involving particularly the frontal and temporal lobes; parietooccipital gyri are commonly less severely affected, and the inferior frontal and inferior occipital gyri are usually least involved. The anterior ends of the superior and middle temporal gyri may be particularly severely involved, and the hippocampus, para-hippocampus, and hippocampal gyrus are often shrunken to the naked eye. Usually the changes are symmetrical, and on coronal sections the appearances of atrophy are heightened by widening of the sulci in all affected areas; broadening of the Sylvian fissure, particularly at its front end; and a moderate or severe dilatation of the lateral and third ventricles. Atrophy may, however, be asymmetrical and focally of great severity in almost any part of the hemispheres, producing circumscribed areas of severely shrunken brain usually superimposed on a lesser degree of generalized atrophy.[12, 125, 176] Brain stem and cerebellum are also small in many instances, though in comparison with the hemispheres they are not as severely affected.

Microscopic Observations

SENILE PLAQUES. Histologically, gross abnormalities are usually present throughout all areas of the cerebral cortex. In the majority of cases it is impossible to find a single microscopic field not involved to some extent. Most striking is the presence throughout the cortex of the so-called senile, or neuritic, plaques and nerve cells affected by Alzheimer's neurofibrillary degeneration. When numerous, and particularly when they have large centers of amyloid material, senile plaques are visible in hematoxylin and eosin preparations as an eosinophilic condensation of the cortical neuropil around which one or two glial nuclei may be visible. In silver impregnations, however, the appearance of the cortex is unmistakable: all the cortical layers from the second to the junction with the white matter, and often apparently slightly into the superficial white matter, are disrupted by silver impregnated masses, many of which are 150 to 200 μ across. Between the well-defined plaques, the neuropil is usually abnormal, containing numerous twisted, thickened, and distorted fibrils. The appearance of the plaques in silver impregnations varies considerably with the method used and from case to case even with the same method. The variation from case to case depends to some extent on the precise composition of each individual plaque and whether or not it has been sectioned through its center but it also partly reflects on the vagaries of silver impregnation procedures. In many preparations the plaques consist of obvious tangled masses of irregular and beaded or club-like fibers, whereas in others the appearance is more of clusters of silver-positive granules which may or may not be well-defined from the surrounding neuropil. Many plaques clearly have a densely stained, central, roughly rounded area surrounded by a less densely stained fibrillary or granular zone, the central area consisting of amyloid. A proportion of the plaques are positive with conventional stains for amyloid, and this is particularly well demonstrated by Congo red stain when polarized or ultraviolet light is used.

In the most severely affected cases, up to 50 percent of the cortex appears involved by these abnormal argyrophilic structures; indeed, in many areas plaques run together to form masses of abnormal fibrillary or granular material sometimes as large as 0.5 mm. in diameter. Particularly in the amygdaloid complex, hippocampus, subiculum, and hippocampal gyrus, plaque formation may be massive and almost continuous. Subcortical structures are much less involved than the cortex. Small numbers of plaques may be found in the basal ganglia, thalamus, hypothalamus, mammillary bodies, and periventricular tissues of the third ventricle. Occasionally they are present in considerable numbers in the mammillary bodies, but nowhere in the subcortical tissues do they reach the concentrations found in the cerebral cortex.

NEUROFIBRILLARY DEGENERATION. Alzheimer's neurofibrillary degeneration, usually only visible in medium or large neurons, consists of alteration of the normal, delicate intraneuronal fibrils into thickened, densely staining fibers which are twisted or distorted within the neuronal perikaryon. Frequently the abnormal structures form loops or rather intricate tangles around the nucleus. With experience affected neurons can be identified with conventional cytological stains, but they are dramatically demonstrated by silver impregnation or when viewed with polarized light after Congo red staining. Although as a rule not as obtrusive as plaques, they can nevertheless be found in large numbers throughout the cerebral cortex. Again in the amygdaloid complex, subiculum, and hippocampal gyrus, the majority of neurons may be affected, but in some instances the lateral temporal, frontal, or even occipital cortex may contain vast numbers. Grossly visible foci of atrophy anywhere in the hemispheres may be found to be particularly involved. Smaller numbers of similarly affected cells can be found in the deeper neuron masses and a few in the upper stem.[94]

GRANULOVACUOLAR DEGENERATION. The third change typical of this disease is largely confined to the pyramidal cells of the hippocampus and subiculum. The term granulovacuolar degeneration sufficiently describes this change, because in hematoxylin and eosin preparations the affected cells are seen to contain within their cytoplasm from one to a dozen or so clear, rounded vesicles 5 to 6 μ across which contain a hematoxyophilic granule 1 to 2 μ across in the center. In severe cases many affected cells are actually ballooned by these inclusions. The eosinophilic spindle-shaped or rod-like paracrystalline bodies, now known as Hirano bodies,[82] also occur in the hippocampus in large numbers in many instances, certainly in excess of what is found in normal old age.[68]

With this gross abnormality throughout the cortex, there is only a slight astrocytic and microglial response and surprisingly little pallor demonstrable in the white matter, though from the dilatation of the ventricles and the finger-like contraction of numerous cortical gyri the white matter is clearly seen to be reduced in quantity. Reduced thickness of the cortical layers may not be obvious, but recent studies have established a small diminution in mean cortical thickness compared with controls.[161] This does not, however, apply to the anterior hippocampal structures where the amygdaloid nucleus, hippocampus, and hippocampal gyrus may be grossly atrophied and reduced in thickness by roughly 50 percent. In these anterior temporal structures, astrocytic proliferation and spongiosis may be moderate (and occasionally very marked) and myelin pallor severe. The same statements apply to any other area of severe circumscribed atrophy.

NEURONAL LOSS. Nerve cell loss throughout the cortex has for many years been considered severe by subjective assessment; but objective evidence of nerve cell loss has been slow to appear, largely because of the difficult and time-consuming nature of this work, and has not yet been entirely satisfactorily established. In some instances, actual gaps among the neurons appear to have been created by the presence of vast numbers of plaques, but comparison of cell counts with those from appropriate age-matched, intellectually normal controls has been performed on few occasions. Colon[37, 38] demonstrated considerable neuron loss in the deeper cortical layers in 3 cases of Alzheimer's disease compared with two controls. However, studies of large groups of demented and normal old people are needed, because variation in cell populations in the latter may be great, and marked cortical cell loss in old age has been demonstrated.[28] Further evidence of cell loss in Alzheimer's disease as compared with normal aging has also been presented by Shefer.[161] Automated analysis of cellular and other components of the central nervous system should make precise statements on such populations possible.

It must be stressed that the amount of change present throughout the majority of the subcortical structures, even in the most severely affected cases, is much less than in the cortex. Plaques in small or moderate numbers are not uncommon in basal ganglia and hypothalamus, and neurofibrillary tangles may be present in certain hypothalamic and brain stem nuclei, apparently with a characteristic distribution.[93] The severe reduction in certain brain enzymes in the caudate and other deeper structures[21] may prove to be of major significance but is difficult to explain on a morphological basis.

With onset of the disorder above the age of 65 years, the term senile dementia is applied by most clinicians and morphologists to the similar if not identical dementing process. However, some variations in the clinical and morphological findings are observed, and certainly the morphological changes are not as consistently severe (in terms of cerebral atrophy, ventricular dilatation, and plaque and tangle formation) in the older group as in the presenile group. In the older group, although cerebral atrophy and ventricular dilatation may be severe,[193] some cases show no more gross atrophy than is present in some intellectually well-preserved old people. There are also, as would be expected in this age group, a larger number with ischemic cerebral lesions. The majority of these lesions are merely co-incidental, but some are large enough to be possible contributors to the dementing process. However, the morphological changes seen by both light and electron microscopy appear essentially similar in the two age groups, the difference largely being that the changes in the older age group are more variable but less severe. Nevertheless, in many cases among the older group vast numbers of senile plaques can be found throughout the cortex with smaller numbers in the subcortical structures as is found in the presenile disease. Also, in many instances numerous neurons affected by neurofibrillary change are present throughout the cortex and particularly in the anterior temporal lobes, but this feature may be more patchy and in some instances less severe than in younger subjects. Occasionally severely demented old people with large numbers of plaques show tangle formation only to a degree which can be found in non-demented old people. At the other end of the scale, occasionally demented old subjects show widespread and severe neurofibrillary tangle formation but have relatively few senile plaques, the number of which may be established by counting as falling within the range that can be found in some normal old people. Similar instances occur in the presenile group, but in my experience variations in morphology are greater in the older individuals. Granulo-vacuolar degeneration in the older group is usually severe as in the presenile group, but in a very occasional case the number of cells in the hippocampus so affected may be similar to that found in nondemented subjects.

Ultrastructural Studies

Electron microscopy has, over the last 12 years, firmly established the ultrastructural changes in the cortex which are constant in this disorder.[70, 98, 99, 106, 112, 179, 183] Senile or dendritic plaques present in a number of forms which have been categorized by both light and electron microscopy and are probably related to the age and stage of development of the lesion.[206] Essentially, plaques consist of collections of bulbous or rounded, grossly enlarged, abnormal neuronal processes. The majority are probably axonal terminals or pre-terminals, many of which apparently still possess a normal synaptic membrane. These abnormal nerve processes, dozens of which may be present in a single plaque, are often swollen to a diameter 5 or 6 times that of their normal counterparts by large numbers of oval or round, lamellated or uniform densely staining bodies largely derived from mitochondria and lysosomes. Many of the swollen neurites also contain masses of proliferated tubular or fibrillary structures, some of which are identical with the structures which form the neurofibrillary tangle. These enlarged nerve-cell processes constitute the club-like, irregular, granular thread-like structures which make up the greater part of many senile plaques in silver impregnation preparations viewed by light microscopy. By light and electron microscopic analysis, neuron bodies are rare within the plaque, and astrocytic and microglial processes form quantitatively a relatively minor element of the structures. Amyloid content varies greatly within the plaque but can be demonstrated in all plaques identified with the light microscope. In some large plaques, amyloid forms a central mass around which relatively few bulbous nerve terminals remain (the so-called "burnt-out" plaque).[181] It is of major importance in the genesis of human plaques that bulbous abnormalities of nerve terminals occur before amyloid fiber deposition, the latter only occurring when a cluster of several abnormal neurites is present.[181] It has also been demonstrated[181] that between the plaques visible by light microscopy, numerous minute clusters of abnormal neurites can be found, the appearance of which clearly coincides with the abnormal fibrillary background of large stretches of cortex seen in silver impregnations viewed by light microscopy. The importance of the electron microscopic delineation of these structures can hardly be overestimated, for until this was accomplished speculation on the origin and structure of the plaques had been rife. Among the many suggestions made over the years, the most favored were that plaques resulted primarily from disintegration of glial reticulum;[17, 166] from degeneration of nerve cells;[110, 171] or from formation within the neuropil of an abnormal metabolic product, identified by Divry[56, 57] as amyloid, the importance of which has been recently propounded by Schwartz.[159] Wisniewski and Terry[206] present an excellent brief review of the theories of origin of senile plaques. Ultramicroscopic evidence, however, has firmly established that the fundamental lesions which form the plaques are abnormal nerve processes (neurites) and that cell bodies themselves are not primarily involved within the plaques. At this time there is no certain knowledge of the state of the neurons which contribute abnormal processes to the plaque.

Neurofibrillary tangles consist ultrastructurally of a massive proliferation of abnormal intracytoplasmic structures which are either paired helical filaments or twisted tubules. In this paper they will be referred to as twisted tubules; although the most recent observations support the view, originally expressed by Kidd,[98] that they are paired helical filaments. Whatever the final decision, they differ in structure from anything normally found in the neuron and appear, when viewed longitudinally, to be tubular and approximately 200 Å in diameter with a constriction or twist about every 800 Å. The fact that they are unlike any normal neuronal fibrillary or tubular element suggests that they are a manifestation of an abnormal protein within the cell. Indeed partial chemical characterization of this abnormal material has been achieved.[92] Other changes within the neuron affected by tangle formation appear to be minor, the other elements of the perikaryon being pushed to one side by the tubular structures rather than being lost or destroyed.

The understanding of granulovacuolar degeneration, which is almost entirely limited to hippocampal pyramidal cells, has not been significantly increased by electron microscopy since it merely consists of a central rather ill-defined electron-dense granular mass within an electron translucent area of cytoplasm. What its contribution can be as a histological counterpart of any of the features of dementia in Alzheimer's disease is totally obscure. Indeed, the circumscribed distribution of granulovacuolar degeneration suggests that it has limited, if any, significance in the dementing process. However, its severity in hippocampal neurons makes it a useful "marker" for the likely presence of the other severe histological changes of the disorder.[191, 209, 210]

Diagnostic Considerations

Senile dementia of Alzheimer type is a more difficult diagnosis to arrive at on morphological grounds in some cases than is the diagnosis of the disease in the presenium. This is largely because senile plaques, neurofibrillary tangles, and granulovacuolar degeneration, changes which characterize Alzheimer's presenile dementia, tend to occur in increasing numbers in the brains of intellectually normal old people.[188, 192] However, quantitative analysis of senile plaques, neurofibrillary tangles, and granulovacuolar degeneration[16, 191, 193] has demonstrated significant differences between demented and normal old people in the quantity and,

124

to some extent, the distribution of these changes. Nevertheless, as one would expect, an overlap exists, particularly in terms of plaques and cells involved by granulovacuolar degeneration, in which sharp distinction on morphological grounds between some demented and some normal old people cannot be made even using fairly precise criteria. The morphological distinction between normal and demented old subjects is briefly as follows: Senile plaque formation occurs in approximately 70 percent of people over the age of 65.[188, 192] The numbers of plaques are few in the great majority of individuals. Some 90 percent of normal subjects have less than 10 plaques per low-power field throughout the cortex, although local concentrations of plaques, particularly at the bottoms of cortical sulci, can be much in excess of this figure. Very rarely, a patient who has been considered intellectually normal in old age is found to have large numbers of senile plaques within the range commonly found in the demented subject.

Neurofibrillary tangles also occur, their frequency increasing with age, in the hippocampus and subiculum of normal old people; and in some instances numerous cells in these areas are involved. However, in the neocortex neurofibrillary tangles are either absent or very scanty in approximately 80 percent of old people and are never found in more than small numbers, the occasional cell most commonly being observed in the temporal lobes but sometimes in other areas. In the author's experience no normal old subject ever shows large numbers of neurofibrillary tangles in the neocortex. Such a finding, even in a single section, would be sufficient to distinguish that brain morphologically from the brain of a non-demented old person. This is not true for the structures of the anterior temporal lobe, including the amygdaloid, uncus, hippocampus, and subiculum, where plaque and tangle formation may be heavy in intellectually well-preserved old people.

Granulovacuolar degeneration serves as a similar criterion in the morphological distinction between normal old subjects and demented subjects with Alzheimer's disease. The great majority of normal old people show some cells involved in Sommer's sector of the hippocampus and the adjacent subicular structures, but only an occasional normal old subject shows more than 10 percent of cells affected. The possibility of basing the total distinction between demented and non-demented subjects on the presence of granulovacuolar degeneration of more than 10 percent of cells as demonstrated by Woodard[209, 210] has not been completely confirmed.[191] An occasional well-preserved old subject with no clinical or other morphological features of Alzheimer's disease shows a degree of granulovacuolar degeneration similar to that shown by the majority of subjects with Alzheimer's disease or senile dementia of Alzheimer type. It seems likely that the older the normal subject group examined, the more frequently one will find high percentages of cells in the hippocampus to be involved by granulovacuolar degeneration.

Pathophysiological Observations

These variations in senile changes which can be found in well-preserved normal old subjects have led to considerable doubt about the significance of plaques and tangles in relation to dementia. Without quantitative studies on cases carefully assessed during life for the presence or absence of dementia, the conclusion has easily and erroneously been drawn[66, 152, 153, 208] that no significant correlation exists between the morphological changes in old age and the presence or absence of dementia. Quantitative studies[16, 151, 193] have demonstrated that among demented

125

old subjects, approximately 50 percent have more senile plaques (accompanied by widespread neurofibrillary tangle formation) than can be found in any non-demented person. Further, in a group of well-preserved subjects and subjects with varying degrees of dementia, the severity of dementia increased with the presence of increasing numbers of senile plaques. In the original cases studied, the mean plaque count in the group of normal old people was 3.3 per field compared with 14.7 for the demented group (p = < 0.001); the latter figure reached a mean of more than 20 per field when dementias of other etiologies were excluded. Investigation of further cases has not significantly altered this position. In more than 150 cases studied, 2 instances of intellectually well-preserved old people with plaque counts in excess of 18 per field have seen seen. Plaque counts this high are usually found only in demented subjects, but the fact remains that the great majority of normal old people have few senile plaques, and the majority of subjects with numerous plaques in the hemispheres are demented. There is some evidence that, among non-demented old subjects, those who show minor evidence of intellectual decline have significantly more plaques than those who are exceptionally well-preserved.[189]

With neurofibrillary degeneration the quantitative relationships of numbers of cells involved to degrees of dementia have not been so well documented for technical reasons. However, as stated, many demented old people have large numbers of cortical neurons containing neurofibrillary tangles, and non-demented subjects never have more than a few cells so involved, except in the anterior temporal lobes where neurofibrillary tangles occur in an increasing proportion of the general population from middle age on.[188, 192] In over 90 percent of cases, the presence of many plaques in the neocortex is associated with dementia; many neocortical neurofibrillary tangles are invariably so associated.

Direct evidence that tangles and plaques interfere with cerebral function is not available. It seems utterly improbable, however, that the grossly swollen and abnormal nerve terminals which constitute the bulk of the plaque do not produce major physiological disturbances at the synaptic level. Similarly, the twisted tubules of the tangle probably represent a major abnormality in the production of neuronal fibrillary protein, added to which the bulk of the tubules often appears sufficient to interfere mechanically with cytoplasmic and axonal flow. That the tangled neuron is functioning normally also seems impossible. The quantitative relationship between these structures and dementia adds weight to the notion that they are of prime importance in the causation of dementia.

Vascular Changes in Alzheimer's Disease.

In the majority of cases of Alzheimer's disease in middle or late life, the entire cerebrovascular supply from aorta to capillaries shows no more changes than are seen in non-demented subjects of similar age. Indeed in many cases in old age, the extra- and intracranial arteries are strikingly free of disease, and the cerebral arterioles are either unremarkable or show only hyalinosis common for the age. In cases with severe concomitant cerebral softening, vascular disease is present in the same form which occurs in cerebral softening unaccompanied by Alzheimer's disease. The detailed report of Arab[9] presents important evidence (morphological, statistical, and topographical) on the lack of association between vascular disease and plaque formation.

126

In a minority of cases, however, Alzheimer's disease is associated with a severe form of amyloid angiopathy which has been investigated recently by Mandybur.[115] The combination has been seen in a number of cases of familial Alzheimer's disease, but the majority of familial cases show no unusual vascular changes. Although a slight degree of amyloid infiltration of small cerebral vessels is not uncommon in old age with or without plaque formation, its severe occurrence, termed "congophilic angiopathy" by Pantelakis[139] and "dyshoric angiopathy" by Morel and Wildi,[129] presents a striking appearance. Numerous cerebral arterioles, both subpial and intracerebral, and less commonly arteries and capillaries are patchily infiltrated and thickened by a hyalin material with the tinctorial and electron microscopic features of amyloid. Amyloid particularly infiltrates and separates the heavily reduplicated basement membrane of the vessel. Amyloid sometimes extends from the vessel into the surrounding parenchyma and may be continuous with deposits forming the core of plaques when these are present. Whether, when Alzheimer's disease and amyloid angiopathy are present together, there is any direct connection between the amyloid and plaque formation is unknown. Such cases often have a distinctive clinical course and always have a striking neurohistological appearance. It is simply not possible at this time to state how the two disorders relate to each other etiologically if, indeed, they do.

Arteriosclerotic or Multi-Infarct Dementia

In subjects with hypertension or evidence of widespread arterial disease the presence of dementia, often progressing in steps, has been well recognized for many years as has the more occasional association of widespread ischemic cerebral lesions with a more insidiously developing dementia not clinically recognizable as resulting from cerebral infarction. When dementia of multi-infarct type occurs in the presenium, runs a typical clinical course, and is associated at autopsy with extensive cerebral softening, it is usually correct to ascribe the dementia to the ischemic lesions. However, in older subjects in whom some cerebral softening is frequent,[192] two sources of confusion have arisen. Firstly, the tendency to ascribe dementia to the ischemic lesion is common among clinicians and pathologists. On the other hand, the occurrence of strokes without evidence of dementia and the presence of cerebral softening at autopsy in normal old people have led others to believe that there is no close correlation between cerebral softening and dementia.

A correlation between dementia and the amount of cerebral softening has been clearly demonstrated by quantitative analysis of the volume of softened brain in normal and demented old subjects.[193] Probably 50 percent of people over 65 who show no evidence of intellectual deterioration can be demonstrated to have small, and sometimes considerable, areas of infarction. This estimate could be higher than the amount present in the normal active population, because the original studies[192, 193] were done on hospitalized patients. A small number of subjects without dementia are found to have considerable areas of cerebral softening, but the amount of destroyed tissue rarely exceeds 50 ml.. In no instance was a well-preserved old subject found with more than 100 ml. of softening. In contrast some 15 to 20 percent of demented old subjects in the original study had massive areas of softening, often in excess of 150 ml. As would be expected, some demented subjects had amounts of softening between 50 and 100 ml., an amount which may rarely be found in old people without clinical evidence of dementia. Once more, as with plaques and tangles, the quantitative element in the determination of dementia in old age becomes apparent in relation to ischemic lesions.

Certain absolute distinctions are present between the two groups in terms of quantity and distribution of tangles and ischemic softening, and in the great majority of cases a clear distinction exists in terms of the number of senile plaques. It is tempting to revert to Rothschild's[152, 153] hypothesis to explain the variations in dementia with the varying extent of these lesions in old age, i.e., that the basic personality of some subjects renders them more susceptible to dementia in the presence of morphological lesions. It seems to the author, however, that the situation is morphologically much more complex than this. In any individual case of ischemic disease, the location of the lesion may be significant in addition to its size. However, good evidence exists[122, 141, 142] that mass lesions in the hemisphere at any site are capable of producing an overall or general deleterious effect on intellectual function as well as specific neurological disturbances according to the site. In addition, many demented old people show combinations of morphological changes, all of which may make some contribution to the dementing process. The most frequent and important combination is that of SDAT and cerebral infarction.[42, 55, 144, 193] If the correct assessment of the origins of dementia in any old subject is to be made, comprehensive neuropathological studies are essential, even when numerous infarcts, perhaps sufficient to account for a dementing process, are found. If such studies are not done, the contribution made by Alzheimer type disease in old age and by occasional other unexpected processes will be underestimated and the amount of dementia attributed to vascular disease falsely elevated.

Recent studies have somewhat altered the view of the morphological changes in subjects who are demented due to vascular lesions. In the past, when considering the etiology of arteriosclerotic dementia, considerable emphasis[125] was placed upon the presence of microinfarctions widely spread throughout the cerebral cortex in association with small vessel disease. However, morphological[43, 193] and clinical[118] evidence now indicates that multiple macroscopic infarcts much more frequently produce dementia than do widespread microscopic lesions due to small vessel disease. In dementias of this type, subjects will usually, though by no means always, have had one or more clinically recognizable strokes and will certainly at autopsy have readily visible large areas of ischemic destruction. The distribution of the ischemic destruction may vary so much from case to case as to support the view that mass lesions whatever their position affect the overall functioning of the brain. In many cases, lesions, often multiple, are present in both hemispheres. An occasional case may present at autopsy with widespread hemispheric softening which did not produce recognizable strokes or neurological dysfunction in life. In my experience these cases have usually had posteriorly placed hemispheric infarcts or widespread small ischemic lesions in the white matter. The latter group come close to the concept of Binswanger's disease, but I have never found multiple ischemic lesions entirely restricted to the white matter. Undoubtedly, cases occur in which the white matter is predominantly affected, but invariably some ischemic lesions within the cortex and subcortical nucleated structures are present also. These lesions are often visible to the naked eye and never absent if widespread histological preparations are studied.

NEURONS AND AGING. Many other factors complicate the subject of the variations found in brain morphology in demented old subjects. One question, presently unresolved, concerns the neuron population of the cortex and the role that a

128

declining cell population plays in precipitating dementia in an elderly subject whose cerebral function is threatened by any other morphological change. Since Brody[28, 29] demonstrated that loss of neurons occurs throughout life in some cortical areas, there has been little to confirm this view. His findings have been quite unjustifiably questioned due to the results of studies of neuron populations in other regions. Because certain brain stem nuclei do not lose neurons throughout life,[86, 103, 104] it has been argued that Brody's original observations on cortical loss of neurons may be inaccurate. It has become increasingly clear that no general conclusions can be drawn about cell populations in the central nervous system from a study of one or two groups. The stability of cell populations in certain nuclei has been adequately demonstrated, but the loss of nerve cells from other particular cell populations in many individuals is also certain. That such loss occurs is true of cerebellar Purkinje cells[76] and of spinal cord anterior horn cells.[190] And using an automatic particle counting and analyzing device which gives results comparable to those of manual counting,[80] we have largely confirmed[189] Brody's finding that there is a considerable loss of neurons throughout life in certain areas of cerebral cortex — sometimes the loss amounts to 50 percent of the neuron population in old subjects who are intellectually well-preserved. Nevertheless, in cell populations known to be reduced in old age such as the cerebellar Purkinje cells, anterior horn cells in the spinal cord, and cortical neurons, some old subjects possess cell counts equivalent to or only slightly lower than the number found in young subjects, while other old subjects show reduced cell numbers.

When one relates these findings to dementia, the parameters of morphological change that are possibly related to the dementing process seem to increase in number with increasing age. Not only do neurofibrillary changes, axonal and dendritic abnormalities (senile plaques), and the amount of ischemic softening have to be considered, but the additional factor of nerve cell loss needs to be taken into account. Nerve cell loss is possibly the third major variable (in addition to senile change and cerebral softening) which accounts for the overlap of morphological findings in the small group of demented and non-demented subjects whose findings are otherwise somewhat similar. Numerous other factors could be involved in the onset of dementia in old age. It has yet to be established that senile plaques and neurofibrillary tangles actually interfere with the function of neurons though the present evidence strongly suggests this, but we need to know much more about the numbers and morphology of cortical synapses in old age (some information about this is already available),[47] the ultrastructural morphology and physiological capabilities of the astrocyte, fluid dynamics, and protein and enzyme neurochemical function in old age. Extensive studies in these areas are now being undertaken.

OTHER DEMENTING PROCESSES WITH NEUROFIBRILLARY ABNORMALITIES AS A MAJOR FEATURE

Parkinsonism-Dementia Complex of Guam

In 1954 Kurland and Mulder[107] reported on the major clinical, pathological, and epidemiological features of amyotrophic lateral sclerosis (ALS) prevalent among the native Chamorros of the island of Guam. The most striking pathological feature was the presence of numerous neurofibrillary tangles[114] with an unusually wide distribution throughout the central nervous system, including the anterior horn cells of the spinal cord, the basal ganglia, and cerebral cortex. Further studies among the same population revealed that a dementing process associated with features of parkinsonism was also common.[84, 85] This dementia often developed in patients with evidence of both upper and lower motor neuron disease and caused death about 5 years after the onset of symptoms. Brains from these patients usually showed marked generalized cortical atrophy, dilatation of the ventricular system, atrophy and depigmentation of the substantia nigra and locus ceruleus, and in some cases marked atrophy of the basal ganglia. In addition to extensive neuron loss throughout the cerebral cortex and other affected areas, the most striking feature microscopically was the very large number of neurofibrillary tangles, which were identical ultrastructurally with those occurring in Alzheimer's disease and senile dementia of Alzheimer type. In the parkinsonism-dementia complex, however, in addition to the greater involvement of the cortex by neurofibrillary tangles in comparison to the usual case of Alzheimer's disease, the distribution of the tangles differs noticeably in that the deeper structures of the brain, particularly the substantia nigra, are severely affected. Senile plaques are absent in the majority of cases, this feature negating any suggestion of an etiological relationship between plaque and tangle formation in Alzheimer's disease. As with the other diseases with heavy neurofibrillary tangle formation, the etiology of the parkinsonism-dementia complex of Guam is obscure. However, there is a strong possibility of a major genetic determinant since the non-Chamorro population of Guam appears free of the disease and a case has been diagnosed in a Chamorro man who had lived outside Guam for 50 years.[83] Efforts to transmit the disease to primates have been unsuccessful. As in other instances of dementia with widespread morphological abnormalities, the symptomatology of these patients can be readily understood on the basis of pathological changes.

Progressive Supranuclear Palsy (The Steele-Richardson-Olszewski Syndrome)

This disorder, first suggested as a distinct clinicopathological syndrome in 1963 and 1964,[145, 172] often presents with relatively mild personality and behavioral changes accompanied by speech or visual disturbances, spastic facies, tonic rigidity of the neck and upper trunk, and a constant ophthalmoplegia with striking loss of conjugate vertical gaze. Although the dementia occasionally becomes severe, in the average case it remains relatively mild even till death occurs 5 to 10 years after onset. To the naked eye, the brain often appears normal apart from some slight or moderate dilatation of the ventricles and aqueduct, but in some cases the brain stem and particularly the superior colliculi appear small, and the aqueduct is markedly dilated. In a few instances, gliosis of the dentate nucleus and atrophy of the superior cerebellar peduncles have been visible. Histologically the significant changes are of 3 kinds, almost all related to structures in or around the brain stem. First, neurofibrillary tangles are numerous in the substantia nigra, pallidum, subthalamic nucleus, and, commonly, many other nuclear groups throughout the midbrain and medulla including the inferior olive, lateral cuneate nucleus, and the supratrochlear nucleus. The dentate nucleus of the cerebellum is occasionally involved. Secondly, in the majority of affected nuclei, extensive loss of neurons mirrors the degree of neurofibrillary degeneration, but in some areas of the stem, such as the vestibular, dentate, and red nuclei, neuron loss greatly exceeds the degree of tangle formation. The third change, more limited but still apparently

130

unique to this disorder, is the presence of granulovacuolar degeneration within some nuclear groups of the stem, particularly the substantia nigra, locus ceruleus, dentate nucleus, and Purkinje cells of the cerebellum. The granulovacuolar degeneration here is apparently identical with that which is found to be largely restricted to the hippocampus and para-hippocampal structures in normal old people and is particularly severe in Alzheimer's disease. The only other significant change in this disease seen on light microscopy is the presence of fibrillary gliosis which is, again, greatest in the deep nuclear and stem structures most affected by nerve cell loss. Demyelination in some fiber tracts appears to mirror the degree of neuronal loss, for instance that found in the superior cerebullar peduncles.

Ultrastructurally the neurofibrillary tangles in this disease are unusual, since they differ from those found in other disorders. In Alzheimer's disease, senile dementia, and the ALS parkinsonism-dementia complex of Guam, tangles are ultrastructurally either twisted tubules or 100 Å filaments. In progressive supranuclear palsy, tangles consist of conglomerates of straight elements of approximately 150 Å diameter. Tellez-Nagel and Wisniewski[178] also found typical Pick bodies in their case, a feature which they suggested[201] might in Pick's disease be the result of trans-synaptic or retrograde change. It is of great interest that neurofibrillary tangles consisting of straight filaments of 150 Å diameter are produced in those cells which in other diseases produce twisted tubules of greater size or 100 Å filaments. This demonstrates that the same cells under different stimulae generate abnormal fibrillary proteins of different constitution. Once more, the extensive cell loss, gliosis, and neuronal abnormalities in the basal ganglia, brain stem, and cerebellar structures in this disorder appear to account for the greater part of the symptomatology. The absence of cortical and significant white matter lesions led Steele, Richardson, and Olszewski[174] to conclude that the mild dementia probably is related to striatal and midbrain lesions, with perhaps some added effects to intellect and emotion from the minor changes in the brain stem reticular formation, thalamus, and hypothalamus.

Dementia in Boxers

The syndrome of progressive neurological disturbance and dementia which occurs mainly in boxers[119, 121, 146] but also possibly in other sports or occupations involving repeated concussive injuries[63] is associated with scattered cerebral lesions of several types. Over the past 20 years, this became clear from reports of isolated cases or several cases,[73, 130] but the pattern and relative constancy of the changes were only established recently through a detailed report on the brains of 15 boxers.[45] The majority of the brains were small, showing some degree of cerebral hemispheric atrophy and moderate or severe ventricular dilatation. There was a high incidence of a large septum of the cavum pellucidum, often with fenestration of the septum, separation of the fornix from the undersurface of the corpus callosum, and thinning of the corpus callosum. The cerebellum frequently showed small cortical scars on its inferomedial surface with loss of Purkinje cells over larger areas. In the majority of cases, there was moderate or severe loss of pigmented neurons in the substantia nigra. Many of those neurons remaining showed neurofibrillary tangles which frequently also involved the locus ceruleus and other brain stem neurons. Vast numbers of neurofibrillary tangles were present in the structures of the anteromedial temporal lobes. There was heavy but patchy in-

131

volvement of the lateral temporal, frontal, and insular cortex with almost total sparing of the parietal and occipital cortex. Senile plaques were usually absent.

The neurological and psychiatric sequelae in these severely affected boxers seems adequately explained by the neuropathological findings. The abnormalities in the septum and cerebellum, loss of white matter with resulting ventricular dilatation and corpus callosal thinning, and some brain stem lesions are probably due to the effects of differential movement and distortion of various parts of the brain produced by closed head injury involving acceleration and deceleration.[174, 185] No explanation can be offered for the intense neurofibrillary degeneration, which is presumably largely responsible for the dementia, except that it seems probable that repeated concussive blows are capable of inducing tangles in neurons in many different sites in the human brain.

No one, to my knowledge, has as yet established the ultrastructural appearance of the tangles in this syndrome.

Dementia in Mongols

Considerable problems exist in characterizing the clinical features of the dementia thought by many to occur in aging mongols. Over the past 20 years, published reports[95, 136, 170] have established that with increasing longevity, senile plaques and neurofibrillary tangles appear in these subjects' brains during the third and fourth decades of life. All surviving to 40 years are affected, the lesions being as severe as in many cases of Alzheimer's disease.[113] This lowered age of appearance of "senile changes" and the high incidence of morphological Alzheimer's disease in a syndrome known to show chromosomal abnormalities demands the investigation of neurochemical (particularly enzymatic) abnormalities in young mongols in the hope of identifying changes which precede and possibly induce plaque and tangle formation.

EXPERIMENTAL PRODUCTION OF ALZHEIMER-TYPE CHANGES

Without attempting a review of the experimental induction of Alzheimer-type neuronal changes, some mention must be made of the growing interest and knowledge in this field. A number of diseases in which neurofibrillary tangle formation is a characteristic feature have been discussed. From this discussion is appears obvious that different etiological agents produce tangles in various sites in the human. It also appears certain that tangles and plaques, though frequently occurring in the same brain, are by no means inevitably present together. Therefore their joint production must depend on factors which may be different in different disease processes.

That a number of experimental procedures for producing tangles and plaques should have been developed is not surprising, nor are the different susceptibilities to induction of the changes among experimental animals. It is clear that neurofibrillary tangles and plaques, apparently identical by light microscopy, require electron microscopy for confirmation of their similarity or dissimilarity in different disease states or in animal experiments. The light microscopic appearance of neurofibrillary tangles in human diseases is predominantly due to the collection of large numbers of twisted tubules in the perikaryon, the major exception being in progressive supranuclear palsy in which straight neurofilaments form the tangles.

132

Until recently, when Nicklowitz[133] reported production of a small number of twisted tubules with a predominance of straight tubules in rabbits following acute tetraethyl lead intoxication, all the induced tangles in animals have consisted of straight filaments or tubules. The agents most studied experimentally have been various aluminium salts[102, 180, 202] and some alkaloid mitotic spindle inhibitors, particularly colchicine[205] and vinblastine and vincristine,[155, 182, 204] all of these being administered intracerebrally or into the cerebrospinal fluid. Administration of these agents has produced tangles consisting of bundles of 100 Å wide filaments. With spindle inhibitors, other changes occur in the cell, but no tubules, straight or twisted, comparable to the human tangle have been observed to result from these procedures. With long survival in animals treated with aluminium, abnormal neurites form, occasionally clustered, particularly after undercutting of the cortex, to produce a plaque-like appearance. Then smaller neurites are ballooned by abnormal mitochondria, dense bodies, and neurofilaments but without evidence of amyloid deposition. Increased aluminium content of the brain in Alzheimer's disease has been demonstrated,[48, 49] but the relationship of aluminium to the development of the disease remains obscure. Confirmation of these findings are awaited from other investigators, since this was not found by Nikaido, Austin, Trueb, and Rinehart[135] nor in the brain of a patient dying of Alzheimer's disease following childhood lead encephalopathy in which high brain-lead levels were still present at death.[134] More recently, plaques consisting of abnormal neuronal processes, amyloid fibrils, and reactive cells which closely resemble the human plaque have been produced in some strains of mice using scrapie agent.[64, 200]

Scrapie is a naturally occurring transmissible disease of sheep of the so-called slow virus type in which neuritic plaques do not occur naturally or experimentally. The experimental production of "plaques" by the use of the agent in mice has produced an animal model for the production of lesions similar to human plaques for the first time. This naturally raises the possibility of transmissible agent involvement in Alzheimer's disease. It must be remembered that virus induction of neurofibrillary tangles has been assumed for many years on the basis of tangle formation in the brain stem of patients with postencephalitic parkinsonism. The mouse model will make possible an experimental study of the relationship between amyloid and neuritic plaques. Such a study has importance since for some years amyloid was postulated to be the primary agent responsible for plaque and tangle formation.[56, 57, 159] Electron microscopy eliminated any possibility that tangles possessed an amyloid component but established that the congophylia of plaques was associated with amyloid fiber deposition. However, small or primitive human plaques are devoid of amyloid, the neurite abnormalities preceeding amyloid deposition.[181] Conversely, abnormal neurites may be few when amyloid deposition is severe and may be absent in the amyloid deposits of familial amyloidosis. If, however, the types of amyloid in the brain differ in different conditions, it seems possible that extracellular amyloid of immunoglobulin type might, as postulated by Glenner, Ein, and Terry,[69] be formed extracellularly following catabolism of antigen-antibody complexes by phagocytes. Such an occurrence might explain the varying neuritic response to amyloid in the human brain according to the neurotoxicity of the antigen-antibody complexes.[207]

In the last 10 years the experimental production of lesions closely similar to the plaques and tangles of human disease states has been achieved. This clearly raises the possibility of studying the changes by using techniques that were previously unavailable. Whether or not any of the methods will prove to have any relevance to the pathogenesis of human disease, particularly to Alzheimer's disease and senile dementia, remains to be seen.

OTHER FORMS OF DEMENTIA IN WHICH CEREBRAL INFARCTION PLAYS A PART

In middle and old age, multiple foci of ischemic infarction, without other apparent significant changes, produce the condition called multi-infarct or arteriosclerotic dementia. In addition, in a considerable number of cases, multiple infarcts occur along with the senile changes of the type seen in Alzheimer's disease. In fact cerebral infarction is the second most common cause of, or contributory factor to, dementia in old age, and probably also in middle age. The dementia which may follow rupture of an intracranial aneurysm and that which occurs following severe brain injury are contributed to by cerebral infarction. Indeed, in dementia following subarachnoid haemorrhage, infarction almost certainly constitutes the major destructive factor.

Cerebral ischemia is common and often severe in cases dying after rupture of intracranial aneurysms with or without operative interference.[15, 50, 147, 184] The distribution of the infarction is most commonly within the territory of the major artery on which the ruptured aneurysm lies,[186] but the infarctions following aneurysmal rupture may also affect other brain areas. Frequently, and particularly with aneurysms on the anterior cerebral or communicating arteries, infarction affects both hemispheres. There is every reason to suppose that the sequelae which are so frequent in patients who have recovered from ruptured intracranial aneurysms[111, 197] are largely determined by the position and extent of the infarction. Information is scanty about the numbers of cases recovering, with or without operation, who become demented. Possibly 5 percent or so[197] can be demonstrated to be so affected within a relatively short time of a bleed, and many others[111] have marked personality changes, especially following recovery from ruptured anterior cerebral or communicating artery aneurysms. Unilateral infarction, particularly that limited to the territory of the middle cerebral artery, may produce disabling sequelae without immediate evidence of a dementing process, but almost certainly many cases who survive without immediately demonstrable dementia have small infarcts in territories other than those producing demonstrable neurological abnormality. The possibility exists that cases of this kind run a heavier risk of developing dementia in later life than do normal subjects.

Dementia following brain injury almost certainly results from lesions of mixed type and site. The clinical manifestations unquestionably vary with extent and type of the injuries. At this time problems exist in the use of the term "dementia" for the post-traumatic state of many severely affected individuals. Those cases who remain in a vegetative state after a period of coma lasting many days or weeks and who never progress significantly toward recovery are not logically included within the group of dementias discussed in this chapter. But a growing number of patients with non-fatal but severe head injuries are sufficiently affected by neurological or neuropsychiatric sequelae that they never return to their previous occupations, and a considerable number never work again. Among these are many cases with memory defects and personality changes who by standard clinical criteria and psychometric testing would be placed within the demented group. A group of this kind should be followed and tested psychometrically to establish whether the state of dementia remains steady or deteriorates with advancing years and to determine at autopsy the changes within the brain.

Certain predictions about the pathology in this group can be made, however, from knowledge of what has occurred in patients dying more rapidly after head injuries, some of which have not been severe. In the latter type of case, Graham and Adams[72] have demonstrated that a large incidence of significant infarction may exist. The studies of Strich[174] and Tomlinson[187] have shown that axon damage within both the hemispheres and the brain stem is frequent in the patient with head injury. Dilatation of the lateral ventricle demonstrated by ventriculography in many post-trauma cases commonly has its origin in the combination of these two lesions. Of course, focal neurological signs may follow direct laceration or contusion of the hemispheres, but this is inevitably followed by a degree of infarction in the immediate vicinity. However, by no means is the infarction always limited to that area.[72] More diffuse lesions of the hemispheres involving scattered infarctions may also occur, but extensive tearing of axons within the hemispheres, a feature not yet widely recognised, is unquestionably an important contributor to the loss of white matter which can be demonstrated both radiologically and at autopsy. Many fatal cases of head injury have severe lesions of the corpus callosum along with small infarcts and extensive damage to specifically located ascending and descending tracts in the brain stem — sometimes specifically the tegmental tracts. The majority of patients in whom recovery of consciousness is minimal several weeks or months after injury can be demonstrated to have extensive lesions resulting from tearing of fiber tracts at the time of the original injury.[187]

A study of the contribution of all the forms and sites of cerebral injury to any individual cases of post-traumatic dementia would be worthwhile and informative. If the clinical follow-up were sufficiently detailed, such a study might well add considerably not only to the knowledge of the neuropsychiatric sequelae of head injury and its anatomical basis but also to the knowledge of the clinicopathology of certain features of dementia per se. The unique combination of changes which occurs in boxers suffering repeated concussion has already been described. The slow progression of symptoms, often continuing for many years after the patient ceases to box, suggests that long term follow-up of patients recovered from a single severe head injury may be profitable.

PICK'S DISEASE

Pick's disease has a known and relatively constant neuropathology; yet it has a curious association with other apparently unrelated disorders, particularly with amyotrophic lateral sclerosis.[23, 26, 127] The occasional association of Pick's disease with other so-called system atrophies naturally results in symptomatic overlap. Surprisingly, recent electron microscopic studies have demonstrated the tendency for a number of disorders, including Pick's disease, to produce tubular and filamentous abnormalities within the neuronal cytoplasm which confuse the boundaries of what used to be regarded as rather distinct morphological groups.

In Pick's disease at autopsy the brain may show considerable generalized hemispheric atrophy, though often either temporal or frontal lobe atrophy or both are particularly severe. The frequency with which this occurs leads to use of the term "lobar sclerosis." As with atrophy in almost all other disorders producing dementia, there is great variation, and the atrophy may not be symmetrical. Not infrequently the left hemisphere is more severely affected.[116] Involvement of subcortical grey masses, particularly the caudate nucleus, is also variable but may be moderately severe. The disease is rare even among cases of presenile dementia. Although the greatest incidence is seen in the fifth and sixth decades of life,[168] cases have been observed as early as the third and as late as the tenth decade.[13]

On light microscopy the changes are usually most characteristic and severe in the most atrophied areas of the cerebrum (usually the frontal and temporal lobes, although the central and precentral gyri and the posterior two-thirds of T1 are often spared). Cell loss in the affected areas may be severe. The degree of cell loss in various parts of the cerebral cortex as compared with age-matched normal controls needs to be established for this disease as for all other dementing processes. Often a dense astrocytosis of the cortex, and to a lesser extent the white matter, is present in the atrophied lobes. But the most characteristic and diagnostic finding is the presence of ballooned cells, some of which contain so-called Pick bodies. These latter are rounded argyrophilic cytoplasmic inclusions which can be faintly seen with the hematoxylin and eosin stains but can be seen well with silver impregnations and in 1μ thick Epon embedded toluidine blue material. In silver impregnations these bodies are large, often being 12 to 15μ across in large neurons, with a clear, rounded outline and a homogenous silver staining central area in which are commonly lighter zones of what may be interfibrillary material.[26] The other swollen or ballooned cells may show some generalized affinity for silver or show the light microscopic appearances typical of central chromatolysis. Numerous other cells may show varying degrees of more nonspecific shrinkage and apparent degeneration.

According to Wisniewski, Coblentz, and Terry,[201] electron microscopic studies show neuronal changes of three types. First, Pick bodies, that is defined silver-positive inclusions within neurons, consist of a mixture of 100 Å neurofilaments and 240 Å normal tubules. Second, some ballooned cells contain an excess of neurofilaments uniformly distributed throughout the cytoplasm; and third, some neurons in addition to an excess of neurofilaments and tubules show prominent multiple vesicles and cisternae of varying shapes and sizes which probably represent the remnants of endoplasmic reticulum.

In a considerable number of cases, senile plaques and sometimes neurofibrillary tangles have been found in association with changes typical of Pick's disease.[131, 156, 168] The combination has been sufficiently severe for some cases to be regarded as combined Alzheimer's and Pick's disease.[12] Although association of the relatively rare Pick's disease with the much more common Alzheimer's disease could be coincidental, the more likely explanation is that these cases represent Pick's disease in a patient showing no more than the relatively early formation of plaques and tangles present in a considerable proportion of people in middle or old age. The plaques found in the biopsy of the second frontal gyrus of the case reported by Wisniewski, Coblentz, and Terry[201] which were unaccompanied by neurofibrillary tangles could well be explained this way, as indeed, could the numerous references to the occasional presence of plaques and tangles in other central nervous system diseases occurring in middle and old age. The rare finding of twisted tubules in Pick bodies[156] could well have a similar explanation, since cells which contain twisted tubules (as some do in the hippocampus of normal old people) can presumably undergo other pathological processes, such as those which result in the production of Pick bodies. This is even more likely if, as Wisniewski, Coblentz, and Terry[201] suggest, Pick bodies and the more diffusely swollen cells common in Pick's disease share a basic etiology and represent various stages and manifestations of central chromatolysis, perhaps with an additional stimulus to neurofilament production initiated by transneuronal degeneration. These same authors suggest that wallerian degeneration (or a dying-back phenomenon) which may stimulate the formation of senile plaques may also apply to Pick's disease and account for plaque formation. However, the occurrence of plaques in well documented Pick's disease is too infrequent to allow this explanation to be thoroughly accepted. A similar statement could apply to the finding of Hirano bodies in Pick's disease, since these structures also occur in the majority of normal people, although they are probably markedly increased in Alzheimer's disease and senile dementia.[68] The same explanation is possibly applicable to the finding of granulovacuolar degeneration, which has been described in Alzheimer's disease particularly[191, 209, 210] but also in Pick's disease.[125] However, according to Brion, Mikol, and Psimaras,[26] the small bead-like structures enclosed in a vacuole in some cells in Pick's disease are different from granulovacuolar degeneration, particularly in the lack of argyrophilia. These authors also make interesting observations on the different appearances of the cells in Ammon's horn and in the allocortex in Pick's disease. In Ammon's horn most of the neurons are moderately ballooned and contain rounded argyrophilic inclusions of Pick type, but in the allocortex many neurons are entirely ballooned, show no evidence of argyrophilia, and have the appearance of central chromatolysis. The latter characteristic, they state, has never been found in Ammon's horn in this disease. They also relate cellular appearance to the length of survival. Longstanding cases show particularly well-formed cytoplasmic inclusions with a limited number of cells having the appearance typical of central chromatolysis. Whereas cases with short clinical histories (death being coincidental) show opposite findings: Pick bodies are much less numerous, particularly in Ammon's horn, and when present are irregular and fragmented rather than being the typical rounded and well-defined shape.

Unfortunately these electron microscopic findings throw no light on the etiology of this disorder in which the paramount importance of genetics has been recognized for many years. The explanation of the dementia poses little problem since all cases show severe loss of neurons with the majority of the remaining neurons being grossly abnormal at both the light microscopic and ultrastructural level. The frequently severe astrocytic gliosis of both cortex and white matter and the more sparse microglial response could well be merely a reaction of glial elements to the changes and loss of neurons, although this is not proven. Extensive loss of neurons with its clear deleterious effect on cortical function and the assumption that many of the remaining neurons almost certainly function defectively seem quite sufficient to explain the dementing process.

HUNTINGTON'S CHOREA AND WILSON'S DISEASE

Two familial diseases, Huntington's chorea and Wilson's disease, with principal pathological changes in the basal ganglia are frequently associated with dementia. Dementia may appear early in the course of either disease but is usually a more striking and eventually more severe manifestation in Huntington's chorea. In Huntington's chorea, mental deterioration or other psychiatric disturbances, particularly depression,[163] may occur long before choreiform movements develop, and some cases die without detected movement abnormalities.[18] Occasionally dementia fails to develop.[78] The age of onset is usually from the late twenties to the mid-forties, but the age range is from early childhood[33] to the early seventies. The disease is usually more severe in the younger than in the older age group,[34] and affected children of males with the disease die sooner than those of affected mothers.[14]

The brain of a Huntington's chorea patient at autopsy occasionally appears normal, but more commonly there is moderate or severe atrophy with the frontal and parietal lobes being most affected. The characteristic feature of the cut brain is the gross diminution in size of the caudate head which is usually reduced to a thin plate of brownish tissue lying adjacent to the markedly enlarged anterior horn of the lateral ventricle. White matter in this area and in the corpus callosum is diminished in quantity but otherwise is not altered in appearance. A lesser degree of atrophy affects the putamen, and some shrinkage is usually apparent in the globus pallidus. Apart from slight reduction in overall size, the midbrain and hindbrain structures appear normal.

Histologically the caudate is devastated by loss of small neurons (but with preservation of some large neurons), astrocytosis, and in severe cases extensive spongiosis. The severity of change is said to vary in different areas of the caudate head and putamen,[44] but all parts of these nuclei are affected in most cases, and neuron loss and some astrocytic proliferation usually extend into the outer part of the globus pallidus. Remaining neurons in the affected areas are often shrunken, and they and the glial cells frequently contain excess pigment. Changes in the brain stem have been described but are usually difficult to detect. Some neuron loss and astrocytosis may be present in the thalamus.

Cortical changes are less dramatic. Microglial and astrocytic proliferation and gliosis appear to be only moderate or slight, but neuronal loss in the middle cortical layers often appears to be severe, and many remaining neurons are shrunken and pigmented. In studies of cortical cell population using an image analyzing computer,[80, 189] the single case of Huntington's chorea so far investigated showed a striking diminution of medium and large neurons in several areas of cortex. However, whether this represents shrinkage rather than, or as well as, loss remains to be determined. Electron microscopy of cortical biopsies[177] confirmed the lipofuschin excess in neurons and glial cells and morphological changes in many remaining neurons—in which almost all subcellular components were abnormal. Remnants of neurons were detected in microglia, and astrocytic hypertophy and proliferation with glial filament production and lipo-pigment deposition in cell bodies and processes were observed.

In Wilson's disease,[199] or hepatolenticular degeneration, a gross excess of copper is found in liver and brain. This is associated with cirrhosis of the liver and abnormalities in many parts of the brain, although the most pronounced changes affect the basal ganglia, particularly the putamen. The putamen is usually atrophied to the naked eye and often shows cavity formation and reddish-brown discoloration. Less severe but similar changes may involve the caudate and globus pallidus, and cavitation occasionally extends to the thalamus, red nucleus, and cerebral and cerebellar white matter.[158] Histologically there is a variable but often severe loss of neurons, with marked proliferation of Alzheimer type II astrocytes and the presence of unusual large round cells with small nuclei (Opalski cells), probably of phagocytic origin, throughout many parts of the brain. Excepting the presence of Opalski cells, the putamen probably is always most severely affected. Astrocytic proliferation, Opalski cells, and varying degrees of neuronal and white matter degeneration have been described in the thalamus, many brain stem nuclei,[89] dentate nucleus, white matter of the cerebral and cerebellar hemispheres, and cerebral cortex.

138

The severe morphological changes in the basal ganglia and cortex in these diseases appear to account for the abnormal movements and dementia, but specific clinicopathological correlations are far from understood. In fact, mental deterioration in Huntington's chorea has been said to be absent in the presence of severe cortical atrophy and present when the cortex was little affected.[52] Modern psychometry, more objective and quantitative assessment of the morphological changes, and ultrastructural studies are needed and might clarify some confused situations. Certainly with few exceptions, where disease states predominantly affect basal ganglia or brain stem and spare hemispheric white matter and cortex, the incidence of dementia tends to be low or mild. Thus, in striatonigral degeneration,[3, 195] in which severe degeneration of basal ganglia, substantia nigra, and many brain stem and cerebellar nuclei may be found, the usual clinical picture is predominantly one of parkinsonism with little or no dementia. The putaminal lesions strongly resemble those of the caudate and putamen in Huntington's chorea, the major difference being the severity of change in the two structures.[175] In striatonigral degeneration there are, as the name implies, invariably lesions in the substantia nigra in addition to other areas. Yet in idiopathic parkinsonism, in which the much more restricted lesions involve principally the substantia nigra (though with wider distribution of Loewi bodies in stem neurons), some degree of dementia is present in a significant proportion of cases.[27, 87, 109] In my experience when severe dementia accompanies parkinsonism, the changes of Alzheimer's disease or extensive hemispheric softening accompany the typical nigral lesions. With mild or moderate dementia in Parkinson's disease, usually no significant cortical or white matter lesions are found. The precise clinical diagnosis in any case of dementia is based on numerous considerations, among which the age of the patient, speed of development, and accompanying neurological disturbances are of major importance. However, claims are made[5, 123] that the pattern of dementia in the predominantly subcortical disorders differs significantly from that in the predominantly cortical disorders. The intensive biochemical studies being undertaken in a wide variety of dementing processes may illuminate clinicopathological correlates. Inevitably biochemical abnormalities will be severe in areas of marked morphological change, but evidence that striking diminution of some cerebral enzymes occurs in senile dementia of Alzheimer type not only in the cerebral cortex but in deeper structures where morphological change is minor[21] may indicate that the subcortical structures, even in this classical "cortical" dementia, have a more significant roll than has been previously thought.

The use of the term "subcortical dementia" to describe a group of disorders with lesions in deep nuclear structures is somewhat unfortunate, since a rare, insidious but progressively dementing disorder called progressive or primary subcortical gliosis[132] has gained considerable recognition as a pathological entity. In this disease, extensive gliosis and astrocytic proliferation affect the hemispheric subcortical white matter and many parts of the basal ganglia, thalamus, and brain stem.

VIRAL DISEASES PRODUCING DEMENTIA

Creutzfeldt-Jakob Disease

Creutzfeldt-Jakob disease (the term is used here to cover a wide spectrum of symptomatology and neuropathology) is important in any consideration of demen-

139

tia. This is true partly because it commonly presents with dementia as a leading feature, but especially because it is a human disorder in which there is growing evidence of causation by a transmissible agent. This agent, usually referred to as a virus, produces a slowly progressive disease which is usually fatal in 3 months to 2 years from the onset of symptoms and neuropathological changes lacking in the conventionally accepted features of infection.

The disease may present with a wide variety of clinical manifestations[100] depending largely on the severity of involvement of different central nervous system structures. This and the wide spectrum of neuropathological change have led to the use of numerous synonyms. Use of the term Creutzfeldt-Jakob disease to cover the numerous syndromes (for a brief and readable summary see Kirschbaum[101]) is justified by (1) the tendency for the disease to present, however varying the detailed manifestations, as a disorder with prominent cortical, striatal, and often spinal and cerebellar components, and (2) evidence that the neuropathological changes though markedly different in individual cases nevertheless show sufficient evidence of similarity and gradation to cause the suspicion that they are members of the same group of closely related disorders. The final inclusion and subdivision of the various disorders in the group will follow the identification of the variety of clinical and neuropathological forms which prove transmissible and the more complete characterization of the disease-producing agent or agents. Only a small proportion of the cases diagnosed as Creutzfeldt-Jakob disease has proved transmissible to chimpanzees and New World monkeys so far.[148]

Patients dying with Creutzfeldt-Jakob disease show in the systemic organs only the terminal changes that are commonly associated with prolonged immobilization or neurological disability. In many instances, the brain shows no significant changes macroscopically. In cases with prominent astrogliosis, there may be cortical and striatal atrophy and marked dilatation of the lateral ventricles. The dilatation appears to some extent in most cases.

Microscopically the changes invariably involve large tracts of the cerebral cortex and consist of neuronal loss, astrocytic proliferation, and some degree, often severe, of status spongiosis. However, the variations in severity of these three changes produce histological appearances which may appear dissimilar. Only experience with cases showing changes which range from one end of the spectrum to the other* leads to the conclusion that they all, almost certainly, belong within the same disease group. The spongiform changes in the cortex and deep grey matter are so striking in many instances that they have led to use of the term subacute spongiform (viral) encephalopathy as a synonym[65, 211] for the whole range of clinical and pathological findings covered by the term Creutzfeldt-Jakob disease. In all cases the significant changes are limited to the neuronal areas of the brain and are usually more severe in the middle and deep cortical layers. In some instances morphological abnormalities are most severe in the striatum or the medial thalamus or even the cerebellum.

On light microscopy, status spongiosis consists of vacuolated, rounded areas within the neuropil of the cortex or other neuronal areas. The vacuoles appear as clear spaces and vary from a few to many minute structures of 1 to 2 μ across up to large and occasionally confluent vacuolated areas of 40 to 50 μ Some vacu-

---

*For examples of the diversity in cases see those of the so-called Heidenhain[79] type and those described by Jones and Nevin[96] and by Brownell and Oppenheimer.[30]

olation occurs within the neuronal perikaryon, but it has been established by electron microscopy[62, 71] that most vacuoles lie within the processes of astrocytes and are less frequent within neurons. In the most severe cases almost the whole thickness of the cerebral cortex appears disrupted by this change.

With this vacuolation, or in its almost total absence, all cases show neuronal loss. In less affected areas of cortex and, therefore, in some biopsy preparations, the neuronal loss can be extremely difficult to appreciate and needs quantitative analysis. The third to the sixth cortical layers undergo more cell loss than elsewhere, and at whatever stage the process is seen, abnormal, shrunken, pale-staining, ghost-like neurons are present among the surviving more normal cells.

Astrocytic proliferation, the third important change, may be easy to distinguish when severe, particularly in cases that show macroscopic cortical atrophy. But in other cases, its recognition may require careful comparison with normal control material, particularly if biopsy specimens are taken early in the course of the disease. In the most severe cases, masses of large, pale, astrocytic nuclei, sometimes lobulated, can be seen throughout the cortex; though, again, they are most consistantly seen in the deep layers. Very occasionally the cytoplasm of these cells is visible in general cytological stains; more commonly Cajal preparations provide the best demonstration. In my experience the predominant type of change, or combination of changes, tends to be reflected in all affected areas in any individual case. That is, if spongiosis is the most obvious feature, it is present in the cerebral cortex and any affected areas of the basal ganglia, cerebellum, or spinal cord; if the principal feature is neuronal loss, then similar change tends to be present in all other areas affected.

The explanation of the dementia in cases of Creutzfeldt-Jakob disease will raise little argument. Neuronal loss is often severe and widespread within the cortex. It and the other changes vary in intensity and site, but it is difficult in many instances to find any area of cortex that is totally uninvolved. In many cases, extensive striatal and thalamic abnormalities as well as mesencephalic and brain stem changes are present and sometimes severe, so that functional changes involving all these structures must be expected. In the majority of cases, the morphological changes are so widespread and severe that severe dementia is inevitable.

The importance of the evidence that at least some forms of this disease are produced by a transmissible agent with many properties similar to those of a virus cannot be overestimated. At no stage in the disorder are the conventional evidences of an inflammatory viral type invasion of the cental nervous system evident histologically. Glial stars are occasional in affected cortex, but infiltration of the subarachnoid space, Virchow-Robin spaces, intracerebral peri-capillary and peri-venular regions, and brain parenchyma with immunocytes has never been described, nor have proliferation of microglia, macrophage formation, active disintegration of neurons, or presence of inclusion bodies. Further, experimental transmission of this disorder into the larger primates,[67] other primates,[148] mice,[30] and guinea pigs[121] has demonstrated the similarity of the responsible agent to that which produces scrapie in sheep and kuru. The agents of Creutzfeldt-Jakob disease, scrapie, and kuru all possess the unusual property of inducing severe neurological disorder after a latent period. The latent period varies with different animals, but in the larger primates and man it extends for months or several years before symptoms appear. The neuropathology of these 3 disorders also has many similarities, none of which would have suggested a virus or any other infective agent 20 years ago. The transmissible agent of Creutzfeldt-Jakob disease

141

has not been visualized or grown but is known to be exceptionally resistant to heat[91] and to various forms of radiation[7] (implying very low or possibly even complete absence of nucleic acid[6]). The response of central nervous system tissue to this agent clearly has implications for other apparently degenerative central nervous disorders and must stimulate intense inquiry into a wide range of poorly understood and so-called degenerative conditions of the central nervous system. In human cases of Creutzfeldt-Jakob disease, senile plaques are either absent or are consistent with the age of the affected person. However, scrapie agent when transmitted to certain strains of mice[200] yields plaques similar if not identical to human senile plaques both at light microscopic and ultrastructural levels. The possibility that human senile plaques might under certain circumstances be induced by a transmissible agent clearly needs to be investigated.

Other Viral Infections Leading to Dementia

Multifocal Leukoencephalopathy

Multifocal leukoencephalopathy is a rare disorder only recognized for the first time as a pathological entity in 1958.[10] The lesions present to the naked eye as numerous small or confluent foci of partial softening and predominantly affect the white matter of the hemispheres, although there are often small lesions elsewhere. The lesions result from focal demyelination with macrophage proliferation and gliosis, the latter associated with the production of large astrocytes with bizarre massive nuclei. Numerous oligodendroglial nuclei, particularly at the periphery of the lesions, contain inclusions. Multifocal leukoencephalopathy usually occurs in association with disorders which are known to have abnormal immunological responses such as Hodgkin's disease and the chronic leukemias. In patients with such disorders or on immunosuppressive therapy, the onset of a fairly rapidly progressive neurological disorder often including paresis, blindness, and dysphasia and, commonly, intellectual disturbance increasing eventually to severe dementia should raise the possibility of this diagnosis. Occasionally it occurs in subjects with no previous suggestion of immunological deficiency.[59] I have seen an elderly woman with long-standing schizophrenia who demented rapidly over the last 9 months of her life, and the dementia proved to be of this origin. A papova-like virus was identified by electron microscopy in 1965,[162, 212] and the presence of such particles in the oligodendroglial nuclei has now been reported on numerous occasions. The virus was subsequently cultivated from a proven case,[138] and more recently, anti-viral chemotherapy has been associated with dramatic though temporary improvement.[41] Remission occasionally occurs spontaneously, however, and has been reported following cerebral biopsy.[124]

Subacute Sclerosing Panencephalitis

Called subacute inclusion body encephalitis for a number of years following its original description by Dawson,[53, 54] subacute sclerosing panencephalitis is an uncommon disorder largely restricted to older children and young adults. It often commences with behavioral and intellectual disturbances, followed over a few weeks by the occurrence of frequent involuntary spasmodic movements, and terminating with severe dementia usually in less than 6 months. The brain may be unremarkable to the naked eye or show some firm, focal cortical atrophy; when present white matter changes are limited to a slight increase in firmness or granularity, mostly in the occipital lobes. Microscopically, the lesions are severe and extensive in the cortex and in most cases immediately suggest a viral infection. In the cortex of any area, perivascular collections of lymphocytes and plasma cells are frequent and often heavy; microglial and astrocytic proliferation is always present, and the latter may be focally severe. These changes are accompanied by obvious neuron damage as evidenced by neuronophagia and loss, the latter again commonly focally severe in areas of astrocytic proliferation. Type A intranuclear inclusions are present in neurons and oligodendroglia, although their numbers vary greatly and may be few, particularly in long surviving cases. White matter lesions may be slight or severe; some perivascular cuffing and microglial and astrocytic proliferation are usually present. Inclusions may be found in oligodendroglia. Gliosis may be severe but is rarely accompanied by much evidence of myelin destruction.

Investigations conducted over the past 10 years have firmly established the relationship of the disease with infection by a paramyxovirus similar or identical to measles. Electron microscopic identification of a myxovirus was reported in 1965;[20] raised measles antibody titres were demonstrated in serum; and measles antigen, identified by fluorescent antibody techniques, was demonstrated in neurons and glial cells in 1967 and 1968.[39, 40] Measles virus was finally isolated from biopsy material in 1969.[88] All these observations have been confirmed on numerous occasions, although association of the disorder with clinical evidence of other viral infections has been reported.[167] The mechanisms which precipitate this unusual manifestation of a common viral infection are not satisfactorily explained.[1]

Herpes Simplex Encephalitis

Herpes simplex encephalitis is a third viral disorder which may result in dementia, although when dementia occurs it follows recovery from the acute infection. The disease is commonly fatal in the first few days or weeks but may result in profound intellectual and particularly memory disturbances in survivors. This results from extensive damage to the temporal lobes by a necrotizing process which constitutes the major gross and microscopic feature of the disorder.[2, 77] In fatal cases, encephalitis commonly involves the frontal lobes also, particularly their inferior and medial surfaces, and in the most severe cases it involves almost any other area of the cerebrum or the stem. Recovery from the initial infection in such cases would be likely to result in permanent neurological and intellectual deficits, and indeed many survivors are so affected.[137] The possibility that successful chemotherapeutic agents will be discovered probably increases rather than decreases the chances of more cases of dementia appearing as a result of this disease. Not only must chemotherapy be extremely rapid to control the virus, but it must be given very early to prevent the necrotic and ischemic destruction of the brain which is a cardinal feature of fatal cases. It seems likely that structural change is already considerably advanced before the patient presents with symptoms and that chemotherapy is unlikely to be started before considerable brain damage has been done. With rare exceptions, therefore, survivors from herpes simplex encephalitis have considerable temporal lobe damage, and it seems likely that at least memory disturbances will occur in such cases. With successful chemotherapy, the number of survivors with severe memory disturbance will increase. The possibility that those only slightly affected are more likely to become demented in late life than normal subjects will be discussed later.

143

POSSIBLE CHANGES AND INCREASING INCIDENCE IN DEMENTIA

Our present inability to affect the course of Alzheimer's disease and senile dementia and to influence materially the incidence of multiple infarctions in subjects with widespread vascular disease means that until effective measures for controlling these disorders are available, they will continue to cause dementia in many old subjects. With increasing life expectancy, the proportion of such affected old subjects in the general population will continue to grow. Effective control of severe hypertension may well diminish the dementia resulting from widespread small vessel disease, and the control of vasculitis in such diseases as polyarteritis and disseminated lupus erythematosus may prevent the development of widespread cerebrovascular lesions in such cases. However, it would seem inevitable that any benefit from successful therapy of these relatively rare disorders would be more than counterbalanced by the increased numbers of demented old people suffering from the vastly more common disorders of senile and arteriosclerotic dementia, alone or in combination.

There is evidence that the quantity of vascular and senile type change is important in the development of dementia, that senile type change in particular tends to occur with greater frequency and severity with increasing age, and that cortical neurons are probably lost throughout life in most people. This raises the possibility that any disorder which produces additional brain damage will lead to an increased possibility of dementia with survival into old age. Therefore, it seems to me inevitable that the development of methods which prevent death from previously fatal disorders of the central nervous system will increase the total population of demented subjects. Indeed, some examples of this are already well established. Perhaps the best known example is that of the dementia which arises in mongols who before antibiotics tended to die in childhood or early adulthood but who now commonly survive into the fourth, fifth, or even sixth decade. That the majority of such survivors undergo a superimposed dementing process is certain. The evidence seems to be established that any mongol surviving into the fourth or fifth decade develops, possibly as the morphological counterpart of that dementia, widespread and severe senile plaque formation. Some less impressive evidence exists that mental deterioration probably occurs in cases of Duchenne muscular dystrophy who now frequently survive into the third decade of life. It should also not be forgotten that dementia in boxers may well not become manifest for 10 to 15 years after they have ceased boxing, although the initial cerebral damage clearly occurred many years earlier. The dementing process must have resulted from some slowly progressive change not dependent upon repeated trauma.

That a similar process will occur with other disorders now being relatively effectively treated seems inevitable. A few examples will illustrate this point. Recovered cases of ruptured intracranial aneurysms who show neurological or psychiatric abnormality unquestionably have areas of ischemic cerebral tissue. Cases of severe and possibly even trivial brain injury will have frontal and temporal lobe lesions as well as widespread ischemic and tract damage in the more severe cases. Both these types of case form a highly susceptible reservoir for dementia in middle and late life as the effects of neuron loss, senile plaques, and neurofibrillary tangles are superimposed on already damaged brains. Patients recovering from severe bacterial or viral disorders of the central nervous system are also clearly susceptible to additional damage in old age. Subjects recovering from disorders known to carry severe sequelae such as tuberculous meningitis and herpes simplex encephalitis probably carry an unusually high risk of dementia supervening with relatively slight additional cerebral abnormality. Cases resuscitated after cardiac arrest may well, if survival is sufficiently long, also fall into this category of susceptibility. Therapy of diseases not primarily affecting the central nervous system at all, such as hemodialysis for chronic renal failure, may carry the risk of new and at the moment unexplained dementia. The etiology of the rapidly developing dementia now being reported from many hemodialysis centres has no well defined morphological basis[32] nor any biochemical explanation although aluminum toxicity is a possible etiological agent.[108] The possibility that future developments while extending life in many currently fatal disorders will leave damaged brains (not necessarily immediately evident from neurological and psychiatric disturbances) is so high that the numbers of middle and old aged individuals susceptible to the "normal" ravages of old age in the brain can only increase. The numbers of cases of dementia in the population and the morphological and etiological forms seem, therefore, destined to grow.

REFERENCES

1. ADAMS, J. H.: Virus diseases of the nervous system, in Blackwood, W., and Corsellis, J.A.N. (eds.): *Greenfield's Neuropathology*, ed. 3. Edward Arnold (Publishers) Ltd., London, 1976.

2. ADAMS, J. H., AND MILLER, D.: *Herpes simplex encephalitis: a clinical and pathological analysis of twenty-two cases*. Postgrad. Med. J. 49: 393, 1973.

3. ADAMS, R. D.; BOGAERT, L. VAN; AND VANDER EECKEN, H.: Striatonigral degeneration. J. Neuropathol. Exp. Neurol. 23: 584, 1964.

4. ADAMS, R. D.; FISHER, C. M.; HAKIM, S.; OJEMANN, R.; AND SWEET, W.: *Symptomatic occult hydrocephalus with "normal" cerebrospinal fluid pressure: a treatable syndrome*. New Engl. J. Med. 273: 117, 1965.

5. ALBERT, M. L.; FELDMAN, R. G.; AND WILLIS, A. L.: *The subcortical dementia of progressive supranuclear palsy*. J. Neurol. Neurosurg. Psychiatry 37: 121, 1974.

6. ALPER, T.; CRAMP, W. A.; HAIG, D. A.; AND CLARKE, M. C.: *Does the agent of scrapie replicate without nucleic acid?* Nature (Lond.) 214: 764, 1967.

7. ALPER, T.; HAIG, D. A.; AND CLARKE, M. C.: *The exceptionally small size of the scrapie agent*. Biochem. Biophys. Res. Commun. 22: 278, 1966.

8. ALZHEIMER, A.: *Über eine eigenartige Erkrankung der Hirnrinde*. Allgemeine Zeitschrift für Psychiatrie, 64:146, 1907.

9. ARAB, A.: *Plaques séniles et artériosclerose cérébrale*. Rev. Neurol. (Paris) 91: 22, 1954.

10. ASTROM, K.-E.; MANCALL, E. L.; AND RICHARDSON, E. P., JR.: *Progressive multifocal leukoencephalopathy; a hitherto unrecognized complication of chronic lymphatic leukaemia and Hodgkin's disease*. Brain 81: 93, 1958.

11. BENSON, D. F.: The hydrocephalic dementias, in Benson, D. F., and Blumer, D. (eds): *Psychiatric Aspects of Neurologic Disease*. Grune and Stratton, New York, 1975.

12. BERLIN, L.: *Presenile Psychosis (Alzheimer's disease) with features resembling Pick's disease*. Arch. Neurol. Psychiat. (Chicago), 61: 369, 1949.

13. BINNS, J. K., AND ROBERTSON, E. E.: *Pick's disease in old age*. Br. J. Psychiatry 108: 804, 1962.

14. BIRD, E. D.; CARO, A. J.; AND PILLING, J. B.: *A sex related factor in the inheritance of Huntington's chorea*. Ann. Hum. Genet. 37:255, 1974.

15. BIRSE, S. H., AND TOM, M. I.: *Incidence of cerebral infarction associated with ruptured intracerebral aneurysms*. Neurology (Minneap.) 10: 101, 1960.

16. BLESSED, G.; TOMLINSON, B. E.; AND ROTH, M.: *The association between quantitative measurements of dementia and of senile changes in the cerebral grey matter of elderly subjects*. Br. J. Psychiatry 114: 797, 1968.

17. BLOCQ, P., AND MARINESCO, G.: *Sur les lésions et la pathogénie de l'epilepsie dite essentielle*. Sem. Med. 12: 445, 1892.

18. BOLT, J. M. W.: *Huntington's chorea in the west of Scotland.* Br. J. Psychiatry 116: 259, 1970.

19. BOUCHER, M.; TOMMASI, M.; DESPIERRES, G., AND MOURET, J.: *A new case of thalamic dementia.* Lyon Med. 231: 417, 1974.

20. BOUTEILLE, M.; FONTAINE, C.; VEDRENNE, C.; AND DELARUE, J.: *Sur un cas d'encéphalite subaigüe à inclusions: étude anatomo-clinique et ultrastructurale.* Rev. Neurol. (Paris) 113: 454, 1965.

21. BOWEN, D. M.; SMITH, C. B.; AND DAVISON, A. N.: *Molecular changes in senile dementia.* Brain 96: 849, 1973.

22. BRAIN, W. R.; DANIEL, P. M.; AND GREENFIELD, J. G.: *Subacute cortical cerebellar degeneration and its relation to carcinoma.* J. Neurol. Neurosurg. Psychiatry 14: 59, 1951.

23. BRAUNMÜHL, A. VON: *Picksche Krankheit und Amyotraphische Lateralsclerose.* Allg. Z. Psychiat. 96: 364, 1932.

24. BRIERLEY, J. B.: The neuropathology of amnesic states, in Whitty, C. W. M., and Zangwill, O. L. (eds.): *Amnesia.* Butterworth, London, 1966.

25. BRINDLEY, G. S., AND JANOTA, I.: *Observations on cortical blindness and on vascular lesions that cause loss of recent memory and blindness.* J. Neurol. Neurosurg. Psychiatry 38: 459, 1975.

26. BRION, S.; MIKOL, J., AND PSIMARAS, A.: Recent findings in Pick's disease, in Zimmerman, H. M. (ed.): *Progress in Neuropathology,* Vol. II. Grune and Stratton, New York, 1973.

27. BRITISH MEDICAL JOURNAL: *Mental changes in parkinsonism.* (Editorial) Br. Med. J. 2: 1, 1974.

28. BRODY, H.: *Organization of the Cerebral Cortex. A study of aging in the human cerebral cortex.* J. Comp. Neurol. 102: 511, 1955.

29. BRODY, H.: *Structural changes in the aging nervous system.* Interdisciplinary topics in Gerontology, 7: 9, 1970.

30. BROWNELL, B., AND OPPENHEIMER, D.: *An ataxic form of subacute presenile polioencephalopathy (Creutzfeldt-Jakob disease).* J. Neurol. Neurosurg. Psychiatry 28:350, 1965.

31. BROWNELL, B.; CAMPBELL, M. J.; GREENHAM, L. W., AND PEACOCK, D. B.: *Experimental transmission of Creutzfeldt-Jakob disease.* Lancet, 2: 186, 1975.

32. BURKS, J. S.; ALFREY, A. C.; HUDDLESTONE, J.; NORENBERG, M. D.; AND LEWIN, E.: *A fatal encephalopathy in chronic haemodialysis patients.* Lancet 1: 764, 1976.

33. CARLIER, G.; REZNIK, M.; FRANCK, G.; AND HUSKINET, H.: *Clinicopathological study of an infantile form of Huntington's chorea.* Acta Neurol. Belg. 74: 36, 1974.

34. CHANDLER, J. H.; REED, T. E.; AND DE JONG, R. N.: *Huntington's chorea in Michigan. III Clinical Observations.* Neurology 10:148, 1960.

35. COBLENZ, J. M; MATTIS, S.; ZINGESSER, L. H.; KASOFF, S. S.; WISNIEWSKI, H. M.; AND KATZMAN, R.: *Presenile Dementia.* Arch. Neurol. 29: 299, 1973.

36. COIFFU, B. L. H.: *Artériosclérose cérébral à forme démentielle.* Thesis, University of Paris, 102, 1958.

37. COLON, E. J.: *The elderly brain. A quantitative analysis of the cerebral cortex in two cases.* Psychiatr. Neurol. Neurochir. (Aust.) 75: 261, 1972.

38. COLON, E. J.: *The cerebral cortex in presenile dementia. A quantitative analysis.* Acta neuropathol. (Berl.) 23: 281, 1973.

39. CONOLLY, J. H.; ALLEN, I. V.; HURWITZ, L. J.; AND MILLER, J. H. D.: *Measles virus antibody and antigen in subacute sclerosing panencephalitis.* Lancet 1:542, 1967.

40. CONOLLY, J. H.; ALLEN, I. V.; HURWITZ, L. J.; AND MILLER, J. H. D.: *Subacute sclerosing panencephalitis; Clinical, pathological, epidemiological and virological findings in three patients.* Q. J. Med. 37:625, 1968.

41. CONOMY, J. P.; BEARD, N. S.; MATSUMOTO, H.; AND ROESSMANN, V.: *Cytarabine (Cytosine arabinoside) treatment of progressive multifocal leukoencephalopathy; clinical course and detection of viral particles after antiviral chemotherapy.* J.A.M.A. 229:1313, 1974.

42. CORSELLI, J. A. N.: *Mental Illness and the Ageing Brain.* Oxford University Press, London, 1962.

43. CORSELLIS. J. A. N.: *The Pathology of Dementia.* Br. J. Hosp. Med. 2:695, 1969.

44. CORSELLIS, J. A. N.: Ageing and the dementias, in Blackwood, W., and Corsellis, J. A. N. (eds.): *Greenfield's Neuropathology,* ed. 3. Edward Arnold (Publishers) Ltd., London, 1976.

45. CORSELLIS, J. A. N.; BRUTON, C. J.; AND FREEMAN-BROWNE, D.: *The aftermath of boxing.* Psychol. Med. 3:270, 1973.

46. CORSELLIS, J. A. N.; GOLDBERG, G. J.; AND NORTON, A. R.: 'Limbic encephalitis' and its association with carcinoma. Brain 91:481, 1968.

47. CRAGG, B. G.: The density of synapses and neurons in normal, mentally defective and ageing human brains. Brain 98:81, 1975.

48. CRAPPER, D. R.; KRISHNAN, S. S.; AND DALTON, A. J.: Brain aluminum distribution in Alzheimer's disease and experimental neurofibrillary degeneration. Science 180:511, 1973.

49. CRAPPER, D. R.; KRISHNAN, S. S.; AND QUITTKAT, S.: Aluminum, neurofibrillary degeneration and Alzheimer's disease. Brain 99:67, 1976.

50. CROMPTON, M. R.: Cerebral infarction following the rupture of cerebral berry aneurysms. Brain 87:491, 1964.

51. CUSHING, H., AND EISENHARDT, L.: Meningiomas: Their Classification, Regional Behaviour, Life History, and Surgical End Results. Hafner, New York, 1962.

52. DAVISON, C.; GOODHART, S. P.; AND SCHLIONSKY, H. S.: Chronic progressive chorea. The pathogenesis and mechanism. Arch. Neurol. Psychiat. 27:906, 1932.

53. DAWSON, J. R.: Cellular inclusions in cerebral lesions of lethargic encephalitis. Am. J. Pathol. 9: 7, 1933.

54. DAWSON, J. R.: Cellular inclusions in cerebral lesions of epidemic encephalitis. Arch. Neurol. Psychiat. 31:685, 1934.

55. DELAY, J.; BRION, S.; ESCOUROLLE, R.; AND DUJARIER, L.: Etude anatomique des artères carotides et vertébrales au cours des démences séniles. Rev. Neurol. (Paris) 106:772, 1962.

56. DIVRY, P.: Etude histo-chimique des plaques séniles. Journal belge de neurologie et de psychiatrie. 27:643, 1927.

57. DIVRY, P.: La pathochimie générale et cellularie des processes sénile et présénile, in 1st International Congress of Neuropathology Proceedings. Rosenberg and Sellier, Turin. 2:312, 1952.

58. ESCOUROLLE, R., AND POIRIER, J.: Manual of Basic Neuropathology. W. B. Saunders Co., Philadelphia, 1973.

59. FARIS, A. A., AND MARTINEZ, A. J.: Primary progressive multifocal leukoencephalopathy. Arch. Neurol. 27:357, 1972.

60. FERGUSON, F. R., AND MAUDSLEY, C.: Chronic encephalopathy in boxers. 8th International Congress of Neurology, Vienna. Wiëner Medizinischen Akademic; Vienna, 1:81, 1965.

61. FISHER, A.: On meningioma presenting with dementia. Proc. Aust. Assoc. Neurol. 6:29, 1969.

62. FONCIN, J. R.; GACHES, J.; AND LE BEAU, J.: Encéphalopathie spongiforme (apparentée à la maladie de Creutzfeldt-Jakob). Biopsie étudiée an microscope electronique, confirmation autopsique. Rev. Neurol. (Paris) 111:507, 1964.

63. FOSTER, J. B.; LEIGUARDA, R.; AND TILLEY, P. J. B.: Brain damage in National Hunt jockeys. Lancet 1:981, 1976.

64. FRASER, H.; AND BRUCE, M. E.: Argyrophilic plaques in mice inoculated with scrapie from particular sources. Lancet 1:617, 1973.

65. GAJDUSEK, D. C.: Kuru and Creutzfeldt-Jakob disease. Experimental models of non-inflammatory degenerative slow virus disease of the central nervous system. Ann. Clin. Res. 5:254, 1973.

66. GELLERSTEDT, N.: Zur Kenntnis der Hirnveränderungen bei der normalen Altersinvolution. Upsala Läk-Fören. Förh. 38:193, 1933.

67. GIBBS, C. J.; GAJDUSEK, D. C.; ASHER, D. M.; ALPERS, M. P.; BECK, E.; DANIEL, P. M.; AND MATTHEWS, W.: Creutzfeldt-Jakob disease (spongiform encephalopathy): Transmission to the chimpanzee. Science 161:388, 1968.

68. GIBSON, P.; AND TOMLINSON, B. E.: Hirano bodies in the hippocampus of normal and demented subjects with Alzheimer's disease. In press.

69. GLENNER, G. G.; EIN, D.; AND TERRY, W. D.: The immoglobulin origin of amyloid. Am. J. Med. 52:141, 1972.

70. GONATAS, N. K.; ANDERSON, A.; AND EVANGELISTA, I.: The contribution of altered synapses in the senile plaque: an electronmicroscopic study in Alzheimer's dementia. J. Neuropath. Exp. Neurol. 26:25, 1967.

71. GONATAS, N. K.; TERRY, R. D.; AND WEISS, M.: Electron microscopic study in two cases of Jakob-Creutzfeldt disease. J. Neuropath. Exp Neurol. 24:575, 1965.

72. GRAHAM, D. I., AND ADAMS, J. H.: Ischaemic brain damage in fatal head injuries. Lancet 1: 265, 1971.

147

73. GRAHMANN, H., AND ULE, G.: *Beitrag zur Kenntnis der chronischen cerebralen Krankheits-bilder bei Boxern.* Psychiatria et neurologia, 134:261, 1957.

74. HAASE, G. R.: Diseases presenting as dementia, in Wells, C. E. (ed.): *Dementia,* ed. 2. F. A. Davis Company, Philadelphia, 1977.

75. HAKIM, S., AND ADAMS, R. D.: *The special clinical problem of symptomatic hydrocephalus with normal cerebrospinal fluid pressure — Observations on cerebrospinal fluid hydrodynamics.* J. Neurol. Sci. 2:307, 1965.

76. HALL, T. C.; MILLER, A. K. H.; AND CORSELLIS, J. A. N.: *Variations in the human Purkinje cell population according to age and sex.* Neuropathology and Applied Neurobiology. 1:267, 1975.

77. HAYMAKER, W.; SMITH, M. G.; VAN BOGAERT, L.; AND DE CHENAR, C.: Pathology of viral disease in man characterised by nuclear inclusions, in Field, W. S., and Blattner, R. L. (eds.): *Viral Encephalitis,* Charles C Thomas, Springfield, Illinois, 95:1958.

78. HEATHFIELD, K. W. G. *Huntington's chorea: Investigation into prevalence in the N.E. Metropolitan Regional Hospital Board area.* Brain 90:203, 1967.

79. HEIDENHAIN, A.: *Klinische und anatomische Untersuchungen über eine eigenartige organische Erkrankung des Zentralnervensystems im Praesenium.* Z. ges. Neurol. Psychia. (Berlin) 118:49, 1928.

80. HENDERSON, G.; TOMLINSON, B. E.; AND WEIGHTMAN, D.:*Cell counts in the human cerebral cortex using a traditional and an automatic method.* J. Neurol. Sci. 25:129, 1975.

81. HENSON, R. A.; HOFFMAN, H. L.; AND URICH, H.: *Encephalomyelitis with carcinoma.* Brain 88:449, 1965.

82. HIRANO, A.: Pathogenesis of amyotrophic lateral sclerosis, in Gajdusek, D. C.; Gibbs, C. J., Jr.; and Alpers, M. (eds.): *Slow, Latent and Temperate Virus Infections.* NINDB Monograph No. 2. National Institutes of Health, PHS Publication No. 1378. U.S. Government Printing Office, Washington, D. C. 1965.

83. HIRANO, A.: Parkinsonism-dementia complex on Guam: Current status of the problem, in Subirana, A., and Espadaler, J. M. (eds.): *Proceedings of the 10th International Congress of Neurology, Barcelona, 1973.* Excerpta Medica, Amsterdam, 1974, p. 348.

84. HIRANO, A., AND KURLAND, L. T.: *Parkinsonism-dementia complex, an endemic disease on the island of Guam. II Pathological features.* Brain 84:662, 1961.

85. HIRANO, A.; KURLAND, L. T.; KROOTH, R. S.; AND LESSELL, S.: *Parkinsonism-dementia complex, an endemic disease on the island of Guam. 1. Clinical features.* Brain 84, 642, 1961.

86. HÖPKER, W. VON.: *Das Altern des Nucleus dentatus.* Z. Alternsforsch. 5:256, 1951.

87. HORNABROOK, R. W.; AND POLLOCK, M.: *The prevalence, natural history and dementia of Parkinson's disease.* Brain 89:429, 1966.

88. HORTA-BARBOSA, L.; FUCCILLO, D. A.; SEVER, J. L.; AND ZEMAN, W.: *Subacute sclerosing panencephalitis; isolation of measles virus from a brain biopsy.* Nature (Lond.) 221:1969.

89. HOWARD, C. P., AND ROYCE, C. E.: *Progressive lenticular degeneration associated with cirrhosis of the liver (Wilson's disease).* Arch. Intern. Med. 24:497, 1919.

90. HUGHES, C. P.; MYERS, F. K.; SMITH, K.; AND TORACK, R. M.: *Nosological problems in dementia. A clinical and pathological study of 11 cases.* Neurology (Minneap.) 23:344, 1973.

91. HUNTER, G. D., AND MILLSON, G. C.: *Studies on the heat stability and chromatographic behaviour of the scrapie agent.* J. Gen. Microbiol. 37:251, 1964.

92. IQBAL, K.; WISNIEWSKI, H. M.; SHELANSKI, M. L.; BROSTOFF, S.; LIWNICZ, B. H.; AND TERRY, R. D.: *Protein changes in senile dementia.* Brain Res. 77:337, 1974.

93. ISHII, T.: *Distribution of Alzheimer's neurofibrillary changes in the brain stem and hypothalamus of senile dementia.* Acta Neuropathol. (Berl.) 6:181, 1966.

94. ISHINO, H.: *Distribution of Alzheimer's neurofibrillary tangles in the basal ganglia and brain stem of progressive supranuclear palsy and Alzheimer's disease.* Brain Nerve (Tokyo) 27:601, 1975.

95. JERVIS, G. A.: *Early senile dementia in mongoloid idiocy.* Am. J. Psychiatry 105:102, 1948.

96. JONES, D., AND NEVIN, S.: *Rapidly progressive cerebral degeneration (subacute vascular encephalopathy) with mental disorder, focal disturbances and myoclonic epilepsy,* J. Neurol. Neurosurg. Psychiat. 17:148, 1954.

97. KAY, D. W. K.; NORRIS, V.; AND POST, F.: *Prognosis in psychiatric disorders of the elderly; an attempt to define indicators of early death and early recovery.* Br. J. Psychiatry 102:129, 1956.

98. KIDD, M.: *Paired helical filaments in electron microscopy in Alzheimer's disease.* Nature (Lond.) 197:192, 1963.

99. KIDD, M.: *Alzheimer's disease — an electron microscopic study.* Brain 87:307, 1964.

100. KIRSCHBAUM, W. R.: *Jakob-Creutzfeldt Disease.* Elsevier Publishing Co., New York, 1968.

101. KIRSCHBAUM, W. R.: Jakob-Creutzfeldt disease, in Minckler, J. (ed.): *The Pathology of the Nervous System,* Vol. 2. McGraw Hill Book Co., New York, 1971, p.1410.

102. KLATZO, I.; WISNIEWSKI, H.; AND STREICHER, E.: *Experimental production of neurofibrillary degeneration. 1. Light microscopic observations.* J. Neuropath. Exp. Neurol. 24:187, 1965.

103. KONIGSMARK, B. W.: *Neuronal population of the ventral cochlea nucleus in man.* Anat. Rec. 163:212, 1969.

104. KONIGSMARK, B. W., AND MURPHY, E. A.: *Volume of the ventral cochlear nucleus in man — its relationship to neuronal population and age.* J. Neuropath. Exp. Neurol. 31:304, 1972.

105. KRAEPELIN, E.: *Klinische Psychiatrie in Psychiatrie,* ed. 8. Vol. 2, Part 1, Barth, Leipzig. 1910.

106. KRIGMAN, M. R.; FELDMAN, R. G.; AND BENSCH, K.: *Alzheimer's presenile dementia. A histochemical and electron-microscopic study.* Lab. Invest. 14:381, 1965.

107. KURLAND, L. T., AND MULDER, D. W.: *Epidemiologic investigations of amyotrophic lateral sclerosis. Part 1. Preliminary report on geographic distribution with special reference to the Mariana Islands, including clinical and pathologic observations.* Neurology (Minneap.) 4:355, 1954.

108. LANCET: *Dialysis dementia; aluminium again?* (Editorial) Lancet 1:349, 1976.

109. LIEBERMAN, A. N.: *Parkinson's disease. A clinical review.* Am. J. Med. Sci. 267:66, 1974.

110. LISS, L.: *Senile brain changes. Histopathology of the ganglion cells.* J. Neuropath. Exp. Neurol. 19:559, 1960.

111. LOGUE, V.; DURWARD, M.; PRATT, R. T. C.; PIERCY, M., AND NIXON, W. L. B.: *The quality of survival after rupture of an anterior cerebral aneurysm.* Br. J. Psychiatry 114:137, 1968.

112. LUSE, S. A., AND SMITH, K. R.: *The ultrastructure of senile plaques.* Am. J. Pathol. 44:553, 1964.

113. MALAMUD, N.: Neuropathology of organic brain syndromes, in Gaitz, C. M. (ed.): *Aging and the Brain.* Plenum Press, New York, 1972, p.63.

114. MALAMUD, N.; HIRANO, A.; AND KURLAND, L. T.: *Pathoanatomic changes in amyotrophic lateral sclerosis on Guam.* Arch. Neurol. 5:401, 1961.

115. MANDYBUR, T. I.: *The incidence of cerebral amyloid angiopathy in Alzheimer's disease.* Neurology (Minneap.) 25:120, 1975.

116. MANSVELT, J. VAN: *Pick's disease. A syndrome of lobar cerebral atrophy.* Enschede, Netherlands, 1954.

117. MANUELDIS, E. E.: *Transmission of Jakob-Creutzfeldt disease from man to guinea pig.* Science 190:571, 1975.

118. MARSDEN, C. G., AND HARRISON, M. J. G.: *Outcome of investigation of patients with presenile dementia.* Br. Med. J. 2:249, 1972.

119. MARTLAND, H. S.: *Punch drunk.* J.A.M.A. 91:1103, 1928.

120. MATHEWS, T.; WISOTZKEY, H.; AND MOOSSY, J.: *Multiple CNS infections in progressive multifocal leukoencephalopathy.* Neurology (Minneap.) 26:51, 1976.

121. MAUDSLEY, C., AND FERGUSON, F. R.: *Neurological disease in boxers.* Lancet 2:795, 1963.

122. MCFIE, J., AND PIERCY, M.: *Intellectual impairment with localised cerebral lesions.* Brain 75:292, 1952.

123. MCHUGH, P. R., AND FOLSTEIN, M. R.: Psychiatric syndromes of Huntington's chorea: A clinical and phenomenological study, in Benson, D. B., and Bulmer, D. (eds.): *Psychiatric Aspects of Neurological Disease.* Grune and Stratton, New York, 1975, p.267.

124. MCMENEMEY, W. H.: *Alzheimer's disease.* J. Neurol. Neurosurg. Psychiat. 3:211, 1940.

125. MCMENEMEY, W. H.: The dementias and progressive diseases of the basal ganglia, in Blackwood, W.; McMenemey, W. H.; Meyer, A.; Norman, R. M.; and Russell, D. S. (eds.): *Greenfield's Neuropathology,* ed. 2. Edward Arnold, London, 1963, p.475.

126. MILNER, B.: Amnesia following operation on the temporal lobes, in Whitty, C. W. M., and Zangwill, O. L. (eds.): *Amnesia.* Butterworth, London, 1966, p.109.

149

127. MINAUF, M., AND JELLINGER, K.: *Kombination von Amyotrophischer Lateralsclerose mit Pickscher Krankheit.* Arch. Psychiatr. Nervenkr. 212:279, 1969.

128. MONAGLE, R. D., AND BRODY, H.: *The effects of age upon the main nucleus of the inferior olive in the human.* J. Comp. Neurol. 155:61, 1974.

129. MOREL, F., AND WILDI, E.: *Contribution à la connaissance des différentes altérations cérébrales du grande âge.* Schweiz. Arch. Neurol. Neurochie. Psychiatr. 76:174, 1955.

130. NEUBERGER, K. T.; SINTON, D. W.; AND DENST, J.: *Cerebral atrophy associated with boxing.* Arch. Neurol. Psychiat. 81:403, 1959.

131. NEUMANN, M. A.: *Pick's disease.* J. Neuropath. Exp. Neurol. 8:255, 1949.

132. NEUMANN, M. A., AND COHN, R.: *Progressive subcortical gliosis, a rare form of presenile dementia.* Brain 90:405, 1967.

133. NICKLOWITZ, W. J.: *Neurofibrillary changes after acute experimental lead poisoning.* Neurology (Minneap.) 25:927, 1975.

134. NICKLOWITZ, W. J., AND MANDYBUR, T. I.: *Neurofibrillary changes following childhood lead encephalopathy.* J. Neuropath. Exp. Neurol. 34:445, 1975.

135. NIKAIDO, T.; AUSTIN, J.; TRUEB, L.; AND RINEHART, T.: *Studies in aging of the brain. II. Microchemical analyses of the nervous system and Alzheimer patients.* Arch. Neurol. 27:549, 1972.

136. OLSON, M. I., AND SHAW, C.: *Presenile dementia and Alzheimer's disease in mongolism.* Brain 92:147, 1969.

137. OXBURY, J. M., AND MCCALLUM, F. O.: *Herpes simplex encephalitis: Clinical features and residual damage.* Postgrad. Med. J. 49:387, 1973.

138. PADGETT, B. L.; WALKER, D. L.; ZURHEIN, G. M.; ECKROADE, R. J., AND DESSEL, B. H.: *Cultivation of papova-like virus from human brain with progressive multifocal leukoencephalopathy.* Lancet 1:1257, 1971.

139. PANTELAKIS, S.: *Un type particulier d'angiopathie sénile du système nerveux central: L'angiopathie congophile. Topographie et frequence.* Monatsschr. Psychiatrie Neurologie, 128:219, 1954.

140. PERUSINI, G.: *Über klinisch und histologisch eigenartige psychische Erkrankugen des späteren Lebensalters.* Histologische und histopathologishe Arbeiten über die Grosshirnrinde 3:297, 1910.

141. PIERCY, M.: *The effects of cerebral lesions on intellectual function: A review of current research trends.* Br. J. Psychiatry 110:310, 1964.

142. PIERCY, M.: Neurological aspects of intelligence, in Vinken, P. J., and Bruyn, G. W. (eds.): *Handbook of Clinical Neurology,* Vol. III. North Holland, Amsterdam, 1969, p.296.

143. PLUM, F. (ed.): *Brain dysfunction in metabolic disorders.* Res. Publ. Assoc. Res. Ment. Nerv. Dis. 1974.

144. POST, F.: *The Clinical Psychiatry of Late Life.* Pergamon Press, Oxford, 1965.

145. RICHARDSON, J. C.; STEELE, J.; AND OLSZEWSKI, J.: *Supranuclear ophthalmoplegia, pseudobulbar palsy, nuchal dystonia and dementia. A clinical report on eight cases of "heterogeneous system degeneration".* Trans. Am. Neurol. Assoc. 88:25, 1963.

146. ROBERTS, A. H.: *Brain damage in boxers. A study of prevalence of traumatic encephalopathy among ex-professional boxers.* Pitman, London, 1969.

147. ROBERTSON, E. G.: *Cerebral lesions due to intracranial aneurysms.* Brain 72: 150, 1949.

148. ROOS, R.; GAJDUSEK, D. C.; AND GIBBS, C. J., JR.: *The clinical characteristic of transmissible Creutzfeldt-Jakob disease.* Brain 96:1, 1973.

149. ROTH, M.: *The natural history of mental disorders arising in the senium.* Br. J. Psychiatry 101:281, 1955.

150. ROTH, M., AND MORRISEY, J. D.: *Problems in the diagnosis and classification of mental disorder in old age.* Br. J. Psychiatry 98:66, 1952.

151. ROTH, M.; TOMLINSON, B. E.; AND BLESSED, G.: *Correlation between scores for dementia and counts of 'senile plaques' in cerebral grey matter of elderly subjects.* Nature (Lond.) 209:109, 1966.

152. ROTHSCHILD, D.: *The pathologic changes in senile psychosis and their psychobiologic significance.* Am. J. Psychiatry 93:757, 1937.

150

153. ROTHSCHILD, D.: *Neuropathologic changes in arteriosclerotic psychoses and their psychiatric significance.* Arch. Neurol. Psychiat. 48:417, 1942.

154. SACHAR, E. J.: Psychiatric disturbances in endocrine disease, in Plum, F. (ed.): *Brain Dysfunction in Metabolic disorders.* Res. Publ. Assoc. Res. Ment. Nerv. Dis. 239, 1974.

155. SCHOCHET, S. S., JR.; LAMPERT, P. W.; AND EARLE, K. M.: *Neuronal changes induced by intrathecal vincristine sulphate.* J. Neuropath. Exp. Neurol. 27:645, 1968.

156. SCHOCHET, S. S., JR.; LAMPERT, P. W.; AND LINDENBERG, R.: *Fine structure of the Pick and Hirano bodies in a case of Pick's disease.* Acta Neuropathol. (Berl.) 11:330, 1968.

157. SCHULMAN, S.: *Bilateral symmetrical degeneration of the thalamus—a clinico-pathological study.* J. Neuropath. Exp. Neurol. 16:446, 1957.

158. SCHULMAN, S.: Wilson's disease, in Minckler, J. (ed.): *Pathology of the Nervous System,* Vol. 1. McGraw Hill, Co., New York, 1968, p.1139.

159. SCHWARTZ, P.: *Amyloidosis: Cause and manifestations of senile degeneration.* Charles C Thomas, Springfield, Illinois, 1970.

160. SEGARA, J. M.; VON STOCKERT, T. R.; AND CURTIS, M.: Thalamic dementias, in Subirana, A., and Espadaler, J. M. (eds.): *Proceedings of the 10th International Congress of Neurology, Barcelona, 1973.* Excerpa Medica, Amsterdam, 1974, p.393.

161. SHEFER, V. F.: *Absolute numbers of neurones and thickness of cerebral cortex during aging, senile and vascular dementia and Pick's and Alzheimer's diseases.* Neurosciences and Behavioral Physiology 6:319, 1973.

162. SILVERMAN, L.; AND RUBINSTEIN, L. J.: *Electron microscopic observations on a case of progressive multifocal leukoencephalopathy.* Acta neuropathol. (Berl.) 5:215, 1965.

163. SIM, M.: *Guide to Psychiatry.* Livingstone, London, 1963.

164. SIM, M.; TURNER, E.; AND SMITH, W. T.: *Cerebral biopsy in the investigation of presenile dementia. I. Clinical Aspects.* Br. J. Psychiatry 112:119, 1966.

165. SIM, M; TURNER, E.; AND SMITH, W. T.: *Cerebral biopsy in the investigation of presenile dementia. II. Pathological Aspects.* Br. J. Psychiatry 112:127, 1966.

166. SIMCHOWICZ, T.: *Histologische Studien über die senile Demenz.* Histologische und histopathologische Arbeiten über die Grosshirnrinde, 4:267, 1911.

167. SINGHAL, B. S.; WADIA, N. H.; VIBHAKAR, B. B.; AND DASTUR, D. K.: *Subacute sclerosing panencephalitis. l. Clinical aspects.* Neurology (Bombay) 22:87, 1974.

168. SJÖGREN, T.; SJÖGREN, H.; AND LINDGREN, A. G. H.: *Morbus Alzheimer and Morbus Pick: A genetic, clinical and patho-anatomical study.* Acta Psychiat. Neurol. Scand. (suppl) 82, 152, 1952.

169. SLABY, A. E., AND WYATT, R. J.: *Dementia in the Presenium.* Charles C Thomas, Springfield, Illinois, 1974.

170. SOLITAIRE, G. B., AND LAMARCHE, J. B.: *Alzheimer's disease and senile dementia as seen in mongoloids.* Am. J. of Ment. Defic. 70:840, 1966.

171. SONIAT, T. L. L.: *Histogenesis of senile plaques.* Arch. Neurol. Psychiat. 46:101, 1941.

172. STEELE, J.; RICHARDSON, J. C.; AND OLSZEWSKI, J.: *Progressive supranuclear palsy.* Arch. Neurol. 10:333, 1964.

173. STERN, K.: *Severe dementia associated with bilateral symmetrical degeneration of the thalamus.* Brain 62:157, 1939.

174. STRICH, S. J.: *Shearing of nerve fibres as a cause of brain damage due to head injury.* Lancet 2, 443, 1961.

175. TAKEI, Y., AND MIRRA, S. S.: *Striatonigral degeneration: a form of multiple system atrophy with clinical parkinsonism,* in Zimmerman, H. M. (ed.): *Progress in Neuropathology,* Vol. 2. Grune and Stratton, New York, 1973.

176. TARISKA, I.: Circumscribed cerebral atrophy in Alzheimer's disease. A pathological study, in Wolstenholme, G. E. W., and O'Connor, M. (eds.): *Alzheimer's Disease and Related Conditions. A Ciba Foundation Symposium.* J. & A. Churchill, London, 1970, p.51.

177. TELLEZ-NAGEL, I.; JOHNSON, A. B.; AND TERRY, R. D.: *Studies on brain biopsies of patients with Huntington's chorea.* J. Neuropath. Exp. Neurol. 33:308, 1974.

178. TELLEZ-NAGEL, I., AND WISNIEWSKI, H. M.: *Ultrastructure of neurofibrillary tangles in Steele-Richardson-Olszewski Syndrome.* Arch. Neurol. 29:324, 1973.

179. TERRY, R. D.: *The fine structure of neurofibrillary tangles in Alzheimer's disease.* J. Neuropath. Exp. Neurol. 22:629, 1963.

180. TERRY, R. D., AND PĒNA, C.: *Experimental production of neurofibrillary degeneration. 2. Electron microscopy, phosphatase histochemistry and electron probe analysis.* J. Neuropath. Exp. Neurol. 24:200, 1965.

181. TERRY, R. D., AND WISNIEWSKI, H.: The ultrastructure of the neurofibrillary tangle and the senile plaque, in Wolstenholme, G. E. W., and O'Connor, M. (eds.): *Alzheimer's disease and related conditions. A Ciba Foundation Symposium.* J. & A. Churchill, London, 1970, p.145.

182. TERRY, R. D., AND WISNIEWSKI, H.: Ultrastructure of senile dementia and of experimental analogs, in Gaitz, C. M. (ed.): *Aging and the Brain.* Plenum Publishing Corp., New York, 1972.

183. TERRY, R. D.; GONATAS, N. K.; AND WEISS, M.: *Ultrastructural studies in Alzheimer's presenile dementia.* Am. J. Pathol. 44:269, 1964.

184. TOMLINSON, B. E.: *Brain changes in ruptured intracranial aneurysm.* J. Clin. Path. 12:391, 1959.

185. TOMLINSON, B. E.: Pathology of brain injury, in Rowbotham, G. F. (ed.): *Acute Injuries of the Head.* E. & S. Livingstone, Edinburgh and London, 1964, p. 93.

186. TOMLINSON, B. E.: *Ischaemic lesions of the central hemispheres following rupture of intracranial aneurysms. Part I.* Newcastle Med. J. 31:81, 1966.

187. TOMLINSON, B. E.: *Brain stem lesions after head injury.* J. Clin. Path. [Suppl.] 23:4, 154, 1970.

188. TOMLINSON, B. E.: Morphological brain changes in non-demented old people, in van Praag, H. M., and Kalverboer, A. F. (eds.): *Ageing of the Central Nervous System.* De Erven F. Bohn N. V., Haarlem, Netherlands, 1972, p. 38.

189. TOMLINSON, B. E.; AND HENDERSON, G.: *Some Quantitative Cerebral Findings in Normal and Demented Old People.* Raven Press, New York. 1976.

190. TOMLINSON, B. E.; AND IRVING, D.: *The numbers of neurons in the lumbosacral spinal cord throughout life.* In press.

191. TOMLINSON, B. E., AND KITCHENER, D.: *Granulovacuolar degeneration of the hippocampal pyramidal cells.* J. Pathol. 106:165, 1972.

192. TOMLINSON, B. E.; BLESSED, G.; AND ROTH, M.: *Observations on the brains of non-demented old people.* J. Neurol. Sci. 7:331, 1968.

193. TOMLINSON, B. E.; BLESSED, G., AND ROTH, M.: *Observations on the brains of demented old people.* J. Neurol. Sci. 11:205, 1970.

194. VAN BUREN, J. M.; AND BORKE, R. D.: *The mesial temporal substratum of memory.* Brain 95: 599, 1972.

195. VANDER EECKEN, H.; ADAMS, R. D.; AND BOGAERT, L. VAN: *Striatopallidalnigral degeneration. An hitherto undescribed lesion in paralysis agitans.* J. Neuropath. Exp. Neurol. 19:159, 1960.

196. VICTOR, M; ANGEVINE, J. B.; MANCALL, E. L.; AND FISHER, C. M.: *Memory loss with lesions of the hippocampal formation.* Arch. Neurol. 5:244, 1961.

197. WALTON, J. N.: *Subarachnoid haemorrhage.* Livingstone, Edinburgh, 1956.

198. WILSON, G.; RIGGS, H. E., AND RUPP, C.: *The pathological anatomy of ruptured cerebral aneurysms.* J. Neurosurg. 11:128, 1954.

199. WILSON, S. A. K.: *Progressive lenticular degeneration: a familial nervous disease associated with cirrhosis of the liver.* Brain 34:295, 1912.

200. WISNIEWSKI, H. M.; BRUCE, M. E.; AND FRASER, H.: *Infectious etiology of neuritic (senile) plaques in mice.* Science 190:1108, 1975.

201. WISNIEWSKI, H.; COBLENZ, J. M.; AND TERRY, R. D.: *Pick's disease. A clinical and ultrastructural study.* Arch. Neurol. 26:97, 1972.

202. WISNIEWSKI, H.; KARCZEWSKI, W.; AND WISNIEWSKI, K.: *Neurofibrillary degeneration in nerve cells after intracerebral injection of aluminium cream.* Acta Neuropathol. (Berl.) 6:211, 1966.

203. WISNIEWSKI, H. M.; NARANG, H. K.; AND TERRY, R. D.: *Neurofibrillary tangles of paired helical filaments.* J. Neurol. Sci. 27:173, 1976.

204. WISNIEWSKI, H.; SHELANSKI, M. L.; AND TERRY, R. D.: *The effects of mitotic spindle inhibitors on neurotubules and neurofilaments in anterior horn cells.* J. Cell Biol. 38:224, 1968.

152

205. WISNIEWSKI, H., AND TERRY, R. D.: *Experimental colchicine encephalopathy. l. Induction of neurofibrillary degeneration.* Lab. Invest. 17:577, 1967.

206. WISNIEWSKI, H., AND TERRY, R. D.: Morphology of the aging brain, human and animal, in Ford, D. H. (ed.): *Progress in Brain Research.* Elsevior Scientific Publishing Co., Amsterdam, 1973, p.167.

207. WISNIEWSKI, H., AND TERRY, R. D.: *Neuropathology of the Aging Brain.* Raven Press, New York, 1976.

208. WOLF, A.: Clinical neuropathology in relation to the process of aging, in Brien, J. E. (ed.): *The Process of Aging in the Nervous System.* Charles C Thomas, Springfield, Ill. 1959.

209. WOODARD, J. S.: *Clinico-pathological significance of granulo-vacuolar degeneration in Alzheimer's disease.* J. Neuropath. Exp. Neurol. 21:85, 1962.

210. WOODARD, J. S.: *Alzheimer's disease in late adult life.* Am. J. Pathol. 49:1157, 1966.

211. ZLOTNIK, I.; GRANT, D. P.; DAYAN, A. D.; AND EARLE, C. J.: *Transmission of Creutzfeldt-Jakob disease from man to squirrel monkey.* Lancet 11:435, 1974.

212. ZURHEIN, G. M.; AND CHOU, S. M.: *Particles resembling papova viruses in human demyelinating disease.* Science 148:1477, 1965.

CHAPTER 7

Biochemical Approaches to Dementia*

James O. McNamara, M.D., and
Stanley H. Appel, M.D.

Other chapters detail the range of mental dysfunction and intellectual deterioration associated with dementia, the term usually applied to diffuse deterioration of mental function, primarily in thought and memory and secondarily in feeling and conduct. Although considerable information has accumulated in the last 5 years as to the etiology of dementia, our understanding of the biochemistry of dementia is still in its infancy. Perhaps the major problem is that dementia is not due to a single cause but may be the result of a wide range of disorders which includes degenerative, metabolic, vascular, inflammatory, malnutritional, toxic, neoplastic, or infectious alterations. In fact, the potential etiologies of dementia are so diverse that it is extremely unlikely that impairment of any single biochemical process will explain all the manifestations of clinical dysfunction seen in dementia. For example, alterations in vitamin intake (thiamine, niacin, B_{12}, folic acid), hormonal levels, or electrolytes are known to be associated with dementia. Yet these constituents are involved in such a wide range of biochemical reactions that it is doubtful a single rate-limiting step is applicable to all cases of dementia.

Careful consideration of those disorders in which the specific inborn error of metabolism has been clarified—such as the aminoacidurias or lipid storage disease—may help us in the future to define those biochemical processes essential for normal mental function, the impairment of which might give rise to dementia. However at present, even in disorders whose specific inherited enzymatic defect is defined—such as phenylketonuria, branched chain aminoaciduria, or Tay Sachs disease—we have no clear insight as to whether the behavioral alterations associated with the specific enzymatic defect can be attributed to focal, multifocal, or diffuse involvement of neurons, glia, or their subcellular compartments. Furthermore, we have little understanding of whether the initial enzymatic defect is itself responsible for the dysfunction or whether the enzymatic defect has led to other biochemical alterations which are responsible for the neuronal or glial dysfunction.

In the previous edition, we posited that impairment of cellular interaction primarily between neurons could give rise to the symptomatology of dementia without necessarily compromising total neuronal or glial function. Since the synapse is

*This work has been supported in part by grants from the National Institutes of Health and the National Multiple Sclerosis Society.

often a key and rate-limiting step in intercellular communication within the nervous system, alterations in the pattern of synaptic organization and the efficiency of synaptic function might well be reflected behaviorally as dementia. Although no direct evidence is presently available to confirm this hypothesis, the increasing recognition of structural alterations in synapses of cases with dementia and the loss of dendritic arborization with age offer circumstantial support for the role of the synapse in dementia.

If the impairment of intercellular communication should be the important factor in the pathogenesis of dementia, any of the factors which affect synaptic functions might well be a target for a dementia-inducing insult. Such factors include axoplasmic flow, neurotransmitter metabolism, neurotransmitter mobilization and release, presynaptic membrane structure and function, the width of the intercellular cleft, the nature of the intercellular matrix, the neurotransmitter receptor, the ion conductance "channels" of both presynaptic and postsynaptic membranes, and the dendritic components responsible for the transmission of ion conductance changes to the soma and axon hillock. One of these factors can already be circumstantially linked with cases of dementia, namely the presumed alteration in axoplasmic flow in cases of adult neuroaxonal dystrophy. With investigations of other cases of dementia, several other steps may well be implicated. Furthermore, recent developments in basic approaches to synaptogenesis and to neuronal recognition and plasticity will play an ever increasing role in future approaches to dementia.

This point of view in no sense excludes the more conventional approach that loss of neurons and/or glia per se may be responsible for dementia. Neurons may differ with respect to their susceptibility to a range of biochemical defects, such as the susceptibility of hippocampal neurons and Purkinje cells to anoxia. Any biochemical process that affected these critical neurons would thereby alter the communal response. Thus, whether the disease were focal, multifocal, or diffuse, compromise of a critical population of neurons or glia could result in dementia. For example, any damage to limbic system structures bilaterally is likely to compromise memory function.

It seems probable that in many forms of dementia both rate-limiting biochemical reactions and rate-limiting neuronal and glial functions contribute to the behavioral aberrations, but in no instance is it completely understood how the biochemical alterations ultimately result in the clinical symptomatology of dementia. Huntington's chorea most likely reflects an inborn error of metabolism resulting in neuronal destruction in selected areas. Adult onset metachromatic leukodystrophy similarly reflects an inborn error of metabolism, but the pathology is mainly seen in the oligodendrocytes and myelin. In both of these diseases, a biochemical defect is probably primary. In contrast, in Creutzfeldt-Jakob disease, the primary cause appears to be a "slow virus." In this instance the biochemical alteration would be secondary to the presumed viral etiology. Regardless of whether the biochemical alterations are primary or secondary, and regardless of whether the disease involves primarily neurons or glia, our major efforts should be to determine the nature of the critical biochemical alterations and how they translate into the symptoms and signs of dementia.

The problem of brain dysfunction in dementia has been studied biochemically through several different research approaches:

1. Direct biochemical and morphological examination of the brain in a particular type of dementia made possible by the increasing sophistication of electron

microscopic techniques, the availability of suitable brain biopsy specimens, and the advances in understanding of protein, nucleic acid, lipid, and neurotransmitter metabolism.

2. Investigation of a variety of demented patients with cerebral blood flow techniques.

3. Investigation of the biochemistry of memory, employing inhibitors of protein and nucleic acid synthesis.

4. Trials of a variety of agents in the therapy of dementia.

In this chapter, we will summarize our present knowledge as developed by each of these approaches.

CORRELATION OF MORPHOLOGICAL AND BIOCHEMICAL CHANGES

Senile Plaque

Three pathological changes have been noted to be markedly increased in patients with presenile and senile dementia: senile plaques, neurofibrillary tangles, and granulovacuolar degeneration. Ultrastructural studies have revealed senile plaques to consist of an extracellular core of fibrils resembling amyloid, surrounded by cytoplasmic processes containing fibrils, multilamellar bodies, and degenerating mitochondria.[42] In the region of senile plaques, changes in axons and in presynaptic and postsynaptic processes have also been described.[11, 23] Enzyme histochemistry of these areas demonstrated increased oxidative function, presumably reflecting an early metabolic reaction to neuronal injury, especially in the neuropil.[7, 8] The cores of the plaques were characterized as amyloid because they exhibited a carbohydrate staining protein with dichromic birefringence when stained with Congo red. The filamentous material of the plaque was shown to be extracellular and appeared to possess the morphological appearance of amyloid noted in other conditions.[19, 44]

Wisniewski and coworkers[50] demonstrated senile plaques in the brains of mice infected with scrapie agent. Some of these plaques were morphologically identical to those observed in humans. This model offers possibilities for fundamental studies of the pathogenesis of senile plaques and supports a possible infectious etiology for many forms of dementia. The presence of senile plaques in brains of nondemented old patients offers proof that such lesions are not exclusively associated with dementia; however, there is a good correlation between the number of senile plaques and the presence of dementia. Thus, it appears reasonable to suggest that they reflect an important aspect of the pathogenesis of dementing disease and constitute a potentially fruitful avenue of investigation.

Neurofibrillary Changes

The etiology of the neurofibrillary alterations and hippocampal pyramidal cell granulovacuolar bodies is likewise unknown. They occur under a variety of pathological conditions ranging from Alzheimer's disease to chronic encephalitis to mongolism. They may also be present in older individuals without evidence of dementia (although such changes are noted in quantitatively smaller concentrations in such patients).[46] Of interest is the fact that they are found only in man and are not observed to occur spontaneously in the dog, cat, rat, monkey, etc. The neurofibrillary tangles are argyrophilic and by electron microscopy they prove to be closely aggregated coarse neurofilaments in a parallel array.[42] Similar changes may be produced experimentally by intracerebral injection of colchicine.[49] Subarachnoid injections of aluminum salt in experimental animals result in a progressive encephalopathy associated with neuronal neurofibrillary tangles.[20] However, these tangles differ both morphologically and histochemically from the neurofibrillary tangles of Alzheimer's disease.[43] Ribosomes are almost entirely absent from the experimental animal tangles in contrast to the human tangle where interspersed ribosomes may account for the mild basophilia. The individual elements which make up the experimental tangle are 100 Å filaments with very narrow lumens; thus they appear somewhat different from the twisted 200 Å tubule with central filament found in the human lesion. Neurons containing neurofibrillary tangles in brain derived from patients with Alzheimer's disease have a very positive basal adenosine triphosphatase stain.[18] No such activity is observed in the neurons with aluminum-induced neurofibrillary tangles. Questions regarding the specificity of neurofibrillary tangles for a given metabolic error or neuronal malfunction, or even their specificity for dementia have not been answered. However, the recent observations of elevated aluminum in brains of patients with Alzheimer's disease[5] provide a possible link between the experimental observations and clinical problems.

Biochemistry of Alzheimer's Disease

The most detailed biochemical investigations of dementia have been reported for Alzheimer's disease. In biopsies of 3 cases of Alzheimer's disease, Suzuki, Katzman, and Korey[40] noted a decrease in total protein and an increase in total lipid in gray matter resulting in a decreased protein-lipid ratio compared to controls. No decreased protein synthesis was noted in microsomes derived from both neurons and glia of brain tissue from cases of Alzheimer's disease.[41] Since microsomes derived selectively from neurons were not studied, the possibility of defective neuronal protein synthesis has not been excluded. These data could also refect neuron cell loss or enhanced proteolysis in either neurons and/or glia.

In Alzheimer's disease, total gangliosides have been noted to be reduced with a chromatographic pattern of the various ganglioside species that is identical in patients with dementia and in controls.[40] Disagreement has been noted with respect to the cerebroside content of tissue of patients with Alzheimer's dementia. Suzuki and associates[40] reported a marked increase in cerebrosides compared to controls; whereas Pope, Hess, and Lewin[30] and Rouser aided by Galli and Kritchevsky,[31, 32] in separate studies, observed a significant decrease. Oxygen uptake, respiratory rate, lactic acid production, and glucose 14C conversion to lipid and amino acid constituents in brain biopsies obtained from patients with Alzheimer's were comparable to controls.[40] Fatty acid elongation in the mitochondrial fraction obtained from biopsies of demented patients did not differ from controls.[51] Nikaido and associates have isolated material with morphological characteristics of senile plaques and their cores from temporal lobe cortex of Alzheimer's patients.[27, 28] This plaque fraction was obtained by sieving the brain followed by fractionation and sucrose density gradients. Chemical studies were limited by the paucity of material. These authors found increased silicon in the isolated cores, in rims of senile plaques, and in Alzheimer neurons containing neurofibrillary tangles.

Several observations have suggested that aluminum may be toxic to the central

158

nervous system. The brain of an aluminum ball-mill worker suffering an encephalopathy with dementia and seizures was found to contain 20 times the normal concentration of aluminum.[25] Aluminum hydroxide applied to cerebral tissue in experimental animals induced epileptogenic foci.[21] Subarachnoid injections of trace amounts of aluminum salts resulted in a progressive encephalopathy.[20] Pathological examination of these animal brains disclosed neurofibrillary degeneration. This latter observation prompted Crapper, Krisman, and Dalton[5] to measure aluminum concentration in brains of Alzheimer patients. While the aluminum in brains of Alzheimer patients approached the level found in experimental animals suffering from toxicity, the experimentally induced neurofibrillary tangles differed both morphologically and histochemically from those of Alzheimer's disease.[18, 43] Whether the aluminum is bound in a toxic or nontoxic form is unclear; the nature of the tissue binding sites of aluminum in both experimental and human diseases is similarly unclear. Although such studies are pertinent only to the neurofibrillary tangles of Alzheimer's disease, the association of aluminum with Alzheimer's disease is sufficiently intriguing to warrant further study.

Iqbal and associates[15] have isolated neurons of hippocampal cortex of patients with Alzheimer's disease and demonstrated twisted tubules in a subfraction of these cells which contains small amounts of rough endoplasmic reticulum and mitochondria. A novel protein band (enriched fraction band or EFB) with an estimated molecular weight of 50,000 was found in sodium dodecyl sulfate gels of this material. The alpha and beta monomers of human brain tubulin have estimated molecular weights of 56,000 and 53,000 daltons respectively. The molecular weight of the major protein band of bovine neurofilament is approximately 51,-000. Since the electrophoretic mobility on sodium dodecyl sulfate gels of the enriched fraction band was very close to that of the major neurofilament protein band, these authors suggested that they may be identical. The reader must be cautioned that estimating molecular weights of proteins using electrophoretic mobility on sodium dodecyl sulfate gels can be hazardous. Furthermore, identity in terms of size does not necessarily imply identity in terms of molecular species. Thus, it is unclear whether the enriched fraction band represents a microtubular or neurofilament protein or a novel protein. Although it does not appear to be a postmortem artifact, the enriched fraction band could represent proteolytic modification of a normal cellular component. The enriched fraction band probably represents a subunit of the twisted tubule, but evidence supporting this contention is circumstantial. Proof of this hypothesis awaits cytological localization of the enriched fraction band and further biochemical characterization.

Biochemistry of Huntington's Chorea

Biochemical investigations of genetic diseases such as Huntington's chorea frequently focus on elucidating an enzymatic deficiency which might constitute the primary metabolic defect. Conversely, such alterations in enzymatic activity may simply reflect death of a particular neuronal population containing this enzyme. This problem is particularly relevant to biochemical investigations of Huntington's disease.

Recent investigations have demonstrated decreased amounts of gamma aminobutyric acid (GABA) in basal ganglia of patients with Huntington's chorea.[29] Subsequent investigations of basal ganglia in such patients disclosed decreased amounts of glutamic acid decarboxylase, the rate-limiting enzyme in gamma ami-

159

nobutyric acid synthesis.[4, 24, 39] Several lines of evidence suggest that this decreased enzymatic activity is not the primary metabolic defect in the disease. First, both gamma aminobutyric acid and glutamic acid decarboxylase activity were normal in the frontal cortex yet decreased in the basal ganglia.[4, 24, 29, 39] Since these patients displayed profound dementia as well as choreiform movements, it is unlikely that the biochemical manifestation of the primary metabolic defect would be limited to the basal ganglia. Second, Stahl and Swanson found normal levels of gamma aminobutyric acid and glutamic acid decarboxylase in the basal ganglia in an early and well documented case of Huntington's chorea.[39] Third, imidazole-4-acetic acid, a GABA-mimetic agent that is absorbed from the gut and passes the blood-brain barrier of rodents, when administered to patients with Huntington's disease had no therapeutic benefit on motor function.[34] Fourth, alterations of dopamine content, choline acetyl transferase activity, and even succinic dehydrogenase have been noted in basal ganglia in Huntington's disease.[1, 3, 39] These observations suggest that enzymatic alterations are not limited to glutamic acid decarboxylase activity or even to enzymes responsible for neurotransmitter synthesis, and that therefore deficiency of glutamic acid decarboxylase activity is not the primary metabolic defect. The alterations in neurotransmitter content and enzymatic activity observed may well reflect death of a particular population of neurons in Huntington's chorea.

Several other approaches have been employed in biochemical investigations of Huntington's disease. Stahl and Swanson found a marked increase of a high molecular weight protein (approximately 230,000 daltons) in the supernatant of homogenates of corpus striatum in three brains from patients with Hungtington's disease.[39] This same protein band was present in smaller amounts in controls and individuals with early Huntington's disease. Its significance is unclear, but it may simply reflect the gliotic response of end-stage disease. Iqbal and coworkers[14] described large amounts of 3 low molecular weight proteins in a microsomal fraction of neuronal soma derived from the cerebral cortex of patients with Huntington's disease. Again, smaller amounts were observed in normal and disease controls. The authors suggested that these proteins might be histones. Identification of these proteins as histones and an understanding of their potential significance has not yet been achieved. Other recent observations have shown that cultured skin fibroblasts from patients with Huntington's disease grew to a significantly higher maximal density than those of controls.[9] This could indicate a genetically determined alteration in cell surface or a metabolic difference in Huntington's disease. In either case, the alteration would not be restricted to the central nervous system and might encourage a strategy of biochemical investigations using easily accessible tissues outside the central nervous system.

Potential Role of the Synapse in Dementia

Sampling of the biochemical constituents of the entire biopsy specimen necessarily excludes specific analysis of neuronal, glial, or synaptic biochemistry. Therefore, it is possible that particular components of the nervous system, such as the synaptic junction, may be the primary but as yet undetected site of the defect in dementia. It has been generally assumed that the synapse plays a secondary role and degenerates in a nonspecific manner following lesions of the perikaryon. Bignami and Forno,[2] however, found morphological evidence of abnormal synapses in a cortical biopsy from a patient with Creutzfeldt-Jakob disease. An electron

160

microscopic study of this material showed the cavities of status spongiosus to be formed by clusters of the distended cell processes, some of which could be identified as preterminal axons and presynaptic endings. Alterations consisting of enlargement of the presynaptic terminal, reduction of the number of synaptic vesicles, and accumulation of fibrillar and vesicular material have been observed in biopsies of patients with Alzheimer's disease.[11] An ultrastructural study of the aging human cortex demonstrated a variety of alterations, the intensity of which appeared to be more a function of the amount of "senility" manifested by the patient than of his calendar age.[33] The sequence of histopathological changes involved: increased swelling and lumpiness in outline of the cell body and proximal dendrites; progressive loss of horizontally oriented dendrite systems, especially the basilar shaft; and an eventual loss of apical shaft with cell death. These findings are of particular interest since horizontal dendrites appear to receive synaptic terminals from intracortically derived fiber systems. These synaptic abnormalities might well cause disturbances in either transmitter output or response of postsynaptic membranes, either of which might affect intercellular communication. Although these studies are not conclusive, they suggest the possibility that synaptic function represents a rate-limiting process in neuronal interaction and that impairment in any facet of such function may have widespread effects upon interneuronal interaction. Clearly any pathological process that prevented interneuronal communication would resemble a process that diffusely destroyed neurons.

CEREBRAL BLOOD FLOW IN DEMENTIA

The first critical question to be raised is whether vascular disease can give rise to dementia. Recent studies attempt to distinguish the clinical correlates of different pathological substrates of dementia.[12] Utilizing features of a clinical profile including acute onset, focal neurological signs, relative preservation of personality, and profound pseudobulbar signs, the clinical diagnosis of multi-infarct dementia has been established. The pathological substrate of this group is atherosclerotic vascular disease with multiple small infarcts including a lacunar state. In contrast, an insidious onset, lack of focal neurological signs, lack of pseudobulbar signs, and the presence of markedly impaired intellectual function constitute the clinical profile of primary degenerative dementia. The pathological correlate of this group is neuronal loss with large numbers of senile plaques, neurofibrillary tangles, and granulovascuolar degeneration. Vascular disease appears to be responsible for the dementia in the multi-infarct dementia group. Whether or not vascular disease plays an important pathogenetic role in patients in the latter group with Alzheimer's dementia is unclear. Electron microscopic studies have revealed abnormalities of the brain capillaries in patients with Alzheimer's disease, but the significance of these findings is unclear.[26]

Another central issue is whether chronic tissue anoxia, independent of actual tissue infarction, can cause dementia. Sokoloff and coworkers[35] found normal cerebral blood flow and oxygen consumption in elderly patients who were free of both dementia and atherosclerotic vascular disease. Their patients with dementia had significantly decreased cerebral blood flow, decreased oxygen consumption, and decreased cerebral venous oxygen partial pressure. The most intriguing finding was that non-demented elderly patients with atherosclerotic vascular disease had decreased blood flow and decreased cerebral venous oxygen partial pressure but normal oxygen consumption. These data prompted Sokoloff and coworkers to suggest that decreases in cerebral blood flow and oxygen consumption are not consequences of chronological aging per se but rather of atherosclerosis. They proposed that the atherosclerosis first caused a relative cerebral circulatory insufficiency and hypoxia. Ultimately, after a protracted period of insufficiency and hypoxia, cerebral tissue damage ensued with a reduction in the cerebral metabolic rate. An alternative viewpoint has been presented by Lassen and his colleagues[22] who also found decreased cerebral blood flow and reduced oxygen uptake in demented patients. They argued, however, that the reduced oxygen uptake could be explained simply by cortical atrophy and endogenous decline in neuronal metabolism. The decreased blood flow would thus represent an intrinsic adjustment of the circulation to the lesser metabolic demands of the tissue.

Recently, Hachinski and associates[12] studied cerebral blood flow in patients with a relatively moderate degree of dementia, in contrast to earlier studies in which the manifestations of dementia were quite severe. These investigators also differentiated multi-infarct dementia and primary degenerative dementia groups on clinical grounds. Cerebral blood flow was normal in the primary degenerative group but was decreased in the multi-infarct group. Hachinski and associates suggested that the blood flow was adequate for the metabolic needs of the brain in patients with primary degenerative dementia but was inadequate for the metabolic needs of patients with multi-infarct dementia. Thus impaired blood flow leading to chronic anoxia could be an important pathogenetic mechanism in multi-infarct dementia. This suggestion assumed the metabolic needs of the brains of the two groups were comparable. Since evidence to support this assumption is lacking, the decreased blood flow in the multi-infarct dementia group does not necessarily imply a pathogenetic role for the decreased flow. Conversely, the finding of normal flow in the primary degenerative group fails to exclude a role for decreased blood flow in the pathogenesis of this disorder. It is important to note that the method of cerebral blood flow measurement employed does not assess the microcirculation. Since patients with Alzheimer's disease have demonstrable abnormalities of their brain capillaries,[26] it is entirely possible that their microcirculation is disturbed. In summary, it is unclear whether chronic tissue anoxia, independent of actual tissue infarction, can cause dementia, and it appears that this issue is not likely to be resolved with present techniques of cerebral blood flow measurement.

BIOCHEMISTRY OF LEARNING AND MEMORY

The manner by which the brain acquires and stores information has long fascinated neuroscientists. Since anatomical correlates of these processes are almost nonexistent and almost impossible to obtain, the major scientific thrust has taken biochemical approaches. The most popular hypothesis has been that learning and memory are accompanied by specific neurochemical events. The nature, site, and sequence of these events, particularly the synthesis of ribonucleic acid and protein, have been the subject of most of these studies. None of the studies of the past 5 years has contributed to an understanding of learning and memory in man. We will attempt to provide some insight into the general problems in this area and the specific problems with the various approaches employed.

A basic problem that pervades all experimental approaches to this area is the comparison of an animal that has learned a task with one that has not. The major difficulty in making this seemingly simple comparison lies in the fact that any training experience exposes the animal to stressful situations such as flashing

162

lights, shock, handling, exercise, and frustration. Controlling these variables is particularly difficult because many of them appear to have effects on brain biochemistry similar to those believed to occur when an animal learns. Indeed many investigators believe that it may be impossible to design appropriate controls for these variables. A second difficulty is the lack of an accurate definition of the term "learning." To define learning simply as a modification of behavior by experience is vague and may well also include behavioral changes that are primarily developmental. Furthermore, there may be different types of learning each of which may initiate different biochemical events in the nervous system.[48]

Another major problem that pervades all approaches to brain biochemistry is the cellular heterogeneity of the brain. Thus, the question is raised whether the observed alterations, such as in ribonucleic acid or protein synthesis, are occurring in the critical population of neurons or astrocytes or oligodendrocytes, etc. Finally, analyses of alterations in ribonucleic acid turnover, protein synthesis, or lipid constituents tell us little about subcellular changes taking place. A critical element may be the tight coupling of membrane function with intracellular metabolism or the interaction of many exquisitely regulated neurons. These are important problems in any attempt to understand the biochemical alterations of learning and memory.

One of the most popular approaches has been to inject a radioactive labeled amino acid or nucleotide precursor into an experimental animal. The incorporation of this labeled precursor into protein or ribonucleic acid has been assessed in association with a particular paradigm purportedly reflecting learning or memory. The ability of the particular precursor to cross the blood-brain barrier is an important consideration. Beyond this, it is very difficult to be certain that the labeled precursor is distributed evenly to all the metabolic compartments of the cells and throughout the tissue of the brain. If increased amounts of the precursor are observed in protein or ribonucleic acid, it is important to determine whether this represents increased synthesis or decreased degradation. Increased blood flow to the particular area involved may simply have provided increased accessibility of the precursor to these cells, and the observed alterations may reflect only the altered blood flow and turnover of the precursor pools. An additional problem is the difficulty of pinpointing the particular cells responsible for these alterations.

Another approach has been to assess the amounts of a particular molecular species present in association with learning or memory. For example, Hyden and his associates[13] have found particularly large increases in S 100 protein in the hippocampus after training. These investigators reasoned that if S 100 were necessary for memory storage, injections of an antiserum for S 100 should retard or inhibit the storage process. The antiserum did have an inhibiting effect on learning; however, any substance that affected brain biochemistry could impair a behavior as complex as learning. A protein which is simply necessary for learning may not be at all related to the actual storage process. Many investigators now believe that learning cannot proceed without stress, sensory stimulation, or arousal, and it may not be possible to separate the biochemical substrate of learning and memory from these other phenomena.

Other investigators have suggested that specific macromolecules might be synthesized in association with each memory. Ungar and his colleagues[47] trained rats to avoid the dark compartment of a two-chambered box and injected extracts of the trained rat brain into untrained rats. They isolated and synthesized a peptide, called scotophobin, which when injected into untrained rats improved their performance. Few laboratories have been able to replicate this memory transfer by the injection of scotophobin. Although other laboratories have reported that scotophobin isolated from rat brain improved dark avoidance learning in mice and goldfish, doubt persists as to whether this peptide actually transmitted the stored memory for dark avoidance or whether it simply improved performance by raising the arousal levels of the untrained animals.[38] Indeed, part of the scotophobin chain resembles adrenocorticotrophic hormone which improves learning performance on many tasks and has specific behavioral effects when injected intracerebrally. The major problem is not whether scotophobin can produce behavioral effects, but whether the behavior it induces is task-specific and whether it provides any greater understanding of animal behavior than administering any neurotransmitter such as norepinephrine or a possible neuronal cell modulator such as adrenocorticotrophic hormone.

Another popular approach has involved the use of drugs which inhibit ribonucleic acid or protein synthesis. These studies attempt to correlate impaired ribonucleic acid or protein synthesis with impaired learning or memory. The dose, route of administration, absorption, half-life, and ability of the drug employed to cross the blood-brain barrier are critical variables in these studies as are the duration of the training tasks and the timing of the injection in relation to the training. Finally, most of these drugs have diverse effects apart from protein or ribonucleic acid synthesis inhibition. Squire and his colleagues[36, 37] sought to circumvent this problem by employing a number of drugs, all of which inhibit the same metabolic pathway but in different ways. These drugs have few or at least nonoverlapping side effects. These studies have generally supported the proposed hypothesis that learning initiates the formation of new ribonucleic acid and protein synthesis.

Despite a large number of recent studies supporting this theory, very few scientists are willing to state unequivocally that learning initiates new ribonucleic acid or protein synthesis. New approaches are necessary to ascertain the manner in which the brain acquires and stores information. Experiments in which lesions are made in various regions of the brain after training may help identify specific areas that are necessary for memory formation. Basic information linking intracellular metabolic processes with surface membrane behavior and interaction with other cells is a critical link to further our understanding of such complex processes as learning and memory. Much basic information regarding biochemical, physiological, and morphological parameters of cell function is still necessary before we can begin to unravel this complex problem.

TREATMENT OF DEMENTIA

Present dementia therapy is not based either upon a sound theoretical framework or upon well documented biochemical defects. Considerable attention has recently been focused on the possible value of hyperbaric oxygenation as a treatment for dementia in the elderly. Since some authors suspect that anoxia may play a role in both multi-infarct and primary degenerative dementia, this therapy is particularly intriguing. Jacobs and her associates[17] initially reported that patients with chronic organic brain syndrome showed improved cognitive function following 15 days of intermittent exposure to high pressure oxygen, that is 100 percent oxygen at 2.5 atmospheres for 90 minutes twice daily. Of the patients in their treatment group 13 improved, whereas 5 control patients showed no change in intellectual function. Improvement was observed in the latter group with subsequent hyperbaric treatment. Later investigations by these workers[16] suggested that the beneficial effects of such treatment might persist for 7 to 10 days. Similar therapeutic results in age-related dementia have been reported by other investigators[6] following hyperbaric oxygenation, but the use of control subjects was notably lacking or the treatment was combined with other types of therapy. In contrast, Goldfarb and colleagues[10] found no significant changes in cognitive functions following hyperbaric oxygenation in elderly patients with organic brain syndrome. Thompson and coworkers[45] treated 21 elderly patients with dementia due to both cerebrovascular disease and presumed cortical atrophy related to degenerative disease. This study was performed double blind, and the patients received treatment identical to that of Jacobs' study. Careful monitoring of clinical performance, a variety of psychological tests, electroencephalogram, and cerebral blood flow failed to disclose any effect of hyperbaric oxygenation. It is difficult to reconcile the findings of Goldfarb and coworkers[10] and Thompson and associates[45] with those of Jacobs and her coworkers. The treatment procedures in all 3 studies were essentially the same. Some of the behavioral measures were identical, and personal communication among the 3 investigators indicated that the time and conditions of testing were similar. The patients treated by Jacobs and coworkers[16] may have been less demented than those of the subsequent studies. However, we must conclude that hyperbaric oxygenation does not appear to be of predictable therapeutic benefit to the cognitive performance of demented patients.

A variety of pharmacological agents appears to enhance learning and memory in experimental animals. Amphetamines, strychnine, and physostigmine are among the most intensively studied agents. Whether these agents influence learning and memory by their known pharmacological effect or by some unknown mechanism is unclear. It is possible that their effects are simply due to nonspecific effects on brain systems involved in arousal. A variety of similar agents has been employed in patients with dementia, none of which has had any demonstrable therapeutic benefit. Two compounds which presumably influenced animal behavior (tricyahoaminopropane [TCAP] and magnesium pemoline) are no longer under active investigation. The use of these compounds was based on their enhancement of nucleic acid metabolism, and at best they seem to have provided stimulant effects on performance. Nevertheless, these results are important because they suggest that despite tissue degeneration, the remaining viable neurons may possibly be made to perform in a more efficient manner. It is not clear whether the use of such stimulants may make excessive cellular energy demands and thereby compromise neuronal longevity.

CONCLUSIONS

Relatively little progress has been made in the past 5 years toward elucidating the biochemical basis of dementia. Our failure to understand the pertinent disease mechanisms is not surprising when one considers our naivete regarding biochemical mechanisms of normal intellectual function and behavior.

The major factor limiting all such investigations is the infinite complexity of the brain. Whether one seeks to study dementia as a synaptic, neuronal, or glial disease, the functional and structural heterogeneity of the brain renders such investigations exceedingly difficult. For example, if one assumes that dementia is a synaptic disease, a number of serious problems limit the biochemical approaches. There may be thousands of unique neurons in the mammalian nervous system, and identification and isolation of the synapses of the critical population(s) in pure form free of cellular or subcellular contaminants are presently impossible. The central nervous system also contains large numbers of neurotransmitters. While the biogenic amines are the most easily measured and thus the most extensively studied, they probably account for only a small percentage of central neurotransmitters. Identification of the important neurotransmitters of the afflicted neuronal population, understanding of the mechanisms underlying their synthesis, release, and interaction with the post-synaptic membrane receptor, and coupling of surface membrane events with intracellular metabolic processes are necessary before a biochemical approach to dementia as a synaptic disease will be fruitful.

Indeed, it appears that much basic information of developmental and molecular neurobiology is needed before we will understand the biochemical mechanisms underlying normal intellectual function and dementia. An understanding of the mechanisms of neuronal recognition and synapse formation is likely to be particularly helpful in this regard. We are just now gaining initial insights into the mechanisms of cell adhesion and aggregation and the extracellular factors which promote such interactions. The relationships of these initial stages of cell recognition to the more differentiated process of synapse formation is presently unresolved. The utilization of simple model systems will likely provide an understanding of important basic mechanisms which can in turn be applied to the complex interactions of the mammalian nervous system.

REFERENCES

1. BARBEAU, A.: *Recent progress: Progress in understanding Huntington's chorea.* Can. J. Neurol. Sci. 2:81, 1975.
2. BIGNAMI, A., AND FORNO, L.: *Status spongiosus in Jakob-Creutzfeldt disease. Electron microscopic study of a cortical biopsy.* Brain 93:89, 1970.
3. BIRD, E., AND IVERSEN, L.: *Huntington's chorea. Post-mortem measurement of glutamic acid decarboxylase, choline acetyl transferase, and dopamine in basal ganglia.* Brain 97:457, 1974.
4. BIRD, E.; MACKAY, A.; RAYNER, C., AND IVERSEN, L.: *Reduced glutamic acid decarboxylase activity of post-mortem brain in Huntington's chorea.* Lancet 1:1090, 1973.
5. CRAPPER, D. R.; KIRSHNAN, S.S.; AND DALTON, A. J.: *Brain aluminum distribution in Alzheimer's disease and experimental neurofibrillary degeneration.* Science 180:511, 1973.
6. EDWARDS, A., AND HART, G.: *Hyperbaric oxygenation and the cognitive functioning of the aged.* J. Am. Geriat. Soc. 22:376, 1974.
7. FRIEDE, R. L.: *Enzyme histochemical studies of senile plaques.* J. Neuropathol. Exp. Neurol. 24: 477, 1965.
8. FRIEDE, R. L., AND MAGEE, K. R.: *Alzheimer's disease. Presentation of a case with pathologic and enzymatic histochemical observations.* Neurology (Minneap.) 12:213, 1962.
9. GOETZ, I.; ROBERTS, E.; AND COMINGS, D.: *Fibroblasts in Huntington's disease.* New Engl. J. Med. 293:1225, 1975.
10. GOLDFARB, A.; HOCHSTADT, N.; JACOBSON, J.; AND WEINSTEIN, E.: *Hyperbaric oxygen treatment of organic mental syndrome in aged persons.* J. Gerontal. 27:212, 1972.
11. GONATAS, N. K.; ANDERSON, W.; AND EVANGELISTA, I.: *The contribution of altered synapses in the senile plaque: An electron microscopic study in Alzheimer's dementia.* J. Neuropathol. Exp. Neurol. 26:25, 1967.
12. HACHINSKI, V.; ILIFF, L.; ZILHKA, E.; DUBOULAY, G.; McALLISTER, V.; MARSHALL, J.; RUSSELL, R.; AND SYMAN, L.: *Cerebral blood flow in dementia.* Arch. Neurol. 32:632, 1975.
13. HYDEN, H., AND LANGE, P.: *S100 brain protein:correlation with behavior.* Proc. Natl. Acad. Sci. USA 67:1959, 1970.
14. IQBAL, K.; TELLEZ-NAGEL, I.; AND GRUNDKE-IQBAL, I.: *Protein abnormalities in Huntington's chorea.* Brain Res. 76:178, 1974.

15. IQBAL, K.; WISNIEWSKI, M.; SHELANSKI, M.; BROSTOFF, S.; LIWNICZ, B.; AND TERRY, R.; *Protein changes in senile dementia.* Brain Res. 77:337, 1974.
16. JACOBS, E.; ALVIS, H.; AND SMALL, S.: *Hyperoxygenation: A central nervous system activator?* J. Geriatric Psychiatry 5:107, 1972.
17. JACOBS, E.; WINTER, P.; ALVIS, H.; AND SMALL, S.: *Hyperoxygenation effects on congitive functioning in the aged.* New Engl. J. Med. 281:753, 1969.
18. JOHNSON, A. B.; AND BLUM, N. R.: *Nucleoside phosphatase activities associated with the tangles and plaques of Alzheimer's disease: A histochemical study of natural and experimental neurofibrillary tangles.* J. Neuropathol. Exp. Neurol. 29:463, 1970.
19. KATZMAN, R., AND SUZUKI, K.: *A search for a chemical correlate of amyloid in senile plaques of Alzheimer's disease.* Trans. Am. Neurol. Assoc. 89:17, 1964.
20. KLATZO, I.; WISNIEWSKI, H.; AND STREICHER, E.: *Experimental production of neurofibrillary degeneration.* J. Neuropathol. Exp. Neurol. 24:187, 1965.
21. KOPELOFF, L.; BARRERA, S.; AND KOPELOFF, N.: *Recurrent convulsive seizures in animals produced by immunologic and chemical means.* Am. J. Psychiatry 98:881, 1942.
22. LASSEN, N. A.; FEINBERG, I.; AND LANE, M. H.: *Bilateral studies of cerebral oxygen uptake in young and aged normal subjects and in patients with organic dementia.* J. Clin. Invest. 39:.491, 1960.
23. LUSE, S. A.; AND SMITH, K. R.: *The ultrastructure of senile plaques.* Am. J. Pathol. 44:553, 1964.
24. McGEER, P.; McGEER, E.; AND FIBIGER, H.: *Choline acetylase and glutamic acid decarboxylase in Huntington's chorea.* Neurology (Minneap.) 23:912, 1973.
25. McLAUGHLIN, A.; KAZAUTZIS, G.; KING, E.; TEARE, D.; PORTER, R.; AND OWEN, R.: *Pulmonary fibrosis and encephalopathy associated with the inhalation of aluminum dust.* Br. J. Ind. Med. 19:253, 1962.
26. MIYAKAWA, T.; SUMIYOSHI, S.; MURAYAMA, E.; AND DESHIMARU, M.: *Ultrastructure of capillary plaque-like degeneration in senile dementia. Mechanism of amyloid production.* Acta Neuropathol. (Berl.) 29:229, 1974.
27. NIKAIDO, T.; AUSTIN, J.; RINEHART, R..; TRUEB, L.; HUTCHINSON, J.; STUKENBROK, H.; AND MILES, B.: *Studies in aging of the brain.* Arch. Neurol. 25:198, 1971.
28. NIKAIDO, T.; AUSTIN, J.; TRUEB, L.; AND RINEHART, R.: *Studies in aging of the brain. II. Microchemical analyses of the nervous system in Alzheimer patients.* Arch. Neurol. 27:549, 1972.
29. PERRY, T.; HANSEN, S.; AND KLOSTER, M.: *Huntington's chorea. Deficiency of gamma-amino butyric acid in brain.* New Engl. J. Med. 288: 337, 1973.
30. POPE, A.; HESS, H.; AND LEWIN, E.: *Microchemical pathology of the cerebral cortex in presenile dementias.* Trans. Am. Neurol. Assoc. 89:15, 1964.
31. ROUSER, G.: *Speculations on the nature of the metabolic defects in Tay-Sachs, Nieman-Pick, Gaucher's and Alzheimer's disease, and metachromatic leukodystrophy.* J. Am. Oil Chem. Soc. 42:412, 1965.
32. ROUSER, G.; GALLI, C.; AND KRITCHEVSKY, G.: *Lipid class composition of normal human brain and variations in metachromatic leukodystrophy, Tay-Sachs, Nieman-Pick, chronic Gaucher's and Alzheimer's disease.* J. Am. Oil Chem. Soc. 42:404, 1965.
33. SCHEIBEL, M.; LINDSAY, R.; TOMIYASU, V.; AND SCHEIBEL, A.: *Progressive dendritic changes in aging human cortex.* Exp. Neurol. 47:392, 1975.
34. SHOULSON, I.; CHASE, T.; ROBERTS, E.; AND VAN BALGOODY, J.: *Huntington's disease: treatment with imidazole-4-acetic acid.* New. Engl. J. Med. 288:337, 1973.
35. SOKOLOFF, L.: *Cerebral circulatory and metabolic changes associated with aging.* Res. Publ. Assoc. Res. Nerv. Ment. Dis. 41:237, 1961.
36. SQUIRE, L., AND BARONDES, S.: *Memory impairment during prolonged training in mice given inhibitors of cerebral protein synthesis.* Brain Res. 56:215, 1973.
37. SQUIRE, L.; AND DAVIS, H.: *Cerebral protein synthesis inhibition and discrimination training.* Behav. Biol. 13:49, 1975.
38. STEWART, W.: *Comments on the chemistry of scotophobin.* Nature 238:202, 1972.
39. STAHL, W., AND SWANSON, P.: *Biochemical abnormalities in Huntington's chorea brains.* Neurology (Minneap.) 24:813, 1974.
40. SUZUKI, K.; KATZMAN, R.; AND KOREY, S. R.: *Chemical studies on Alzheimer's disease.* J. Neuropathol. Exp. Neurol. 24:211, 1965.

167

41. SUZUKI, K.; KOREY, S. R.; AND TERRY, R. D.: *Studies on protein synthesis in brain microsomal system.* J. Neurochem. 11:403, 1964.

42. TERRY, R. D.: *The fine structure of neurofibrillary tangles in Alzheimer's disease.* J. Neuropathal. Exp. Neurol. 22:629, 1963.

43. TERRY, R. D.: Electron microscopic studies of Alzheimer's disease and of experimental neuro-fibrillary tangles, in Bailey, O., and Smith, D. (eds.): *The Central Nervous System.* The Williams & Wilkins Co., Baltimore, 1968.

44. TERRY, R. D.; GONATAS, N. K.; AND WEISS, M.: *Ultrastructural studies in Alzheimer's presenile dementia.* Am. J. Pathol. 44:269, 1964.

45. THOMPSON, L.; DAVIS, G.; OBRIST, W.; AND HEYMAN, A.: *Effects of hyperbaric oxygen on behavorial and physiological measures in elderly demented patients.* J. Gerontol. 31:23, 1976.

46. TOMLINSON, B. E.; BLESSED, G., AND ROTH, M.: *Observations on the brain of nondemented old people.* J. Neurol. Sci. 7:331, 1968.

47. UNGAR, G.; DESIDERIO, D.; AND PARR, W.: *Isolation, identification, and synthesis of a specific-behavior-inducing brain peptide.* Nature (Lond.) 238:198, 1972.

48. WALLACE, P.: *Neurochemistry: Unraveling the mechanism of memory.* Science 190:1076, 1975.

49. WISNIEWSKI, H.; AND TERRY, R. D.: *Further studies on experimental neurofibrillary tangles.* J. Neuropathol. Exp. Neurol. 27:149, 1968.

50. WISNIEWSKI, H.; BRUCE, M.; AND FRASER, H.: *Infectious etiology of neuritic (senile) plaques in mice.* Science 190:1108, 1975.

51. YATSU, F.; MOSS, S.; CONNOLLY, E.; AND NELSON, L: *Elongation of fatty acids in human brain tissue.* J. Neurochem. 20:621, 1973.

168

CHAPTER 8

The Neurological Examination in Dementia

George W. Paulson, M.D.

Special features characterize the neurological examination of patients with dementia. This chapter hypothesizes that these special features relate primarily to the diffuse brain disorder that underlies dementia rather than to localized cerebral pathology. Signs that do not specify focal disease and do not reflect systemic lesions will be emphasized; thus signs typifying diffuse cerebral dysfunction will be stressed. This approach does not imply that the neurological examination in patients who are demented is peculiar or difficult but rather intends to emphasize signs commonly found but often overlooked in demented individuals. In patients with dementia, sensitivity to environmental change is often diminished, and the rapidity and appropriateness of both specific and overall responses may be jeopardized. It is primarily the overall or total responses that are reviewed here. This chapter seeks to answer two questions: In the patient whose history suggests but does not confirm a diagnosis of dementia, are there observations which might be particularly valuable in establishing the presence of diffuse brain disease? In the patient known to be demented, which neurological changes point toward diffuse rather than focal brain disease?

NEUROLOGICAL EXAMINATION OF THE AGED[17, 32, 39, 57]

Despite youthful testimony to the contrary, advanced age is not inevitably coexistent with dementia. Many peculiarities of the nervous system of the elderly do not indicate loss of higher integrative function, although it is often difficult to separate the "normal" or common findings in aged patients from those findings that suggest disease. It is, of course, conceivable that many of the aspects of aging, even the calm "wisdom of age," are secondary to insidious loss of neuronal function. The fact that certain changes seem inevitable, if one lives long enough, does not imply disease. Most observers have noted numerous degenerative changes common to people of advancing years regardless of whether the observer interprets aging as a potentially avoidable disease or a regrettable but entirely normal state. Loss of tissue elasticity, arthritic changes of "wear and tear," chronic pain, changes in nutrition, diminution of total blood flow, and frank insufficiency of both large and small blood vessels, as well as other non-neurological phenomena—all can influence the neurological examination. In addition, the examiner must contend with both his own and the patient's psychological handicaps while evaluating the aged person. A feeble octogenarian with decreased hearing, slow motor responses, and a petulant unwillingness to be disturbed is not the ideal subject for extensive tests. The examination may be lengthened by the patient's apathy or weakness, by his decreased powers of memory, or by his persistent rumination on past events, significant to the patient but trivial to the physician. A harried physician, late to his rounds, conscious of his vigor, and jealously guarding his time in the interests of efficiency may not be the right one to perform the examination. Therefore, it is fortunate that many of the significant neurological manifestations of aging can be seen by purposeful observation alone. Awareness of these easily observable characteristics of age allows us to adopt a proper standard for normality while performing a reasonably complete neurological examination on an individual who happens to be aged. As in pediatric neurology, the best testing may consist of an imaginative survey with later repetitions rather than an obsessively complete examination performed at one exhaustive sitting.

When an aged patient is first seen, it is commonly noted that gait is slow and that arm swing, head turning, and other associated movements are less conspicuous than in younger individuals. Moderate generalized stiffness, secondary to changes in joints and ligaments, and muscular hypertonicity are often observed. Fatigue, anxiety, or an arduous examination may exaggerate a mild, underlying tremor. The patient's posture may be bent, and he may relate his complaint in a quavering high pitched voice that fatigues early in the interview. These extrapyramidal phenomena of aging are so easily recognized that actors tend to imitate parkinsonism when they wish to depict an old person.

Examination of the eyes of an aged person reveals a decreased ability or unwillingness to converge, and upward gaze may be limited. Constricted pupils are the rule, complicating evaluation of the light reflex as well as of the fundus. It has been suggested that it is the physician, not the patient's pupil, that is sluggish in recording "sluggish pupils," but the aged pupil does react less briskly to light. Funduscopic examination reveals a waxy and indistinct disc, the choroidal vessels are more visible, and a diffuse granular pigmentation may be observed.[37, 42] Elderly patients lose as much as 50 percent of their sensitivity to both taste and smell. Hearing ability, particularly of high pitched sounds and background noise, is reduced. The lack of perception of background sound often combined with a decrease in visual perception must potentiate the sense of isolation that often accompanies aging. In an effort to maintain orientation despite the attrition of years, some geriatric services utilize surprisingly loud background music. Tinnitus and vertigo may occur and be accentuated by positional changes. Gag reflex is reduced, and this plus a decrease in the cough reflex leads to an accumulation of secretions in the bronchial tree and probably to death in many aged patients. In addition to mildly increased muscle tone and inconstant action tremors that are reminiscent of benign familial tremor, some patients also manifest a generalized weakness of the muscles. Frank weakness is usually much less apparent than an overall decrease in quick coordinative functions. Many a grandson has been amazed to discover the residual strength of his old grandfather; on the other hand, many a grandfather has been discomfited by the quick movements, talk, or driving of the grandson. Muscular wasting, particularly in the calves and interossei, may be pronounced in the very old, and a few scattered fasciculations in the calves, not rare at any age, are often present.

The results of a carefully performed sensory examination can be normal, but decreased vibratory sensation at the ankles is almost the rule. Even though they

170

are difficult to measure quantiatively, pain and touch sensitivity are also some-what reduced in many aged patients. The ankle jerks are often absent though re-flexes in the upper extremities may be more brisk than at a younger age. Abdom-inal reflexes,[38] possibly because of a pendulous abdomen and lax muscles, may be hard to elicit.[27] A pathological plantar response should not be observed, but the plantar response is often difficult to confirm in this age group, perhaps partially as a result of insensitivity of the sole and stiffness of the joints.

Numerous neurophysiological changes occur in normal aging, some of which are reflected in the clinical observation of the aging patient. Studies of ocular func-tion have included measurement of latency of blinking, electroretinography, and electro-oculography. Electroencephalographers have written extensively on EEG changes, and the changes in evoked cerebral responses in late life have been studied. Audiologic, olfactory, and gustatory function in the aged have been studied; none improve with advanced age. Peripheral nerves have been assessed by use of conduction time, evaluation of the H-reflex, and tests of peripheral end organ sensitivity. Reflex responses and habituation do change with age,[27, 38] par-ticularly in the length of time required for transmission of some of the responses with longer reflex arcs. The threshold for ischemic pain is measurably different as is the extent of nerve damage caused by ischemia.

Detailed review of these neurophysiological aspects of aging is not appropriate here, but generalization is possible. Advanced age is associated with decreased rapidity of transmission, raised threshold, and relative insensitivity in almost all the phenomena mentioned above. The fatigability of response to stimulation is increased and the latency of responses prolonged as aging advances. Amplitude of response tends to diminish slightly in advanced years, and responses may be more fragmentary. Responses to drugs are modified, even distorted, and a paradoxical response to excitants or sedatives is well recognized as a geriatric hazard. Matura-tion from childhood to adulthood tends to stabilize neurophysiological respon-ses, at a cost of the flexibility and plasticity of childhood. The transition to senility does not restore plasticity or flexibility, however, but instead is associated with a loss of neurophysiological stability and progressively lessened rapidity of re-sponse.

GAIT AND POSTURE IN DEMENTIA

Even the most superficial tour of institutions for chronically demented patients reveals that such individuals, young and old, walk in a clumsy, graceless fashion. Rocking movements of the trunk and neck, inappropriate associated gestures of the hands or similar "stereotypies," and a "slewfooted" and clumsy placement of the feet are particularly noticeable in younger demented patients. Myoclonic jerks or facial grimaces are characteristic of some of the progressive degenerative dis-eases, and athetoid posturing and tremors are seen with chronic or progressive diseases involving the basal ganglia.

Older patients, both demented ones and those with normal intelligence, often have an unsteady gait that is marked by tremor of the hands and limbs. There is some tendency toward an overall flexion and though a rigorously upright posture is not typical of the average noncompulsive person, a military stance certainly does not appear in late life except in association with muscle spasm or low back pain. Associated movements of the hands during walking have not been specifical-ly studied in elderly or demented patients, although in children with hemiplegia or with chronic diffuse brain damage the presence of associational patterns is more prominent than in normal children of the same age.[1] I have the impression that along with the other extrapyramidal features of aging there is also a loss of involuntary associated movements.

Yakovlev,[63] perhaps the most philosophical of writers in this area, has discussed the tendency toward progressive changes in stance in the very aged as well as in demented patients. Except in its advanced stages, he did not find such loss of postural control to correlate well with dementia. He has conceptualized the following 3 stages of progressive change in station and posture:

1. *The flexion attitude,* as mentioned, is typical of the aging patient in that he tends to sit or stand in a bent position with the neck slouched forward and hands cupped while the thumb is held in opposition to the forefinger. Such flexion tendencies are exaggerated when the patient walks, and he may tend to tumble forward in a heap if he is not warned as he starts rapidly. If left to his own devices, spontaneous ambulation is infrequent and may be preceded by a "to-and-fro" inefficient foot shuffle. This is similar to the "slipping clutch" gait often attributed to arteriosclerotic brain damage. Some patients are incoordinated and ataxic of gait, and during their hesitant ramblings they lean forward while grasping a side rail or touching a wall for support. Progressive dementia with increasing flexion may lead to a reluctance of the attending staff to get the patient up into a chair, since he tends to curl forward and slump from the seat.

2. *Paratonic rigidity,* or *gegenhalten* (opposition), refers to the increased tone noted with passive manipulation of the limb. At times, *gegenhalten* seems even more obvious if the manipulation is done impatiently and repeatedly while the patient is urged to "relax, relax." Slow movements may avoid the resistance. "Involuntary rigidity," "perservation," "postural fixation," "negativism," and similar phrases are used to describe this phenomenon. It is certain that some of these patients do attempt to cooperate but to no avail. It is logical to assume that the inability to shift muscle tone rapidly is accompanied by an inability to shift mental set, but there is no proof of such an association. The inconstant rigidity of *gegenhalten* is in contrast to the plastic rigidity of parkinsonism, which is consistent and usually best demonstrated in the neck and shoulder groups. *Gegenhalten* must also be distinguished from spasticity due to activation of the stretch reflex as seen in the biceps or hamstrings of patients with corticospinal tract disease. Paratonic rigidity is frequent in dementia and usually becomes more obvious as cerebral deterioration progresses.

3. *Pelvicrural flexion contracture* (Fig. 1) is a much more striking phenomenon, and it is not at all rare when one surveys chronically bedridden patients in a de-

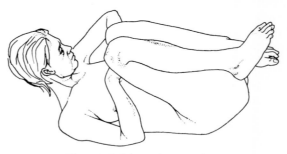

Figure 1. Pelvicrural contraction.

mented and aged population.[18] A similar phenomenon is common in the late stages of progressive degenerative diseases in childhood and has been reported to follow repeated seizures. As a rule seizures, myoclonic jerks, chorea, and other abnormal movements tend to diminish as pelvicrural contraction becomes permanent. In this position the knees are flexed toward the abdomen, and the heels often rest against the posterior thighs. Although the ankle and knee jerks may be diminished, the hamstring reflexes are usually quite brisk. Even a gentle stimulus of the lower limbs may produce massive contractions of the proximal muscles which can usually be distinguished from the defensive reactions elicited with lower spinal cord disease. In the latter response, sometimes called the "triple flexion response," the foot tends to contract and secondary movements occur higher throughout the limb; all movements occur at about the same time and finally subside. In pelvicrural flexion the entire lower portion of the body contracts rapidly and inappropriately, with both limbs usually contracting at the same time and tending to remain contracted. Some of the same patients have an explosive crying, "pseudo-affective hyperpathia."

REFLEXES

Grasp Reflex

A distal moving contact in the palm may elicit flexion of the fingers, with grasping of the stimulating object (Fig. 2). When present, this response can be elicited in any position of the limbs and is not related to spasticity. In patients with more extensive brain lesions, the hand may not only clasp the stimulus but trap it as well or may pursue or grope after it in space. A firm stroking movement on the back of the hand may effect release, and there has been some attempt to select out a subgroup in which stimulation on the back of the hand eliminates the tonic grasping. The variations and significance of the grasp reflex and grasping have been discussed at length during the past 5 decades.[2, 6, 21, 53, 55, 60] The grasp reflex can be incorrectly identified in patients in whom a traction response secondary to stretch occurs and in whom it signifies corticospinal tract disease. Perhaps most

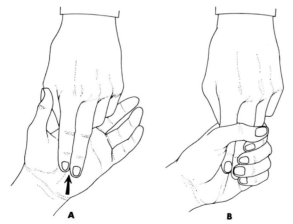

Figure 2. Grasp reflex. (A) Palmar stimulation; (B) grasp response.

difficult is the distinction between a genuine grasp reflex and a grasp secondary to habit, an attempt to cooperate, or simple hand holding for politeness. One of the distortions of the grasp may be the clutching of bedsheets, or picking at real or imaginary lint. Nevertheless, the experienced clinician will usually have no trouble detecting a typical and pathological grasp response.

The reflex may be predominantly a subcortical one, but most authors link the grasp reflex to frontal lobe disease even though lesions of the frontal lobe may either release or abolish a prior grasp reflex. A grasp reflex has been observed in patients with frontal lobe tumors, and Bucy[15] has reported its presence with occipital lobe tumors as well. Vascular lesions and bilateral atrophic cortical disease are common associated disorders, and bilateral thalamic degeneration has been reported in association with this reflex. At one time it was stated that section of the corpus callosum plus destruction of one frontal lobe was sufficient to produce a grasp reflex, but neither uncomplicated section of the corpus callosum nor frontal lobotomy necessarily produces the reflex.[6, 60]

Probably as many as 20 percent of aged and demented patients have a grasp reflex, and in many its presence reflects the severity of the disease more than it reflects an exact localization to the frontal poles.[47] Although usually contralateral to the frontal lobe lesion, a grasp reflex can be present on either the ipsilateral or the contralateral side. When it appears ipsilateral to a focal lesion, most writers invoke transitory diaschisis, acute cerebral edema, or extension of the lesion to the other side. It is also possible, of course, that such an appearance relates largely to a release phenomenon from the opposite frontal pole. It has been suggested that the pelvicrural contraction described above represents only a larger elaboration of the grasp reflex.

One author has suggested that the characteristic pointing position of normal humans, with the index finger extended and the others flexed into the palm, may have originated as an enfeebled or sublimated grasp reflex. Grünbaum[26] has noted preservation of what he calls the "pointing reflex" as an abnormal phenomenon in children with diffuse brain damage. He reports that under favorable circumstances whenever the index finger is passively extended, the others tend to curl reflexly into the palm, at least until about 2 to 3 years of age. This response is not easy to elicit in healthy adults but might be expected to appear when brain damage is present. It may be similar to the traction response defined by Denny-Brown.[19] So far as I know, the pointing reflex has never been studied in adults, but it seems possible that it might reappear in dementia.

Tonic Foot Response

In 1938, Goldstein[24] discussed at length the tendency for the toes to turn down when the ball of the foot is stimulated (Fig. 3). The phenomenon is best elicited by direct pressure on the ball or sole of the foot, in contrast to the stroking necessary for a Babinski's reflex. When a tonic foot response is present, the toes curl down in response to the stimulus, and there may be wrinkling of the skin of the sole plus flexion and adduction movements of the toes.

The reflex has been associated with damage to the frontal lobe,[14] particularly its medial portions, and may represent a response related to the "turning to" phenomenon of childhood. The tonic foot response may be similar to the palmar grasp; both these reflexes are almost always present in infancy but are absent in normal adults.[22] In each instance a stimulus on the extensor portion of the hand or foot

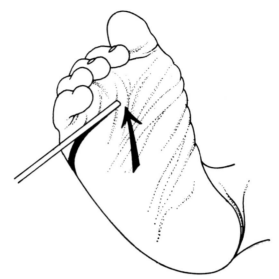

Figure 3. Tonic foot response.

tends to counteract the grasping. It has been said that the presence of the tonic foot response on the homolateral side in patients with brain tumors suggests either increased intracranial pressure or extension across the midline.

Oral Responses

Several reflex responses result from a stimulus applied to the mouth area. The best recognized are the snout and sucking reflexes. These are elicited by percussion (snout reflex) or stroking of the oral region (Figs. 4 and 5). Normal subjects manifest little or no response to such stimuli. A positive response consists of a puckering movement as the orbicularis oris contracts. Some patients pucker and also turn toward the stimulus as if "rooting." Sucking and puckering movements occur via the nuclei of the fifth, seventh, and twelfth cranial nerves, and some mouth movements are probably possible without dependence on any areas other than these low-level centers.[29, 30] Hydranencephalic infants lacking cortical strata may still manifest yawning, hiccups, and a host of low-level reflexes such as snout, grasp, and tonic foot reflexes. The range of mouthing, "rooting," and sucking responses is at least as wide in normal or decorticate infants as in demented adult

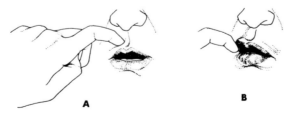

Figure 4. Snout reflex. (A) Puckering of lips in response to gentle percussion in the oral region; (B) turning to a stroking stimulus in oral region.

175

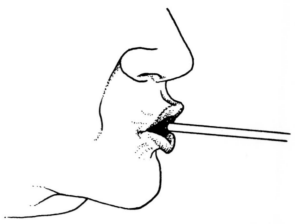

Figure 5. Sucking reflex, sucking movement of the lips in response to tactile stimulation in oral region.

patients in whom similar primitive responses have been released by cortical dissolution.

Some patients with dementia show, particularly in the late stages of deterioration, not only incessant mouthing and licking movements but a persistent pursing of the lips that Darwin described many years ago.[50] The snout and sucking responses, either or both, may be present in dementia; it seems unlikely that either one implies a lower or a more severe lesion than the other. In general, a snout reflex in a person with delicate mouth muscles is probably more significant than a sucking reflex. Normal individuals with powerful oral musculature sometimes manifest fragments of these responses.

De Ajuriaguerra, Rego, and Rissot[5] attempted to quantify these oral responses and found that patients with severe Alzheimer's disease are particularly likely to show all the types of primitive mouth responses. In some patients the typical rooting reflex of infancy, which consists of a turning toward the finger or tongue blade that has stroked the cheek, is also observed.[23] The latter phenomenon suggests even more loss of normal inhibition than does a simple snout or sucking reflex produced by a stimulus at the lips.

Three major explanations are commonly offered for these oral phenomena: (1) A decline in overall levels of activation and awareness leads to movements that ordinarily would be inhibited.[58] (2) Specific localization has been postulated as a cause, particularly lesions between frontal cortex and globus pallidus, and bitemporal lesions. (3) The most commonly offered explanation is that these reflexes are ontogenetic or phylogenetic "release" phenomena: "Once a man, twice a child."

Some of the mouthing disorders seen in demented patients are not related to these reflexes and can be quite confusing. Any large group of old people is likely to include examples of lip-smacking and involuntary jaw movements, and a large and overactive tongue is commonly observed in edentulous patients. Reactions to certain drugs such as the phenothiazines may cause tardive or buccolingual dyskinesia in senile patients.[45, 54]

Aside from the tardive dyskinesias and distinct from senile chorea and benign tremor, many involuntary mouth movements occur in aged patients that do not

176

indicate any measurable decline in cortical function; at least, no one has yet reported such correlative measurements.

Nuchocephalic Reflex

In 1974, Jenkyn and associates[33] described a reflex which had not previously been noted and which they termed the nuchocephalic reflex. It is elicited by rapidly turning the shoulders of a standing subject to right or left, preferably while the subject wears +20 lenses to avoid visual fixation. The reflex is considered present, uninhibited, if the head holds its original position through active contraction of the cervical musculature. In a normal adult the reflex is inhibited, and the subject turns his head in the direction of the shoulder after a brief time lag. The reflex is fully present in infants and becomes inhibited by 4 years of age. With diffuse cerebral dysfunction the reflex reappears ("disinhibited"); it was considered by these authors to be the most sensitive single indicator of early dementia.

Palmomental Reflex

The palmomental, or "palm-chin," reflex consists of unilateral contraction of the mentalis muscle when the thenar eminence of the ipsilateral hand is simulated briskly (Fig. 6). Along with the common association of grasping and sucking, this reflex is one of several phenomena that illustrate the neurological association of hand and mouth areas in early life.[10, 11, 44]

The palmomental reflex was originally described in adults with damage of the corticobulbar tracts.[12] One reason for the persistent interest in this somewhat inconsequential reflex is the long distance between the point of stimulation and place of observation. As might be anticipated, it can be asymmetrical or absent when there is a facial weakness or an injury of the brachial plexus. The palmomental reflex is almost universally present in infancy but is usually absent or inconstant in normal adult life.[43] However, the reflex becomes more prominent with age and is particularly common with severe dementia. It seems more common after a hemiplegic insult and is often prominent in patients with parkinsonism or presenile dementia. Nevertheless, the presence or absence of this particular reflex does not indicate either health or disease.

It is not clear why the wince-like movement adjacent to the mouth in response to a scratch of the palm is observed at all. Why should the chin move when the hand is stimulated? It has been suggested that the reflex might relate to the spatially close representation of the mouth and thumb in the cerebrum, but the cerebral cortex is probably not required for presence of the reflex. Others have suggested a "short circuit" between the sensory and mouth areas. Bracha[13] suggested that palmomental reflexes may be an early sign of lesions of the frontal lobe, because he so readily demonstrated the reflex in patients with a frontal tumor and after posterior frontal lobotomy. This may have been indicative of nothing more remarkable than the fact that widely separated areas of the nervous system may be involved in the production of any one reflex.

In interpreting this reflex, it should be emphasized that its reported frequency in normal individuals has varied with different observers and techniques and that it is difficult to quantify.[41] It seems likely that many, even most, normal subjects have a weakly positive response if it is measured electrically, but in many situations

177

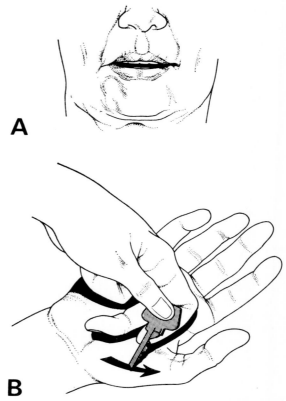

Figure 6. Palmomental reflex. (A) Ipsilateral response of mentalis muscle; (B) stimulation of thenar eminence.

involving suprasegmental damage the reflex will be easily seen, markedly exaggerated, and persistent.

Corneomandibular Reflex

Although generally ignored by American neurologists, the corneomandibular reflex has been recognized for many decades.[25] Wartenburg[61] emphasized it as a useful sign of supranuclear trigeminal involvement. It is best elicited by a firm stimulus (Wartenburg used a rounded glass rod) such as a cotton tip applied quickly to the cornea. A strenuous contraction of the eyelid is associated with a contralateral movement of the chin (Fig. 7). The mentalis muscle is likely to move even when the complete chin movement does not occur. If the reflex is bilaterally present and both corneal areas are stimulated synchronously, then the chin moves forward. The corneomandibular response is an associated movement between the muscles innervated by the facial and trigeminal nerves. This "oculopterygoid" response relates directly to the forceful blink of the eye and must be distinguished from numerous other facial synkinesias, such as that following Bell's palsy when (after partial recovery from damage to the facial nerve) the deep facial muscles contract jointly with the orbicularis oculi or that following partial recovery from

178

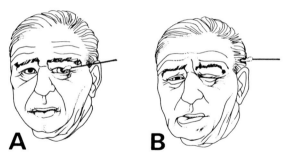

Figure 7. Corneomandibular reflex. (A) Corneal stimulation; (B) ipsilateral strong blink and contralateral movement of chin in response.

an ocular motor palsy when there may be an associated movement between the levator palpebrae and the rectus internus. None of these latter facial synkinesias are related to the corneomandibular response.

Movements such as the corneomandibular response probably represent a dedifferentiation of (or dissolution down to) an association that was present at earlier phases of development in the various muscles about the face. If this is true, then any state of heightened reflexivity may be expected to be associated with an overflow of facial movements from one area to another. The range of normal associated movements about the face can be quite high; for example, even without prior injury of the facial nerve one ala may move in response to a blink. A rare normal patient, and perhaps more commonly a patient with a disease such as multiple sclerosis, will manifest a side to side movement of the chin as the eyes move from side to side.

The corneomandibular reflex is often unilaterally present in patients with hemiplegia and is likely to be brisk bilaterally in patients with amyotrophic lateral sclerosis when the disease has extended rostral to the pons. It is also observed in patients with bilateral subcortical disease, as, for example, in patients with lacunar infarcts. It has also been observed in patients with degenerative cerebral diseases, such as Alzheimer's disease. It can be postulated that the presence of this reflex is one more indication of diffuse brain disease. Wartenburg specifically stated that this reflex in its fully developed form is not noted in normal persons. Having subjected one patient with migraine to angiography and pneumoencephalography solely on the basis of this reflex, I feel confident that Wartenburg was incorrect this once; from this case and several others it can be stated that the reflex does occur occasionally in normal individuals.

In an effort to check the ontogenetic hypothesis or cause for this reflex, a series of newborns was examined,[46] and over 50 percent manifested a partial or fully developed corneomandibular response. However, the reflex is not present in most normal ambulatory children.

Glabella Tap Reflex

Light tapping over the glabella in a normal subject elicits reflex blinking, but with repetition the response quickly disappears. In many types of degenerative disease, but most particularly in parkinsonism, this glabella tap reflex may be accentuated and fail to fatigue (Fig. 8). The most striking feature of the positive response is the absence of habituation on repeated testing.[48] It seems likely that this

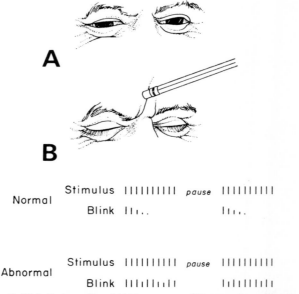

Normal   Stimulus |||||||||| *pause* ||||||||||
         Blink ||... ||...

Abnormal Stimulus |||||||||| *pause* ||||||||||
         Blink ||||||||||| ||||||||||

Figure 8. Glabella tap reflex. (A) Eyes at rest; (B) response to stimulus.

primitive response, found by Minkowski to be present in a 21.5cm. fetus, would be present in other diseases in which cortical inhibition is diminished or in which there are degenerative lesions in the basal ganglia. In situations in which the level of cortical control is progressively diminishing, as in insulin shock therapy, the reflex may be initially increased and then disappear.[36]

Some General Comments on the Ontogenetic Approach to These Reflexes

It is unlikely that a modern clinician would use the reflex responses discussed above as a primary means of localization. Neurology is not reflexology. Nevertheless, the responses are of interest and utility as monitors of central nervous system function, development, and deterioration. For example, the patient with an acute cerebral accident who gradually acquires an ipsilateral grasp reflex may be worsening because of brain swelling that involves both hemispheres. An elderly man with no clear evidence of intellectual deterioration may fall under suspicion, though not under indictment, of having cortical atrophy if there is a prominent snout or sucking reflex. These reflexes are also of theoretical interest since the ontogenetic approach is a useful general explanation for most of them. It must be recognized that any single ontogenetic explanation represents interpretation through a narrow viewpoint, is overly simplified, and may inhibit anatomical explanations. Nevertheless, it is one obvious explanation and can offer directions for future observation.

Coghill,[16] who viewed the central nervous system as a tool for maintaining the integrity of the individual, repeatedly emphasized the innate solidarity of the total organism. From his experience in Amblystoma he defined development as proceeding from the center to the periphery and originating from the innate developmental potentials of the organism. In 1929, he wrote, "During later periods pro-

180

cesses of conduction in established tracts may be one activating factor in directing the line of growth, vascularization may be another. But, in the nerve cell as in the seed, growth as such must be regarded as the expression of an intrinsic potential of the cell." In addition to this spontaneous, dynamic view of growth, Coghill conceived development as a uniting of partial but discrete smaller patterns. Many embryonic responses can be interpreted in this fashion: that out of general and broad patterns more precise and appropriate local responses appear.

The initial reaction to stimulation in amphibian and fish embryos consists of a contraction in a lateral plane, with partial or localized responses in later developmental phases. Hooker and his remarkably productive student Tryphena Humphrey[31] demonstrated that flexion is the first motor response in human embryos and that such flexion is an avoidance response. Extension of the embryo, perhaps having to do with postural and locomotor responses, is a latter acquisition. Reflex "turning toward" a stimulus generally appears later in fetal life than "turning away." Throughout fetal life the intensity of the stimulus may affect the response, and a seeking after, or "turning toward," response can be converted into an equally intense "turning away" if the stimulus is preceived as noxious.

Humphrey[29] has stated that the first reaction to stimulation of the oral area is simple mouth movement at 7 to 9 weeks in the human fetus. Sucking is a later and more complex phenomenon, and the common rooting reflex is quite variable in the fetus. Premature infants, and some term infants as well, appear to have an initial confusion and may display inappropriate turning away or rejection movements while seeking the nipple.

Although it is tempting to believe that there is a regular and orderly progression of responses such as those listed by Humphrey,[30] and that skin responses, nociceptive sensitivity, smell, nerve conduction rates, and a host of other unrelated phenomena are explainable on the basis of an orderly progression from (1) more variable, inappropriate, slow, and diffuse responses to (2) more consistent, precise, rapid, and discrete responses—the situation is just not that simple. It is, of course, true that the pelvicrural response depicted in Figure 1 is somewhat like an embryonic flexion response and the oral responses in dementia are similar to those of an infant. In the ontogenetic sense one assumes that rooting or grasping responses in demented patients indicate less severe disturbances than prominent rejection or apparent "hyperpathic" withdrawal, but such general conclusions are probably overstated. One can speculate also that persistent turning toward will represent a less severe dissolution than persistent avoidance.

Another concept similar to the ontogenetic one was offered by Thomson[59] in 1903 in an effort to explain associated movements. In certain clinical situations such as with basilar impression, after a cerebrovascular accident (particularly in childhood), or even as a benign familial trait, subtle or obvious mirror movements mimic activity in the contralateral limb. When one hand contracts, so does the other. To some extent this phenomenon is part of daily experience—every school boy discovers how hard it is to pat his head and rub his stomach at the same time. Pursing of the lips or mouth movements are often associated with difficult hand movements. Thomson stated that such associated movements, particularly flexion or extension movements of a lower limb when an upper limb is used, are explicable only in evolutionary terms. He also theorized that during normal development the constant presence of inhibitory influences leads to a gradual disuse of commissural fibers. More primitive creatures than man would retain more associated or combined movements. An alternative explanation would be that the more mature or trained commissural fibers themselves serve to inhibit the associated movements; in other words, it is not diminished but perfected connections that eliminate automatic associated responses.

The concept of higher levels serving as a damper to lower levels has been prominent in neurology for many years. Coghill's concept[16] of a patterned or predestined developmental template is attractive but incomplete. Modification, distortion, or development of normal interrelationships in the nervous system is directly dependent on the utilization, nutrition, and exercise of the central nervous system area involved. The ontogenetic and dynamic interpretation of growth has been enlarged by the additional emphasis on levels and mutual interaction.

As part of his lifetime attention to the ontogenetic, evolutionary, and anatomicoclinical explanation, Denny-Brown[19] has been interested in what he has termed "positive" and "negative" phenomena. Although greatly oversimplified here, in general he linked positive aspects to frontal lobe disease and negative features to parietal lobe disease. The normal equilibrium may be disturbed, or there may be a predominance of either aspect. Frontal lobe lesions (positive or seeking) may lead to overreaction to natural visual or sensory stimuli, tactile automatisms such as the grasping reflex, and perhaps to such phenomena as preoccupation with the present and a loss of response to disagreeable situations. Parietal lesions (negative or withdrawal) may be reflected in primitive avoiding reactions, both visual and tactile, as well as in phenomena such as denial of disability, apathy, and anosognosia.

Other Phenomena Seen with Diffuse Disease

In addition to the primitive reflexes discussed above there are many phenomena that are, to varying degrees, explicable by the Jacksonian concept of a loss of higher levels, a decomposition, or (in Jackson's words) a "dissolution" that leads to release of phenomena that had been submerged or repressed since the earliest developmental phases. A few such phenomena are discussed below.

Impersistence and Perseveration

Motor impersistence has been picked out of the large repository of ignored neurological observations by Miller Fisher.[20] Among the tests that can demonstrate this phenomenon are: (1) keeping eyes closed, (2) keeping tongue out, (3) maintaining fixation of gaze laterally, (4) persistence in a sound such as "ah" or "ee," (5) persistence of grip, and (6) combinations of these.

Although Fisher emphasized that motor impersistence is associated predominantly with right parietal lesions, studies by Ben-Yishay and his colleagues[8, 9] suggest that motor impersistence correlates best with diffuse brain damage. Most neurologists would agree that although right parietal lesions are particularly likely to be correlated with this phenomenon, motor impersistence is also seen in many patients with diffuse lesions.[35] One well recognized example seen with bilateral cerebral disease is the difficulty patients with Huntington's chorea often have in maintaining protrusion of the tongue. As a general rule, when a demented patient manifests marked motor impersistence, attention should first be directed toward the right parietal lobe.

Perseveration, the repetitious performance of a motor or verbal action, has been associated with left inferior temporal and parietal lesions. The definition has alternately broadened and narrowed over the last 50 years, and it is now clear that many different mechanisms can lead to what has been called perseveration. Severely demented patients, normal children, or even extremely fatigued normal adults may repetitiously write the same letter or perform an act requested of them. Perhaps the idle repetitive doodling seen at any meeting may represent a similar primitive release under the influence of fantasy or boredom. When critical faculties are dulled, or if intermediate memory is impaired, the same concept may be uttered again and again. In one striking example of a lack of awareness of recent events, transient global amnesia, a phenomenon akin to preseveration is noted.[56] In this condition, patients seem unable to remember anything current for longer than approximately 2 minutes, although distant memory and social actions are entirely normal. During the brief period of illness, which usually lasts only hours or a few days, the patient may repeat the same phrase again and again, using slightly different words. The phenomenon is reminiscent of the repetition of stories by individuals who have forgotten that they have previously told them.

Allison and Hurwitz[4] studied perseveration in aphasia, which they distinguish from palilalia, recurrent utterances, stereotypes, and afterimages. They stressed the involuntary nature of perseveration and devised specific tests of verbal and motor performance that might elicit this response. Perseveration occurred in most aphasics and might be one of the few residual indicators of a formerly severe aphasia after the general clouding of consciousness had disappeared. Although data suggest that either frontal or temporal lobes, particularly on the dominant side, are likely to be involved, a deeply placed midline lesion that disturbs the upper brain stem and interrupts subcortical connections was considered the most likely explanation for perseveration in most cases.

Apraxia

Although this chapter is chiefly intended to discuss generalized phenomena and although apraxia may have more focal significance than impersistence or perseveration, persistent apraxia sometimes occurs in patients with diffuse and bilateral brain lesions and sometimes is absent in patients with focal brain lesions, regardless of the site. Von Monakow considered apraxia to be "an answer of the entire nervous system to a massive regional or general insult."[40] There are localities of predilection, especially the entire territory supplied by the middle cerebral artery, particularly on the left. Although the local coloring of the apraxia may relate to the area involved by being predominantly motor or sensory, Brun and others[62] have emphasized that lasting apraxia is usually associated with bilateral and diffuse disease. Total disturbance of the left frontal or of the left inferior parietal area does not always result in apraxia, but severe damage of almost any region of the brain may result in a temporary apractic state. It has been suggested that each kinetic experience from childhood on leaves a complex engram that is superimposed on other engrams; it is thus not surprising that lesions of many areas may lead to perseveration of earlier and more rigidity formed or "instinctive" actions with a loss of willed performance of the same act. For example, the apractic patient may eat and relish a meal placed in front of him but be unable to imitate the eating of an imaginary meal. Pick found typical apraxia in senile dementia, and others have noted its presence in presenile dementia, usually as a fairly late sign.

The importance of complex neuronal circuits is particularly apparent in aphasia. Some varieties of aphasia may reflect a breakdown in connections between areas rather than a destruction of one particular area. More neuronal connections are involved in conceptualizing and uttering a thought than in understanding one. One reason expressive or fluent aphasia is more common than receptive or non-fluent aphasia may be the involvement of more neurons in speaking a thought clearly than in perceiving one. Similarly an automatic response that can be performed without thought may require fewer neuronal connections or less energy than a carefully organized new concept. In daily learning of a new act, such as riding a bicycle, skiing, or developing a new "move" on the basketball court, the performer's goal is to shift the cortical plan into a series of automatic lower level responses that are quicker and more efficient than intellectualized or planned action.

Social and Affectual Preservation

Among the changes classically listed in the old descriptions of "chronic brain syndrome" were changes in affect along with loss of social control. These phenomena when they occur are often present only in far advanced disease. It is possible indeed that the *single* most valuable diagnostic clue to disorders such as Alzheimer's disease is the *relative* preservation of the neurological state and social graces in the presence of disintegrated memory and intellectual deterioration. This phenomenon is hard to particularize, and there is no label that is satisfactory, yet all neurologists look for such a dissociation. The patient retains obvious marks of his cultural and educational background in the midst of fluctuating confusion and a profound memory deficit. The personality and cultural background may even be used to conceal the deficit with a pleasant smile and facile excuse offered to gloss over obvious errors as if they never existed. Hats are lifted in greeting, modesty is preserved, the physician is greeted like a guest — while the patient may be totally befuddled as to what the situation entails. The preservation of personality, motor power, and sensory ability in the face of profound amnesia and intellectual loss suggests bilateral cortical damage to the neurologist and further suggests that the damage is bilateral and therefore not due to tumor or vascular accident.

Janice Barnes, in an unpublished study of the PICA (Porch Index of Communications Ability) Scale of verbal skill in presenile dementias, noted that all of her patients tended to over verbalize. A repetition of instructions was necessary, and particular deficits in gestural scales and in one series of verbal scales were noted in these patients. Similar observations have been made in other studies using various psychological tests but are hard to quantify. There can be combinations of any of the responses reviewed above, but again they are hard to quantify. Some clinicians who utilize the face-hand tests (stimulating each separately and then at the same time while the patients have their eyes closed) found not only the relative extinction of the "peripheral" or hand stimulus as compared to that of the face in demented patients but often so much impersistence or perservation that the testing is hard to quantify. A simple test to quantify dementia is one of the techniques most needed to sharpen the validity of clinical research in this area.

Pseudobulbar Palsy

Diffuse bilateral subcortical and cortical disease of many causes can lead to pseudobulbar palsy. This phenomenon consists particularly of a loss of emotional control, usually as brief, affectless crying with reddening of the face and a wide-open mouth.[7] In rare patients the emotional incontinence is manifested as laughter. Spasticity of the oral or lingual areas and dysarthric speech is commonly observed. Swallowing may be limited, and salivation can be distressingly obvious. Atrophy of the tongue, as is seen with bulbar palsy, is not a feature. The syndrome is considered to represent supranuclear involvement with secondary brain stem release. The emotional incontinence of pseudobulbar palsy accompanies many conditions including bilateral strokes. It is particularly likely with small subcortical infarcts or multiple cortical ones. When a patient has dementia plus pseudobulbar palsy, bilateral cerebral disease can be assumed.

Distortion in Speed of Responses

Albert, Feldman, and Willis[3] have suggested that "subcortical" disease that leads to dementia can be distinguished from cortical dementia. They have described the characteristic features of the "subcortical dementias," as in patients with progressive supranuclear palsy, to be impairment of timing and activation. The cortical systems for manipulating knowledge are intact but when activated involve an inordinately long delay for processing. Answers are so postponed that responses are ignored or missed by the audience, and the patient is falsely labeled as being seriously demented. Measurements such as the temporal ones suggested by these workers will also be hard to quantify but, as with the dissociation mentioned above (social skills present, memory and intellectual skills absent) can be clues to the diagnosis.

Iivanainen[32] has correlated diffuse ventricular atrophy with disturbances in precise finger movements. He has also demonstrated a positive relationship between loss in kinesthetic, vibratory, and touch sensation and tactile gnostic sensibility in dementia and the extent of combined ventricular and cortical atrophy as measured by pneumoencephalography.

Respiratory Abnormalities

Among the numerous physiological alternations of aging is a change in response to carbon dioxide inhalation and to forced hyperventilation in the presence of diffuse brain disease. Patients with severe bilateral cortical disease appear overly responsive to the effect of carbon dioxide and may hyperventilate markedly on breathing air with a high level of carbon dioxide.[28] On the other hand, apnea may be prolonged after voluntary overbreathing of room air.[51, 52] The phenomenon of posthyperventilation apnea (PHVA) can be tested by having patients take 5 deep in-and-out breaths, which lowers the arterial carbon dioxide tension transiently. Alert patients with normal brains rarely experience significant apnea, but subjects with brain damage often experience a period of apnea lasting 12 to 30 seconds or more. Both the excessive response to carbon dioxide and the prolonged posthyperventilation apnea may relate to loss of forebrain control. Jennett, Ashbridge, and North[34] confirmed that brief voluntary hyperventilation commonly causes apnea in patients with supramedullary lesions. These researchers considered the apnea to be related to drowsiness rather than to the extent of the lesion; they concluded that the test for posthyperventilation apnea is not useful in identifying bilateral cerebral dysfunction. Studies of this phenomenon in presenile dementia are lacking.

Irregularities in respiration are common both in the very old and in the very young. Cheyne-Stokes respiration is particularly common in aged patients, especially at times of drowsiness. This abnormality of rhythm does not have grave prognostic significance and is not known to correlate with the degree of dementia.

Kluver-Bucy Syndrome

This syndrome is not properly discussed in a chapter that deals with nonfocal neurological aspects of diffuse brain disease since traditionally the syndrome is observed after bitemporal lobectomy in monkeys. However, Pilleri[49] has stated that a similar syndrome can develop with atrophic disorders such as Alezheimer's or Pick's disease. The major features include: (1) visual agnosia such that the animal seems unable to differentiate between living and nonliving objects; (2) oral behavior that includes licking or oral experimentation; (3) hypermetamorphosis, which implies a restless need to touch objects that are perceived; (4) decrease in emotional responsiveness, such as loss of fear; (5) hypersexuality or pansexuality; and (6) changes in feeding patterns.

This rather rigid instinctive behavior is, according to Pilleri,[50] similar to the physiological repertory of normal infants. He suggests that lesions involve both the limbic and neocortical areas if the syndrome is evident in humans. Other authors have questioned the precise temporal localization of this syndrome. The full range of symptoms seen in monkeys and particularly the hypersexuality is not usually present in humans, but portions of the syndrome are quite common with Alzheimer's and Pick's disease.

SUMMARY

The thesis of this chapter is that the neurological phenomena discussed and numerous others omitted or not yet recognized relate primarily to a release of primitive activity when diffuse brain damage erodes cerebral inhibition mechanisms. Anatomical correlations are always difficult when there are multiple lesions, and those that have been made have not completely explained these phenomena.

A phylogenetic explanation is not completely adequate either but certainly does not bar further investigations. Indeed such a concept points out the necessity to continue to search for other fetal or developmental responses in dementia, to assess the interrelationships between these reflexes, and to quantify the stimulus as well as the response. The prognostic value of these reflexes is not emphasized, because it is not known. In the evaluation of dementia, one of the last obvious frontiers of neurological science, both specific observations and general principles await discovery.

REFERENCES

1. ABERCROMBIE, M. L. M.; LINDON, R. L.; AND TYSON, M. C.: *Associated movements in normal and physically handicapped children.* Dev. Med. Child Neurol. 6:573, 1964.
2. ADIE, W. J., AND CRITCHLEY, M.: *Forced grasping and groping.* Brain 50:142, 1927.
3. ALBERT, M. L.; FELDMAN, R. G.; AND WILLIS, A. L.: *The "subcortical dementia" of progressive supranuclear palsy.* J. Neurol. Neurosurg. Psychiatry 37:121, 1974.
4. ALLISON, R. S., AND HURWITZ, L. J.: *On perseveration in aphasics.* Brain 90:429, 1967.
5. AJURIAGUERRA, J. DE; REGO, A.; AND RISSOT, R.: *Le réflexe oral et quelques activitiés orales dans les syndromes démentiels du grand âge.* L'Encephale 52:189, 1963.

6. AKELAITES, A. J.; RISTEEN, W. A.; AND VAN WAGENEN, W. P.: *Studies on the corpus callosum. IX. Relationship of the grasp reflex to section of the corpus callosum.* Arch. Neurol. Psychiat. 49: 820, 1943.

7. ARING, C. D.: *Supranuclear (Pseudobulbar) palsy.* Arch. Intern. Med. 115:198, 1965.

8. BEN-YISHAY, Y.; DILLER, L.; GERSTMAN, L.; AND HAAS, A.: *The relationship between impersistence, intellectual function and outcome of rehabilitation in patients with left hemiplegia.* Neurology (Minneap.) 18:852, 1968.

9. BEN-YISHAY, Y.; HAAS, A.; AND DILLER, L.: *The effects of oxygen inhalation on motor impersistence in brain-damaged individuals: A double-blind study.* Neurology (Minneap.) 17:1003, 1967.

10. BERLIN, L.: *Compulsive eye opening and associated phenomena.* Arch. Neurol. Psychiat. 73:597, 1955.

11. BIEBER, I.: *Grasping and sucking.* J. Nerv. Ment. Dis. 91:31, 1940.

12. BLAKE, J. R., AND KUNKLE, E. C.: *The palmomental reflex.* Arch. Neurol. Psychiat. 65:.337, 1951.

13. BRACHA, S.: *The clinical value of the pollicomental reflex in neuropathology.* J. Nerv. Ment. Dis. 127:91, 1958.

14. BRAIN, W. R., AND CURRAN, R. D.: *The grasp-reflex of the foot.* Brain 55:347, 1932.

15. BUCY, P. C.: *Reflex-grasping associated with tumors not involving the frontal lobes.* Brain 54: 480, 1931.

16. COGHILL, G. E.: *Anatomy and the Problems of Behavior.* Cambridge University Press, New York, 1929.

17. CRITCHLEY, M.: *Neurologic changes in the aged.* J. Chronic Dis. 3:459, 1956.

18. DANIELS, L. E.: *Paraplegia in flexion.* Arch. Neurol. Psychiat. 43:736, 1940.

19. DENNY-BROWN, D.: *Positive and negative aspects of cerebral cortical functions.* N. C. Med. J. 17:295, 1956.

20. FISHER, M.: *Left hemiplegia and motor impersistence.* J. Nerv. Ment. Dis. 123:201, 1956.

21. FULTON, J. F.; JACOBSEN, C. F.; AND KENNARD, M. A. *A note concerning the relation of the frontal lobes to posture and forced grasping in monkeys.* Brain 55:524, 1932.

22. GENTRY, E. F., AND ALDRICH, C. A.: *Toe reflexes in infancy.* Am. J. Dis. Child. 76:389, 1948.

23. GENTRY, E. F., AND ALDRICH, C. A.: *Rooting reflex in newborn infants.* Am. J. Dis. Child. 75: 528, 1948.

24. GOLDSTEIN, K.: *The tonic foot response to stimulation of the sole: Its physiological significance and diagnostic value.* Brain 61:269, 1938.

25. GORDON, R. M., AND BENDER, M. B.: *The corneomandibular reflex.* J. Neurol. Neurosurg. Psychiatry 34:236, 1971.

26. GRUNBAÜM, A. A.: *The pointing position of the hand as a pathological and primitive reflex.* Brain 53:267, 1930.

27. HAGBARTH, K. E., AND KUGELBERG, E.: *Plasticity of the human abdominal skin reflex.* Brain 81: 305, 1958.

28. HEYMAN, A.; BIRCHFIELD, R. I.; AND SIEKER, H. O.: *Effects of bilateral cerebral infarction on respiratory center sensitivity.* Neurology (Minneap.) 8:694, 1958.

29. HUMPHREY, T.: *The development of mouth opening and related reflexes involving the oral area of human fetuses.* Ala. J. Med. Sci. 5:126, 1968.

30. HUMPHREY, T.: *Embryology of the central nervous system: With some correlations with functional development.* Ala. J. Med. Sci. 1:60, 1964.

31. HUMPHREY, T.: *Some correlations between the appearance of human fetal reflexes and the development of the nervous system.* Prog. Brain Res. 4:93, 1964.

32. IIVANAINEN, M.: *Statistical correlations of diffuse cerebral atrophy, with special reference to diagnostic and aetiological clues.* Acta. Neurol. Scand. 51:365, 1975.

33. JENKYN, L. R.; WALSH D.; CULVER, C.; AND REEVES, A. G.: *The nuchocephalic reflex in diffuse cerebral disease.* Neurology (Minneap.) 24:358, 1974.

34. JENNETT, S.; ASHBRIDGE, K.; AND NORTH, J. B.: *Post-hyperventilation apnea in patients with brain damage.* J. Neurol. Neurosurg. Psychiatry 37:288, 1974.

35. JOYNT, R. J.; BENTON, A. L.; AND FOGEL, M. L.: *Behavioral and pathological correlates of motor impersistence.* Neurology (Minneap.) 12:876, 1962.

36. KINO, F. F.: *Nasopalpebral reflex: Application to neuropsychiatry, particularly to insulin shock treatment.* Br. J. Psychiatry 95:143, 1949.

37. KORNZWEIG, A. I.: *Ocular conditions of the aged.* Geriatrics 19:24, 1964.

38. KUGELBURG, E.; AND HAGBARTH, K. E.: *Spinal mechanisms of the abdominal and erector spinal skin reflexes.* Brain 81:290, 1958.

39. LOCKE, S.: *The neurological concomitants of aging.* Geriatrics 19:722, 1964.

40. MAYER-GROSS, W.: *Further observations on apraxia.* J. Ment. Sci. 82:744, 1936.

41. McDONALD, J. K.; KELLEY, J. J.; BROCK, L. D.; AND BARTUNEK, E. J.: *Variability of the palmomental reflex.* J. Nerv. Ment. Dis. 136:207, 1963.

42. OKUN, E.; RUBIN, L. F., AND COLLINS, E. M.: *Retinal breaks in the senile dog eye.* Arch. Ophthalmol. 66:702, 1961.

43. OTOMO, E.: *The palmomental reflex in the aged.* Geriatrics 20:901, 1965.

44. PARMALEE, A. H.: *The palmomental reflex in premature infants.* Dev. Med. Child Neurol. 5:381, 1963.

45. PAULSON, G. W.: *Tardive dyskinesia.* Annu. Rev. Med. 26:75, 1975.

46. PAULSON, G. W., AND BIRD, M. T.: *Corneomandibular reflex.* Conf. Neurol. 33:116, 1971.

47. PAULSON, G. W., AND GOTTLIEB, G.: *Developmental reflexes: The reappearance of foetal and neonatal reflexes in aged patients.* Brain 91:37, 1968.

48. PEARCE, J.; AZIZ, H.; AND GALLAGHER, J. C.: *Primitive reflex activity in primary and symptomatic parkinsonism.* J. Neurol. Neurosurg. Psychiatry 31:501, 1968.

49. PILLERI, G.: *The Klüver-Bucy syndrome in man.* Psychiat. Neurol. 152:65, 1966.

50. PILLERI, G.: *Schippenzeichen von Darwin "pursing of the lips" beim morbus Alzheimer.* Psychiat. Clin. (Basel) 152:301, 1966.

51. PLUM, F., AND POSNER, J. B.: *Diagnosis of Stupor and Coma.* F. A. Davis Co., Philadelphia, 1966.

52. PLUM, F.; BROWN, H. W.; AND SNOEP, E.: *Neurologic significance of posthyperventilation apnea* J. A. M. A. 181:1050, 1962.

53. RICHTER, C. P., AND PATERSON, A. S.: *On the pharmacology of the grasp reflex.* Brain 55:391, 1932.

54. SCHMIDT, W. R., AND JARCHO, W. W.: *Persistent dyskinesias following phenothiazine therapy.* Arch. Neurol. 14:369, 1966.

55. SEYFFARTH, H., AND DENNY-BROWN, D.: *The grasp reflex and the instinctive grasp reaction.* Brain 71:109, 1948.

56. SHUTTLEWORTH, E. C.: *The transient global amnesia syndrome.* Editorial. J.A.M.A. 198:778, 1966.

57. SKRE, H.: *Neurological signs in a normal population.* Acta. Neurol. Scand. 48:575, 1972.

58. STERJILEVICH, S. M.: *La turbulence nocturne du vieillard psychotique.* L'Endéphale 51:238, 1962.

59. THOMSON, H. C.: *Associated movements in hemiplegia: Their origin and physiological significance.* Brain 26:514, 1903.

60. WALSHE, F. M. R.: *Syndrome of the premotor cortex.* Brain 58:49, 1935.

61. WARTENBURG, R.: *Winking-jaw phenomenon.* Arch. Neurol. Psychiat. 59:734, 1948.

62. WOLTMAN, H.: *Review of clinical and anatomical studies of apraxia, with special reference to papers by R. Brun.* Arch. Neurol. Psychiat. 10:344, 1923.

63. YAKOVLEV, P. I.: *Paraplegia in flexion of cerebral origin.* J. Neuropath. Exp. Neurol. 13:267, 1954.

CHAPTER 9

The Clinical Use of Psychological
Testing in Evaluation for Dementia

Charles E. Wells, M.D., and
Denton C. Buchanan, Ph.D.

The multiplicity of psychological tests available and their potentialities to evaluate dementia were described by Horenstein[32] in the first edition of this volume and by others elsewhere.[7, 8, 40] In this chapter we will endeavor to demonstrate both the usefulness and the limitations of selected psychological tests as ancillary diagnostic procedures for the patient with suspected dementia and as evaluative procedures for the patient with identified dementia.

Appropriate use of psychological testing in dementia, as in other disorders, requires familiarity with the various tests utilized and appreciation of the many varying factors that produce deviations in performance. Only with such understanding will the physician be able to make appropriate use of the testing and interpretive skills of the psychologist.

RELATIONSHIP OF PSYCHOLOGICAL TESTING TO OTHER
ANCILLARY DIAGNOSTIC PROCEDURES

Physicians are prone to regard psychological testing as being more precise a technique for qualitatively and quantitatively measuring brain function than it really is. In fact, psychological testing is a refined, reliable, and reproducible method for *testing behavior*. As Benton[8] emphasized, ". . . the aspects of behavior sampled by clinical observation and by neuropsychological tests are the same;" these tests do not measure "infrabehavioral events." Psychological tests per se rarely, if ever, are sufficiently discriminating to establish a diagnosis in the absence of confirmatory clinical findings.[32] Rather, psychological tests provide alternative and complementary measurements of behavior which, in conjunction with historical and clinical observations, often help to establish a diagnosis and to understand the patient's behavioral alterations. Psychological testing should serve as an aid in clinical evaluation, not as a primary diagnostic instrument.

Behavioral measurements lack the specificity of biochemical tests that measure subcellular phenomena. Yet, physicians unfamiliar with individual tests and testing procedures sometimes accord them unmerited validity. When an unforeseen interpretation appears in a psychological report, the physician's response is often that he *must* have "missed that" in his examination, whereas were a blood chemistry determination unexpectedly abnormal, he would first try to replicate the finding and then evaluate its meaning. It is usually the physician and not the psychologist who assigns certitude to the interpretation of psychological tests. The psychologist seldom denies the possibility (or sometimes even the probability) of alternate interpretations.

Certain problems arise in the use of ancillary testing procedures. One important consideration is that the identification of an observation as normal or abnormal is frequently imprecise. Usually there is a range of values which is definitely normal, another definitely abnormal, and those in between which may be either. This is true for observational methods as accurate as radiology and pathology (as emphasized in Chapter 6 by Tomlinson[53] and Chapter 11 by Lowry and coworkers[39]) as well as for psychological testing. Humans are not readily separable into unequivocally normal and unequivocally abnormal groups regardless of what is being measured, and the range of uncertainty often widens as the complexity of the quality being measured increases.

Even if psychological test results are unquestionably "normal" or "abnormal," stumbling blocks may arise in their interpretation. An Intelligence Quotient (I.Q.) of 100 on the Wechsler Adult Intelligence Scale (WAIS) represents the statistically described normal. On the other hand, the score may reflect defective function if the history suggests previously superior intellectual performance. For example, we recently saw a prominent professional man suffering from normal pressure hydrocephalus who had a full scale I.Q. of 106. Certainly, his premorbid score would have been 30 to 40 points higher. Another patient may demonstrate defective short-term memory measured by a low digit span on the WAIS, a classical finding in dementia, but this is also frequent with hysteria, anxiety, poor cooperation, and dissimulation.

In evaluating patients with dementia or suspected of having dementia the physician may appropriately ask the clinical psychologist the following questions:

1. In the patient whose diagnosis is uncertain, do psychological tests reveal abnormalities supporting a diagnosis of organic dysfunction or suggesting this to be unlikely?

2. In the patient with identified organic disease, can you identify any specific defects suggesting a focal lesion?

3. In the patient with identified organic disease, can you measure the severity of cerebral dysfunction (or the level of cerebral function) to provide a base line for follow-up?

4. In the patient with identified organic disease, can you identify areas of cognitive and emotional strength or weakness that can be utilized in clinical management?

TESTING PROCEDURES

Brief Screening Tests for Dementia

Many attempts have been made to find brief screening procedures that reliably detect dementia and can be administered by relatively unskilled persons. Unfortunately, none have yet been devised that detect less than moderately advanced dementia. Nevertheless brief tests may be useful in specific situations. Tests for memory and information, memory and fluency, and visuomotor performance have been proposed and will be discussed here.

Some years ago Kahn, Pollack, and Goldfarb[37] developed a set of 10 memory-information type questions (Table 1) to measure the severity of dementia.

190

Table 1. Mental status questionnaire
of Kahn, Pollack, and Goldfarb[37]

What is the name of this place?

Where is it located?

What is today's date?

What is the month?

What is the year?

How old are you?

When were you born (month)?

When were you born (year)?

Who is the President of the United States?

Who was the President before him?

These questions subsequently were employed extensively by Goldfarb[20] to evaluate demented patients. Pfeiffer[43] recently modified the questions (Table 2) and standardized the test for differences in race and educational achievement. Although Pfeiffer's test has been thoroughly studied in a "normal" aged population, there is reason to doubt that it will be sensitive enough to detect incipient and mild dementia. A similar, but shorter, questionnaire (for temporal orientation alone) was prepared by Benton, Van Allen, and Fogel.[9] They found nearly perfect performance not only in their controls but also in a significant proportion of their patients with identified brain damage. On the other hand, substantial errors were confined almost entirely to brain damaged patients. This study suggests that although false positive findings are rare, false negatives are frequent. A factor hampering interpretation is that clinical evaluation of these simpler tests has not been reported in large groups of patients with known psychiatric dysfunction.

A similar but more detailed measure was drawn up and used by Blessed, Tomlinson, and Roth.[10] The test has two parts, a "Dementia Scale," which is essentially a measure of multiple aspects of behavior as observed by attendants, and an "Information-Memory-Concentration Test," which is a longer and more detailed memory-information type questionnaire similar to those described above. This

Table 2. Mental status questionnaire of Pfeiffer[43]

What is the date today?_____		
Month	Day	Year

What day of the week is it? _____

What is the name of this place? _____

What is your telephone number? _____

What is your street address? _____
(Ask only if patient does not have a telephone)

How old are you? _____

When were you born? _____

Who is the President of the U.S. now? _____

Who was President just before him? _____

What was your mother's maiden name?_____

Substract 3 from 20 and keep subtracting 3 from each new number you get, all the way down.

measure served Blessed, Tomlinson, and Roth well in their studies of demented patients and of hospitalized patients without dementia; it has also been used by Hachinski and coworkers[28] to study patients with diagnosed dementia. The items in this test are probably better at uncovering dementia than are those in the shorter tests described, but the measure has not been widely evaluated using normal nonhospitalized subjects of varying ages or patients with nonorganic psychiatric dysfunction.

Several short tests for dementia have been proposed that measure both memory and fluency. Borkowski and coworkers[11] modified a test originally devised by Thurstone and asked subjects to name as many words beginning with a given letter as they could in 1 minute. The test differentiated between groups of brain damaged patients and controls, but overlap was considerable. More recently Isaacs and coworkers[33, 34] described the Set Test for detecting dementia. In this test, the subject is asked to name as many items as he can recall in each of 4 categories or "sets"—colors, animals, fruits, and towns. A maximum of 10 items are accepted for each set, resulting in a possible maximum score of 40. Scores of less than 15 were closely related to diagnoses of dementia; scores between 15 and 24 were less reliably associated with dementia, whereas no subject who scored over 25 was diagnosed as demented. Again, the test was studied in a relatively small group of subjects, and its use has not been reported in patients with functional psychiatric disorders.

Short visuomotor performance tests have also been used as an index of cerebral function. Among the many tests available, the Trail-Making Test[49] appears to be a useful screening instrument for organic involvement,[12] although as with any individual psychological test, it is not foolproof.[23] Its benefit lies in its brevity and ease of administration; with normal performance the entire test can be administered in less than 3 minutes. It consists of 2 printed pages. On Part A, the subject is asked to draw a line to connect 25 numbers that are scattered over the page, and his performance is timed. The primary task components are active visual search for the spatial array and fine movement. Part B requires the subject to drawn a line connecting numbers and letters alternately and in sequence. Good performance is unusual in the presence of significant organic disease; poor performance, however, by no means proves organic disease and should only be a stimulus for more intensive evaluation.

In summary, brief psychological tests may be useful in certain circumstances. For example, Pfeiffer's[43] questionnaire and the test used by Blessed, Tomlinson and Roth[10] are valuable in assessment of moderate to severe dysfunction in high-risk groups. Most screening questionnaires, however, probably fail to identify patients with mild dementia. Tests which combine requirements for memory and fluency hold promise and deserve more extensive testing. High level performance on visuomotor tasks is helpful in ruling out significant organic disease, but poor performance may reflect a variety of causes other than organicity.

Tests of General Brain Function

Most tests used to provide an index of overall brain function have been outgrowths of attempts to predict school performance (Binet) or to measure an abstract concept usually called intelligence (Wechsler). Argument persists as to whether intelligence is a unitary capacity or a composite of a variety of functions.[54, 59] The European emphasis has been on a unitary capacity, and intelligence tests, such as Raven's Progressive Matrices,[46] are used to assess intelligence in general as well as to investigate the influence of brain damage.[55] The North American bias has been toward assessing intelligence as a composite of many factors. This argument will not concern us here.

Wechsler Adult Intelligence Scale

The most widely used intelligence test is the Wechsler Adult Intelligence Scale (WAIS)[58] which fortunately has proven especially useful in the assessment of dementia. The WAIS has been standardized for a wide age range. Since many aspects of performance decline with aging and most dementia begins in middle and old age, this standardization is of considerable importance. An additional advantage is that the test can be repeated without a learning effect invalidating the results.

Nevertheless, the WAIS has drawbacks. It must be administered individually and requires considerable time, effort, and attention from both examiner and subject. Training is required for administration, scoring, and interpretation. Also results are to some extent influenced by culture and education of the subject.

The WAIS is made up of 11 subtests: 6 classified as "verbal" — Information (old and general in nature), Comprehension (judgment and social understanding), Arithmetic, Similarities (e.g. coat-dress; praise-punishment), Digit Span, Vocabulary; and 5 classified as "performance" — Digit Symbol (transcription of numbers into symbols), Picture Completion (identification of missing parts in drawings), Block Design (arrangement of blocks to form specified patterns), Picture Arrangement (placing pictures in logical pattern to tell story), Object Assembly (assembling parts to make a manikin, profile, hand, and elephant). Performance on the 6 verbal tasks may be combined to form a verbal score from which a verbal Intelligence Quotient (I.Q.) can be derived by reference to an age specific table; the same can be done for the 5 performance subtests. The verbal score and performance score can then be combined for a full scale score from which the full scale I.Q. is derived. Normally the scaled scores for the specific subtests vary little in a given individual; the same is generally true for mentally retarded subjects but not necessarily for patients with brain lesions occurring in later life. The verbal and performance I.Q.s are seldom separated by more than a few points in normal subjects but may be separated by 20 or more points in demented patients.

By definition, an I.Q. of 100 reflects the median of an age defined population, I.Q. being merely a comparison of an individual's performance with that of peers of the same age. With increasing age, an increasing percentage of the population experiences decreased performance on testing; therefore, in an absolute sense, the performance level of the population decreases. It requires less and less functional ability of the individual to maintain an average I.Q. Maintaining the same I.Q. over a long span of years then denotes considerable decline in performance on the standardized tests of the WAIS. An elderly patient can have considerable impairment of function (compared to that of earlier years) with an I.Q. within the normal range.

The WAIS is usually modified by the disorders that produce dementia. This is most convincingly demonstrated when the scores decline in the same person tested repeatedly over time. Unfortunately this does not help in the initial assessment of the patient except for those rare instances in which the test was performed earlier for another purpose (and where the records have been retained and are available). Several methods have been employed in attempts to assess organic dysfunction from a single WAIS. These include: (1) a decline in present full scale I.Q. from that which might have been predicted on the basis of education and vocational attainments, (2) a wider than normal spread between verbal and performance I.Q.s, and (3) increased intertest score variation with low scores on subtests considered to be particularly vulnerable to organic lesions.

Intelligence tests, originally designed to predict school performance, correlate well with educational attainment and vocational success. However, the relationship is far from exact in the individual patient. Not infrequently a person is encountered with a high I.Q. and little education or a person with an average or below average I.Q. and a college degree. Nevertheless, Fogel[18] demonstrated, in a comparison of brain damaged patients with carefully selected controls, that a low measured I.Q. in comparison to the predicted I.Q. (based on educational attainment) points toward organic brain disease. Accurate figures for predicted I.Q.s are not generally available, however, and the studies have not been extended to patients with functional psychiatric disorders.

A greater than normal spread between verbal and performance I.Q.s (especially with a lower performance I.Q.) has often been considered characteristic of organic brain disease. Nevertheless, considerable question persists as to the reliability of this observation.[18, 56] Most physicians and psychologists consider a performance I.Q. of 20 or more points below the verbal I.Q. to be a strong indicator of possible cerebral disease. However, this spread often fails to appear, particularly if left hemispheric involvement causes impaired language function which is reflected in a decline of the verbal I.Q.

An extension of this approach has been the attempt to use interest variation as a measure of organic dysfunction. Specifically, certain subtests (information, vocabulary, picture completion, object assembly) have been noted to be relatively unaffected by deterioration in organic brain disease (the so-called "hold" items). (Different authorities assign different subtests to the "hold" or "don't hold" categories.) Low scores on "don't hold" subtests in combination with relatively normal scores on "hold" subtests suggest organic brain disease. Various mathematical formulae have been devised to quantitate these changes and derive a "deterioration" index:

$$\frac{\text{Scores on "hold" tests} - \text{Scores on "don't hold" tests}}{\text{Scores on "hold" tests}} = \text{Deterioration Index}$$

Studies have cast doubt on the applicability of these methods as well as those described earlier.[60]

Other researchers have suggested that certain "don't hold" subtests (e.g., block design, digit symbol) might alone reflect organic dysfunction. Indeed, Violon and Rustin[56] found that low scores on the digit symbol subtest alone indicated organic dysfunction as accurately as did information derived from the full WAIS. Fogel found the same for the block design subtest in one study[18] and for the picture arrangement subtest in another.[19] This area obviously needs further study.

In summary, the WAIS is a valuable though not infallible tool for the detection of organic brain disease. Detection of early or minimal organic disease may be difficult, and false negatives should be expected. False positives are probably less frequent, but are not unknown.[37]

Halstead and Reitan Batteries

Halstead,[30] in his studies of frontal lobe function, developed several neuropsychological tests in an attempt to devise a sensitive instrument for measuring "biolgical intelligence" and, coincidentally, for detecting organic brain disease. The Halstead "battery" consists of 10 measures: I. Category Test (primarily abstractional ability); II. Critical Flicker Frequency Test; III. Critical Flicker Frequency-Deviation Test; IV. Tactual Performance (form board) Test, Time Component; V. Tactual Performance Test, Memory Component; VI. Tactual Performance Test, Localization Component; VII. Rhythm Subtest; VIII. Speech-Sound Perception Test; IX. Finger Oscillation (tapping) Test; and X. Time Sense Test, Memory Component. From these 10 measures Halstead derived an overall Impairment Index. Reitan[47] applied this battery to 50 brain damaged patients and to a finely matched control group and found that the Impairment Index provided excellent though not perfect separation of the two groups.

Reitan has added to and refined these and other tests seeking a finer instrument for the detection of organic disease. With the WAIS and the Halstead battery he variously combined the Wheeler-Reitan modification of the Halstead-Wepman Aphasia Screening Test, the Trail-Making Test, tests of peripheral sensory and perceptual function, examination for lateral dominance, measurement of strength of grip, and the Minnesota Multiphasic Personality Index (MMPI).[26] Filskov and Goldstein[17] compared the accuracy of the Reitan battery with 6 other ancillary neurological diagnostic procedures in the identification of neurological disease and found it to be generally superior to any of the other individual procedures. However, their experimental design was such that false positives were impossible and false negatives were not followed up over time. Nevertheless, there is no question that the Reitan battery is a sensitive test for organic brain dysfunction. However, the battery is complex and expensive, requires approximately 5 hours to administer, and demands considerable effort from both subject and examiner. Also its interpretation requires considerable skill. It is probably the best instrument available for research purposes.

Wechsler Memory Scale

The Wechsler Memory Scale (WMS)[57] assesses both general and discrete brain function. It tests various aspects of memory including orientation to person, time, place, and current events; mental control items such as counting backwards, counting by 3s, and reciting the alphabet; immediate recall of paragraphs presented verbally; digit span similar to the WAIS; reproduction of geometric designs after 10 seconds observation; and the learning of 10 paired associations presented and tested 3 times.

The test is designed to determine a memory quotient (M.Q.) in the same manner that I.Q. is determined. It is widely used clinically; but its use far exceeds its usefulness. The content of the subtests is out of date, and Cohen[14] has demonstrated that the M.Q. does not differentiate between psychoneurotic, organic, and schizophrenic groups.

In a factor analysis of normal subjects' performances on the WMS, Dujovne and Levy[16] found that 1 of the 3 factors in the M.Q. is simple learning ability. This finding points to a major deficiency in research on intellectual functioning in dementia. Investigators have concentrated on the ability of the subject to retain material presented once and tested after a delay. Only recently has the ability of the subject to learn new material presented repeatedly begun to receive attention.[13] Such information may be both valuable diagnostically and useful in making recommendations for patient management.

Tests Designed to Measure More Discrete Qualities

Tests for Abstraction, Reasoning, and Problem Solving

The qualities of abstraction, reasoning, and problem solving, which many consider the highest integrative functions of the nervous system, are perhaps as difficult to define as to measure. Nevertheless, the capacity to conceptualize, abstract, reason, and solve problems—especially with flexibility and ease in new situations—is commonly observed to be defective in the brain damaged patient. A wide variety of approaches has been used in attempts to measure this elusive capacity, but the dependence of these functions upon the integrity of others (language, memory, perception) makes their measurement more difficult. We will consider only a few of the more commonly used tests.

HALSTEAD'S CATEGORY TEST. This subtest of Halstead's battery,[30] designed initially to measure frontal lobe damage, is generally considered to primarily test concept formation. Problems are presented visually, and the subject is asked to look for similarities and differences in the stimulus material, to formulate a hypothesis as to the correct concept (variables include size, shape, position, oddity, etc.), and to respond by pressing 1 of 4 keys. Positive or negative reinforcement (bell or buzzer) tells the subject whether the decisions are accurate or not. After a series of problems with similar solutions, the correct solution is changed, thus making the test a complex evaluation of "learning to learn," ability to utilize reinforcement, and capacity to alter strategies or hypotheses. Performance has been shown[47] to be strikingly deficient in patients with identified brain damage, but again the test is not perfect, and a few patients with brain damage doubtless perform within the usually accepted range of normal.

GOLDSTEIN-SCHEERER TEST OF ABSTRACT AND CONCRETE THINKING.[21] This test is based on the propositions that abstract thinking typifies efficient brain function and concrete thinking typifies deficient brain function. There are five subtests: Goldstein-Scheerer Cube Test, The Goldstein-Sheerer Stick Test, Gelb-Goldstein Color Sorting Test, Weigle-Goldstein-Sheerer Color-Form Sorting Test, and the Goldstein-Sheerer Object Sorting Test. The Cube Test and the Stick Test assess visuomotor skills by requiring the subject to copy designs with blocks or sticks respectively. The other three tests require the subject to sort objects on the basis of various concepts (e.g., color, shape, class) and then to shift sets. They are nonverbal, making them useful in some patients with language deficits. These tests are relatively sensitive, but they are not specific for brain damage. They have also been criticized for the absence of data on their reliability and the influence of age and intelligence on results.[32]

GORHAM PROVERBS TEST.[24] The ability to interpret proverbs has long been considered a manifestation of the capacity for abstract thinking. Conversely the inability to interpret proverbs has been considered a manifestation of impaired brain function. Proverb interpretation has been part of the usual mental status examination, and defects have been recognized in cases of cultural deprivation, mental retardation, schizophrenia, and organic brain damage. However, the usual

196

clinical examination has relied on anecdotal observations and quantification has been difficult. Gorham devised a multiple choice proverbs test with interpretations of each proverb that vary in degrees of abstraction and concreteness. From the responses chosen by the subject, both an "abstract score" and a "concrete score" were obtained. Taking good abstraction as an indication of high level brain function and concreteness as evidence of impaired brain function, the Proverbs Test proved to be a good test for organic brain disease, although it failed to identify some patients with documented disease.[19] The same test has demonstrated impaired function in schizophrenics.[25]

Tests of Visuomotor Performance

Various tests have been devised in which the subject is asked to draw a common object from memory, copy a series of geometric line drawings, or copy illustrated designs with sticks or blocks. Often some of these tests are included in mental status examinations performed by neurologists and psychiatrists. Patients are commonly asked to draw a picture of a clock, house, person, or tree. Spatial neglect, distortion, rotation, fragmentation, lack of integration, or perservation in these drawings suggest organic dysfunction and call for more complete testing. In addition, some psychologists and psychiatrists have developed skills in utilizing these drawings as projective tests revealing of feelings and conflicts perhaps not consciously accessible.

BENDER GESTALT TEST.[2] This is probably the most commonly used test of visuomotor ability. The subject is asked to copy 9 geometric figures. Errors in reproduction may be scored,[29] but often observation is sufficient and scoring is unnecessary. This test is nonverbal and thus largely independent of educational attainment, although some types of errors, such as rotations, have been related to intelligence independent of organic disease.[27] Performance obviously depends on visual and motor function, so that the test is used mainly when these functions are intact on neurological examination. When visual and motor functions are impaired, interpretation of the test is difficult. Poor reproduction of the designs by a cooperative patient with intact visual and motor functions usually indicates disease of the cerebral hemispheres.

A memory component may be added by asking the patient to reproduce the designs from memory after having copied them. This test measures "visual retention" in contrast to most tests of memory which measure auditory or verbal memory. Assessment of this component relies on clinical judgment, for no good scoring system is available.

BENTON VISUAL RETENTION TEST.[6] This test was originally designed to test immediate memory plus visuomotor ability. More recently it has been used for visuomotor ability alone.[5] Subjects are presented a series of line drawings varying from simple to complex. If immediate memory is to be tested, the subject is allowed to view each drawing for 5 to 10 seconds and asked to reproduce the drawing following a delay of 15 seconds. If visuomotor ability alone is to be tested, the subject is asked to draw the design shown and maintained in his visual field. Errors of omission, addition, distortion, perserveration, rotation, misplacement, and size are noted and scored. A recently revised scoring system has improved the accuracy of the test as used to assess memory.[39] When presented as a copying task, normal subjects perform at perfect or nearly perfect levels. Brain damaged patients as a group perform defectively[5]; however some brain damaged subjects perform well despite clear evidence of brain disease on other diagnostic procedures.

WAIS BLOCK DESIGN AND DIGIT SYMBOL SUBTESTS. Both these subtests measure visuomotor ability and cerebral integration. As mentioned above, these are "don't hold" subtests in the WAIS, the scores of which are frequently depressed in organic brain disease.

IMPLICATIONS. Visuomotor ability and constructional ability are nonverbal and may be missed both on mental status and neurological examinations. The tests described above are designed to reveal defects in these areas. Deficiencies in performance are, however, of limited localizing value. Although the parietal lobes (especially the right) are perhaps most important in maintaining these functions, performance may be impaired by either diffuse or localized lesions elsewhere. However, a severe deficiency in these tasks with good capacities otherwise would most strongly suggest a right parietal lobe lesion. These tests probably present few false positives, but false negatives are not infrequent.

Tests of Language Function

It is unlikely that gross evidence of aphasia or other language defect would be missed on thorough mental status examination by either a neurologist or psychiatrist (except perhaps mistaking fluent aphasia for the "word salad" of schizophrenia as emphasized by Benson[3, 4]). On the other hand, mild defects in language function are easily overlooked and may be recognized only by appropriate testing. The complete mental status examination contains procedures to test auditory comprehension, articulation, verbal fluency, object naming, grammar and syntax, paraphasia, reading, and writing. When rigorously performed, this portion of the mental status examination probably leads to recognition of most patients with language function defects. However, the usual level of examination is not very sophisticated, and probably mild language defects are frequently overlooked.

Many psychological tests in common use (including some already mentioned) evaluate one or another aspect of language function, yet few have this as the primary objective. Considering the importance of language in human thinking and communication and the importance of language defects as evidence of focal cerebral disease, it is surprising that so few tests for this specific function have achieved popularity and that virtually none are routinely used. Most tests in regular use are designed to measure the scope and specificity of the language defect in a patient already recognized as "aphasic," the most familiar being those used in speech therapy centers to evaluate patients referred for treatment.

DeRenzi and Vignolo[15] described a Token Test to uncover receptive disorders that are not evident "during normal conversation." The test utilized tokens of different sizes, shapes, and colors which the subject was asked to manipulate in various ways in response to 5 sets of verbal instructions of increasing complexity. The test as originally described showed promise but was not standardized for age and intelligence nor were patients with non-aphasic disorders studied.

The Wheeler-Reitan Modification of the Halstead-Wepman Aphasia Screening Test is perhaps the one most frequently utilized in a psychological test battery. It requires only a few minutes and is designed to demonstrate agnosia, anomia, articulation defects, paraphasia, and aphasic defects. Unfortunately it is not well standardized for different ages, educational achievements, and intelligence levels. Although there is considerable dependence on the examiner's interpretive skills,

198

errors are generally considered pathognomonic of brain damage. The Porch Index of Communicative Ability (PICA),[45] the Boston Diagnostic Aphasia Examination,[22] and the Minnesota Test[31] are longer and more elaborate and make extensive demands on examiner and subject. They are generally used to define, with more precision, defects which are apparent clinically.

In summary, lengthy, sophisticated, and expensive tests are available to explore and define with considerable accuracy and detail the nature of speech and language defects. However, patients who are so evaluated generally have already been recognized on clinical grounds to have language impairment. Still lacking are short, easily administered, well standardized tests which effectively screen for those aphasic defects that are not apparent on routine clinical examination. It is likely that a more rigorous and meticulous routine mental status examination could identify most of these defects.

Personality Assessment

Tests of personality are not generally utilized for the recognition and assessment of organic dysfunction. Although personality changes certainly occur with brain impairment, the types of change are idiosyncratic to each person and thus not diagnostic. More important is the help which psychological tests of personality provide in the thorny diagnostic problem of pseudo-dementia.[39] As discussed in Chapters 1 and 12, depression and other functional disorders often masquerade as dementia. With contradictory evidence of dementia from neuropsychological tests and confirmatory evidence of depression and other functional disorders from personality tests, the clinician may be encouraged to pursue a thorough psychiatric evaluation.

Personality assessment may also help in planning for patient management. Demented patients may adopt any of a number of coping devices such as compulsive ordering of life events, agitated behavior, depression in reaction to declining abilities, and sporadic and unpredictable outbursts of irritability due to frustration. Tests may provide insight into the dynamics of this behavior and assist the family in adjusting to the patient's changed behavior and in arranging the environment to provide more support.

The most commonly used projective tests for personality assessment are the Rorschach,[51] Thematic Apperception Test (TAT),[41] and the Sentence Completion Test.[52] Projective techniques use the patient's responses to relatively nonspecific stimuli as clues to feelings, worries, conflicts, defense mechanisms, and behavioral patterns. In the Rorschach, the subject is shown a series of 10 ink blots (either black and white or color), and his perceptions of and associations to the individual blots are recorded in detail. Elaborate scoring systems may be used.[1] Piotrowski[44] and a number of other investigators have attempted to develop a scoring system for organic impairment. Reitan,[48, 50] in a series of well controlled studies, concluded that although there are distinguishing features, the test is inferior to others in the diagnosis of organic states.

In the Thematic Apperception Test (TAT),[41] the subject is presented a series of pictures of structured scenes and asked to make up a story about each. This test is not used as an indicator of organic dysfunction[42] but may identify important dynamic features. In the Sentence Completion Test,[52] the subject is given a series of incomplete sentences and asked to supply the predicates. This latter test taps problems and conflicts present at a more conscious level than the other two.

199

The most commonly used personality test is the Minnesota Multiphasic Personality Inventory (MMPI),[31] a true-false questionnaire made up of several hundred items that has been well standardized and is even subject to interpretation by computer. It is useful both as an indicator of personality structure and of current dynamics and distress. Again abnormalities may occur with organic dysfunction but the test does not measure them directly.

Projective and personality techniques serve mainly here to help in understanding the character structure and dynamics of the patient with organic brain disease, not in establishing the diagnosis or measuring the dysfunction.

CASE STUDIES

Two examples of the clinical application of psychological testing are presented below. They have been chosen to demonstrate the usefulness of psychological test procedures in patients presenting problems in diagnosis and treatment.

> The patient, a prominent 60-year-old professional man referred for neuropsychiatric evaluation and treatment by his internist, complained chiefly of trouble concentrating and inability to accomplish as much work as he thought he should. His symptoms had begun insidiously 1 to 2 years earlier and had been slowly progressive. He perceived his efficiency to be reduced, although others had not remarked on this. He found it easy to put off chores and had trouble initiating new tasks, especially if these involved creativity. Concentrating on new topics and planning new projects were particularly difficult. He noted increased forgetfulness and had been embarrassed by this. He found letters in his files which he had written and forgotten. For several months insomnia had worsened, and his alcoholic intake had increased moderately. Frustration tolerance was lowered. Some feelings of anxiety and depression were acknowledged, but he attributed them to concern about his symptoms.
>
> There was history of long and steady superior professional accomplishments. He had been happily married for many years. There was no history of previous neurological or psychiatric disorders. His general health was good.

The patient was cooperative and behaved appropriately during the examination. Neurological examination was entirely normal. On mental status examination, he was noted to have difficulty describing his symptoms with precision, and he rambled in his speech. When he spoke of remote events, his descriptions were much more tightly organized than were his descriptions of recent events. At times he had difficulty in recalling a memory, and at other times he hesitated in choosing a word. However, detailed testing of orientation, language, memory, and general intellectual functions revealed no defects. He appeared worried and moderately depressed.

In summary, this man presented a history rather typical of that described in dementia, but specific cognitive defects were lacking on mental status evaluation. In addition he evinced more awareness of decline in his capacities than do most patients with dementia, and he appeared depressed. Psychological evaluation was requested, the question being if psychological tests could reveal abnormalities to support a diagnosis of organic brain disease or evidence to cast doubt on this diagnosis.

200

On the WAIS, the patient had a full scale I.Q. of 137 (commensurate with his educational level) without significant spread between verbal and performance scores and without significant intertest variability. Tactual Performance Tests were quickly and accurately performed as were parts A and B of the Trail-Making Test. The Benton Visual Retention Test was carried out better than would have been expected for a man of his age. Rorschach and MMPI revealed considerable depression and anxiety in a man with high aspirations and expectations of nearly perfect performance. In summary, psychological testing revealed excellent performance on tests usually most sensitive to organic dysfunction plus evidence of significant depression.

A diagnosis of neurotic depression was made, and the patient was treated with psychotherapy with significant improvement. Follow-up after 2 years has provided no additional evidence of organic disease.

In this instance, the patient's very high level of performance on the psychological tests usually sensitive to organicity obviated the need for further neurological diagnostic procedures and directed attention to treatment of his basic psychiatric disorder. Follow-up confirmed the soundness of this approach.

A 50-year-old man, complained of "nerves" and "memory troubles" so severe that he feared he could not keep going. His symptoms dated back to World War II when he had been knocked unconscious by an explosion, awoke on a hospital ship several days later, and had never been the same since. A dissociative reaction was diagnosed at that time and he had since been admitted repeatedly to VA hospitals for depressive and anxious states which had been helped minimally by the varied treatments employed.

A more detailed history revealed that his memory problem had been unchanged since its onset. He had operated a dry-cleaning establishment but gave this up because he was unable to remember customers' names (a significant problem when he had to make charges to their accounts). He went into industry and was promoted by steps to a position of supervisory responsibility over 40 men. Still his memory troubles persisted, causing him more and more difficulty with each added responsibility. Although he knew his men well, he forgot their names, and he regularly failed to recall the names of objects and of tasks he needed to direct them to do. He lived in a small town and knew everyone but could never recall their names when greeted on the street. Periodically he perceived his memory trouble as unbearable and became depressed, requiring hospitalization.

On examination the patient was alert and cooperative but preoccupied with his symptoms, anxious, and depressed. He cried easily but was not suicidal. He spoke hesitantly and slowly, especially in answer to specific questions, but more fluently when the examiner was non-directive. At times he stuttered. Orientation was correct, and immediate recall was good. Memory for recent and remote events and overall intellectual function for his educational level appeared excellent. Testing for language function was difficult because he became agitated whenever he could not think of a specific word, and this occurred repeatedly. Comprehension appeared good. The patient could discuss many details about recent presidents but was unable to name any. He could not write well from dictation but expressed himself well, though slowly, in writing spontaneously. Neurological examination was entirely normal.

Hospitalization was advised because of the intensity of his distress and the need for more thorough neurological and psychiatric evaluation. The history strongly suggested some longstanding brain damage with language impairment, but his affective distress was so striking that it suggested depressive psychosis with associated features of pseudo-dementia. Psychological consultation was requested to determine if testing might uncover evidence of organic impairment, specifically any focal damage which might account for a portion of his symptoms.

The WAIS revealed a verbal I.Q. of 96 and a performance I.Q. of 121. On the Wechsler Memory Scale, he had much difficulty in memory for auditory input. Performance was below normal on the Benton Visual Retention Test. Part B of the Trail-Making Test was strikingly impaired in relation to Part A, indicating particular difficulty with alphabetical symbols. The Tactile Performance Test was carried out slowly, with the right hand slower than the left. These tests thus strongly supported the presence of organic brain dysfunction particularly involving the left hemisphere. Personality appraisal (Rorschach, TAT, Sentence Completion Test, MMPI) indicated an "acute panic reaction in an obsessive compulsive personality."

Skull x-rays, radioisotope scanning, and electroencephalograms were all normal. It was concluded that this man had suffered brain damage involving the left hemisphere during the World War II episode which he described. His basic intellectual capacity and his obsessive-compulsive personality led to his being placed and retained in jobs of considerable responsibility, jobs which were very stressful to him because of the unrecognized deficits imposed by his left hemispheric damage. In addition, he had suffered for many years because his organic defects were attributed to his "nerves" thus leading to further frustrations.

Explanations as to the nature and extent of his organic impairment, counseling, medication, and environmental changes to reduce demands upon the patient led to considerable symptomatic improvement

In this patient, organic and emotional dysfunctions were intimately intertwined as they so often are. Psychological testing helped define each aspect of the patient's disorder so that they could be better dealt with individually and concurrently.

REFERENCES

1. BECK, S. J.: *Rorschach's Test,* Vols. I, II, and III. Grune and Stratton, New York, 1944.

2. BENDER, L.: *A Visual Motor Gestalt Test and Its Clinical Use.* Research Monograph No. 3, American Orthopsychiatric Association, New York, 1938.

3. BENSON, D. F.: *Psychiatric aspects of aphasia.* Br. J. Psychiatry 123:555, 1973.

4. BENSON, D. F.: Disorders of verbal expression, in Benson, D. F., and Blumer, D. (eds.): *Psychiatric Aspects of Neurological Disease.* Grune & Stratton, New York, 1975.

5. BENTON, A. L.: *The visual retention test as a constructional praxis task.* Confin. Neurol. 22:141, 1962.

6. BENTON, A. L.: *The Visual Retention Test. Clinical and Experimental Applications,* ed. 3. Psychological Corporation, New York, 1963.

7. BENTON, A. L.: Psychologic testing, in Baker, A. B., and Baker, L H. (eds.): *Clinical Neurology.* Harper and Row, Publishers, Hagerstown, Md., 1974.

8. BENTON, A. L.: Psychological tests for brain damage, in Freedman, A. M.; Kaplan, H. I.; and Sadock, B. J. (Eds.): *Comprehensive Textbook of Psychiatry — II.* The Williams & Wilkins Co., Baltimore, 1975.

9. BENTON, A. L.; VAN ALLEN, M. W.; AND FOGEL, M. L.: *Temporal orientation in cerebral disease.* J. Nerv. Ment. Dis. 139:110, 1964.

10. BLESSED, G.; TOMLINSON, B. E.; AND ROTH, M.: *The association between quantitative measures of dementia and of senile change in the cerebral grey matter of elderly subjects.* Br. J. Psychiatry 114:797, 1968.

11. BORKOWSKI, J. G.; BENTON, A. L.; AND SPREEN, O.: *Word fluency and brain damage.* Neuropsychologia 5:135, 1967.

12. BROWN, E.; CASEY, A.; FISCH, C., ET AL.: *Trail making test as a screening device for the detection of brain damage.* J. Consult. Psychol. 22:469, 1958.

13. BUSCHKE, H., AND FULD, P.A.: *Evaluating storage, retention, and retrieval in disordered memory and learning.* Neurology (Minneap.) 24:1019, 1974.

14. COHEN, J.: *Wechsler memory scale performance of psychoneurotic, organic and schizophrenic groups.* J. Consult. Clin. Psychol. 14:371, 1950.

15. DERENZI, E., AND VIGNOLO, L. A.: *The token test: A sensitive test to detect receptive disturbances in aphasics.* Brain 85:665, 1962.

16. DUJOVNE, B. E., AND LEVY, B. I.: *The psychometric structure of the Wechsler Memory Scale.* J. Clin. Psychol. 27:351, 1971.

17. FILSKOV, S. B., AND GOLDSTEIN, S. G.: *Diagnostic validity of the Halstead-Reitan neuropsychological battery.* J. Consult. Clin. Psychol. 42:382, 1974.

18. FOGEL, M. L.: *The intelligence quotient as an index of brain damage.* Am. J. Orthopsychiatry 34:555, 1964.

19. FOGEL, M. L.: *The proverbs test in the appraisal of cerebral disease.* J. Gen. Psychol. 72:269, 1965.

20. GOLDFARB, A. I.: *Predicting mortality in the institutionalized aged. A seven-year follow-up.* Arch. Gen. Psychiatry 21:172, 1969.

21. GOLDSTEIN, K., AND SCHEERER, M.: *Abstract and concrete behavior: An experimental study with special tests.* Psychol. Monogr. 53:2, 1941.

22. GOODGLASS, H., AND KAPLAN, E.: *The Assessment of Aphasia and Related Disorders.* Lea & Febiger, Philadelphia, 1972.

23. GORDON, N. G.: *The trail making test of neuropsychological diagnosis.* J. Clin. Psychol. 28:167, 1972.

24. GORHAM, D. R.: *A proverbs test for clinical and experimental use.* Psychol. Rep. 2 (Monog. Suppl. No. 1) 1–12, 1956.

25. GORHAM, D. R.: *Use of the proverbs test for differentiating schizophrenics from normals.* J. Consult. Clin. Psychol. 20:435, 1956.

26. GRANT, I.; MOHNS, L.; MILLER, M.; AND REITAN, R. M.: *A neuropsychological study of polydrug users.* Arch. Gen. Psychiatry 33:973, 1976.

27. GRIFFITH, R. M., AND TAYLOR, V. H.: *Bender-Gestalt figure rotations: A stimulus factor.* J. Consult. Clin. Psychol. 25:89, 1961.

28. HACHINSKI, V. C.; ILIFF, L. D.; ZILHKA, E.; DUBOULAY, G. H.; MCALLISTER, V. L.; MARSHALL, J.; RUSSELL, R. W. R.; AND SYMON, L.: *Cerebral blood flow in dementia.* Arch. Neurol. 32:632, 1975.

29. HAIN, J. D.: *The Bender-Gestalt Test: A scoring method for identifying brain damage.* J. Consult. Clin. Psychol. 28:34, 1964.

30. HALSTEAD, W. C.: *Brain and Intelligence.* University of Chicago Press, Chicago, 1947.

31. HATHAWAY, S. R., AND MCKINLEY, J. C.: *The Minnesota Multiphasic Personality Inventory.* The Psychological Corporation, New York, 1942.

32. HORENSTEIN, S.: The clinical use of psychological testing in dementia, in Wells, C. E. (ed.): *Dementia,* ed. 1. F. A. Davis Co., Phileladelphia, 1971.

33. ISAACS, B., AND AKHTAR, A. J.: *The set test.* Age and Aging 1:222, 1972.

34. ISAACS, B., AND KENNIE, A. T.: *The set test as an aid to the detection of dementia in old people.* Br. J. Psychiatry 123:467, 1973.

35. JENKINS, J. J.; JIMENEZ-PABON, E.; SHAW, R. E.; AND SEFER, J. W.: *Schuell's Aphasia in Adults,* ed. 2. Harper & Row, Publishers, Hagerstown, Md., 1975.

36. KAHN, R. L., POLLOCK, M.; AND GOLDFARB, A. I.: Factors related to individual differences in mental status of institutionalized aged, in Hoch, P. H., and Zubin, J. (eds.): *Psychopathology of Aging.* Grune and Stratton, New York, 1961.

37. KILOH, L. G.: *Pseudo-dementia.* Acta Psychiatr. Scand. 37:336, 1961.

38. LACKS, P. B.: *Revised interpretation of Benton visual retention test scores.* J. Clin. Psychol. 27: 481, 1971.

39. LOWRY, J.; BAHR, A. L.; ALLEN, J. H., JR.; MEACHAM, W. F.; AND JAMES, A. E., JR.: Radiological techniques in the diagnostic evaluation of dementia, in Wells, C. E. (ed.): *Dementia,* ed. 2. F. A. Davis Co., Philadelphia, 1977.

40. MILLER, E.: Psychological testing, in Pearce, J. and Miller, E. (eds.): *Clinical Aspects of Dementia.* Balliére-Tindall, London, 1973.

41. MURRAY, H. A.: *Thematic Apperception Test.* Harvard University Press, Cambridge, Mass., 1943.

42. MURSTEIN, B. I.: *Theory and Research in Projective Techniques.* (Emphasizing the TAT). John Wiley and Sons, New York, 1963.

43. PFEIFFER, E.: *A short portable mental status questionnaire for the assessment of organic brain deficit in elderly patients.* J. Am. Geriatr. Soc. 23:433, 1975.

44. PIOTROWSKI, Z.: *On the Rorschach method and its application in organic disturbances of the central nervous system.* Rorschach Res. Exchange 1:23, 1936–37.

45. PORCH, B. E.: *Porch Index of Communicative Ability.* Consulting Psychologists Press, Palo Alto, 1971.

46. RAVEN, J.: *Guide to Using Progressive Matrices,* (revised order, 1956). H. R. Lewis Co., London, 1956.

47. REITAN, R. M.: *Investigation of the validity of Halstead's measures of biological intelligence.* Arch. Neurol. Psychiat. 73:28, 1955.

48. REITAN, R. M.: *Validity of Rorschach test as measure of psychological effects of brain damage.* Arch. Neurol. Psychiat. 73:445, 1955.

49. REITAN, R. M.: *Trail Making Test: Manual for Administration, Scoring, and Interpretation.* Indiana University, Indianapolis, 1956.

50. REITAN, R. M.: Methodological problems in clinical neuropsychology, in Reitan, R. M., and Davison, L. A. (eds.): *Clinical Neuropsychology: Current Status and Applications.* John Wiley and Sons, New York, 1974.

51. RORSCHACH, H.: *Psychodiagnostics. A Diagnostic Test Based on Perception.* (Lemkau, P., and Kronenberg, R., translators) Grune and Stratton, New York, 1942.

52. ROTTER, J. B.: *Rotter Incomplete Sentence Blank.* The Psychological Corporation, New York, 1950.

53. TOMLINSON, B. E.: The pathology of dementia, in Wells, C. E. (ed.): *Dementia,* ed. 2. F. A. Davis Co., Philadelphia, 1977.

54. TUDDENHAM, R. D.: The nature and measurement of intelligence, in Postman, L. P. (ed.): *Psychology in the Making.* Alfred A. Knopf, New York, 1964.

55. URMER, A.; MORRIS, A.; AND WENDLAND, I.: *The effect of brain damage on Raven's progressive matrices.* J. Clin. Psychol. 16:182, 1960.

56. VIOLON, A., AND RUSTIN, R. M.: *Etude des critères d'évaluation de la détérioration mentale d'étiologie organique à partir de l èchelle d'intelligence de Wechsler-Bellevue pour adultes.* Acta Psychiatr. Belg. 71:449, 1971.

57. WECHSLER, D.: *A standardized memory scale for clinical use.* J. Psychol. 19:87, 1945.

58. WECHSLER, D.: *The Measurement and Appraisal of Adult Intelligence,* ed. 4. The Williams & Wilkins Co., Baltimore, 1958.

59. ZANGWILL, O. L.: *Dsicussion on the psychopathology of dementia.* Proc. R. Soc. Med. 57:914, 1964.

60. ZIMMERMAN, I. L., AND WOO-SAM, J. M.: *Clinical Interpretation of the Wechsler Adult Intelligence Scale.* Grune and Stratton, New York, 1973.

CHAPTER 10

The Electroencephalogram in Dementia*

William P. Wilson, M.D.; Lilli Musella, Ph.D., and
M. J. Short, M.D.

In the clinical evaluation of dementia, electroencephalography is an important tool which extends the clinical examination into the pathophysiological realm. It is simple, easy to do, and repeatable, allowing its use in both diagnosis and assessment of progressive disease processes.

We will discuss first the specific clinical uses to which the electroencephalogram (EEG) may be put in evaluating the patient suspected of having dementia. We will then discuss in detail the electroencephalographic changes of normal aging and those which occur in a variety of dementing illnesses.

THE ELECTROENCEPHALOGRAM IN PATIENT EVALUATION

The EEG may be useful at each step of patient evaluation, but it is especially so as the clinician seeks to answer the following specific questions: (1) Is the disorder organic or functional? (2) Is the disorder diffuse or focal? (3) Is the disease process progressive, stable, or resolving? Rarely, the EEG may also identify the pathophysiological disorder itself with some degree of specificity, but this is not usually its prime objective.

First, the EEG may help define the disorder as functional or organic. A normal EEG never rules out organic cerebral disease; the EEG may be normal in a variety of dementing processes, especially in their early stages or when the dementia is mild.[78] On the other hand, an abnormal EEG suggests organicity and the need for further studies which might identify the specific disease responsible for the clinical picture. Harner[31] suggests that the EEG is abnormal early in the course of dementia in a high percentage of cases where the dementia is due to a treatable cause, thus perhaps increasing the value of the EEG as an early screening procedure. Of course, recognition of an EEG abnormality does not necessarily imply that it is related to the observed clinical dysfunction. False negative and false positive EEGs do occur, but they do not negate the considerable help that the EEG offers the clinician, particularly in the earliest phase of the diagnostic process.

Second, in the patient with recognized organic brain disease, the EEG often provides evidence that the pathological process is either focal or diffuse. Since

---

*From the Division of Biological Psychiatry of the Department of Psychiatry, Duke University Medical Center, Durham, North Carolina.

choice of further ancillary diagnostic procedures often depends upon whether a focal or diffuse lesion is suspected, the EEG may help define the studies required.

Third, it is often important for the physician to ascertain the temporal characteristics of the disease process, that is, whether it is progressive, stable, or resolving. When the EEG is repeated several times over a period of weeks or months, this question can often be answered with certainty.

Lastly, although the characteristics of the EEG seldom if ever permit positive identification of any specific disease process, there are rare situations in which a characteristic wave pattern strongly suggests a precise diagnosis. Examples of this, which will be discussed below, include the periodic sharp wave complexes seen in Creutzfeldt-Jakob disease and the triphasic waves that often accompany metabolic encephalopathy.

THE ELECTROENCEPHALOGRAM IN OLD AGE

Normal Aging

Studies by Blessed, Tomlinson, and Roth[5] have demonstrated a good correlation between total plaque counts in the grey matter and the degree of functional deterioration of "normal" aged subjects. They showed a range of pathological change from minimal to severe and suggested that pathological changes are part of the normal aging process.

Change in alpha rhythms has served as one of the basic parameters in EEG evaluation of aging. In his pioneering investigation of EEG and aging (carried out with aging neuropsychiatric patients), Davis[12] demonstrated a slowing of the alpha frequency with a reduction of the alpha index (equivalent to percent times alpha expressed in decimals) accompanied by increased slow activity (Fig. 1). It was not until 1952 that an EEG investigation was carried out on a group of normal old people to contrast and supplement earlier reports of abnormal EEGs in aged psychotic and demented patients. In a study of 329 persons over 60 years of age, Busse and associates[10] noted much variation in the EEGs of psychologically normal old people; in fact, they found both normal and abnormal EEGs. There

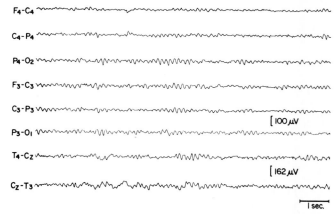

Figure 1. A 78-year-old female with normal mental function. The EEG demonstrates slowing of the alpha frequency to 7 and 7½ Hz. There is also bitemporal slowing, which is a common finding in this age group without clinical significance or correlation.

was a tendency for the basic background frequencies to decrease. Their most frequent observation was the occurrence of focal theta, particularly in the left anterior temporal region, not correlated with cerebral dominance. Incidence of this focal abnormality increased with age.

The work of Obrist[55] not only corroborated the earlier observations of Busse and his group[10] but extended our understanding of the variety of EEG findings in healthy older persons. Obrist noted that the mean occipital alpha frequency shifted from 11 to 12 Hz. (Hertz) in middle age to 7 to 8 Hz. in old age with an accompanying reduction in the alpha index. Focal slowing occurred in the temporo-occipital region in 4 percent of normal aged males, while 8 percent showed bilateral synchronous slowing in the frontoparietal region, and 2 percent had bilateral independent slowing. Obrist also observed, as had others,[23, 49, 71] that the EEG response to hyperventilation was either minimal or absent in older individuals. In a more recent study, Drachman and Hughes[15] compared the EEGs and psychological tests of normal aged subjects and of patients with circumscribed bilateral hippocampal lesions. They concluded that the EEG and cognitive findings in the normal aged subject reflected a more diffuse degenerative process rather than any primary degenerative process within the hippocampal complex. These findings were in keeping with the previously cited studies.

In summary, the electrical activity of the brain changes with age, whether or not there is clinically recognizable cerebral disease. Typical EEG changes of the senium are decreasing frequency of alpha rhythm, lower percent time alpha, unilateral temporal slowing or symmetrical anterior slowing, and decreased sensitivity to hyperventilation.

Dementia in Old Age

Studies on the dementing disorders in old age have generally suffered from a failure to define the underlying pathological processes. In addition, many of the systematic studies used diagnostic classificiations for the psychoses of old age which have been superseded by newer and more exact classifications, making comparison with current experience difficult.

Although earlier investigators[13] noted EEG changes in the organic deteriorations of old age, Mundy-Castle and coworkers[52] were the first systematically to study normal elderly subjects and to compare their EEGs with those of elderly patients with severe cerebral dysfunction. In their study of 50 mentally normal elderly persons and 104 patients with "senile psychosis," 24 percent of the normal group were found to have abnormal EEGs whereas 44 percent of the senile psychotic group had abnormal EEGs. Of their 104 patients, 44 suffered from "simple senile deterioration" which is probably equivalent to the senile dementia of Alzheimer type (SDAT) (see Chap. 6 by Tomlinson). The characteristic abnormality which they observed in this as in other forms of senile psychosis was diffuse slowing to theta and even delta frequencies (Fig. 2) along with a reduction in beta activity. These authors identified a significant relationship between increased clinical evidence of dementia, increased diffuse theta activity, and reduced alpha index.

Weiner and Schuster[78] studied 71 patients with dementia due to a variety of causes and reported the predominant encephalographic change to be increased slow activity, either diffuse or scattered, but not focal or seizure-like. The EEG was abnormal in 8 of their 9 cases of "senile dementia" and in 55 of their total of

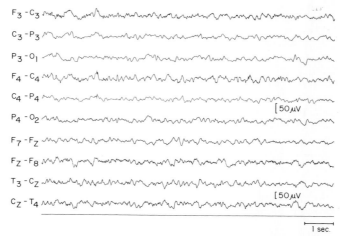

Figure 2. A 75-year-old male patient with senile dementia. The EEG demonstrates diffuse bilateral slowing in theta and delta frequencies.

71 patients. They also noted that increased low voltage fast activity, usually prominent in the elderly, was rare in dementia, occurring in only 3 of their patients. (Fig. 3)

Weiner and Schuster[78] further described a strong correlation between the severity of EEG involvement and the degree of dementia. Short, Mussela, and Wilson[70] observed that in the early stages of dementia, there is less correlation of intellectual and affective symptoms with EEG findings than when the dementia is more advanced. Their observations corroborated and extended the earlier reports of Greenblatt, Levin, and Atwell[29] and Romano and Engel.[63] In contrast, McAdam and Robinson[47] reported a linear relationship between intellectual impairment and EEG abnormalities. The latter relationship might have been predicted from the pathological findings of Blessed, Tomlinson, and Roth.[5]

Muller and Kral[51] described the appearance of bilaterally synchronous slow wave discharges of a triphasic character (similar to those seen in hepatic coma) in

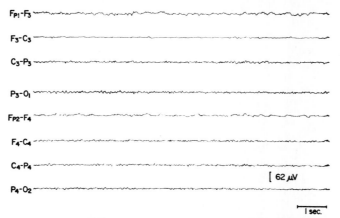

Figure 3. A 67-year-old female with classical senile dementia. The EEG demonstrates a low voltage fast record with generalized slowing, an infrequent finding in senile dementia.

208

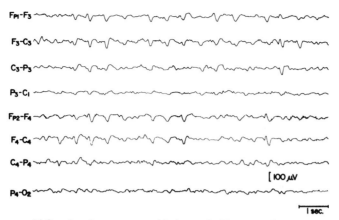

Figure 4. A 71-year-old female who presents with dementia The EEG is characterized by triphasic waves that appear bilaterally in the anterior head regions. Laboratory evaluations demonstrated compromised liver function with hyperammonemia.

elderly patients with severe dementia but without alteration of consciousness (Fig. 4). They were most frequent with senile dementia but also occurred with arteriosclerotic dementia. The prognosis for these patients was poor. In our own laboratories, however, we have found that almost all patients with triphasic waves have metabolic encephalopathy (most commonly liver failure with hyperammonemia).

Harner,[31] in an excellent review of his experiences with demented patients, observed that patients with increasingly serious neurological symptoms had a progressively increasing incidence of EEG abnormalities. Whereas, only 17 percent of patients with minimal, nonspecific neurological complaints had EEG abnormalities, 75 percent of patients with dementia of varied etiologies had abnormal EEGs. Seizures, confusion, cerebrovascular accidents, and coma were almost always associated with abnormal EEGs.

In summary, the EEG in elderly patients with dementia is characterized by diffuse slowing, the severity of which is well correlated with the degree of functional loss. The alpha index is reduced, and prominent low voltage fast activity is rare. In many studies the nature of the underlying pathological process has not been definitely established, so that in the elderly correlation between EEG changes and specific disease entities is inexact. However, the presence of EEG rhythms other than diffuse slowing suggests an etiology other than a cerebral degenerative process.

DIFFUSE PARENCHYMATOUS DISEASES—PRESENILE DEMENTIAS

The abiotrophic theory[27] of presenile dementia (the theory that the presenile dementias result from a premature loss of brain cells or, more simply, early aging) anticipates EEG findings in these conditions qualitatively similar to and probably quantitatively worse than those seen in senile dementia. In 17 cases of pathologically verified Alzheimer's disease, Letemendia and Pampiglione[43] found generalized 2 to 7 Hz. activity which responded minimally to external stimuli. There was, however, a paradoxical increase in frequency with hyperventilation and drowsiness. Sleep spindles were recognizable but of low voltage. The degree of EEG

209

abnormality correlated uniformly with the severity of the dementia. Differing somewhat from Letemendia and Pampiglione, Liddell[44] characterized the EEG patterns of Alzheimer's disease as having "a generalized basic rhythm of diffuse medium amplitude theta or slow alpha activity at 6 to 8 cycles per second (cps). Superimposed on this basic activity, paroxysmal bursts of synchronous high amplitude delta waves occurred. These bursts had a tendency to repeat themselves rhythmically and were of greatest amplitude in the frontal and temporal regions." Liddell did not correlate the degree of EEG involvement with the severity of the dementia.

In a longitudinal EEG study of the major presenile dementias, including Alzheimer's, Pick's and Creutzfeldt-Jakob diseases, Gordon and Sim[26] found the important factor when interpreting EEGs to be the stage of the dementing process. They demonstrated a reduction or absence of alpha rhythm, often with a concomitant flattening of the record, in the early stages. Later, low to medium voltage theta and delta discharges appeared rhythmically or diffusely (Fig. 5). Focal abnormalities were rare. The EEG was abnormal in all their cases of Alzheimer's disease but was sometimes normal in Pick's disease, Creutzfeldt-Jakob disease, and nonspecific presenile dementias. Otherwise there were no EEG characteristics distinguishing between the various disease groups. Records displaying prominent low voltage fast frequencies are uncommon in the presenile dementias as they are in senile dementia.

Gustafson and associates[30] in a recent article reported that in presenile dementia a reduction of cerebral blood flow in the temporal and temporoparietal areas correlated with memory deficits and agnosic symptoms including speech disturbances. Analysis of the EEG demonstrated a relationship between the degree of intellectual impairment and the severity of the EEG abnormalities.

Although recent studies[25] indicate that Creutzfeldt-Jakob is a transmissible rather than a degenerative disease, it will be discussed here with the other presenile dementias. Creutzfeldt-Jakob disease exhibits a succession of EEG changes that have interested both neurologists and electroencephalographers. Abbott[1] aroused this interest by his description of regularly recurring diffuse high voltage

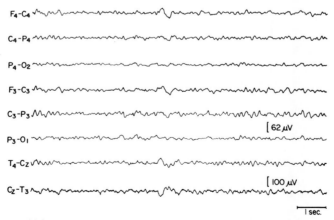

Figure 5. A 60-year-old female with a 3 year history of cerebral degenerative disease diagnosed at autopsy as Pick's disease. The EEG is characterized by the absence of alpha rhythm and the presence of theta and delta activity occurring symmetrically in the central regions and bitemporally.

210

sharp waves (up to 350 μv.) in 2 patients. Early slowing and later flattening of the background activity between the sharp wave discharges was seen (Fig. 6). Similar high voltage sharp waves have been observed in a number of patients with Creutzfeldt-Jakob disease, usually in advanced stages in the presence of both changes in level of consciousness and myoclonic jerks. Although they have been consistent enough to be called "pathognomonic" of the disorder,[21] Hoefer[36] disputed this contention, and there can be little doubt that discharges indistinguishable from these have been observed in other conditions.[42, 48]

During the final stage of Creutzfeldt-Jakob disease, Nelson[54] stereotactically placed depth electrodes in the midline and lateral thalamus, caudate nucleus, internal capsule, subcortical white matter, and upper reticular formation. Recordings showed synchronous discharges occurring in the subcortical areas. He suggested that these sharp wave discharges do not arise from the cortex but are volume-conducted potentials generated by a single source within the upper brain stem.

Further studies[9, 18, 41] have established the 2 characteristic EEG changes for Creutzfeldt-Jakob disease to be progressive slowing and eventual suppression of the background rhythms and evolution of the periodic sharp wave complexes.

In 1961 Hirano and associates,[34] reporting their extensive studies of an endemic parkinsonism-dementia syndrome that occurred among the Chamorros on Guam, noted a high incidence of abnormal EEGs in these patients. They reported a dominant alpha rhythm at 8 to 9 Hz. with diffuse theta activity superimposed, sometimes most markedly present in the temporal regions. The severity of the EEG abnormality appeared to be correlated with the severity of the mental deterioration. Although the syndrome clinically resembled Creutzfeldt-Jakob disease, the EEG findings were quite dissimilar. Extensive neurofibrillary degeneration was found throughout the brain but especially in the cortex, substantia nigra, locus ceruleus, and other subcortical nuclei.[35] We interpreted the EEG changes and dementia as probably being related to the cortical involvement.

In Huntington's chorea, the characteristic pattern for the EEG consists of an absence of rhythmic background activity along with low voltage intermittent random activity of theta and delta frequencies in some cases. As in other heredode-

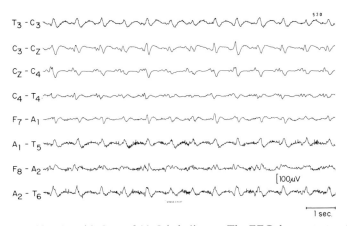

Figure 6. A 64-year-old male, with Creutzfeldt-Jakob disease. The EEG demonstrates rhythmic bilateral sharp and slow waves with suppression of background rhythms.

generative states, there is either minimal or no change with hyperventilation.[33] Sishta and coworkers[69] have recently reviewed the literature and demonstrated altered sleep patterns in Huntington's chorea. Sleep EEGs were of low voltage, had few sigma rhythms, and did not respond with K-complexes to sound stimuli. They considered the records to be abnormal in all 16 of their patients. Green, Dickinson, and Gunderman[28] observed epileptic discharges occasionally in adults and frequently in children with Huntington's chorea. Finally, Scott and associates[67] have reported an EEG-neuropathological study and described a correlation between a low voltage EEG and generalized cortical atrophy.

Although Parkinson's disease, whether of presenile or senile origin, is not generally classified among the dementing illnesses, a significant portion of patients suffering from Parkinson's disease are found to be demented.[8, 60] Patients with parkinsonism frequently have abnormal EEGs,[19, 66, 72] the usual abnormalities being diffuse slowing, bilateral and synchronous or random. Mild to severe shifts to the theta and delta frequencies occur. Sleep is often disturbed, the characteristic change being a marked decrease in delta sleep (stages 3 and 4).[7] The EEG has proven useful in predicting the outcome of neurolytic surgery,[72] an abnormal preoperative EEG being most frequently associated with a failure of postoperative rehabilitation efforts.

METABOLIC DISORDERS

We will consider only briefly the metabolic problems that can be associated with the clinical picture of dementia. Prominent among these are endocrinopathies. For the most part, disturbances of thyroid, parathyroid,[62] and adrenal[79] function produce affective symptomatology, but disturbances of sensorium and cognition may be seen. Since the EEG abnormalities in these states are usually characterized by the same changes found in normal aging or in dementia of other origins, they must be considered in the differential diagnosis of patients with complaints and findings that are often associated with dementia.[16, 57, 79]

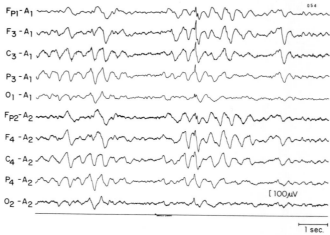

Figure 7. A 45-year-old male with polycystic kidney disease and dialysis dementia. The EEG reveals high voltage bilaterally synchronous 3–3½ Hz. slow wave discharges with sharp components on a background of 5–6 Hz. activity.

212

The long, repeated use of renal dialysis has resulted in a new syndrome called dialysis dementia. First described by Alfrey and his associates,[2] the entity, which tends to run a fatal course, is characterized by dementia, myoclonic jerks, dyspraxia, and characteristic EEG changes. The EEG changes are best described as high voltage polyphasic slow waves which are for the most part bilateral and synchronous (Fig. 7). They are often asymmetrical.[47, 53]

Finally, hepatic encephalopathy, due to liver failure of various causes, may present as dementia. Most often these patients have triphasic waves in the EEG or diffuse slow wave abnormalities. However, these triphasic waves are not pathognomonic for hepatic encephalopathy for they sometimes appear in other metabolic encephalopathies.[32]

VASCULAR DISORDERS

When evaluating the EEG in relation to cerebral vascular disorders, it should be kept in mind that the usual electrode array records only 25 percent of the cerebral cortex. The remainder of the cortex is buried in depths of sulci and underneath the frontal, temporal, and occipital lobes. Thus, routine EEGs record mainly over the area supplied by the middle cerebral artery. In addition, any resulting EEG abnormality depends upon the quantity of infarcted tissue and the integrity of collateral circulation.[65]

The differentiation of dementia due to generalized cerebral arteriosclerosis (multi-infarct dementia) from senile dementia is difficult if not impossible electroencephalographically.[56] However, when clinical evidence points to cerebral vascular disease, the EEG does tend to have focal abnormalities. In a study[4] carried out for cerebral localization of infarction and ischemia, EEG abnormalities during the acute phase correlated poorly with the specific site and severity of infarction. In massive infarction, there was diffuse low amplitude delta activity or suppression of electrical activity over the affected hemisphere, whereas high voltage slow waves seemed to be associated with more localized lesions. Thrombosis of the middle cerebral artery produced diffuse delta activity over the involved hemisphere with theta activity frequently involving the margins of the lesion, although on occasion all activity in the hemisphere might be suppressed (Fig. 8).

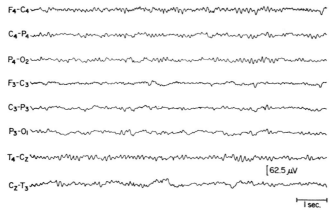

Figure 8. Patient with cerebral infarction due to a left middle cerebral artery obstruction. In the EEG recording there is suppression of background activity and low voltage slowing.

In 48 cases of supratentorial occlusive vascular lesions, slow wave foci occurred in 32.[20] Alpha rhythm on the side of the lesion was slowed in the presence of slow wave foci in 50 percent of the cases. This slowing of the temporo-parieto-occipital rhythm was most characteristic at the border of the lesion rather than in the occipital pole as such. There was a preponderance of fast activity in the opposite hemisphere in 28 of the 48 patients, sufficiently marked to be considered a slightly abnormal sign itself.

Paddison and Ferris[58] reported a high proportion of abnormal EEGs in patients with cerebral hemisphere infarction secondary to occlusion of the carotid artery and middle cerebral circulation in contrast to the frequency of normal records in patients with brain stem infarction due to vertebral or basilar artery disease. The EEG effects of carotid artery disease have also been evaluated by Shimizu and Garoutte.[68] Clinical records, EEGs, and carotid arteriograms were studied in 44 aged patients, and the EEG was abnormal in 30 (19 focal and 11 diffuse). Unilateral stenosis of the internal carotid artery was present in 24 and bilateral stenosis in 5. When definite EEG focal changes were seen, they were always on the same side as the arterial lesions. On the other hand, unilateral carotid artery abnormalities were associated with focal EEG abnormalities on the same side in only 10 of 24 cases.

Phillips[59] evaluated 40 patients with major and minor syndromes of the basilar-vertebral circulation. Nineteen had EEGs within normal limits. Phillips pointed out that the EEG was correlated with the disease only in about half of the patients. Birchfield, Wilson, and Heyman[4] reported that in basilar artery thrombosis there was bilateral theta activity in the occipital and posterior temporal regions. Similarly Paddison and Ferris[58] noted that 14 of 20 patients with vertebral-basilar artery disease had abnormal EEGs characterized by asymmetry of the occipital amplitude and suppression of alpha activity.

Correlative studies of cerebral blood flow and the EEG have usually indicated a relationship between diminished regional blood flow and slow waves. Ingvar[38] and Magnus, Venderberg, and Vanderdrift[46] demonstrated a significant relationship between the two. There was, however, a significant number of cases in which there was no correlation. Both these studies indicated that slow waves were a

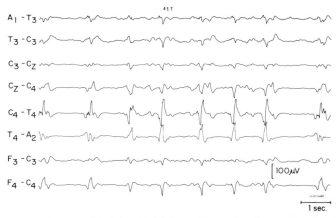

Figure 9. A 75-year-old female with right-sided infarct. The patient is unresponsive. Periodic lateralized epileptiform discharges (PLED's) are recorded over the right centrotemporal region.

good indicator of decreased blood flow or metabolism or both, although Loeb and Fieschi[45] were less enthusiastic.

The reports of Chatrian, Shaw, and Leffman,[11] describing an EEG abnormality which they named PLEDs (periodic lateralized epileptiform discharges), linked these abnormalities to vascular disease in a large percentage of cases (Fig. 9). In most instances, these EEG disturbances were associated with altered states of consciousness. Two of the most common symptoms were psychosis and confusion-disorientation. PLEDs are associated with poor prognosis for survival and high morbidity of the surviving cases. Many of the surviving patients developed chronic mental symptoms. Other workers have reported similar findings.[37, 73]

In summary, focal or hemispheric EEG abnormalities are characteristic for cerebral ischemia resulting from disorders in the anterior cerebral circulation. Disorders of the vertebral-basilar circulation tend to result in fewer localizing defects.

NORMAL PRESSURE HYDROCEPHALUS

Recently attention has been focused on the syndrome known as "normal pressure hydrocephalus." Although considerable doubt exists as to the unity of the pathophysiological alterations underlying this clinical concept, there has been one study devoted to the electroencephalographic manifestations of the condition. Brown and Goldensohn[6] reported the EEG findings in 11 cases who met the criteria for diagnosis as defined by Benson and coworkers.[3] In the 11 cases, 6 had normal records and 5 had abnormalities varying from focal delta to diffuse theta and delta activity. The findings were considered nonspecific.

DEFICIENCY DISEASES

Patients with the Wernicke-Korsakoff syndrome are often hard to examine electroencephalographically in the early, acute phases of illness, and EEG studies are correspondingly scanty. Victor and associates[75] described adequate EEG studies in the initial phases in only 36 of their large series of patients. In half, the EEGs were abnormal, the most usual change being "diffuse decrease in the fre-

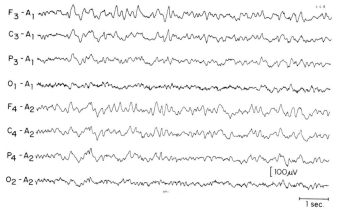

Figure 10. A 72-year-old female patient with pernicious anemia and dementia. The EEG demonstrates diffuse bilateral slowing.

quency of the brain waves, mild to moderate in degree." They also observed the EEG to be entirely normal in some patients who presented the full-blown clinical syndrome.

Of significance also is the diagnosis of pernicious anemia. The classic study of Walton and his collaborators[77] has not been repeated and remains the best description of the EEG and clinical findings in this disorder. Generalized slowing is the usual EEG change (Fig. 10).

TRAUMA

Some comments on cerebral trauma and its sequalae are necessary in order to be complete in our discussion of dementia, although post-traumatic dementia is not a focus of this book. Cerebral trauma frequently results in varying degrees of dementia,[64] and associated with it one can find a variety of EEG changes. The most complete summary is to be found in Rowbothan's 1964 monograph.[64] A more recent but less complete review is by Kiloh, McComas, and Osselton.[39]

The EEG changes associated with post-traumatic dementia are usually characterized by slowing, either focal or generalized. A correlation can be demonstrated between the severity of the EEG abnormality and the degree to which intellectual function is compromised. There is also a correlation between the degree of abnormality seen a few days after an injury and the prognosis for full recovery of mental faculties.

INTRACRANIAL MASSES

Friedman and Odom[24] have recently called attention to the frequency of intracranial neoplasms and hematomas in the elderly population. They emphasized the occurrence of progressive intellectual and personality deterioration as the presenting symptoms. It was not surprising that some patients had been considered to have the more common forms of dementia and, as a result, had been admitted to psychiatric facilities.

Of the 227 patients studied by Friedman and Odom, 69 percent had intracranial neoplasms, 21 percent subdural hematomas, 8 percent intracerebral hematomas, and another 2 percent lesions due to epidural hematoma, abscess, and intracerebral cyst. The EEGs in 86 percent of these patients were abnormal. The EEG was highly accurate in determining the presence of intracerebral neoplasms (93 percent) and subdural hematomas (100 percent), less accurate in meningioma and intracerebral hematomas (75 percent), and even less so in patients with neurinomas (50 percent).

Brain tumors produce changes in the EEG that are dependent on 2 factors.[22] The first is the site, for tumors involving the subcortical structures do not produce the same changes that occur with cortical lesions, nor does a temporal lobe tumor affect the EEG in the same way as one in the parietal lobe. The second is the histological and gross anatomical growth characteristics of the lesion; for example, the EEG changes with an oligodendroglioma are frequently not the same as those that occur with a meningioma.

In gliomas, which invade the brain substance locally and destroy its histological integrity, epileptic discharges are more or less common, depending on the growth rate. Glioblastomas produce the least epileptic discharge and oligodendrogliomas, the most. Slow wave abnormalities (Fig. 11), on the other hand, are the predomi-

216

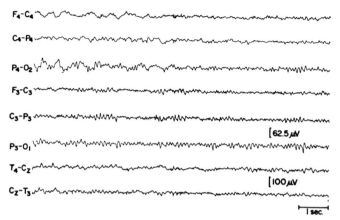

Figure 11. Patient with right parietal lobe tumor. Histopathological diagnosis was mixed glioma. The EEG demonstrates localization of the abnormality to the right central region.

nant abnormality with glioblastomas and may be inconspicuous with oligodendrogliomas. Bilateral slow wave abnormalities that arise as a result of subcortical distortion are most likely to occur with rapidly expanding lesions or with those invading subcortical structures. Thus, glioblastomas produce these abnormalities much quicker than oligodendrogliomas.

In contrast are those neoplasms that grow as a homogenous mass within the substance of the brain, not disturbing the histological picture of the surrounding brain except as they cause distortion with the pressure of their growth or result in a foreign body reaction of the brain. In this group, minimal epileptic discharge occurs, and slowing is the predominant change. Such observations correlate well with the studies of Fischer-Williams and associates,[22] Ellingson and Lundy,[17] and Klass and Bickford,[40] all of whom noted the paucity of epileptic discharge in metastatic tumors. Ellingson and Lundy's excellent study of patients suspected of having metastatic brain lesions also emphasized the high frequency of intellectual

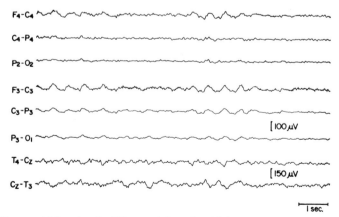

Figure 12. A 79-year-old female who fell, sustaining a head injury. The EEG prior to surgery demonstrated lateralizing slow wave activity over the left frontocentral region. Subsequently, a subdural hematoma was evacuated from the left central region.

deficits in patients with metastatic lesions. They made several generalizations that are useful in the diagnosis of dementia: (1) A focal abnormality correlates highly with a solitary metastasis. (2) Diffuse abnormalities do not correlate with single or multiple metastases unless progression is shown in serial records. (3) A normal record suggests that a metastasis does not exist. (4) Localization of metastases is less accurate than localization of primary tumors of the brain.

Extrinsic lesions, such as meningiomas[76] and subdural hematomas[61, 74] produce similar changes, suppressing background alpha rhythms in at least one-half of the cases. Lateralized and localized slowing is the primary finding in both; epileptic discharges appear in about one-half of the patients with meningiomas but are relatively rare in subdural hematomas. Lateralization and localization are accurate in about 86 percent of cases of meningiomas, and lateralization is apparent in 75 percent of patients with subdural hematomas (Fig. 12).

SUMMARY

The EEG in normal aging and in dementia due to a variety of diseases has been described. In dementia due to degenerative diseases, metabolic disorders, normal pressure hydrocephalus, and deficiency states, the diffuseness of the abnormalities observed has been emphasized; whereas with cerebrovascular disease and with intracranial masses, the focal nature of the changes has been stressed. Although a normal EEG does not rule out the diagnosis of dementia especially in its early stages, the EEG can nevertheless be a significant instrument in the identification of organic processes when the diagnosis is uncertain, in differentiating diffuse from focal cerebral lesions, and in following the course of the disease. Because electroencephalography is easily performed, is safe, and can be frequently repeated, it should be considered one of the more useful tools in the clinical evaluation of patients with dementia.

REFERENCES

1. ABBOTT, J.: *The EEG in Jakob-Creutzfeldt's disease.* Electroencepholog. Clin. Neurophysiol. 11: 184, 1959.
2. ALFREY, A. C.; MISHELL, J. M.; BURKS, J.; CONTIGUGLIA, S. R.; RUDOLPH, H.; LEWIN, E.; AND HOLMES, J. H.: *Syndrome of dyspraxia and multifocal seizures associated with chronic hemodialysis.* Trans. Am. Soc. Artif. Intern. Organs. 18:257, 1972.
3. BENSON, D. F.; LE MAY, M.; PATTEN, D. H.; AND RUBENS, A. B.: *Diagnosis of normal pressure hydrocephalus.* New Engl. J. Med. 283:609, 1970.
4. BIRCHFIELD, R. I.; WILSON, W. P.; AND HEYMAN, A.: *An evaluation of EEG in cerebral infarction and ischemia due to arteriosclerosis.* Neurology (Minneap.) 9:859, 1959.
5. BLESSED, G.; TOMLINSON, B. E.; AND ROTH, M.: *The association between quantitative measures of dementia and of senile change in the cerebral grey matter of elderly subjects.* Br. J. Psychiatry 114:797, 1968.
6. BROWN, D. G., AND GOLDENSOHN, E. S.: *The electroencephalogram in normal pressure hydrocephalus.* Arch. Neurol. 29:70, 1973.
7. BROWN, G. L., AND WILSON, W. P.: *Parkinsonism and depression.* South Med. J. 65:540, 1972.
8. BROWN, G. L.; WILSON, W. P.; AND GREEN, R. L.: Mental aspects of parkinsonism and their management, in *Proceedings of the Fourth International Symposium on Parkinson's Disease.* Vol. 2: *Selected Communication on Topics.* Topic III: *Behavior.* H. Huber, Bern, 1972, pp. 265-278.
9. BURGER, L. J.; ROWAN, A. J.; AND GOLDENSOHN, E. S.: *Creutzfeldt-Jakob disease. An electroencephalographic study.* Arch. Neurol. 26: 428, 1972.

218

10. Busse, E. W.; Barnes, R. H.; Friedman, E. L.; and Kelty, E. J.: *Psychological functioning of aged individuals with normal and abnormal electroencephalograms. I. A Study of non-hospitalized community volunteers.* J. Nerv. Ment. Dis. 124: 135, 1956.

11. Chatrian, G. E.; Shaw, C. M.; and Leffman, H.: *The significance of periodic lateralized epileptiform discharged in EEG: An electrographic, clinical and pathological study.* Electroencephalogr. Clin. Neurophysiol 17:177, 1964.

12. Davis. P. A.: *The electroencephalogram in old age.* Dis. Nerv. Syst. 2: 77, 1941.

13. Davis. P. A., and Davis. H.: *The electroencephalograms of psychotic patients.* Am. J. Psychiatry 95: 1007, 1939.

14. Demedts, M.; Pillen, E.; De Groote, J., and Van De Woestijne, K. P.: *Hepatic encephalopathy: Comparative Study of EEG abnormalities, neuropsychic disturbances and blood ammonia.* Acta Neurol. Belg. 73: 281, 1973.

15. Drachman, D. A., and Hughes, J. R.: *Memory and the hippocampal complexes. III Aging and temporal EEG abnormalities.* Neurology (Minneap.) 21: 1, 1971.

16. Dunleavy, D. L. F.; Oswald, I.; Brown, P.; and Strong, J. A.: *Hyperthyroidism, sleep and growth hormone.* Electroencephalog. Clin. Neurophysiol. 36: 259, 1974.

17. Ellingson, R. J., and Lundy, B. W.: *EEG's in patients suspected of having metastatic lesions of the brain.* Cancer 15: 1138, 1953.

18. Elliott, F.; Gardner-Thorpe, C.; Barwick, D. D.; and Foster, J. B.: *Modification of clinical and electroencephalographic activity with methylphenidate and diazepam.* J. Neurol. Neurosurg. Psychiatry 37: 879, 1974.

19. England, A. C.; Schwab, R. S.; and Peterson, E.: *The EEG and Parkinson's syndrome.* Electroencepholog. Clin. Neurophysiol. 11: 723, 1959.

20. Farbrot, O.: *EEG study in cases of cerebral vascular accidents.* Electroencepholog. Clin. Neurophysiol. 6: 678, 1954.

21. Fisher, C. M.: *The clinical picture in Creutzfeldt-Jakob disease.* Trans. Am. Neurol. Assoc. 85: 147, 1960.

22. Fischer-Williams, M.; Last, S. L.; Lyberi, G., and Northfield, D. W. C.: *Clinico-EEG study of 128 gliomas and 50 intracranial metastatic tumors.* Brain 85: 1, 1962.

23. Friedlander, W. J.: *Electroencephalographic alpha rate in adults as a function of age.* Geriatrics 13: 29, 1958.

24. Friedman, H., and Odom, G. L.: *Expanding intracranial lesions in geriatric patients.* Geriatrics 27: 105, 1972.

25. Gibbs, C. J., Jr., and Gajdusek, D. C.: *Infection as the etiology of spongiform encephalopathy (Creutzfeldt-Jakob disease).* Science 165: 1023, 1969.

26. Gordon, E. G., and Sim, M.: *The EEG in pre-senile dementia.* J. Neurol. Neurosurg. Psychiatry 30: 285, 1967.

27. Gowers, W. R.: *Heredity in disease of the central nervous system.* Br. Med. J. 2: 1541, 1908.

28. Green, J. B.; Dickinson, E. S.; and Gunderman, J. R.: *Epilepsy in Huntington's Chorea: Clinical and neurophysiological studies.* Adv. Neurol. 1: 105, 1973.

29. Greenblatt, M.; Levin, S.; and Atwell, C.: *Comparative value of electroencephalogram and abstraction tests in diagnosis of brain damage.* J. Nerv. Ment. Dis. 102: 383, 1945.

30. Gustafson, L.; Risberg, J.; Hagberg, B.; Hougaard, K.; Nilssen, L.; and Ingvar, D. H.: *Cerebral blood flow, EEG and psychometric variables related to clinical findings in presenile dementia.* Acta Neurol. Scand. (Suppl.) 51: 439, 1972.

31. Harner, R. N.: *EEG evaluation of the patient with dementia,* in Benson, D. F., and Blumer, D. (eds.): *Psychiatric aspects of neurological disease.* Grune and Stratton, New York, 1975.

32. Harner, R. N., and Katz, R. I.: *Electroencephalography in metabolic coma.* In press.

33. Hill. D.: *Discussion on the electroencephalogram in organic cerebral disease.* Proc. R. Soc. Med. 41: 242, 1948.

34. Hirano, A.; Kurland, L. T.; Krooth, R. S.; and Lessell, S.: *Parkinsonism-dementia complex, an endemic disease on the island of Guam. I. Clinical features.* Brain 84: 642, 1961.

35. Hirano, A.; Malamud, N.; Elizan, T. S.; and Kurland, L. T.: *Amyotrophic lateral sclerosis and Parkinsonism-dementia complex on Guam. Further pathologic studies.* Arch. Neurol. 15: 35, 1966.

36. HOEFER, P. F. A.: Discussion of paper by C. M. Fisher.[21]

37. HUGHES, J. R., AND SCHLAGENHAUFF, R. E.: *The periodically recurring focal discharge.* Epilepsia 6: 156, 1965.

38. INGVAR, D. H.: *Cerebral metabolism, cerebral blood flow and EEG.* Electroencepholog. Clin. Neurophysiol. (Suppl.) 25: 102, 1967.

39. KILOH, L. G.; McCOMAS, A. J.; AND OSSELTON, J. W.: *Clinical Electroencephalography,* ed. 3. Butterworth and Co., London, 1972, pp. 125–130.

40. KLASS, D. W., AND BICKFORD, R. G.: *The EEG in metastatic tumours of the brain.* Neurology (Minneap.) 8: 333, 1958.

41. LEE, R. G., AND BLAIR, R. D. G.: *Evolution of EEG and visual evoked response changes in Jakob-Creuzfeldt disease.* Electroencepholog. Clin. Neurophysiol. 35: 133, 1973.

42. LESSE, S.; HOEFER, P. F. A.; AND AUSTIN, J. H.: *The electroencephalogram in diffuse encephalopathies.* Arch. Neurol. Psychiat. 79:359, 1958.

43. LETEMENDIA, F., AND PAMPIGLIONE, G.: *Clinical and EEG observations in Alzheimer's disease.* J. Neurol. Neurosurg. Psychiatry 21: 167, 1958.

44. LIDDELL, D. W.: *Investigations of EEG findings in presenile dementia.* J. Neurol. Neurosurg. Psychiatry 21: 173, 1958.

45. LOEB, C., AND FIESCHI, C.: *EEG's and regional cerebral blood flow in cases of brain infarction.* Electroencepholog. Clin. Neurophysiol. (Suppl.) 25: 111, 1967.

46. MAGNUS, O.; VENDERBERG, D.; AND VANDERDRIFT, H. A.: *EEG and cerebral circulation-isotope technique.* Electroencepholog. Clin. Neurophysiol. (Suppl.) 25: 107, 1967.

47. MAHURKAR, S. D.; DHAR, S. K.; SALTA, R.; MEYERS, L., JR.; SMITH, E. C.; AND DUNEA, G.: *Dialysis dementia.* Lancet 1: 1412, 1973.

48. MAY, W. W.: *Creutzfeldt-Jakob disease.* Acta Neurol. Scand. 44: 1, 1968.

49. McADAM, W., AND McCLATCHEY, W. T.: *The electroencephalogram in aged patients of a mental hospital.* J. Ment. Sci. 98: 711, 1952.

50. McADAM, W., AND ROBINSON, R. A.: *Senile intellectual deterioration and the electroencephalogram: A quantitative correlation.* Br. J. Psychiatry 102: 819, 1956.

51. MULLER, H. F., AND KRAL, V. A.: *The electroencephalogram in advanced senile dementia.* J. Am. Geriatr. Soc. 15: 415, 1967.

52. MUNDY-CASTLE, A. C.; HURST, L. A.; BEERSTECHEN, D. M.; AND PRINSLOV., T.: *The electroencephalogram in the senile psychoses.* Electroencepholog. Clin. Neurophysiol. 6:245, 1954.

53. NADEL, A. M., AND WILSON, W. P.: Unpublished data.

54. NELSON, J.: *On the origin of diffuse spikes in Jakob-Creutzfeldt's disease.* Electroencepholog. Clin. Neurophysiol. 24: 395, 1968.

55. OBRIST, W. D.: *The electroencephalogram of normal aged adults.* Electroencepholog. Clin. Neurophysiol. 6: 235, 1954.

56. OBRIST, W. D., AND BUSSE, E. W.: The electroencephalogram in old age, in Wilson, W. P. (ed.): *Applications of Electroencephalography in Psychiatry.* Duke University Press, Durham, N. C., 1965.

57. OLSEN, P. Z.; STOIER, K.; SIERSBAEK-NIELSEN, J.; HANSEN, J. M.; SCHIOLER, M.; AND KRISTENSEN, M.: *Electroencephalographic findings in hyperthyroidism.* Electroencepholog. Clin. Neurophysiol. 32: 171, 1972.

58. PADDISON, R. M., AND FERRIS, G. S.: *EEG in cerebral vascular disease.* Electroencepholog. Clin. Neurophysiol. 13: 99, 1961.

59. PHILLIPS, B. M.: *Temporal lobe changes associated with the syndromes of basilar-vertebral insufficiency: An EEG study.* Br. Med. J. 2: 1104, 1964.

60. POLLOCK, M., AND HORNABROOK, R. W.: *The prevalence, natural history and dementia of Parkinson's disease.* Brain 89: 429, 1966.

61. PUECH, P.; BOUNES, G. C.; AND LUQUET, P.: *Chronic latent, subdural hematoma. Neuropsychiatric signs and EEG studies.* Ann. Med. Psychiat. 11: 158, 1947.

62. REILLY, E. L., AND WILSON, W. P.: *Mental symptoms in hyperparathyroidism.* Dis. Nerv. Syst. 26: 361, 1965.

63. ROMANO, J., AND ENGEL, G. I.: *Delirium. I Electroencephalographic data.* Arch. Neurol. Psychiat. (Chicago) 51: 356, 1944.

64. ROWBOTHAM, G. F.: *Acute Injuries of the Head,* ed. 4. The Williams & Wilkins Co., Baltimore, 1964, pp. 458–485.

65. SCHWAB, R. S.: EEG studies and their significance in cerebral vascular disease, in Wright, I. S. (ed.): *Cerebral Vascular Diseases.* Grune and Stratton, New York, 1955.

66. SCHWAB, R. S., AND COBB, S.: *Simultaneous electromyograms and EEGs in paralysis agitans.* J. Neurophysiol. 2: 36, 1939.

67. SCOTT, D. F.; HEATHFIELD, K. W. G.; TOONE, B.; AND MARGERISON, J. H.: *The EEG in Huntington's Chorea. A clinical and neuropathological study.* J. Neurol. Neurosurg. Psychiatry 35: 97, 1972.

68. SHIMIZU, M., AND GAROUTTE, B.: *EEG and carotid arteriography in elderly patients.* Electroencepholog. Clin. Neurophysiol. 24: 394, 1968.

69. SHISTA, S. K.; TROUPE, A.; MARSZALEK, K. S.; AND KREMER, L. M.: *Huntington's Chorea: An electroencephalographic and psychometric study.* Electroencepholog. Clin. Neurophysiol. 36: 387, 1974.

70. SHORT, M. J.; MUSELLA, L.; AND WILSON, W. P.: *Correlation of affect and EEG in senile psychoses.* J. Gerontol. 23: 324, 1968.

71. SILVERMAN, A. J.; BUSSE, E. W.; AND BARNES, R. H.: *Studies in the process of aging: Electroencephalographic findings in 400 elderly subjects.* Electroencepholog. Clin. Neurophysiol. 7: 67, 1955.

72. TASKER, R. R., AND SCOTT, J. W.: *The prognostic value of the EEG in thalamotomy for parkinsonism.* Electroencepholog. Clin. Neurophysiol. 21: 620, 1966.

73. TOYONAGA, K.; SCHLAGENHAUFF, R. E.; AND SMITH, B. H.: *Periodic lateralized epileptiform discharges in subdural hematoma: Case reports and review of the literature.* Clin. Electroencepholog. 5: 113, 1974.

74. TURRELL, R. C.; LEVY, L. L.; AND ROSEMAN, E.: *The value of EEG in selected cases of subdural hematomas.* J. Neurosurg. 13: 449, 1956.

75. VICTOR, M.; ADAMS, R. D.; AND COLLINS, G. H.: *The Wernicke-Korsakoff Syndrome.* F. A. Davis Co., Philadelphia, 1971.

76. WAJSBORT, J.; LAVY, S.; SAHAR, A.; AND CARMON, A.: *The value of EEG in the diagnosis and localization of meningioma.* Confin. Neurol. 28: 375, 1966.

77. WALTON, J. N.; KILOH, L. G.; OSSELTON, J. W.; AND FARRALL, J.: *The electroencephalogram in pernicious anaemia and subacute combined degeneration of the cord.* Electroencepholog. Clin. Neurophysiol. 6: 45, 1954.

78. WEINER, H., AND SCHUSTER, D. B.: *The electroencephalogram in dementia—some preliminary observations and correlations.* Electroencepholog. Clin. Neurophysiol. 8: 479, 1956.

79. WILSON, W. P.: The EEG in endocrine disorders, in Wilson, W. P. (ed.): *Applications of Electroencephalography in Psychiatry.* Duke University Press, Durham, N. C., 1965.

221

CHAPTER 11

Radiological Techniques in the Diagnostic Evaluation of Dementia

James Lowry, M.D., A. Lee Bahr, M.D., Joseph H. Allen, Jr., M.D., William F. Meacham, M.D., and A. Everette James, Jr., Sc.M., M.D.

In patients undergoing diagnostic evaluation for dementia, the clinician has a number of choices as to which examinations are most likely to yield the necessary clinical information. Choosing the appropriate sequence of studies may be difficult. Diagnostic radiological procedures are utilized in two ways: (1) in the patient whose clinical evaluation fails to establish with certainty a diagnosis of dementia, radiological studies may serve to confirm or to refute, within limits, the presence of structural brain disease; and (2) in the patient whose dementia is established on clinical grounds, radiological diagnostic procedures may reveal the nature of the underlying cerebral disorder. In the latter case, appropriate radiographic studies will be obtained initially in order to demonstrate any focal lesion which is the etiology of the presenting symptoms. If a significant focal lesion is reasonably excluded, the physician will seek to determine if a diffuse degenerative process is the cause of the clinical presentation. Radiological techniques often provide the only specific evidence, except for histological proof, that such a diffuse process exists.

In this chapter we will present some of the characteristics of the various radiological techniques now available, consider their virtues and limitations, and present data of our own and others detailing experience in the evaluation of patients with dementia.

Many modalities pertaining to the radiological evaluation of the demented patient are included under the general discipline of diagnostic radiology. Plain skull radiographs, cerebral angiography, pneumoencephalography, radionuclide brain scans, isotope cisternography, and computerized cranial tomography are the principal methods of investigation. Of these, computerized cranial tomography (CT scan) is the newest, coming into clinical use since the publication of the first edition of this monograph. This exciting development has revolutionized neuroradiology, and although definitive answers to some questions await sufficient clinical experience, it will doubtless prove fundamental in the radiological evaluation of dementia. Because this technique is relatively new and not yet available to all physicians, we will present material covering the more traditional radiological methods first and later consider the impact and importance of computerized cranial tomography in the evaluation of dementia. Table 1, Diseases Causing Dementia, abbreviated from Haase[19] (see Chap. 3), will serve as our organizational guide in the presentation of material on radiological assessment in the various disease categories.

Table 1. Diseases causing dementia

Diffuse parenchymatous diseases
Metabolic disorders
Vascular disorders
Normal pressure hydrocephalus
Brain tumors
Trauma
Infections

PLAIN SKULL RADIOGRAPHS

Although familiar, plain skull radiographic findings warrant review and comment because of their availability and frequent use. Skull radiographs are usually normal in the diffuse parenchymatous diseases of the central nervous system. Thus, the majority of patients evaluated for dementia will have normal plain skull examinations.

Among the disorders of metabolism that cause dementia, parathyroid disease and Cushing's syndrome may show changes on skull radiographs. Radiographic surveys in hyperparathyroidism reveal abnormalities in approximately one-third of patients, and one-half of these show skull alterations with a mottled demineralization of the calvaria being the most frequent finding.[30] However, even with good radiographic technique, a bone mineralization change of approximately 50 percent can escape detection. Rarely, an area of focal bone resorption in the skull is seen in these patients. These changes may be reversible with treatment.

Approximately 50 percent of hypoparathyroid patients demonstrate the characteristic but unexplained radiographic finding of calcification of the basal ganglia.[5] However, patients with pseudohypoparathyroidism may also show basal ganglia calcification,[30] and the two conditions cannot be differentiated by its presence.

In patients with Cushing's syndrome due to basophilic adenoma there is usually no evidence of sella turcica enlargement, but a variable degree of osteoporosis of the skull is apparent in most patients.[30] Occasionally this decrease in mineralization may be severe.

Some vascular disorders show plain skull radiographic abnormalities. In older patients skull radiographs commonly reveal internal carotid siphon calcification. Some authors do not believe that this calcification reflects stenosis. Di Chiro and Libow,[15] however, separate carotid siphon calcification into medial and intimal groups based on radiological appearance and conclude that the intimal type of calcification is associated with a decrease in cerebral blood flow while the medial type is not.[15]

Arteriovenous malformations cause enlarged vascular grooves which can be seen in plain skull examinations in approximately 40 percent of patients with the disorder.[34] Less commonly, calcification is detected in the arteriovenous malformation. These calcifications histologically represent metaplastic change that is probably related to delayed blood flow in the abnormal vessels.

Intracranial tumors, especially slow growing ones, may produce radiographic changes on plain skull films. Alterations in bony texture and calcification are the most commonly encountered manifestations, the incidence and nature of these changes varying with the type of tumor and location. Focal thinning of calvarial bone may be seen with slow growing gliomas, meningiomas, and rarer lesions such as epidermoid tumors and cholesteatomas. Such a finding frequently is difficult to detect by casual observation. Hyperostosis is associated with meningiomas in as many as 50 percent of cases according to the literature, although prospective studies suggest that clearly abnormal manifestations are probably present only in approximately 20 to 30 percent. Tumor calcification can be detected with a variable frequency on plain skull radiographs: detection of gliomas averages 6 percent and meningiomas 10 to 15 percent.[34] Stereoscopic lateral skull radiographs are invaluable in detecting such calcifications. They are also useful in localizing the finding and in excluding extraneous abnormalities and artifacts due to technique.

In patients with dementia as sequela to trauma, plain skull films may or may not reflect the previous injury. Fractures may heal and be invisible by the time the patient presents with symptoms of dementia. Rarely, a rent in the dura mater is associated with the trauma, and a leptomeningeal cyst results. The radiographic appearance of these cysts is characteristic with enlarging lucent space between the bony fracture edges. Dementia related to antecedent trauma may have associated subdural hematoma which may be suggested by pineal shift or calcification within the hematoma.[34] For the process of organization and calcium deposition to occur, the hematoma must have been present for at least several months.

Dementia secondary to infection is not usually accompanied by abnormalities in the plain skull examination. Tuberculous meningitis may be manifest by characteristic "cluster-like" calcifications detected by plain skull radiography, but usually do not appear until 1 to 3 years after onset of the condition. Certain dementing infectious processes of childhood, such as cytomegalic inclusion disease and toxoplasmosis, also may result in characteristic intracranial calcifications, but these primarily childhood diseases are not considered in detail in this volume.

In summary, although the plain skull radiograph may demonstrate some helpful signs in evaluation of patients with dementia, it is not a sensitive diagnostic study. Normal studies are to be anticipated and should not preclude further investigation utilizing other imaging techniques.

CEREBRAL ANGIOGRAPHY

Diffuse degenerative brain processes have no distinctive angiographic findings. Analysis of the position and arrangement of the deep veins may disclose enlargement of the ventricular system, but the many possible anatomical variations of the deep venous system must be recognized to avoid errors in interpretation. Several angiographic manifestations have been described in cerebral atrophy. These include not only the appearance of contrast media in various identifiable vessels but in the capillary blush that delineates the position of the cerebral cortical margin. Several authors propose that measurements between the individual cortical vessels and between the inner table of the calvaria and the cortex as delineated by the capillary blush have diagnostic utility. We have not found these measurements as reliable as corresponding ones found at pneumoencephalography.

The vascular disorders associated with dementia are best evaluated by cerebral angiography. In arteriosclerosis the presence and extent of the disease in the cerebral vessels may be clearly shown, expecially with radiographic magnification techniques.[3, 26] Irregularities in vessel caliber, occlusions, changes in circulation time, and retrograde filling are frequent findings secondary to atherosclerotic disease in the cerebral vessels.[25] Less specifically, ectasia and tortuosity of the vessels may be noted.

Patients with normal pressure hydrocephalus have no diagnostic features on angiography. Lateral bowing of the thalamostriate vein may be present which reflects the ventricular enlargement accompanying normal pressure hydrocephalus.[43]

Inflammatory diseases of the cerebral vascular system may also show changes on arteriography. For example, systemic lupus erythematosus may cause small and large vessel occlusions and even multiple aneurysms secondary to fibrinoid necrosis.[44] Arch aortography reveals fusiform narrowing at the origin of the great vessels in Takayasu's arteritis.[16, 20]

For many years evaluation of intracranial tumors depended primarily on cerebral angiography. Displacements of arteries, alteration in circulation time, and abnormal appearance of the individual vessels are the well described angiographic manifestations of cerebral tumors.[11, 18] Improved techniques of selected internal and external angiography[3, 26] have greatly helped in the detection of abnormalities.

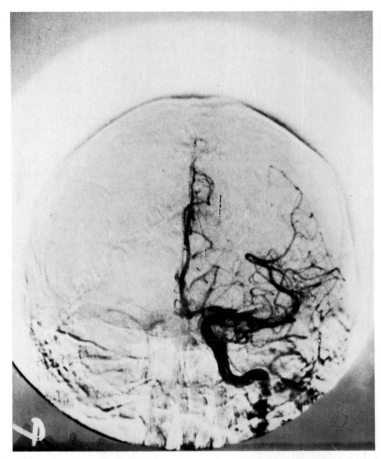

Figure 1. Carotid angiogram (AP view): Failure of vessels to reach the inner table of the skull is characteristic of subdural hematomas. When this displacement occurs without shift of the midline vessels, the possibility that subdural hematomas may be present bilaterally is suggested. Note the use of subtraction technique by which the contrast media within the cranial vasculature is accentuated.

Frequently, not only the presence but the histological type of the tumor can be inferred.

Dementia following trauma may be due to chronic subdural hematomas, and angiography is an expedient, reliable procedure in the diagnosis of extracerebral fluid collections.[37] An avascular space is demonstrated between the cortical arteries and veins and the inner table of the skull. Typically, chronic subdural hematomas have a biconvex or lentiform configuration, whereas acute subdural hematomas are crescent shaped. Midline shifts of the anterior cerebral artery and internal cerebral vein should be appropriate for the size of the subdural hematoma demonstrated. Absence of a midline shift at angiography in the presence of a defined unilateral subdural hematoma suggests the presence of bilateral hematomas (Fig. 1) which occur in 10 to 20 percent of cases.[37]

Areas of narrowing in large and small intracranial vessels, a smooth beaded appearance to the vessels, early venous filling, and occlusions are changes described in a variety of infectious processes which may result in dementia.[16] Basal vascular involvement is more common with mycotic organisms, while peripheral involvement is typical for bacterial organisms.[17] Meningovascular syphilis shows similar vascular changes. It should be emphasized that these angiographic changes are nonspecific and similar to occlusive vascular disease of atherosclerotic origin.

PNEUMOENCEPHALOGRAPHY

Computerized cranial tomography has had an enormous impact on the use of pneumoencephalography(PEG), making it an infrequent procedure in many institutions. The following is presented to put pneumoencephalography in perspective, particularly for those who do not have access to a CT scanner, although we believe that in the near future all patients will have access to this technique and in most instances will not have to risk the morbidity of pneumoencephalography.

In the past, pneumoencephalography and radioisotope cisternography have dominated the radiologic evaluation of patients presenting with dementia. Specifically, diagnostic categories such as a diffuse brain parenchymatous diseases and normal pressure hydrocephalus were evaluated most definitively by pneumoencephalography. Also, pneumoencephalography frequently was employed to evaluate patients developing dementia following trauma, subarachnoid hemorrhage, and infections involving the brain and meninges.

Cerebral Atrophy

The main features upon which the pneumoencephalographic diagnosis of cerebral atrophy has been based are controversial. For example, what constitutes brain atrophy with regard either to the ventricular system or to the subarachnoid space over the cerebral convexities has not been defined to everyone's satisfaction. Burhenne and Davies[9] found few anatomical studies on brain aging, and Nielsen and coworkers[33] cited Lindgren's observation that radiological knowledge of cerebral age involution was deficient. Observations have been made on patients studied for some underlying neurological problem but not for exclusion of brain atrophy. Another difficulty in establishing a range of normal measurements has been the insufficient number of normal patients in each age group, because pneumoencephalography with its attendant morbidity has obviously not been performed on many normal subjects. Despite these disadvantages, the pneumoencephalogram has been valuable in the assessment of many atrophic lesions of the brain. Direct measurements and index values have been described,[9, 32, 33] but index values have been less reliable than direct measurements.[32]

The pneumoencephalogram reveals abnormalities in ventricular size, the cerebral sulci, the basal cisterns, and interhemispheric fissure that make the diagnosis of atrophy possible.

VENTRICULAR SIZE. In the anteroposterior brow-up projection, the width of the air-filled frontal horns may be measured (the so-called ventricular span, Fig. 2). Most authors agree that 40 mm. is the maximum normal value for this measurement.[9, 32, 39, 43] Enlargement of the third ventricle width in the frontal projection, although occasionally striking, is generally less reliable.[9] While generalized ventricular enlargement is the rule in diffuse atrophic disease, focal frontal and temporal horn enlargement occurs selectively in some diseases such as normal pressure hydrocephalus. Other alterations in ventricular shape include focal atrophy of the caudate nuclei in Huntington's chorea resulting in concave lateral borders of the frontal horns.[6] In the evaluation of early hydrocephalus affecting the lateral ventricles, some authors have emphasized that the shape of the superior lateral ventricular angle changes to become rounded. This may be the earliest sign of hydrocephalus in the pneumoencephalogram.

CEREBRAL SULCI. Although Burhenne and Davies[9] conclude that sulcal width measurement is neither "accurate or practical," Taveras,[43] Robertson,[39] and Niel-

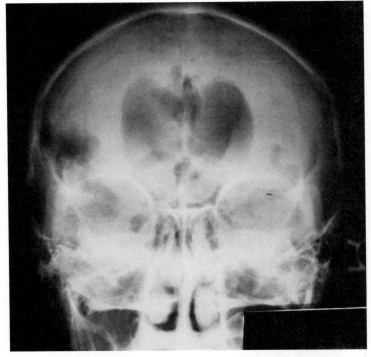

Figure 2. Pneumoencephalogram (AP view): This image is obtained in the brow-up position, filling principally the frontal and body areas of the ventricles. Ventricular span measurement is 70 mm. Corpus callosal angle measurement is 105 degrees. No air is seen over the convexities.

sen and coworkers[33] accept a maximum normal value of 3 mm. for cortical sulcal width. This measurement was originally described by Davidoff and Dyke.[12] All authors stress the importance of technical factors in obtaining reliable and reproducible radiographs. Factors such as the degree and uniformity of air filling of the subarachnoid space and the patient's position in relation to the x-ray beam during exposure influence the apparent cortical size.

BASAL CISTERNS AND INTERHEMISPHERIC FISSURE. Although measurements for the basal cisterns and interhemispheric fissure have not been established, most authors note varying degrees of enlargement of these subarachnoid spaces in atrophic conditions. Considerable importance has been attached to the finding of dilated basal cisterns and widened interhemispheric fissure when convexity air block is also present.[28] This has been related to the hypothesis that normally some relative net current of cerebral spinal fluid flow exists with a tendency to move toward the cerebral convexities and that interference with this flow over the convexities results in dilatation of the basal pathways.

Diffuse Parenchymatous Diseases of the Central Nervous System

There has been considerable debate over the characteristic and reliable pneumoencephalographic findings in the diffuse parenchymatous diseases of the central nervous system. Many of the primary degenerative diseases of the nervous system have no distinguishing features revealed by pneumoencephalography.[43] Moreover, some authors note that minimal widening of cerebral sulci may be a normal consequence of advancing age.[39] Lying-Tunell and Marions[28] state that widening of the cerebral sulci on a pneumoencephalogram should not be equated with brain atrophy. Others, including Mann[29] and Nielsen and associates,[33] specifically correlating pneumoencephalographic findings with intellectual impairment, describe a general tendency to find severe cortical atrophy in patients with severe dementia. With milder degrees of intellectual impairment, results are less reliable. Occasionally unexplained widening of cortical sulci has been observed without any signs of intellectual impairment on psychological testing. Nielsen and coworkers, in two communications[32, 33] relating pneumoencephalographic cortical sulcal and ventricular size to intellectual impairment, found cortical atrophy to be a more sensitive indicator of the disease process in demented patients than ventricular enlargement. Usually, patients with normal or slightly dilated cortical sulci had correspondingly normal or slightly dilated ventricles, while those patients with marked cortical sulcal dilatation had widely varying ventricular sizes. These workers noted that not all patients with diffuse degenerative diseases exhibited cortical atrophy on pneumoencephalogram. This has also been our experience.

In summary, pneumoencephalography in patients with dementia due to diffuse parenchymatous diseases frequently shows marked atrophy by the criteria listed above. In advanced stages when dementia is pronounced, the findings are quite reliable. With lesser degrees of atrophy, the overlap with normal nondemented patients is considerable. Care should be exercised in making a diagnosis of dementia on the basis of pneumoencephalography in these patients.

Normal Pressure Hydrocephalus

Since the description by Adams and associates of normal pressure hydrocephalus over a decade ago,[1] much attention has been given to the pneumoencephalographic criteria of diagnosis. The commonly described pneumoencephalographic findings in normal pressure hydrocephalus are dilated lateral ventricles, enlarged basal cisterns, and relative lack of air filling the subarachnoid spaces over the cortex, the so-called convexity air block (Fig. 2 and 3). Observations by LeMay and New[27] led to the suggestion that a corpus callosal angle which measures less than 120 degrees is characteristic of normal pressure hydrocephalus, while patients with enlargement of ventricles due to other degenerative processes have angles greater than 120 degrees. Observers have varied in their enthusiasm regarding the reliability and usefulness of each of these criteria. While some support convexity air block as the finding of diagnostic significance, others regard this as unreliable. Two important facts to keep in mind are that the classic pneumoencephalogic findings are not present in all patients who clinically have the syndrome of normal pressure hydrocephalus[42, 45] and, conversely, that the same findings are occasionally present in patients with diffuse cerebral atrophy. An example of this lack of specificity is Coblentz and associates'[10] description of 5 patients with documented Alzheimer's disease who exhibited convexity air block on pneumoencephalography.

The radiological diagnosis of normal pressure hydrocephalus by pneumoencephalography is thus based on criteria which lack specificity. The findings described are compatible with a variety of etiologies. As Katzman emphasized in Chapter 4, enlarging ventricles in a patient with antecedent subarachnoid hemor-

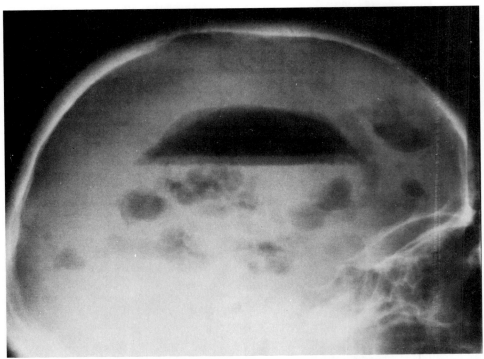

Figure 3. Pneumoencephalogram (lateral view): Enlargement of the lateral ventricles and basal cisterns can be seen, without visible air over the cerebral convexities despite appropriate positioning of the patient.

rhage, trauma, or meningitis present little difficulty in diagnosis, but the pneumoencephalographic diagnosis becomes problematical in the patient with idiopathic normal pressure hydrocephalus. Finally, we emphasize that pneumoencephalographic findings compatible with normal pressure hydrocephalus cannot predict the value of a shunting procedure in a particular patient and should be utilized only in correlation with clinical findings. Ventricular and cisternal size, corpus callosal angle, and cortical air block can be employed only as supplementary documentation and never as criteria to determine the advisability of a cerebrospinal fluid diversionary shunt. It should also be noted that some patients with normal pressure hydrocephalus appear sensitive to pneumoencephalography, and the procedure has sometimes been followed by rapid deterioration in the patient's condition.

RADIONUCLIDE CISTERNOGRAPHY

Radionuclide images obtained after placing an appropriate radioactive material in the subarachnoid space have provided valuable information regarding cerebrospinal fluid (CSF) dynamics and have proven useful in the diagnosis of varied neurological abnormalities. Although anatomical detail is greater with radiographic techniques, CSF imaging provides a more physiological method of assessing CSF dynamics. The relative safety and comfort of the procedure as compared to pneumoencephalography have increased the use of cisternography in neurological evaluation of certain diseases.

A number of radiopharmaceuticals have been employed for CSF imaging.[21] Anticipated length of study, pre-injection radiopharmaceutical testing, physical properties, and radionuclide availability must be considered in making an appropriate choice. Serum albumin, labeled diethylene triamine pentaacetic acid (DTPA), chelates, and ^{99m}Tc-albumin (HSA) have all been employed. If the examination is to be completed in 1 day, ^{99m}Tc($T\frac{1}{2}$, 6 hours) is the radionuclide of choice. If delayed studies at 24 to 72 hours are anticipated, one would probably choose ^{111}In-DTPA ($T\frac{1}{2}$, 2.8 days). Chelated radionuclides (molecular weight, 600 to 800) have been shown to have a movement pattern similar to labeled albumin (molecular weight, 69,000), although somewhat less parasagittal concentration on later views is frequently observed.[21] The radiopharmaceutical is injected using standard lumbar puncture techniques. Ventricular and cisterna magna injections should be performed only by physicians skilled in these methods and only when specific questions are asked which require these routes of injection. Although faulty injections often involve deposition of the radiopharmaceutical outside of the subarachnoid compartment, the study should not be abandoned because the clinician recognizes a faulty injection. Significant anatomical information may still occasionally be obtained from later images, but no attempt to assess the rate of absorption of CSF should be made.

When the radiopharmaceutical is injected into the lumbar subarachnoid space, it normally reaches the basal cisterns in 1 hour, the frontal poles and sylvian fissure in 2 to 6 hours, the cerebral convexities in 12 hours, and the arachnoid villi in the sagittal sinus area in 24 hours. At 24 hours the radiopharmaceutical should be virtually absent from the basal cisterns and distributed over the cerebral convexities or concentrated in the region of the sagittal sinus (Fig. 4A, B, and C). The radiopharmaceutical does not normally enter the ventricular system, reflecting bulk flow of CSF from areas of greatest production (choroid plexus of the lateral ven-

232

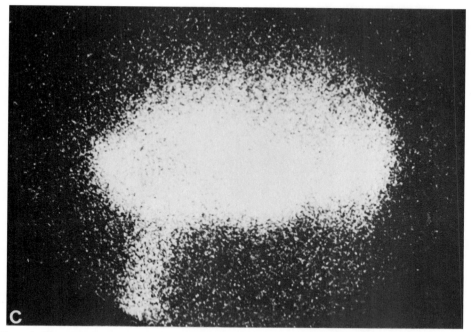

Figure 4. Cisternogram (A, frontal view, B, left lateral view, C, right lateral view) made after injection of 169 Yb diethylene triamine pentaacetic acid (DTPA): This study was performed 24 hours after injection of 1 millicurie of the radiopharmaceutical into the lumbar subarachnoid space. The frontal view and both lateral views reveal movement of the radiopharmaceutical over the cerebral convexities and failure of concentration in the ventricular system in this normal patient.

tricles) to those of greatest resorption (arachnoid granulations in the parasagittal region).

Figures 5A and B demonstrate a typical pattern of communicating hydrocephalus, a diagnosis made whenever ventricular entry of radionuclide is observed on the standard cisternogram.[22] Entry is evidence that no obstruction exists between the outlets of the fourth ventricle and the cisterna magna. In communicating hydrocephalus, two basic patterns are observed. In the first, rapid ventricular entry is seen on the early views, and later views (24 to 72 hours) reveal persistence of ventricular activity with little or no ascension of radiopharmaceutical over the cerebral convexities. Some authors find this pattern correlates with benefit from surgical CSF drainage procedures, but others do not.[42, 45] In the second pattern, relatively rapid ventricular entry is observed, but ventricular clearance is also rapid so that little activity is seen in the ventricles at 24 to 36 hours. This suggests that partial compensation of the hydrocephalus exists and that surgical treatment should probably be deferred. This pattern is most commonly observed in patients with primary atrophic processes. Careful follow-up must be obtained, however, since these patients will occasionally decompensate. Quantitative cisternography may be helpful in serially monitoring these patients.

The pattern of ventricular stasis with dilated ventricles is probably the end stage of a process that begins with obliteration of subarachnoid CSF pathways secondary perhaps to meningitis or subarachnoid hemorrhage. These patients

233

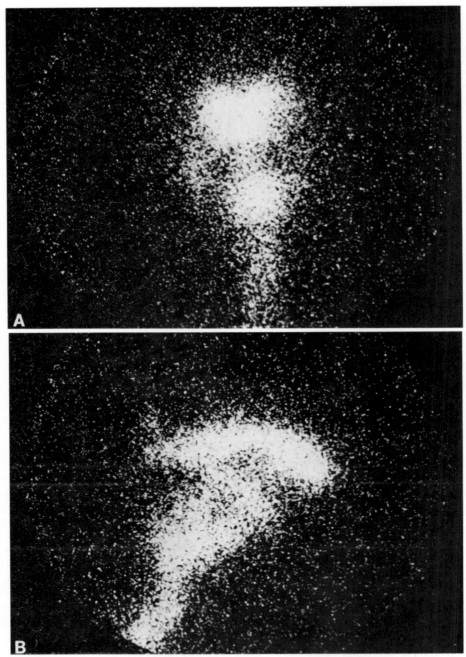

Figure 5. Cisternogram (A, frontal view, B, right lateral view) made with 169 Yb DTPA: Frontal and lateral views 24 hours after injection of 1 millicurie of the radiopharmaceutical. There is persistence of ventricular activity with failure of movement over the convexities. No concentration of radioactivity is seen in the parasagittal area. This type of pattern, when seen at 24 hours, is consistent with the diagnosis of chronic communicating hydrocephalus.

234

recover from the initial episode but on serial cisternograms show progression from a pattern of delayed CSF movement, often with localized block, to ventricular dilatation with some clearing, and finally to ventricular enlargement with marked stasis. The cause of this ventricular "penetration" and the reason the radiopharmaceutical remains there are not known. It cannot be explained by molecular diffusion, nor can it be accounted for by rapid transfer into blood and secretion by the choroid plexus.

COMPUTERIZED CRANIAL TOMOGRAPHY

In 1972 computerized cranial tomography (other terms used for this procedure include computerized axial tomography, CAT, and CT scan) was introduced into clinical neuroradiology by Hounsfield working with Ambrose.[35] The basic principles of mathematical reconstruction of images with observations at a number of angles had been known for some time and had actually been applied to astronomy and electron microscopy.[8] As opposed to conventional radiographic and radioisotopic tomography in which layers outside the focal plane are blurred, in reconstructive tomography the radiation to be detected passes through or originates from the desired anatomical plane. Multiple projections of this plane obtained from many different angles are used with the aid of a computer to reconstruct the anatomical layer or slice. In the past 4 years the application of this technique to the radiological evaluation of the central nervous system has been used extensively throughout the United States and in certain other areas. The rapidity with which this method of scanning has replaced more conventional radiological techniques can be attributed to the remarkable amount of information obtained in the absence of patient morbidity and risk. Where available, CT scanning has become the initial procedure of choice in the evaluation of patients with diseases related to the brain, has virtually replaced pneumoencephalography, and has reduced the need in many instances for arteriography and radionuclide brain scanning.[4, 13, 31, 35, 36]

The system and its technique have been described many times and will be only briefly summarized here. The reader is referred to two excellent descriptions for more elaborate treatment: that of Ambrose[2] and that of Brooks and DiChiro.[8] Basically, this method transmits a narrowly collimated x-ray beam (140 kVp, 69.9 keV mean) directed by a gantry in a transverse orientation across the patient's cranium. With each transverse motion, detectors on the opposite side of the patient's head record the transmission of photons in 160 separate readings. The entire gantry then shifts 1 degree and another 160 readings are taken as the patient's head is scanned. This continues through 180 degrees resulting in 28,800 readings being obtained for the tomographic slice. Simultaneous equations for these 28,800 readings are then solved by computer with the solutions transformed into absorption algorithm coefficients, and the image is analytically reconstructed. A cathode ray tube displays the varying x-ray absorption patterns within the brain for each slice. An arbitrary scale has been chosen with values from -500 (black) to $+500$ (white). Values commonly seen in the reconstructed image include cerebrospinal fluid $= 0 - 5$, white matter $= 12 - 15$, grey matter $= 15 - 18$, blood $= 2 - 40$, calcium $= 50$, and bone $= 500$. Figures 6A, B, and C are Polaroid photographs of a normal CT scan demonstrating the excellent resolution of intracranial structures obtained by this technique. The CT scan can clearly distinguish the ventricular and subarachnoid spaces from the brain parenchyma. Numerous reports have

235

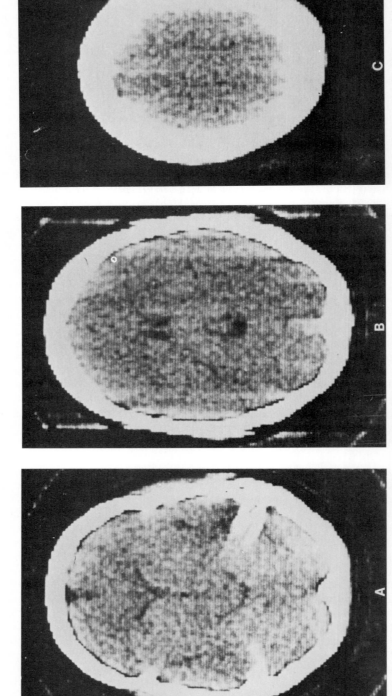

Figure 6. CT scan in a normal patient. A, Horizontal plane above the petrous region shows the frontal horns of the lateral ventricles and the third ventricle. The cortical sulci at this level appear normal. B, Horizontal section through the plane of the frontal horns of the lateral ventricles demonstrates the septum pellucidum. Posteriorly the midline cistern containing the noncalcified pineal gland is noted. C, The most superior horizontal section shows only minimal visualization of the cortical sulci. This lack of demonstration of the cortical sulci is normal and is regarded as evidence that no significant sulcal dilatation is present.

documented the diagnostic value of this technique in virtually all neuropathologically demonstrable abnormalities of the brain.[7, 14, 28, 31, 35]

What is the place of the CT scan among the conventional modalities discussed in this chapter? From the wide experience with the CT scan reported from many institutions, it is evident that this is the method of choice in the initial evaluation of virtually all patients with neurological symptoms relating to the brain. We emphasize that the CT scan, while being utilized as a screening test is sufficiently diagnostic in many instances to preclude further studies. Most investigators who have studied the statistical impact of the CT scanner on other neuroradiological procedures report a marked decrease in the number of pneumoencephalograms and radionuclide brain scans performed.[4, 36] Plain skull radiographs are frequently helpful in correlating areas of calcification and other abnormalities that may be seen on the CT scan; thus these methods are complementary. The need for arteriography is less clearly defined. Although the CT scan is of diagnostic value in vascular lesions such as infarcts,[14] intracerebral hemorrhage, and subarachnoid hemorrhage,[40] the need for arteriography frequently is not obviated by the CT scan. Obviously, vascular lesions such as cerebral arteritis are still definitively studied by the arteriogram. The need for arteriography in lesions such as tumors is less well defined, however, and its use frequently depends upon problems in differential diagnosis and therapeutic considerations.

Degenerative Disorders

What is the impact of the CT scan on evaluation of the patient with dementia or suspected of having dementia? The pneumoencephalogram can be avoided in vir-

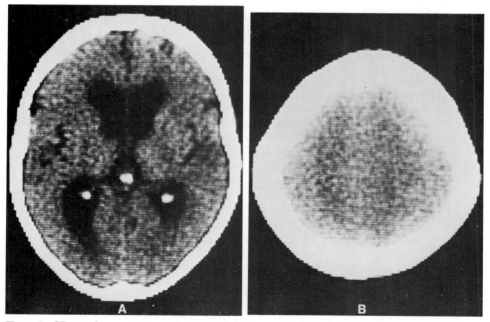

Figure 7. CT scan in a nondemented patient. A, CT scan shows marked enlargement of the ventricles as well as minimal enlargement of the basal cisterns. The three dense areas contain calcium. B, Most superior horizontal section shows no enlargement of the cortical sulci.

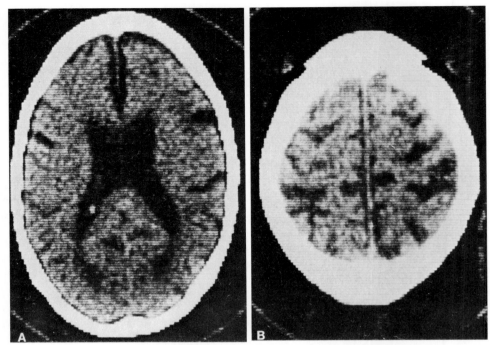

Figure 8. CT scan in a patient with diffuse cerebral atrophy. A, Enlargement of the ventricles and striking enlargement of the cortical sulci can be seen. B, The most superior horizontal plane shows marked enlargement of the cortical sulci. These findings together are regarded as most consistent with a diffuse atrophic process.

tually all cases of cerebral atrophy. As in the initial reports of Paxton and Ambrose[35] who described 20 patients with enlarged ventricles and enlarged cortical sulci diagnosed by CT scan with confirmation by pneumoencephalography, subsequent series have demonstrated that enlarged ventricles and sulci are easily detected by the technique of CT scanning (Figs. 7A and B, 8A and B, and 9). However, the difficulties encountered in evaluating demented patients by pneumoencephalography remain to some extent even with the CT scan. The significance of cortical atrophy diagnosed by demonstration of enlarged sulci on the CT scan is not yet known. Furthermore, the normal CT scan usually fails to visualize the cortical sulci. Thus, it is not possible by CT scan to differentiate normal small sulci from the obliterated subarachnoid spaces seen in the various diseases causing normal pressure hydrocephalus. While grossly dilated ventricles and markedly dilated cortical sulci are easily appreciated, patients who have less marked changes by CT scanning will probably have to be regarded in the equivocal range. Experience sufficient to establish normal limits of ventricular and cortical sulcal size for the varying age groups on the CT scan has not yet been accumulated. For example, patients with large cortical sulci on the CT scan may be without signs or symptoms of dementia. These findings are reminiscent of Mann's observations[29] mentioned earlier in regard to large cortical sulci demonstrated by pneumoencephalography in patients without clinical evidence of dementia.

In the first published description dealing with the validity of criteria for evaluat-

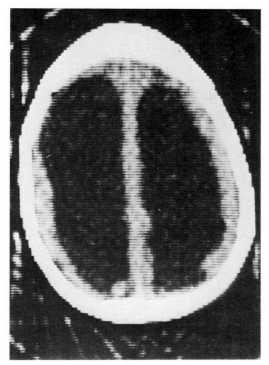

Figure 9. CT scan in a patient with marked hydrocephalus. Ventricles are so enlarged that little is seen in the way of "cortical mantle." This marked ventricular enlargement is usually due to obstruction within the ventricular system.

ing cerebral atrophy by CT scanning, Huckman and coworkers[22] noted that the accuracy of the CT scan in dementia seems to be limited by factors similar to those limiting pneumoencephalography. Diagnosis of atrophy was based upon a measurement method derived initially from the authors' experiences and then correlated with previous anatomical studies. In their subjects, a reasonably close correlation between CT scan diagnosis of atrophy and anatomical studies is described. In patients without dementia, 90 percent had minimal or no cortical atrophy by CT scan. In demented patients, on the other hand, two-thirds had slight and one-third had moderate to severe cortical atrophy by CT scanning. One of the important findings of this initial study was that absence of " major atrophy" by CT scanning in a demented patient should make the physician particularly suspicious of a treatable illness such as a metabolic disease or a deficiency state as a cause for the patient's dementia. Of their patients, 3 were discovered to have treatable causes of dementia — 2 had hypothyroidism and one had pernicious anemia.

Normal Pressure Hydrocephalus

The characteristic appearance of normal pressure hydrocephalus by CT scanning is described by large ventricles with no visualization of the cortical sulci (Fig. 10). The specificity of this finding awaits further clinical experience for confirma-

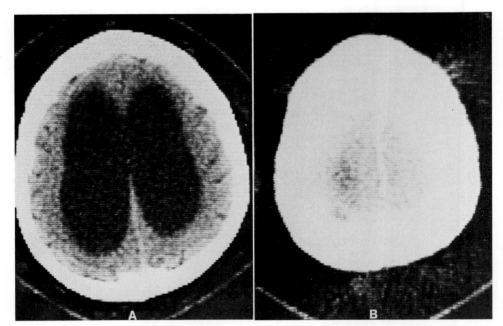

Figure 10. CT scan in a patient with characteristic normal pressure hydrocephalus syndrome. A, This image shows marked enlargement of the lateral ventricles without striking enlargement of the sulci. B, The most superior horizontal section reveals non-visualization of the cortical sulci.

tion for we have seen similar findings in patients without clinical manifestations of this syndrome. Nevertheless, the CT scan demonstration of dilated ventricles with nonvisualization of the cortical sulci does suggest normal pressure hydrocephalus. This set of findings is distinct from that of dilated ventricles and markedly dilated cortical sulci. Davis and coworkers[14] have recommended that in the patient who has increased ventricular size demonstrated by CT scan with no visualization of the cortical sulci, isotope cisternography should be performed to evaluate for normal pressure hydrocephalus. At our institution, the decision to perform a diversionary CSF shunting procedure in a particular patient is based primarily on the clinical presentation of the patient. Consequently, if the CT scan shows findings compatible with normal pressure hydrocephalus, no further diagnostic radiological evaluation is deemed necessary since it would not have therapeutic implications.

Focal Lesions

Since computed cranial tomography is the procedure of choice in the initial evaluation of the variety of focal cerebral lesions, it is evident that the occasional patient with dementia who proves to have a focal lesion is best studied by this technique. We alluded at the outset of this chapter to one of the major tasks confronting the radiologist in evaluating the demented patient: to make sure that the patient does not have a treatable focal lesion causing his symptoms. In this regard,

240

also, the CT scan shows its value. It is especially important to evaluate patients with large lateral ventricles for unsuspected posterior fossa, midbrain, and third ventricular lesions. Figures 11A through F illustrate the value of CT scanning in the diagnosis of a difficult clinical and neuroradiological problem. The initial CT scan, including contrast enhancement, revealed no definite abnormality in a 60-year-old woman with generalized seizures (Figs. 11A and B). Examination six months later (Figs. 11C and D) showed interval enlargement of the supratentorial ventricles with normal sulci. The clinical diagnosis at this time suggested normal pressure hydrocephalus, and the CT scan findings were compatible with this diagnosis though not characteristic. Subsequently, the patient underwent atrioventricular shunting following which she developed increased lethargy. The final CT scan (Figs. 11E and F) demonstrated an area of increased density in the posterior third ventricle and adjacent midbrain with striking enhancement following intravenous contrast media. The patient subsequently died, and at autopsy a malignant infiltrating glioma was found in the midbrain and posterior thalamus obstructing the aqueduct.

Computed cranial tomography thus has become the procedure of choice in the initial evaluation of most patients with symptoms referable to the brain, including the demented patient. Focal abnormalities are easily and accurately diagnosed, and changes of marked cerebral atrophy are readily apparent. Ventricular size may be assessed and followed serially. Further experience will no doubt determine the accuracy of the diagnosis of atrophy by CT scanning as well as its therapeutic implications.

SUMMARY

No radiographic protocol can be devised which is suitable for the evaluation of all cases of dementia. In general, however, computerized cranial tomography is the initial and often the only diagnostic radiographic procedure needed in cases of suspected or identified dementia. Enlarged ventricles and widened cortical sulci are the changes usually demonstrated in patients with significant dementia, and their absence suggests certain diagnostic implications. In the demented patient whose CT scan reveals no significant brain atrophy, the possibility that the dementia is due to a treatable and reversible disorder should be seriously considered and explored. In the patient whose dementia is doubtful and whose CT scan is normal, the likelihood of a functional psychiatric disorder should be entertained. Focal lesions which result in the clinical picture of dementia are also usually demonstrated by computed tomography.

Plain skull radiographs, cerebral angiography, pneumoencephalography, and radionuclide cisternography remain useful and sometimes necessary radiographic procedures in the study of many patients with dementia. However, they no longer make up the routine diagnostic radiographic battery in dementia. Rather, their use is determined individually when some particular feature of the history or clinical examination suggests that the specific procedure might be helpful.

In geographic areas where computerized tomography is unavailable, plain skull radiographs plus pneumoencephalograms remain the sequential diagnostic procedures of choice in dementia, although specific clinical features might require a considerably different radiographic approach.

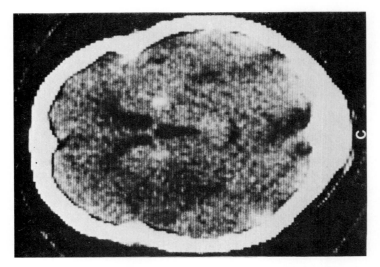

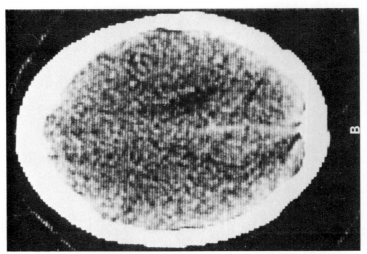

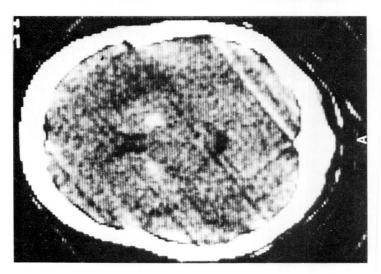

242

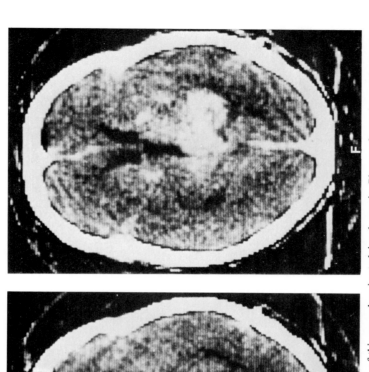

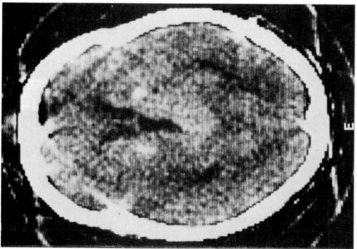

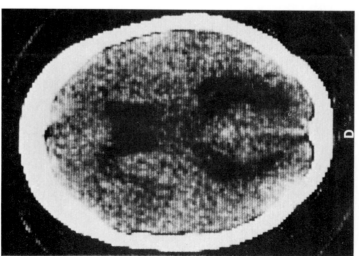

Figure 11A through F. The CT scan performed serially in this patient demonstrates the value of this procedure in studying dementia. Please refer to the text for the description of this particular image sequence.

243

REFERENCES

1. ADAMS, R. D.; FISHER, C. M.; HAKIM, S.; OJEMANN, R. G.; AND SWEET, W. H.: *Symptomatic occult hydrocephalus with "normal" cerebrospinal fluid pressure.* New Engl. J. Med. 273:117, 1965.

2. AMBROSE, J.: *Computerized x-ray scanning of the brain.* J. Neurosurg. 40:679, 1974.

3. BAKER, H. L.: *The clinical usefulness of magnification cerebral angiography.* Radiology 98:587, 1971.

4. BAKER, H. L.; CAMPBELL, J. K.; HOUSER, D. W.; AND REESE, D. F.: *Early experience with the EMI scanner for study of the brain.* Radiology 116:327, 1975.

5. BENNETT, J. C.; MOFFLY, R. H.; AND STEINBACH, H. L.: *The significance of bilateral basal ganglial calcification.* Radiology 72:368, 1959.

6. BLINDERMAN, E. E.; WEIDNER, W.; AND MARKHAM, C. H.: *The pneumoencephalogram in Huntington's chorea.* Neurology (Minneap.) 14:601, 1964.

7. BOGDANOFF, B. M.; STAFFORD, C. R.; GREER, L.; AND GONZALEZ, C. F.: *Computerized transaxial tomography in the evaluation of patients with focal epilepsy.* Neurology (Minneap.) 25: 1013, 1975.

8. BROOKS, R. A., AND DiCHIRO, G.: *Theory of image reconstruction in computed tomography.* Radiology 117:561, 1975.

9. BURHENNE, H. J., AND DAVIES, H.: *The ventricular span in cerebral pneumography.* Am. J. Roentgenol. Radium Ther. Nucl. Med. 90:1176, 1963.

10. COBLENTZ, J. M.; MATTIS, S.; ZINGESSER, L. H.; KASOFF, S. S.; WISNIEWSKI, H. M.; AND KATZMAN, R.: *Presenile dementia.* Arch. Neurol. 29:299, 1973.

11. CRONQVIST, S., AND AGEE, F.: *Regional cerebral blood flow in intracranial tumors.* Acta Radiol. (Diagn.) 7:393, 1968.

12. DAVIDOFF, L. M., AND DYKE, C. G.: *The Normal Encephalogram,* ed. 2. Lea & Febiger, Philadelphia, 1946.

13. DAVIS, D. O., AND PRESSMAN, B. D.: *Computerized tomography of the brain.* Radiol. Clin. North Am. 12:297, 1974.

14. DAVIS, K. R.; TAVERAS, J. M.; NEW, P. F. J.; SCHNUR, J. A.; AND ROBERSON, G. H.: *Cerebral infarction diagnosis by computerized tomography.* Am. J. Roentgenol. Radium Ther. Nucl. Med. 124:643, 1975.

15. DiCHIRO, G., AND LIBOW, L. S.: *Carotid siphon calcification and cerebral blood flow in the healthy aged male.* Radiology 99:103, 1971.

16. FERRIS, E. J.; RUDIKOFF, J. C.; AND SHAPIRO, J. H.: *Cerebral angiography of bacterial infection.* Radiology 90:727, 1968.

17. GREITZ, T.: *Angiography in tuberculous meningitis.* Acta Radiol. (Diagn.) 2:369, 1964.

18. GREITZ, T., AND LINDGREN, E.: Angiographic determination of brain tumor pathology, in Abrams, H. L. (ed.): *Angiography.* Little, Brown and Co., Boston, 1971.

19. HAASE, G. R.: Diseases presenting as dementia, in Wells, C. E. (ed.): *Dementia,* ed. 2. F. A. Davis Co., Philadelphia, 1977.

20. HIRSCH, M. S.; AIKIT, B. K.; AND BASU, A. K.: *Takayasu's arteritis.* Bull. Johns Hopkins Hosp. 115: 29, 1964.

21. HOSAIN, F.; SAM, P.; JAMES, A. E.; DEBLANC, H. J.; AND WAGNER, H. N.: Radioactive chelates for cisternography: The basis and the choice, in Harbert, J. C. (ed.): *Cisternography and Hydrocephalus.* Charles C Thomas, Springfield, Illinois, 1972.

22. HUCKMAN, M. J.; FOX, J., AND TOPEL, J.: *The validity of criteria for the evaluation of cerebral atrophy by computerized tomography.* Radiology 116:85, 1975.

23. KATZMAN, R.: Normal pressure hydrocephalus, in Wells, C. E. (ed.): *Dementia,* ed. 2. F.A. Davis Co., Philadelphia, 1977.

24. JAMES, A. E.; NEW, P. F. J.; HEINZ, E. R.; HODGES, F. J.; AND DELAND, F. H.: *A cisternographic classification of hydrocephalus.* Am. J. Roentgenol. Radium Ther. Nucl. Med. 115:39, 1972.

25. KILGORE, B. B.; AND FIELDS, W. S.: Arterial occlusive disease in adults, in Newton, T. H. and Potts, D. G. (eds.): *Radiology of the Skull and Brain,* Vol. 2. C.V. Mosby Co., St. Louis, 1971.

26. LEEDS, N. E.; ISARD, H. S.; GOLDBERG, H.; AND CULLINAN, J. E.: *Serial magnification cerebral angiography.* Radiology 90:1171, 1968.

27. LeMAY, M., AND NEW, P. F. J.: *Radiological diagnosis of occult normal pressure hydrocephalus.* Radiology 96:347, 1973.

28. LYING-TUNELL, U., AND MARIONS, O.: *A triad of air encephalographic findings in patients with mental impairment: A controlled prospective study.* Neuroradiology 9:251, 1975.

29. MANN, H. H.: *Cortical atrophy and air encephalography: A clinical and radiological study.* Psychol. Med. 3:374, 1973.

30. MINAGI, H.: Skull changes in endocrine disease, in Newton, T. H., and Potts, D. G. (eds.): *Radiology of the Skull and Brain,* Vol. 1. C.V. Mosby Co., St. Louis, 1971.

31. NEW, P. F. J.; SCOTT, W. R.; SCHNUR, J. A.; DAVIS, K. R.; TAVERAS, J. M.; AND HOCHBERG, F. H.: *Computerized tomography with the EMI scanner in the diagnosis of primary and metastatic intracranial neoplasm.* Radiology 114:75, 1975.

32. NIELSEN, R.; PETERSEN, O.; THYGESEN, P.; AND WILLANGER, R.: *Encephalographic ventricular atrophy.* Acta Radiol. (Diagn.) 4:240, 1966.

33. NIELSEN, R.; PETERSEN, O.; THYGESEN, P.; AND WILLANGER, R.: *Encephalographic cortical atrophy.* Acta Radiol. (Diagn.) 4:437, 1966.

34. OZONOFF, M. G., AND BORROWS, E. H.: Intracranial calcification, in Newton, T. H., and Potts, D. G. (eds.): *Radiology of the Skull and Brain,* Vol. 1. C.V. Mosby Co., St. Louis, 1971.

35. PAXTON, R., AND AMBROSE, J.: *The EMI scanner. A brief review of the first 650 patients.* Br. J. Radiol. 47:530, 1974.

36. PENDERGRASS, H. P.; McKUSICK, K. A.; NEW, P. F. J.; AND POTSAID, M.: *Relative efficacy of radionuclide imaging and computed tomography of the brain.* Radiology 116:363, 1975.

37. RADCLIFFE, W. B.; GUINTO, F. C.; AND SCATLIFF, J. H.: *Cerebral and extracerebral hematomas.* Semin. Roentgenol. 6:103, 1971.

38. RUGGIERO, G.; CALABRO, A.; METZGER, J.; AND SIMON, J.: *Arteriography of the external carotid artery.* Acta Radiol. (Diagn.) 1:395, 1963.

39. ROBERTSON, E. G.: *Pneumoencephalography.* Charles C Thomas, Springfield, Illinois, 1967.

40. SCOTT, W. R.; NEW, P. F. J.; DAVIS, K. R.; AND SCHNUR, J. A.: *Computerized axial tomography of intracerebral and intraventricular hemorrhage.* Radiology 112:73, 1974.

41. SEARS, A. D.; MILLER, J. E.; AND KILGORE, B. B.: *Diagnosis of cerebral atrophy from the AP carotid phlebogram.* Am. J. Roentgenol. Radium Ther. Nucl. Med. 85:1128, 1961.

42. STAAB, E. V.; ALLEN, J. H.; YOUNG, B. A.; SOPER, B. A.; AND MEACHAM, W.: ^{131}I-HSA cisternograms and pneumoencephalograms in evaluation of hydrocephalus, in Harbert, J. C. (ed.): *Cisternography and Hydrocephalus.* Charles C Thomas, Springfield, Illinois, 1972.

43. TAVERAS, J. M., AND WOOD, E. H.: *Diagnostic Neuroradiology.* The Williams & Wilkins Co., Baltimore, 1964.

44. TREVOR, R. P.; SONDHEIMER, F. K.; FESSEL, W. J.; AND WOLPERT, S. M.: *Angiographic demonstration of major vessel occlusion in systemic lupus erythematosus.* Neuroradiology 4:202, 1972.

45. WOOD, J. H.; BARTLET, D.; JAMES, A. E.; AND UDVARHELYI, G. B.: *Normal-pressure hydrocephalus: Diagnosis and patient selection for shunt surgery.* Neurology (Minneap.) 24:517, 1974.

CHAPTER 12

Diagnostic Evaluation and Treatment in Dementia

Charles E. Wells, M.D.

Providing optimal medical care for the demented patient entails a complex series of observations, suppositions, and decision making processes. These processes are so complicated and involve so many variables that no single recommended procedure can be proposed that will include all eventualities. Even if it were possible to disregard considerations of time, cost, and personal comfort, it is highly unlikely that any preprogrammed diagnostic evaluation and treatment plan could be developed. In this chapter the problems most commonly confronted are dealt with and a rational approach to patient care, which has general if not universal applicability, is proposed.

The specific problems faced by the individual practitioner depend significantly upon the nature and setting of his practice. The difficulties confronting the generalist, the psychiatrist, and the neurologist, at least early in the process of patient evaluation, are likely to be significantly different. The physician providing primary care (whether family physician, internist, or even gynecologist or surgeon) is likely to have initial and recurring contact with the patient. The primary care physician must learn to recognize the texture of cerebral dysfunction in the warp and woof of the patient's complaints and behavior. As Arie[6] pointed out, it is both easy and common for the primary care physician to fail to recognize dementia even in his regular patient population. Both Coblentz and coworkers[20] and Epstein and Simon[28] emphasized that a long delay from the onset of symptoms of dementia to the time of a definitive diagnostic evaluation is common. Although this may partly reflect the attitude of therapeutic nihilism to be considered below, it also undeniably reflects a failure to recognize the early signs and symptoms of dementia which results in postponement of adequate evaluation at the time when therapeutic efforts might be most beneficial.

For the patient who comes or is brought to the psychiatrist for evaluation and treatment, the assumption has already been made that cerebral function is disordered; the question now largely concerns the nature of the disorder — is it functional or organic? Although neuropathologists continue to report[53] cases occasioning their surprise when structural brain disease is uncovered in patients diagnosed as suffering from functional disorders, this does not much surprise the knowledgeable psychiatrist. The real problem for the psychiatrist arises not because he fails to consider the possibility of organic brain disease (for this is an essential feature of all psychiatric evaluations), but the pressing problem arises when the psychiatrist *does* consider that there is a significant possibility of a primary organic etiology or of a secondary organic contribution to the patient's presenting complaints. Certainly subjecting each patient for whom such suspicion arises to the full gamut of neurological diagnostic procedures is not an acceptable solution. Rather the psychiatrist must evaluate the features of the patient's history, character of complaints, and clinical evaluation which alert him to the likelihood of underlying neurological disease and persuade himself to advise the patient to undergo time-consuming, costly, sometimes uncomfortable, and occasionally even dangerous neurodiagnostic studies.

The neurologist generally encounters a different set of problems. The patient is not usually referred to the neurologist unless there is strong suspicion or likelihood of organic disease. With dementia, in most cases, the neurologist must inquire whether the disordered mentation results from diffuse or focal cerebral disease and pursue diagnosis of the underlying pathological process. Even so, the neurologist must ascertain from the clinical examination whether or not the findings sufficiently suggest organic disease to warrant detailed evaluation. And then the neurologist must choose the appropriate evaluative procedure so that diagnosis is achieved as quickly, safely, and inexpensively as possible. Unless laboratory examinations are to supplant clinical evaluation, the neurologist may often have to decide that the clinical evidence does not merit an exhaustive laboratory search.

Proper clinical management of the demented patient thus presents varied diagnostic and therapeutic problems to each physician who encounters the patient. Common to them all, however, is the discouragement that the physician often feels when he must face this situation. Dementia is so common, particularly in the aged, and its etiology so rarely established definitively that there is an ever present tendency to ascribe the dementia to "old age" without sufficient justification. Were there a readily available therapeutic regimen promising dramatic relief of symptoms, then at least therapeutic pessimism might not be joined to the diagnostic dilemma. Unfortunately, save for the relatively few dementias of specific known cause and treatment, there are no therapeutic measures that assure clinical improvement. Thus neither the patient nor the physician can realistically confront the situation with any degree of optimism.

As patients with dementia are studied with increasing thoroughness, more treatable cases of dementia are being uncovered. It is essential, therefore, that the patient with a treatable disease not be overlooked. Several recent papers[7, 46, 56, 61, 64, 67, 83, 84] attest to the current view that early and exact diagnosis of dementia is vital. To accomplish such diagnosis, the physician must ask and answer several sequential questions (Fig. 1).

The physician must be trained to suspect dementia even on the basis of inadequate evidence. Once the question is raised, the history and mental status evaluation are used to test this possibility. Adding to this the observations obtained from general physical and neurological examinations, the physician makes hypotheses as to the nature of the disorder and the site of involvement. These hypotheses are tested by further diagnostic studies, so that a firm diagnosis and a rational plan of treatment can be reached. The physician must thus formulate a systematic plan for patient care by which he can: (1) prove or disprove the presence of dementia, (2) arrive at a correct diagnosis of its cause, and (3) treat the patient by the best means available. In a volume devoted to dementia, as would be expected, this chapter is focused primarily on identification of the diffuse disorders which result in dementia and their prevention and treatment.

248

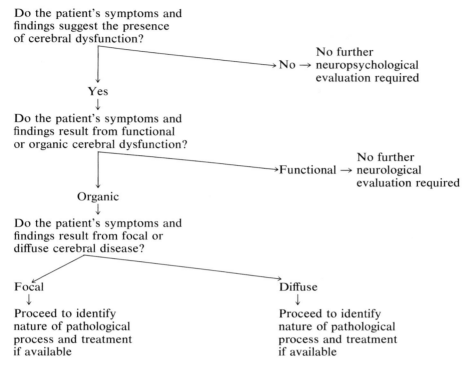

Figure 1. Sequential decisions in patient evaluation.

PREVIOUS STUDIES

It is reasonable and, indeed, necessary to pose the question, "What can be expected from a thorough medical, psychiatric, and neurological evaluation of patients thought to be demented?" In other words, what will the payoff be? Only recently have a few studies emerged which provide some tentative answers to this question.

In 1972 Marsden and Harrison[54, 55] reported the results of their retrospective study of 106 patients who had been admitted to the National Hospital, Queen Square, in 1968 and 1969 with a presumptive diagnosis of dementia, all of whom had been evaluated by a neurologist or a psychiatrist or both before admission. Katzman[43] studied 56 patients consecutively admitted to Jacobi Hospital, a municipal hospital in New York City, with a presumptive diagnosis of dementia. And Freemon[30] evaluated another 60 patients admitted to the Nashville Veterans Administration Hospital with an admission diagnosis of dementia. In each of the three series, patients were evaluated with a full complement of diagnostic procedures, including pneumoencephalography in most instances. Table 1 presents the results of the individual studies as well as the combined figures. The similarities in the findings among the three studies are far more striking than the differences. Each study reflects some differences in patient populations and in triage procedures, but in each group atrophy of unknown cause (doubtless largely Alzheimer's disease or senile dementia) was by far the most frequent diagnosis, this

Table 1. Statistical summary of reported series of demented patients studied

	Marsden and Harrison	Katzman	Freemon	Total Number	Percent
Established Diagnoses	106	56	60	222	
Atrophy of unknown cause (largely Alzheimer's disease and senile dementia)	48	39	26	113	50.9
Intracranial masses	8	1	3	12	5.4
Dementia due to vascular disease	8	4	5	17	7.7
Dementia in alcoholics	6	3	4	13	5.9
Normal pressure hydrocephalus	5	2	7	14	6.3
Creutzfeldt-Jakob disease	3	0	0	3	1.4
Huntington's chorea	3	3	4	10	4.5
Post-traumatic dementia	1	0	1	2	<1
Post-subarachnoid hemorrhage	1	0	0	1	<1
Post-encephalitic dementia	1	0	1	2	<1
Neurosyphilis	0	0	1	1	<1
Dementia with amytrophic lateral sclerosis	0	1	0	1	<1
Dementia with Parkinson's disease	0	1	0	1	<1
Thyroid disease (hypo- or hyper-function)	0	1	1	2	<1
Pernicious anemia	0	1	0	1	<1
Hepatic failure	0	0	1	1	<1
Drug toxicity	2	0	5	7	3.2
Epilepsy	1	0	0	1	<1
Depression	8	0	1	9	4.1
Other psychiatric disease	2	0	0	2	<1
Not demented — no definite diagnosis	2	0	0	2	<1
Dementia uncertain	7	0	0	7	3.2

diagnosis being assigned from four to nine times more often than any other diagnostic subcategory in the three groups studied. These findings are also remarkably consistent with the detailed postmortem studies carried out by Tomlinson, Blessed, and Roth.[79]

From the evidence accumulated in these three studies, a thorough evaluation of demented patients may be expected to result in diagnoses of potentially correctable disorders in approximately 15 percent. These disorders include instances of depression, drug toxicity, normal pressure hydrocephalus, benign intracranial masses, mania, hypothyroidism, hyperthyroidism, pernicious anemia, epilepsy, and hepatic failure. In an additional 20 to 25 percent of patients, disorders will be identified in which therapeutic measures may be beneficial and important even though restoration to health may be impossible. Such measures include control of hypertension in multi-infarct dementia, palliative treatment for malignant brain tumors, withdrawal from alcohol in demented alcoholics, surgical treatment of normal pressure hydrocephalus even where brain damage cannot be reversed, treatment of neurosyphilis, and genetic counseling for families of patients with Huntington's chorea. To summarize, in 35 to 40 percent of demented patients, conditions will be uncovered in which some form of therapeutic intervention other than purely symptomatic treatment is important.

PATIENT EVALUATION

History

When the patient comes to the physician complaining of the classic symptoms of organic brain disease as outlined in the A.P.A.'s *Diagnostic and Statistical Manual*[4] (loss of memory, inability to calculate, disorientation, for example), only a little perspicacity is required to suspect dementia and to confirm the diagnosis. However, the classic symptoms and signs of dementia may occur late in the course and the initial events, when the patient is most amenable to treatment, may prove hazy and evanescent.[85] In the initial evaluation of the patient, three situations should particularly signal the diagnostic possibility of dementia:

1. The physician should be suspicious if the patient presents multiple physical complaints that fit into no discernible pattern of physical disease. He should be particularly suspicious if these complaints do not fit into the previous life style of the individual.

2. The physician should be suspicious if a patient presents a variety of "psychiatric" symptoms, such as depression, anxiety, and irritability. He should be even more suspicious when the symptoms fit into no specific functional diagnostic category and the patient has no history of previous emotional difficulties.

3. The physician should be suspicious if the patient presents a story that remains vague and unclear to the examiner even after a lengthy and sympathetic hearing. This occurs with other illnesses, but the possibility of dementia should always be raised by its observation.

To these should be added that the physician must be wary of the possibility of underlying dementia whenever delirium occurs upon apparently slight provocation. For example, the patient admitted in a delirium following a minor mix-up in taking prescribed medications at home will not infrequently upon recovery from the delirium be found to have a mild, previously unrecognized dementia, which caused the error in the first place. At the same time it should be recalled that commonly prescribed medications when administered in usual dosages seldom cause delirium unless there is preexisting compromised brain function.

When the patient's symptoms center upon emotional experiences, two tendencies must particularly be guarded against. The first tendency is to regard, in an almost automatic fashion, all mental dysfunction in the young as functional or nonorganic in origin, thereby neglecting the possibility of organic cerebral disease in younger patients. The converse tendency is to regard all mental symptoms presenting in old age as being due to cerebral deterioration. In old age particularly, there is danger that a depressive illness may be masked by pseudo-dementia. Kiloh[47] stated the danger clearly: "At any age, including the senium, every time the diagnosis of dementia is being considered, the possibility of depression is worth bearing in mind." Several authors[17, 69] emphasized the frequency of nonorganic mental disorders, particularly depressive illness, in the aged and their relatively good prognosis with appropriate treatment.

Once dementia is suspected, there are a number of historical factors to be investigated. Obtaining a precise description of the presenting symptoms is essential if the patient or his family and friends can provide it. Are there complaints of memory loss and, if so, are these voiced by the patient or by others? The relative rarity of memory loss as a complaint raised by patients with dementia has already been remarked upon as has the good correlation between complaints of memory disturbance and depression.[39, 85] Even when organic brain dysfunction is established, a complaint of memory disturbance correlates better with the degree of depression than with the extent of organic impairment. On the other hand, impairment of memory is an early complaint voiced by the family of virtually every demented patient. Has there been difficulty in concentrating, dealing with complex materials, keeping facts and schedules in order? Is the nature of the complaints largely within the cognitive and intellectual sphere or are they largely affectual? At times affectual symptoms may be prominent in dementia. Post[65] noted that severe depression is seen more often in dementia due to vascular disease than in senile dementia.

The mode of onset and progression is of special importance in suggesting the etiology. Abruptness of onset and a stuttering course are characteristic of vascular disease, as are the appearance and resolution of focal neurological symptoms and signs. Such a progression is not foreign, however, to the primary cerebral degenerative processes. Have there been headaches, changes in level of consciousness, or epileptic seizures? A history of even slight cranial trauma may prove important. With the increasing use of sedatives, tranquilizers, and antidepressant medications, a thorough history of the patient's use of drugs, including alcohol, is essential. The appearance of a drug-induced delirium in a patient taking moderate amounts of commonly prescribed drugs should suggest the possibility of a dementing disorder rendering the brain sensitive to drugs at levels usually well tolerated. Is there a history of anemia? Has the patient experienced malaise, loss of energy, anorexia, or weight loss—all of which might suggest the presence of occult malignancy? Has there been fever or is there a history of chronic infectious processes? Are there symptoms that suggest Parkinson's disease?

The patient must also be questioned about specific symptoms that suggest focal cerebral dysfunction. Have there been language difficulties? Has he had difficulty understanding or reading words? Does he have trouble finding words? It should be recalled that word finding problems occur in many situations other than aphasia and that a diagnosis of aphasia based on word finding defects alone is, as Benson[10] said, "treacherous." Has he forgotten "how to do" things? Is there difficulty attending to and following instructions? Is there loss of recent memory, trouble recognizing people and objects? Has neglect of one side of the body or one-half of space been noted? Are there symptoms of focal weakness or sensory loss?

Since dementia occurs with many systemic diseases,[34] a thorough review of systems is essential. Are there symptoms or a history of syphilis? Does dyspnea, cough, or sputum production suggest chronic pulmonary disease? Does hematuria, scant urine, or edema point toward chronic renal dysfunction? Is there jaundice, itching, dark urine, or light stools compatible with liver dysfunction? Do changes in habitus, heat and cold tolerance, and hair texture and distribution suggest an endocrinological disorder?

Mental Status Evaluation

Often the presence of dementia can be established by a simple mental status examination demonstrating loss of memory for recent events, spatial and temporal disorientation, and generally diminished intellectual capacities; or its presence can safely be disallowed by a thoroughgoing psychiatric examination that reveals none of the features of organic brain disease. Commonly, however, the suspicion of organic brain dysfunction is not easily put to rest. The person suspected of

252

dementia is often elderly when some decline in mental capacity is accepted as normal.[81] In younger individuals, massive employment of defenses such as denial and repression may suggest an hysterical memory loss and hide the underlying organic process.[48] A systematic assay of the patient's mental status usually provides the physician some certainty in the diagnosis.

A significant portion of the mental status examination is performed in taking the history. In general, this establishes the level and competence of the patient's mentative capacities over a wide range of functions, including recent and remote memory, affect, and capacity for logical thought. The patient should be approached in an unhurried manner and be given plenty of time to formulate and present his answers. This applies whether or not the physician suspects a diagnosis of subcortical dementia.[2] Insofar as possible, questioning should be permitted to evolve naturally from the opening remarks, taking the form of a sympathetic and interested conversation. A compulsively ritualized or formal mental status examination may be far less revealing than intelligently directed and selective questioning.

On the other hand, the more formal portions of the mental status examination (described below) may be useful specifically: (1) to establish with more certainty the presence of dementia which is suspected but not proved on the basis of history, (2) to establish a quantitative base line of function from which further progression or regression can be measured, and (3) to delineate specific mentative dysfunctions (particularly amnestic, agnosic, apractic, aphasic features)[39] that have focal significance. A schema for the systematic mental status evaluation is given in Table 2; this follows in large part the examination suggested by McDowell and Wolff.[57]

APPEARANCE AND BEHAVIOR. How does the patient present himself? Is he clean, neatly dressed, and appropriately groomed, or is he unclean with clothing in disarray? Does he look older or younger than his years? Does his appearance reflect his position in the world? Is he alert and responsive or dull and apathetic? Is he drowsy and unable to attend to the questioner? Are his movements slow and sparse, or is he tremulous, changing positions frequently, wringing his hands, or unable to sit for the examination? Is he friendly, cooperative, distant, or truculent? Is he uninhibited and indiscreet in discussion of topics usually considered intimate and private? (A frequent observation in organic deterioration.) Can he attend to the examination, or does his mind frequently wander from the point? Is there any consistency in the nature of the inadequate responses to questions? Post[65] observed, "By and large, 'near miss' answers are suggestive of cerebral defects, while 'don't know' answers are more typical of the unwilling and possibly depressed patient."

ORIENTATION. Unless orientation is established without question from the his-

Table 2. Mental status examinations

Appearance and behavior
Orientation
Language
Mood
Memory
General intellectual evaluation
Special preoccupations and experiences
Understanding

tory, it must be proved by direct questioning. Arie[6] observed, "The important thing is to ask the questions, and never simply to assume the answers. . . ." Does the patient know his name, where he is, the time of day, the day of the week, the date, the year, the season? Benton, Van Allen, and Fogel[11] suggested that neurologists often do not set sufficiently stringent demands for orientation in their patients and thereby fail to recognize disorientation.

LANGUAGE. Is there a paucity of speech, or is the patient loquacious? Are words clearly pronounced? Are there defects in sentence structure? Does he misuse words, seem to have trouble finding words, talk "around" a missing word, or use nonexistent words? Is there perseveration or blocking of speech? Is his speech relevant to the question asked, and does the flow of talk follow a logical course? Can the patient comprehend spoken language? Can he name objects? Is he capable of understanding and following directions? Can he read and comprehend written words and instructions? Can he write his name and that which is dictated to him?

MOOD. Although mood can often be inferred from the general tenor of the conversation, it should be delineated by specific questions. "How are your spirits?" "Are you afraid, fearful, anxious?" If the patient's mood is elevated, is it inappropriate? If his mood is sad, does he have thoughts, plans, or fears of suicide?

MEMORY. Several categories of memory must be tested.

Immediate Recall. This is generally measured by asking the patient to repeat digits after the examiner, beginning with three and increasing the number of digits until the patient begins to fail. The patient is tested first for recall of digits to be repeated just as the examiner said them; then he is asked to repeat them backward. In general, most patients can repeat at least six digits forward and four backward without significant difficulty.

The patient may also be asked to repeat three unrelated words immediately and then after 5 minutes (the latter testing recent memory).

Recent Memory. The patient is asked to tell the examiner of events in his immediate past. How did he get to the doctor's office? If hospitalized, for how long? What did he eat last? What are the names of doctors, nurses, and family who have attended him?

Remote Memory. Can the patient tell the examiner the date of his birth, parents' names, schools attended and their order, jobs held and their sequence, date of marriage, names of children? Can he recall names of Presidents who served during his youth? Can he recount details of significant national and local events which took place in his earlier years?

The demonstration of defects in immediate, recent, and remote memory concurrently is most characteristic of cerebral disease.

General Grasp and Recall. The patient is given a series of increasingly complex tasks: "Raise your right arm." "Put your left index finger on your nose." "Put your right index finger on your left eye." "Put your right index finger on your left ear and your left index finger on your right eye." Frequently the examiner will note the patient's performance to falter as the tasks grow more difficult. These tasks also test for right-left disorientation.

The examiner may read the following story, asking the patient to recount its details immediately afterward: "A cowboy from Arizona went to San Francisco with his dog, which he left with a friend while he purchased a new suit of clothes. Dressed finely, he went back to the dog, whistled to him, called him by name, and patted him. But the dog would have nothing to do with him in his new hat and coat and gave a mournful howl. Coaxing had no effect, so the cowboy went away and donned his old garments whereupon the dog immediately showed his wild joy on seeing his master." The patient's version may be recorded and its accuracy verified.

GENERAL INTELLECTUAL EVALUATION. The patient's responses to this portion of the examination will depend to a large extent upon his past experience. A better performance is expected from a college graduate than from one who dropped out of school in the eighth grade. In the sophisticated patient, a general intellectual evaluation is often best obtained through the general history. However, when there is deterioration or if the patient has a limited background, specific questions may be valuable.

General Information. "Who is President of the United States?" "Name the Presidents going backward as far as you can recall." "Who is the Vice-President, Governor of your state, Senators who represent your state in Congress?" "Name 5 of the largest cities in the United States." "Name the states that border on your home state." "Give an explanation of the seasons of the year."

Calculation. "Subtract 7 from 100, then continue subtracting 7 from each sum obtained." "Compute 2×3, 5×8, 9×12, 12×13."

Can the patient perform the multiplication tables? "If eggs are $1.20 per dozen, what would be the cost of three eggs?"

Discrimination and Judgment. Can the patient describe the difference or similarity between a child and a dwarf, a tree and a bush, a river and a canal, a lie and a mistake, a coat and a dress? Can he explain the difference between idleness and laziness, poverty and misery, character and reputation? Can he interpret proverbs appropriately or does he describe their meaning in concrete terms?

Ask the patient to answer the following questions: (1) "If you drove into an unfamiliar city seeking to find a friend living there, how would you go about reaching him?" (2) "If you got into your automobile one morning planning to go to work but found the car would not start, how would you handle the situation?"

SPECIAL PREOCCUPATIONS AND EXPERIENCES. *Preoccupations.* Are there feelings, thoughts, worries, or concerns that stay on the patient's mind that he cannot stop thinking about?

Hallucinations. The examiner must determine if the patient has visual, olfactory, gustatory, auditory, or tactile hallucinations. Questions that may elicit these symptoms are: "Do you see or hear things that you know aren't there?" "Have you ever had visions?" "Do you hear noises or voices or see objects that others appear unaware of?" "Have you experienced strange tastes or smells for which you could find no cause?"

Illusions. Does the patient misinterpret sensory stimuli; for example, is a fluttering curtain misinterpreted as someone climbing through the window; are specks of dirt misinterpreted as small insects; is a shadow upon the wall misinterpreted as an animal?

Delusions. Does the patient possess false beliefs involving extreme poverty or wealth, wickedness or guilt, health or disease, unusual bodily changes, persecutions or dangers? Some appropriate questions to elicit these beliefs are: "Have people treated you strangely?" "Do you feel people take undue notice of you?" "Has anyone attempted to hurt or injure you?" "Do you believe outside forces such as electricity or television influence your mind or body?" "Do you seem to be under outside control?"

255

Obsessions, Compulsions, Phobias, and Rituals. "Do you have habits that bother you?" "Do you have special ways of doing things, so that it disturbs you if you are not able to do them in this fashion?" "Do you have recurrent thoughts or ideas that you cannot get out of your mind?" "Do you feel compelled to perform certain acts that seem to you to have no reason?"

UNDERSTANDING. To what extent does the patient comprehend his current situation and recognize his difficulties? Does he know that he is ill? Does he feel that all of this attention is unnecessary? Does he feel that nothing is wrong with him and that he should be elsewhere? Does he understand why he is being examined?

Such is the makeup of a thorough mental status evaluation. It is valuable not only to determine whether or not a patient has evidence of organic mental dysfunction but also to establish a level of functioning with precision, so that future changes can be measured against it.

The physician may find it useful to give a few brief, easily administered psychological tests to supplement and extend the observations made on mental status examination. Pfeiffer's short portable mental status questionnaire, the Bender-Gestalt figures, and the Trail-Making Test might together prove especially valuable. They can be given without much difficulty (and can be administered by a technician), and performance on them is usually not hard to evaluate. Several other tests might serve equally as well (See Chap. 9 by Wells and Buchanan). A group of these tests, which would require no more than a few minutes to administer, might be useful in routine screening of patients of advancing age.

The Hard to Examine Patient

The agitated, uncooperative, suspicious, or belligerent patient may prove particularly difficult to examine for organic cerebral dysfunction. The examiner's attempt to carry out an organized mental status evaluation may be perceived as a threat, and persistence in questioning may prove counterproductive. In such instances, the status of cognitive and intellectual functions may have to be inferred from the totality of behavioral observations rather than proved by direct questioning. For example, the patient who refuses to answer questions as to orientation may be observed to learn the geographical arrangement of the ward quickly, easily finding bed, bathroom, lounges, and the like, thus demonstrating the capacity for assimilating well new and complex orienting details. Another patient may refuse to cooperate in tests for recent memory but in conversation mention newly introduced staff and other patients by name—good evidence of the capacity to learn and recall new information. One patient, extremely paranoid, digressed into paranoid ruminations whenever questioned about recent events in an effort to assay his recent memory. However, when another examiner questioned him a few hours later about a skin lesion, his immediate response was, "Oh! So we're back to that again, are we?" thus demonstrating his recall of questioning by the original examiner. By such tangential means a fair measure of memory, cognition, and intellectual function can often be made even in the hard to examine patient.

Physical Examination

The patient suspected of dementia requires not only a thorough psychiatric examination but a complete medical and neurological evaluation as well. The general medical evaluation is directed at uncovering those systemic disorders that

256

might account for the dementia.[34] Does the patient have fever suggesting an infectious process? Is the blood pressure elevated so that cerebrovascular disease might be suspected? Is the pulse irregular, a common finding with cerebral embolism? Does examination of the skin suggest anemia, jaundice, polycythemia, endocrine dysfunction, malnutrition? Does the breath smell of urea or alcohol? Are the lymph nodes enlarged such as might be found with a chronic granulomatous process or Hodgkin's disease?

The cardiovascular system is thoroughly evaluated for evidence of cardiac enlargement, venous engorgement, and pulmonary and peripheral edema. The physician evaluates pulmonary function also, looking for dyspnea, cyanosis, pulmonary congestion, and impaired respiratory movements. The abdomen is palpated for evidence of an enlarged or nodular liver and splenic or renal enlargement. The patient's habitus, hair texture, hair distribution, and skin texture are observed for evidence of endocrinological disorder.

Neurological Examination

A careful, thorough neurological examination is required for each subject suspected of dementia. Directions for the complete neurological examination are not given here, for this is covered in standard neurological texts. Rather the specific aims of the neurological examination in dementia will be enumerated and specific features of the examination emphasized.

When dementia is suspected, neurological examination will reveal either: (1) clear evidence of focal, circumscribed brain disease accounting for the patient's symptoms; (2) clear evidence of diffuse, bilateral brain dysfunction accounting for the patient's symptoms; or (3) no evidence of neurological dysfunction.

The "routine" neurological examination as described in most textbooks is designed to establish the first or last position. These portions of the evaluation will not be considered further here.

Evidence of diffuse brain dysfunction on neurological examination is generally subtle and hard to come by, as Paulson[62] emphasized. At the outset attention is directed toward the patient's level of consciousness, attentiveness to the examiner, comprehension, and performance of requested tasks. Note is also made of facial expressions, quality of speech, posture, respiratory rhythm, and gait. Specific signs of diffuse brain dysfunction may be present. These include: persistence of glabella-tap response, corneomandibular reflex, sucking reflex, snout reflex, palmomental reflex, grasp reflex, and toe grasp reflex. Although these signs may occasionally have focal import, they are much more likely to reflect diffuse brain dysfunction. Paratonic rigidity, motor perseveration, and motor impersistence are other features pointing toward disease.

DIAGNOSTIC CONCLUSIONS AND FURTHER STUDIES

On the basis of the history plus the examinations detailed above, the physician usually reaches one of several possible tentative conclusions that dictate further specific diagnostic studies:

1. The patient has no dementia but rather a functional disorder for which psychiatric treatment is indicated.

2. The patient has dementia secondary to a focal cerebral lesion the nature of which must be elucidated.

3. The patient may have dementia, but this is not definite. If present, the dementia is probably secondary to diffuse cerebral dysfunction.

4. The patient has dementia, probably secondary to diffuse cerebral dysfunction.

5. The patient has dementia, probably secondary to diffuse cerebral dysfunction, with a superimposed functional disorder.

The Patient with a Functional Disorder

The physician reaches the conclusion that the patient has a functional disorder in the absence of dementia with varying degrees of certainty. If the absence of dementia is strongly supported by history and examination, and if a definite psychiatric diagnosis is warranted on the same bases, then the physician proceeds at once either to initiate psychiatric therapy himself or to refer the patient to a psychiatrist for appropriate treatment.

If this conclusion appears likely but cannot be justified by the history and clinical examination alone, then further diagnostic studies are appropriate. Psychological testing may be especially useful in this instance, both by failing to uncover evidence suggesting organic brain impairment and by revealing evidence warranting the diagnosis of a specific functional disorder.[87] Sometimes additional studies — skull radiographs, electroencephalogram (EEG), and computerized axial tomographs (CAT) — may be employed to adduce further evidence against an organic etiology. However, it must be emphasized that no diagnostic testing procedures rule out organic brain disease. The results of all tests may be within normal limits even with significant underlying brain disease, especially if its extent is limited or the process is just beginning. Indeed, the belief that negative diagnostic studies rule out organicity may induce an unjustified sense of security and the patient might have been better served had diagnostic procedures been withheld until clearer evidence for their use appeared.

The Patient with Dementia Due to a Focal Cerebral Lesion

The conclusion that the patient has dementia due to a focal lesion is usually reached because: (1) the history and mental status examination reveal a defect (for example, aphasia) that is probably due to dysfunction within a limited area of brain; or (2) the neurological examination indicates a focal cerebral lesion. In either event, the patient will usually be admitted to the hospital for an evaluation. Although the exact makeup and order of diagnostic tests differ from patient to patient, skull x-ray studies, EEG, examination of cerebrospinal fluid, and CAT usually are the initial procedures, followed by cerebral angiography or air encephalography or both. These procedures aim to demonstrate a treatable focal lesion. When such a lesion is revealed (as with subdural hematoma), surgical treatment is generally indicated. When untreatable focal lesions (such as brain infarction) are revealed, therapy must be largely symptomatic.

The Patient with Possible or Proved Dementia, Probably Due to Diffuse Cerebral Disease

When the physician concludes that the patient has possible or proved dementia that is probably due to diffuse cerebral disease, an extensive diagnostic evaluation is needed.

PSYCHOLOGICAL TESTING. If the presence of dementia is uncertain on the basis of history and mental status evaluation, the physician frequently turns first to the psychologist for assistance. This is reasonable providing the physician recognizes that where "the clinical assessment suggests doubtful impairment, psychologic testing usually produces equally doubtful results. Only occasionally is the psychologist able to allay the clinician's doubts by obtaining test results that definitely exclude cerebral failure."[65] Kiloh's observation of 1961 remains true: "At present it seems that clinical methods of judging early dementia and of distinguishing cases of true from pseudo-dementia are still more sensitive and reliable than psychometric tests."[47] The physician should not expect the psychologist to be able to establish a diagnosis of dementia when the diagnosis cannot be made with certainty on mental status evaluation.

However, when a diagnosis of dementia is established by mental status evaluation, psychological testing may help significantly in determining the extent and severity of the mentative incapacity. Many of the psychological tests and measures have been discussed in Chapter 9. The psychologist is likely to prove most useful to the physician: (1) when the physician states precisely the problem for which he seeks assistance; and (2) when the physician is familiar enough with the psychological testing procedures that he is personally able to evaluate and criticize the results.

Certain observations — a discrepancy between verbal and performance I.Q.s on the Wechsler Adult Intelligence Scale (WAIS); an abnormal "deterioration index" on the WAIS; poor reproduction of the Bender Visual Motor Gestalt Test; poverty of production, poor percepts, and failure to see movement on the Rorschach Test; poor performance on the Trail-Making Test — individually suggest the presence of organic brain dysfunction. When these psychological dysfunctions occur in a constellation, the probability that the patient has organic brain disease is increased.

Psychological testing is also valuable in setting a base line from which the progression or resolution of the disease process may be followed and in evaluating residual function so that realistic treatment and rehabilitation plans can be made. Lijtmaer, Fuld, and Katzman[49] suggested that all patients with a diagnosis of dementia should have psychological testing repeated several months after initial evaluation. Failure to demonstrate progressive decrease in function should throw the original diagnosis into question. In view of the frequency of inaccurate diagnosis reported by Nott and Fleminger,[61] this is certainly a reasonable procedure to follow whenever any doubt exists as to the validity of the original diagnosis. Psychological testing also may be useful in pointing toward a focal or hemispheric lesion when the mental status examination has suggested a more diffuse disorder.

BASIC EVALUATION PROCEDURES. Even if dementia cannot be proved, the physician may assume its presence and proceed to further diagnostic procedures; on the other hand, if dementia is established, then diffuse brain disease is presumed and a search for its cause initiated. Although most of the contemplated medical and neurological diagnostic procedures can be performed on an outpatient basis, hospitalization will often be advised both for its convenience and to assure a thorough and unhurried evaluation. Outpatient examination alone for such serious disorders invites superficiality. In the young or middle-aged patient presenting with dementia, it is unlikely that a full evaluation will not be performed whether it is performed inside or outside the hospital. However, in the elderly, scrupulous attention to detail may be hard to achieve, particularly on an outpatient basis, and the patient might, by default, be assigned a diagnosis of cerebral vascular disease or senile dementia. While these are frequent causes of dementia in old age, they are nevertheless discrete entities and should not be "wastebasket" diagnoses. Eschewing facile diagnoses, the physician should admit almost every patient presenting with dementia to the hospital for thorough medical, neurological, and psychiatric evaluation. However, it is not the place where the evaluation is performed but the thoroughness with which it is performed that is of first importance.

Table 3 lists the ancillary diagnostic procedures often requested for patients admitted for diagnosis of dementia believed to be due to diffuse brain disease, along with the rationale for each test. By no means is every procedure required for every patient; the indiscriminate and uncritical assembly of all possibly relevant measurements is deplorable. Sometimes only one or a few critically chosen diagnostic procedures will be sufficient for diagnosis. For example, a slowed relaxation of the Achilles tendon jerk may suggest hypothyroidism, and a single serum thyroxine may establish the diagnosis. More often, no such valuable clue emerges, and the physician must determine which laboratory studies to use when no specific etiology is suggested.

Table 4 lists the procedures that I would recommend for most patients with dementia whose history and clinical examination suggest no specific disease (other than Alzheimer's disease or senile dementia). I want to emphasize that in the individual patient there may be many valid reasons for a different choice of diagnostic studies. However, these tests will lead to identification of virtually all treatable causes of dementia. In fact, the use of these procedures in conjunction with history and clinical examination would lead to identification of all the treatable disorders identified in the three series of patients in whom the cause for dementia was sought systematically.[30, 43, 54] Most of the patients in these series had

Table 3. Ancillary diagnostic procedures for evaluating dementia believed due to diffuse brain disease

Test	Rationale
Blood tests	
Complete blood count	Anemia (megaloblastic or hypochromic), infection
Serological test for syphilis (STS)	Syphilis
Drug levels (barbiturates, bromides, etc.)	Drug intoxication
Electrolytes (sodium potassium, chloride, carbon dioxide, calcium)	Pulmonary dysfunction, renal dysfunction, endocrine dysfunction
Urea nitrogen	Renal dysfunction
Liver function tests (bilirubin, enzymes, ammonia)	Hepatic dysfunction
Serum thyroxine by column (CT4)	Thyroid dysfunction
Vitamin B_{12} and folate levels	Vitamin B_{12} and folate deficiency
Urinalysis	Renal disease, hepatic disease
Electroencephalogram	Unsuspected focal lesion or diffuse cerebral dysfunction
Chest x-ray	Infectious process, primary or metastatic tumor, chronic lung disease
Skull x-ray	Unsuspected focal lesion, pineal shift, evidence of increased intracranial pressure, disordered calcium metabolism
Computerized axial tomography	Focal or diffuse cerebral atrophy, intracranial masses, hydrocephalus
Brain scan	Unsuspected focal lesion
Isotope cisternography	Impaired spinal fluid flow and absorption
Psychological testing	Focal or diffuse cerebral dysfunction

Table 4. Suggested laboratory studies for patients with dementia

---

Blood tests
    Complete blood count
    Serological test for syphilis
    SMA-12 or other standard metabolic screening tests
    Serum thyroxine by column (CT4)
    Vitamin B_{12} and folate levels
Urinalysis
Chest x-ray
Computerized axial tomography

---

much more elaborate diagnostic protocols in keeping with the research objectives (including most of the tests in Table 3 plus pneumoencephalography and excluding CAT which was not then available), but use of diagnostic tests beyond those suggested in Table 4 did not significantly increase the diagnostic and therapeutic yield.

It should not be implied that diagnostic tests other than those listed in Table 4 may not be of value in specific patients. The EEG, for example, may establish the existence of brain dysfunction when dementia is uncertain clinically, or it may confirm a diagnosis of epilepsy when there is a history of episodic exacerbations. However, in these instances, specific facets of the clinical presentation lead to the *choice* of the EEG as a diagnostic procedure.

Regrettably, regular use of the tests suggested in Table 4 does not guarantee identification of all treatable causes of dementia, and a rare treatable disease (such as cryptococcal meningitis) could be missed. On the other hand, not a single case of cryptococcal meningitis was identified among the 222 patients listed in Table 1, all of whom had examination of the cerebrospinal fluid for inflammatory changes. Widening the suggested diagnostic procedures so that every conceivable cause of treatable dementia is identified appears unwise, both medically and economically.

The cost of seeking a treatable cause for dementia should be considered in economic as well as human terms. The charges for performing the tests suggested in Table 4 are approximately 350 dollars;* this does not include hospitalization or physician's fees. This cost is moderate when one considers the likelihood that a treatable disorder can be identified or when one considers the cost in human suffering, in productivity, and in nursing care when such a cause is overlooked.

In the past, complete neurological evaluation of the demented patient often included cranial angiography and/or pneumoencephalography. In medical centers where computerized axial tomography is available, these procedures are now little used in patients suspected of diffuse brain disease. Cranial angiography and pneumoencephalography continue to prove valuable in patients with focal intracranial lesions and with vascular lesions. Otherwise they are employed in dementia generally only when special diagnostic problems arise or in geographical areas where computerized axial tomography is unavailable.

DIAGNOSIS AND THERAPY OF SPECIFICALLY TREATABLE DISORDERS

The diagnostic process outlined above is designed to reveal causes of dementia for which specific therapeutic measures are available. In this section, these dis-

---

*Based on standard Vanderbilt University Medical Center charges in the summer of 1976.

crete disorders are discussed, with attention to specific diagnostic and treatment requirements. These have also been dealt with in some detail in Chapter 3 by Haase and are treated here in the same order.

Parkinson's Disease

Dementia, along with depression, is a frequent accompaniment of Parkinson's disease. However, in general the disturbance in motility has been so serious an impediment to normal function that it has overshadowed the mental dysfunction. When dementia was noted, it was usually attributed to "arteriosclerosis," as might be the movement disorder as well. The introduction of L-Dopa treatment for the disordered motility has led to a reassessment of this problem. When studied by psychological testing methods, intellectual impairment is often detected[50] in patients with Parkinson's disease, and improvement in intellectual function can be demonstrated after treatment with appropriate amounts of L-Dopa.[51] Unfortunately this improvement does not persist on long term follow-up.[77]

Huntington's Chorea

Although Huntington's chorea is not a treatable disease in the usual sense, its recognition is important both because of the possibility for genetic counseling and because of the need for provision of long term care. Whereas the diagnosis is easy when the chorea and dementia are concurrent, the dementia may precede the movement disorder by a significant period and thereby confound early diagnosis. McHugh and Folstein[58] studied such patients and suggested "three distinctive features of the dementia syndrome in Huntington's chorea: (1) a slowly progressive dilapidation of all cognitive powers; (2) a prominent psychic apathy and inertia that worsens to an akinetic mute state; and (3) an *absence* of aphasia, alexia, cortical blindness, or Korsakov-type amnesia." The concurrence of these three features in young or middle-aged demented patients should alert the examiner to the possibility of this diagnosis.

Wilson's Disease

Wilson's disease (hepatolenticular degeneration) may in rare cases have dementia as the salient feature, but its presentation as dementia alone is so unusual that its routine exclusion by laboratory tests cannot be advised. The possibility of Wilson's disease should be considered if the onset of dementia occurs before age 40, especially if there is evidence of hepatic dysfunction or extrapyramidal involvement such as rigidity, bradykinesis, or involuntary movements. Diagnosis can be confirmed by demonstration of Kayser-Fleischer rings, elevated serum copper, decreased serum ceruloplasmin, and increased urinary copper. Patients may be treated with some hope of improvement by reducing dietary copper intake and administering potassium sulfide 20 to 40 mg. with meals to decrease copper absorption[31] plus penicillamine[80] (up to 4 gm. D-penicillamine orally per day in adults[32]) to augment copper excretion and decrease the body's accumulation of copper.

Thyroid Disease

Both hypothyroidism and hyperthyroidism are accompanied by symptoms and signs of dementia.[88] In general, the dysfunction is greatest in the hypothyroid patient in whom depression plus cognitive and intellectual deficits may be prominent. The severity of the mental dysfunction correlates roughly with the severity of thyroid dysfunction.

With even mild degrees of thyroid dysfunction, changes in cerebration can be demonstrated. The diagnosis of thyroid disease is usually suspected on the basis of the physical examination and confirmed by laboratory studies. The serum thyroxine by column (CT4) determination (normal 3.0 to 6.5 μg./100 ml.) is probably the most readily available and most reliable of the tests commonly used to evaluate thyroid function. Even mild deviations from normal should suggest that thyroid dysfunction is contributing to the mental trouble and lead to appropriate treatment. A variety of other tests of thyroid function may be used to supplement or confirm the presence of thyroid dysfunction.

The treatment of hyperthyroidism, a complex topic, will not be dealt with here. Treatment for hypothyroidism is generally desiccated thyroid, 0.1 to 0.2 gm. daily at the outset, with the dose being regulated later on the basis of clinical response. In older patients, smaller amounts of thyroid are usually employed initially.

Cushing's Syndrome

Mental changes are common in Cushing's syndrome. The diagnosis is usually suspected on the basis of the patient's habitus, plus skin changes and alterations in hair texture and distribution. The diagnosis is confirmed by the demonstration of excessive excretion of urinary glucocorticoids and of elevated plasma corticosteroids. For further details concerning the diagnosis and treatment of Cushing's syndrome, the reader is referred to textbooks of endocrinology.

Chronic Pulmonary, Hepatic, and Renal Disease

Dementia occurs in chronic lung, liver, and kidney disease. In each disorder, however, the appearance of dementia is determined by multiple factors and cannot be related to a single feature of the disease or to a single biochemical abnormality. In general, dementia occurs only in severe chronic lung, liver, or kidney disease with severe metabolic derangement. Individual susceptibility to the development of cerebral symptoms is marked. Treatment is directed toward the primary disease which is not always apparent clinically. For example, in Freemon's[30] patient with dementia due to hepatic dysfunction, the only clinical hint of liver failure was a history of alcoholism, yet liver enzymes were seriously deranged, and the patient's cerebral function improved with treatment of his liver disease.

Cerebral Arteriosclerosis

Cerebral arteriosclerosis or cerebral vascular disease is probably the most common diagnosis assigned to the patient with dementia, especially if the patient is elderly. The diagnosis is often incorrect and carries a cachet of untreatability which may divert the physician from the identification of treatable vascular disease, especially hypertension and multiple embolic phenomena, and other treatable disorders.

It must be emphasized that cerebral vascular disease is not the usual cause for progressive deterioration of brain function accompanied by neurological signs supporting diffuse brain disease. There is ample clinical and pathological evidence

263

Table 5. Features suggesting dementia
due to cerebral vascular disease

Abrupt onset
Stepwise deterioration
Fluctuating course
History or presence of hypertension
History of "strokes"
Focal neurological symptoms
Focal neurological signs

---

that this clinical picture is far more likely to result from Alzheimer's disease or senile dementia than from cerebral arteriosclerosis. In the 3 series of patients with this clinical picture studied clinically in detail,[30, 43, 54] the disorder was identified as being of vascular origin in only 7.7 percent. In their meticulous study of 50 demented patients at autopsy and clinically before death, Tomlinson, Blessed, and Roth[79] found one-half to have senile dementia alone, whereas approximately one-third had either cerebral vascular disease alone or varying combinations of vascular disease plus senile dementia.

It is agreed that dementia due to the cerebral atrophic diseases and dementia due to cerebral vascular disease usually cannot be differentiated by mental status evaluation. They are differentiated clinically by history and neurological examination. Fisher[29] stressed that dementia due to cerebral vascular disease is generally manifested by abrupt onset, a stuttering course, and symptoms and signs of focal cerebral damage. Birkett,[12] in a clinicopathological correlation, agreed that sudden onset along with focal neurological symptoms and signs were strong points in favor of a diagnosis of cerebral vascular disease. Tomlinson, Blessed, and Roth[79] observed cerebral vascular disease more often in males than in females and in patients who were younger at death than their patients with senile dementia.

Based on the studies in pathology of Corsellis[21] and Tomlinson, Blessed, and Roth,[79] Hachinski and coworkers[35] developed an ischemia scale which they used clinically to differentiate "primary degenerative dementia" from "multi-infarct dementia." Although certain features in their scale are open to question, Table 5 lists features selected from their scale which should strongly suggest dementia due to vascular disease. Except for the presence of hypertension, evidence of peripheral vascular disease does not permit the assumption that a dementia is likely to be of vascular origin, for it has been known for years that the cerebral vessels do not predictably reflect the degree of atherosclerosis seen in peripheral and retinal vessels.[3] However, hypertension is undeniably an occasional cause of dementia which cannot be differentiated from the primary degenerative dementias.[26] Since both hypertension and multiple embolic phenomena are potentially treatable, their accurate identification is important.

Normal Pressure Hydrocephalus

This disorder is discussed in detail by Katzman in Chapter 4, so only a few salient points will be mentioned here. Normal pressure hydrocephalus is a relatively rare but nonetheless significant cause of dementia. It should be suspected especially if a mild or moderate dementia is accompanied by significant gait abnormalities and urinary incontinence. Abnormalities uncovered by computerized axial tomography may point to the diagnosis which can be confirmed by pneumoen-

264

cephalography and isotope cisternography. Improvement following surgical shunting procedures may be dramatic or completely absent, but to date no methods are available which permit prediction of response. Clearly improvement is not solely a reflection of change in ventricular size after surgery.[72]

Vitamin B₁₂ and Folate Deficiency

Both vitamin B_{12} (cyanocobalamin) and folate deficiency may be associated with mentative abnormalities.[63, 68, 75, 76] Although the cerebral dysfunction is usually associated with the megaloblastic anemia which results from these deficiencies, it does not correlate well with the degree of anemia. Indeed, there are well documented cases of deficiencies with nervous system dysfunction without anemia. Thus while the presence of megaloblastic anemia in a demented patient strongly suggests vitamin B_{12} or folate deficiency, its absence does not rule out this possibility.

Although there may be some variation among laboratories, in general a serum B_{12} below 100 pg./ml. is diagnostic for primary B_{12} deficiency, and both a serum folate of less than 3 ng./ml. and a red cell folate below 150 ng./ml. are diagnostic for primary folate deficiency.[37] If any test is abnormal, further diagnostic procedures are required to ascertain the source of the deficiency.

Dreyfus[25] suggested that patients with nervous system dysfunction secondary to vitamin B_{12} deficiency should be treated with daily intramuscular injections of 50 µg. of cyanocobalamin for 2 weeks, then 100 µg. twice weekly for 8 weeks, and then 100 µg. monthly. Patients with folate deficiency should receive 20 mg. folic acid orally daily initially[63, 76] which may later be reduced to 1 to 5 mg. for daily maintenance[76] or if there is an absorptive defect, 200 µg. intramuscularly daily. Restitution to previous levels of function may not follow if treatment is delayed.

Chronic Drug Intoxication

Symptoms and signs of dementia are a common by-product of excessive and prolonged use of drugs (see Table 1), particularly tranquilizers, barbiturates, and bromides. The diagnosis should be suspected whenever there is a history of chronic drug ingestion or, even without such history, whenever a patient's dementia shows remarkable improvement without specific treatment during a period of hospitalization. The diagnosis can be confirmed with the demonstration of elevated levels of the specific agent in the blood or urine. In practice, routine screening procedures are seldom productive in the absence of a positive history.[30]

There is some question as to whether prolonged and excessive use of centrally acting drugs can produce cerebral atrophy. Certainly cerebral atrophy can be demonstrated in some patients who chronically abuse drugs, but it cannot be proved that the atrophy is due to the drugs. In patients with proved cerebral atrophy and a history of excessive drug use, improvement in mentation may follow discontinuance of the drugs.[41]

Chronic Alcoholism

Much said about chronic drug intoxication is also true for dementia accompanying chronic alcoholism and, indeed, the two are often associated. This situation is perhaps even more complex because vitamin deficiencies, malnutrition, trauma, and multiple systemic disorders often complicate alcoholism. The importance of alcoholism in the genesis of dementia is emphasized in the 3 studies detailed in Table 1 as well as in the earlier study of Epstein and Simon.[28] Even if the dementia is long standing and profound, remarkable improvement may occur with abstinence from alcohol and the institution of a nutritious diet.[86]

Cryptococcal Meningitis

Cryptococcal meningitis, a rare though treatable cause of dementia, seldom presents as dementia alone without evidence of meningoencephalitis. Routine diagnostic screening procedures for this disorder have a low yield[30] and are not recommended. Only when dementia is associated with a meningoencephalitis should the possibility of cryptococcal infection be entertained seriously and appropriate diagnostic procedures pursued. India ink preparations of cerebrospinal fluid may provide a quick and presumptive diagnosis if positive, but negative preparations do not rule out the diagnosis. About 70 to 80 percent of patients with cryptococcal meningitis have detectable cryptococcal antigen in serum and/or cerebrospinal fluid.[9] Definite diagnosis depends on positive culture of the organism from cerebrospinal fluid. Prolonged treatment with intravenous amphotericin B has proven effective.

Syphilis

General paresis, a frequent cause of dementia only a few years ago, is now so uncommon that it is likely to be overlooked. In general paresis, both blood and cerebrospinal fluid reagin tests are usually strongly positive. However, in rare instances the spinal fluid reagin test is positive while the blood is negative, and initially negative reagin tests in both blood and spinal fluid from cases of paresis have been reported.[19] A negative reagin test on blood or spinal fluid thus does not rule our central nervous system syphilis absolutely. In the rare patient with progressive dementia, a history of untreated syphilis, and negative reagin tests, the Fluorescent Treponemal Antibody-Absorption (FTA-ABS) test or perhaps the Treponema Pallidum Immobilization (TPI) test should be employed on blood and spinal fluid.[33] Even without a history of syphilis these tests should be utilized in any patient with progressive dementia and evidence of meningeal inflammation for which no cause is quickly discovered.

General paresis is most confidently treated with a total of 18 to 24-million units of penicillin given in equal daily doses over a period of 2 to 3 weeks,[24] although smaller amounts have been advised.[36]

THE CEREBRAL ATROPHIES

Close attention to diagnostic detail is essential if we are to identify each example of dementia that is amenable to treatment before irreversible brain damage has occurred, but the yield is not high, and the results are often disappointing. At the present stage of our knowledge and with currently available diagnostic techniques, most patients with dementia will not present evidence sufficient to *confirm* diagnosis of a specific disease antemortem. When the diagnostic procedures outlined above have failed to establish a disease diagnosis, what presumptive diagnosis should the physician make? In the past this dilemma has been solved by label-

266

ing the condition as cerebral atrophy of unknown cause.[30, 54] Such caution appears excessive. Excellent pathological studies[78, 79] have demonstrated that Alzheimer's disease causes these diffuse atrophies in the preponderance of cases, and the hesitancy to assign this diagnostic label appears unwarranted.

A diagnosis of Alzheimer's disease should be made when the adult patient presents: (1) chronic symptoms of dementia, (2) evidence of diffuse cerebral dysfunction on mental status evaluation with or without specific changes on neurological examination, (3) evidence of diffuse cerebral atrophy by CAT or other radiological diagnostic procedures, and (4) absence of clinical or laboratory features which allow the diagnosis of another disease process. An occasional error will be made (for example, Pick's disease might be mislabeled as Alzheimer's), but these will be few. The advantages of making a diagnosis of Alzheimer's disease in terms of knowledge of prognosis (see below) and of planning for future care far outweigh the disadvantages of an occasional incorrect diagnosis.

NONSPECIFIC TREATMENT

Many problems arise when the diagnosis is made of Alzheimer's disease or of other disease entities for which no specific remedies are available. In all likelihood the destructive process and its accompanying clinical deterioration will proceed despite all the physician's efforts. This situation of apparent hopelessness is ripe for the rejection of the patient by the physician and the family. We are apt to forget that it is in just such situations where there is no specific treatment that the treatment of the patient himself becomes most important. In just such "hopeless" situations the acts and powers of the physician, as opposed to the effects of his medicines, become of greatest value.

It is recognized that most patients with dementia will not receive their ongoing medical care from practicing neurologists. In general, the neurologist serves as a diagnostic and therapeutic consultant for special problems in patient management rather than as the primary physician. Patients with dementia complicated prominently by general somatic diseases will continue to be cared for by the general physician or internist, whereas patients with dementia complicated prominently by severe behavioral problems will be cared for by the psychiatrist. Indeed, such a division of responsibility has recently been recommended in the United Kingdom.[27] Although behavioral aberrations may not be sufficiently severe to require specific treatment by psychiatrists or psychiatric hospitalization, the psychiatric evaluation of the patient and the psychiatric aspects of his care are important throughout the course of illness.

The behavior of the demented patient often suggests that medical care is not wanted, needed, or possible. Frequently, the patient appears oblivious to his plight, untroubled by his failures, and unaffected by his deterioration. While such loss of contact with reality does occur in the most profound stages of dementia, one is apt to be misled by such facades in earlier stages of the illness. As Brosin[15] pointed out:

> Injury to the cerebral cortex means injury also to the ego functions, not only mechanically but psychologically, for the cerebral functions are highly valued by man, and any diminution in their efficacy causes apprehension and concern, which in turn arouse defensive measures to protect the total organism from pain and harm. An organism uncertain of its spatial-temporal-social

relations (disturbance of the comprehension of the environment), as brain-damaged cases are, is much more vulnerable to suffering than the normal person, even though much of the basic core of the ego be intact—as it so often is.

It is easy for the physician to be deluded into believing there is an absence of pain and vulnerability to suffering in the demented patient who so blatantly denies his losses and limitations. At a deeper level of realization, however, we cannot conceive the disintegration of the mind as anything other than an agonizing process for the affected individual. The denials and evasions employed by the demented person to hide his failures[40] can then be seen as naive and feeble defense mechanisms, and the physician can no longer hide from himself the inevitable pain of mental disintegration. This was poignantly illustrated by a patient who in the course of a rapidly progressing dementia never complained of failing mental powers but who in rare moments of clarity would turn to the physician and ask, "Why can't it end? Why can't it all end?" A realistic awareness of his situation is not necessarily therapeutic for the patient. In this situation, denial is therapeutic, and the physician should do all in his power to support this defense and do nothing to weaken it.

The needs of the family should also be heeded. "An illness of this kind affects others besides those who suffer from it, and the idea that a loved person—or oneself for that matter—might be transformed into something alien is disquieting. Pain and incapacity and disfigurement can be faced with fortitude, but the sight of a disease which seems to rot the self is hard to bear."[5] Close consultation with the family is needed not only to provide for their needs but because they often possess that intimate knowledge of the patient's premorbid personality which is essential for his optimal care. Help for the family may require more than support and information. Families often are as capable of denying the patient's loss of function as is the patient himself. In such instances, the physician may have to help the family acknowledge the severity of the patient's symptoms, accept the inevitability of further decline, and make adequate provision for the patient's long term care.[22]

The care of the demented patient can be formulated simply and easily; its execution, however, is difficult. In essence, the patient's care is based upon thorough assessment of physical and psychological liabilities (lost functions) and assets (preserved functions) coupled with a knowledge of the premorbid personality characteristics. Treatment is aimed at: (1) restitution of those lost functions which are susceptible to restitution, (2) reduction of the patient's need to employ those functions that have been lost, and (3) maximal utilization of residual functions. The value of such an approach has been proved by Sklar and O'Neill[73] and by others before them.

Restitution of Lost Functions

Restitution of lost functions aims predominantly at correction of medical and physical limitations. Many demented patients are debilitated and cachectic through neglect of physical ailments, nutritional needs, and exercise requirements. It is unwise to expect other measures to effect significant improvement unless the patient is in the best possible physical condition. If anything, prompt and thorough treatment of medical disorders is more important in the demented patient than in the one not so affected. The vulnerability of the diseased brain to fever, infection, and toxins is well recognized but often poorly recalled. Its vulnerability to deficient and distorted perceptions is likewise easily overlooked. The patient with poor vision and hearing plus dementia is in double jeopardy. Properly fitted spectacles and hearing aids may be helpful, and the patient should be encouraged in their use.

The nutritional needs of the patient may be hard to satisfy because of inattention and lack of concern which result in vitamin deficiencies and inanition. Continuous efforts to assure an adequate and judicious dietary intake are essential. Often the patient eats if meals are prepared and served but "forgets" otherwise. Public service agencies (such as "Meals on Wheels") may help greatly. Physiotherapy can promote restitution of lost motor function and prevent its loss in ambulatory patients. Since the physical, psychiatric, and social problems of the bedridden or chair-ridden patient with dementia are infinitely more formidable than those faced by the ambulatory patient, every effort should be made to preserve and promote motility.

Surgical shunting procedures to promote draining of spinal fluid from the ventricles have been advocated for virtually all patients who are demented and have ventricular enlargement.[71] Evidence for the predictable usefulness of these procedures and their lack of harm is not sufficient at present to warrant general application except when there are definable cerebrospinal fluid absorption abnormalities.[45]

Reduction of the Patient's Need for Lost Functions

An accurate assessment of functions that are irretrievably lost is essential. The pressures suffered by the demented patient who battles to perform impossible tasks or struggles to hide his failures are apparent to all observers. Often, at least up to the terminal phases of the disorder, the patient is helpless to give up the fight. Thus Katz, Neal, and Simon[42] have recorded the multiple defenses used by demented patients to avoid acquiescing to failure, to avoid admitting, "I don't know." They also emphasize that demands for task performance are stressful and that immediate stress is often a determinant of symptomatology. Whereas stress in the intact individual may enhance the ego, stress in the demented patient may lead to ego disintegration.

This has been eloquently described by one author writing of her father's illness.[5] Although she knew her father had failing mental powers, she unwisely agreed to accompany him to a foreign resort. There the foreign language and unfamiliar surroundings markedly accentuated his bewilderment and his anxiety.

> He was still potentially rational. His delusions were not determined by a warped mental outlook, but were a reasonable attempt to make sense out of what was subjectively a hopelessly confusing situation. In days gone by I had learned to follow his train of thought intuitively, and I could still keep close to him in spite of his difficulty with speech. I found that if I got him away from other people and steered his mind to topics which he had handled with ease in the past he became rational quite quickly. I sometimes led him into long and interesting discussions on subjects which he knew and cared about, and when he got the sense of being on familiar ground, where he could still tread firmly, the black cloud of depression lifted and he became his old self. As soon as he returned to the strain of new and unfamiliar situations he relapsed.

Using such techniques she was able to maintain some self-control in her father until World War II intervened, providing a stress that she was powerless to control. "Faced with a threat which involved his own country and all that was dear to him, my father let go his last faint hold on reason. . . ." This emphasizes the importance of maintaining the demented patient in a familiar environment as long as possible. Travel, a move to new living quarters, redecorating — in general, anything novel may prove disruptive and result in further functional decompensation.

Environmental manipulation can be used to maintain calm and nontaxing surroundings, arranging things insofar as possible so that the patient does not have to confront his inadequacies. Ingenious techniques may be employed to achieve this objective. One patient, for example, who was disoriented in space but still able to read, was greatly calmed by messages appropriately placed by her family all over the house, saying, "You're in your bedroom," "You're in your parlor," and similar notes.[1]

Change is stressful even for the healthy; it often results in decompensation in patients with compromised brain function. New people and new situations rather than being diverting are disruptive. Patients usually do best if they can be maintained in quiet and familiar surroundings with adequate but familiar distractions. Old friends and old places are most comfortable and most therapeutic. The darkness and silence of nights may prove particularly disturbing, and a soft night light often helps in maintaining a sense of security. If the patient must be moved to a nursing home or hospital, placement of some cherished objects from home in the new environment may reduce the stress of the new and unfamiliar surroundings.

Utilization of Residual Functions

For the demented person to utilize his remaining functions fully, the physician must assume dual roles. He serves as personal physician to the individual patient and as organizer of health care functions by various individuals and agencies.

One of his responsibilities as personal physician is the prescribing of medications for the relief of symptoms. In the demented patient, medications may be employed to: (1) relieve anxiety, (2) improve mood, (3) reduce paranoid and other psychotic symptoms, (4) control harmful behavior such as hyperactivity and assaultiveness, and (5) improve sleep. Treatment is employed to relieve symptoms arising from organic brain disease; treatment cannot presume to restore functions which have been lost secondary to tissue destruction or atrophy. Symptomatic results with psychotropic agents are not as good as when they are employed in the functional psychiatric disorders. However, at times, medications may be remarkably effective, and they certainly should be tried. Increased interest in the pharmacological treatment of patients with dementia has been demonstrated by several recent publications,[23, 38, 70] yet there are few controlled studies of pharmacotherapy in discrete patient populations.[8]

Two points concerning drug treatment in organic dementias should be underscored: (1) Sedatives are poorly tolerated in the presence of structural brain disease; therefore, barbiturates and like medications should be avoided. (2) The damaged central nervous system may be exquisitely sensitive to psychotropic agents; thus treatment should be begun with doses quite small in comparison to those employed in functional brain disorders.[17] In a recent overview of the subject, Hollister[38] suggested that the antidepressants and antipsychotics are most consistently of value, yet the response to these widely used agents remains unpredictable in organic deterioration. Salzman, Shader, and Harmatz[70] suggested that this results from altered drug sensitivity in these usually older patients, heterogeneity of these patient populations, and differences between the elderly and young in perception of and reporting of internal mood states. They also emphasized the increased possibilities for confusing drug-drug interactions in these patients so likely to be suffering from concomitant medical disorders requiring drug treatment. Bender[8] earlier reviewed the effect of increasing age on drug activity.

For relief of nonpsychotic anxiety, chlordiazepoxide (Librium) 5 mg. twice daily, or diazepam (Valium) 2 mg. twice daily, may prove useful. The dosage may be raised to achieve better symptom relief, but only slowly, cautiously, and under close medical supervision. These medications tend to lose their effectiveness with continued use.

For depression, amitriptyline (Elavil, Endep), nortriptyline (Aventyl), imipramine (Imavate, Janimine, Presamine, SK-Pramine, Tofranil), or doxepin (Adapin, Sinequan) may be employed. There are at present no firm guidelines for choice of any particular medication, although in general amitriptyline and doxepin may be preferable when some sedative effect is also desired. In patients with dementia plus depression, starting dosage should probably be more than 10 mg. 3 or 4 times daily for any of these antidepressant medications. As with the minor tranquilizers, the dosage can be raised, but only under close supervision. It has been suggested that since 25 percent of all demented patients have significant depression as well, since depressive psychosis may mimic dementia (pseudo-dementia), and since dementia is not infrequently misdiagnosed,[61] all "demented" patients should be given a period of trial therapy with antidepressant medications.[74] This may be overly inclusive, but it would appear worthwhile to try antidepressants in all patients in whom the diagnosis of dementia is considered who also have clinical evidence of significant depression.

For paranoid and other psychotic symptoms and for control of harmful behaviors, the major tranquilizers should be employed. Chlorpromazine (Thorazine) or thioridazine (Mellaril) 25 mg. 3 or 4 times daily or haloperidol (Haldol) 0.5 mg. 2 or 3 times daily should be tried. Again doses may be adjusted upward with close supervision.

In patients with insomnia, drugs with minimal sedative effects should be employed to help achieve sleep. Promethazine hydrochloride (Phenergan) 25 to 50 mg. at bedtime or chlorpromazine (Thorazine), 50 mg. at bedtime is often effective. For the acutely disturbed patient, chlorpromazine 25 mg. intramuscularly is the drug of choice.

All of these medications when given in sufficient quantities have undesirable central and peripheral nervous system effects that must be monitored. Many of the medications precipitate postural hypotension, cardiac irregularities, urinary retention, and the like, all unfortunate side effects particularly in the aged. Usually the troublesome side effects must be weighed against the benefits of medication and a decision made as to the worth of the treatment. All of these drugs may cause delirium, and they not infrequently do so in this susceptible population. In these situations, the recognition of delirium becomes especially important so that increasing amounts of drugs are not given to control symptoms that are mistakenly attributed to a worsening dementia.

Whether it is called providing supportive psychotherapy or performing the physician's role, the physician furnishes another essential service to the patient.

The foreign doctor came and went again, leaving a sedative which was unfortunately a proprietary brand with the contents printed outside the container. My father feared we were intent on drugging him for some nefarious purpose, and he would not touch it. He had, however, recognized the doctor for what he was, and the visit sobered him a little. Even that much relief was something to be thankful for. . . .[5]

Thus, the physician's presence alone may be important. He supports and encourages the patient to develop interests, to continue social activities, to partake in group activities, to exercise, to be productive in ways in which he can be appreciated by others for as long as is possible.[17, 73] He allows the patient to ventilate feelings of anger, rejection, fear, and hurt—accepting them, appreciating them, and thus "detoxifying" them. The role of the physician's expectations in both symptom production and in symptom relief has never been fully explored in these situations, but it is probably of great importance.[18, 52]

The second responsibility of the physician is to organize the various health professionals and nonprofessionals who participate in the patient's care. This may involve weaving together the ministrations of physician, nurse, social worker, occupational therapist, recreational therapist, physiotherapist, and family—and each role may be crucial. For example, Sklar and O'Neill[73] observed that little can be accomplished by psychiatric treatment "in the absence of successful solution of the patient's social problem." The social problem cannot be solved of course without the cooperation of the family and others. The melding of these various individuals to create a successful treatment program is difficult even in the hospital. Outside, the problems of creating such a treatment program are staggering but worthy of effort.

Special intensive treatment approaches may not only benefit the demented patients in long term custodial care facilities but also the demented patient with an acute disturbance. Arie[6] stressed the frequency with which demented patients come to medical attention in emergency situations. Often only custodial facilities are available for their treatment, but Prinsley[66] demonstrated the feasibility and usefulness of an acute psychogeriatric ward for the treatment of mentally disturbed elderly patients. Many of these patients were discharged improved after a relatively short hospitalization, and most did not require transfer to long term psychiatric facilities. However, the discharged patients continued to present many medical and social problems which required the combined efforts of family, social workers, visiting nurses, physicians, and other care giving persons. Prinsley[66] did not find that the use of day hospitalization significantly ameliorated these problems.

The study of Prinsley and those by others[14, 28] emphasize the poor prognosis and high mortality of demented patients who require institutional care for their medical or psychiatric problems. Whereas evidence of some organic brain impairment may not be a particularly poor prognostic sign (so far as survival is concerned) in aged persons still functioning acceptably in the community,[81] it is undeniable that the mortality is high and survival brief in patients institutionalized for serious dementia. The "malignant" character of Alzheimer's disease has recently been underscored in studies by Katzman[44] and his coworkers.[20, 49] Of 18 patients reported in 1973 who had Alzheimer's disease,[20] 14 were dead when followed-up in 1976.[49] "Life expectancy in Alzheimer's disease is reduced by 50% to 67% based on the age at the time of onset of symptoms."[49]

These three avenues—restitution of lost functions, reduction of patient needs, utilization of residual functions—constitute the essential approaches to the symptomatic treatment of dementia. None aims directly to improve function of diseased neurons; rather the aims are to permit the still functioning neurons to perform optimally. Recently a number of therapeutic measures have been reported to improve brain function per se, and their widespread use has been advocated. We face a serious problem in evaluating these reports. The use of the therapeutic measures advocated above has resulted in rather striking clinical improvement in groups of patients[73] as did group activities to provide sensory stimulation[13] and placebos.[60] Will other measures enhance our results? The difficulties of evaluating the effects of drugs on cerebral function have already been detailed by McNamara and Appel in Chapter 7 who conclude that no drug presently available has proved of value in improving cerebral function in the demented patient, though there are suggestions that one or two chemicals may improve performance secondary to their general stimulant effects. The authors also raised the possibility that stimulation of the failing neuron might hasten its demise, though they carefully pointed out there is no specific evidence for this at present. There is presently available no medication that will predictably improve cerebral function in the demented patient; furthermore, the benefits or desirability of use of the stimulant drugs is unconvincing. This is nevertheless an important area for investigation, and it should not be abandoned because of past failures.

CONCLUSION

In many ways, dementia remains a vast lacuna in our neuropsychiatric knowledge, unfulfilling in its study because so much is unknown and so little understood. Our knowledge of the various disorders that produce dementia is steadily increasing, yet new information often raises more puzzling questions rather than satisfactorily answering the old ones. Were the condition rare, we might take comfort in devoting our efforts to other pressing problems. Unfortunately dementia is common and becoming more so. The pain and suffering it causes patients and their families are great, as are the frustration and discouragement it provokes in their physicians. The proper care of the demented patient requires uncommon time, effort, and devotion and makes uncommon demands upon the family and community resources. There is little question that these unfortunate individuals do not now generally receive the best care possible, even allowing that the best care possible falls short of our goals. Perhaps we should be reminded, as was another physician by the husband of a woman with irreversible brain damage, "Doctor—you should have seen her as the wonderful person she is."[16]

REFERENCES

1. ACKNER, B.: Personal communication.
2. ALBERT, M. L.; FELDMAN, R. G.; AND WILLIS, A. L.: The "subcortical dementia" of progressive supranuclear palsy. J. Neurol. Neurosurg. Psychiatry 37:121, 1974.
3. ALPERS, B. J.; FORSTER, F. M.; AND HERBUT, P. A.: Retinal, cerebral and systemic arteriosclerosis; a histopathologic study. Arch. Neurol. Psychiat. 60:440, 1948.
4. AMERICAN PSYCHIATRIC ASSOCIATION: Diagnostic and Statistical Manual of Mental Disorders, ed. 2. American Psychiatric Association, Washington, D.C., 1968.
5. ANONYMOUS AUTHOR: Death of a mind: A study of disintegration. Lancet 1:1012, 1950.
6. ARIE, T.: Dementia in the elderly: Diagnosis and assessment. Br. Med. J. 4:540, 1973.
7. BARRETT, R. E.: Dementia in adults. Med. Clin. North Am. 56:1405, 1972.

8. BENDER, A. D.: *Pharmacologic aspects of aging: A survey of the effect of increasing age on drug activity in adults.* J. Am. Geriatr. Soc. 12:114, 1964.

9. BENNETT, J. E.: Cryptococcosis, in Beeson, P. B., and McDermott, W. (eds.): *Textbook of Medicine,* ed. 14. W. B. Saunders Co., Philadelphia, 1975.

10. BENSON, D. F.: *Psychiatric aspects of aphasia.* Br. J. Psychiatry 123:555, 1973.

11. BENTON, A. L.; VAN ALLEN, M. W.; AND FOGEL, M. L.: *Temporal orientation in cerebral disease.* J. Nerv. Ment. Dis. 139:110, 1964.

12. BIRKETT, D. P.: *The psychiatric differentiation of senility and arteriosclerosis.* Br. J. Psychiatry 120:321, 1972.

13. BOWER, H. M.: *Sensory stimulation and the treatment of senile dementia.* Med. J. Aust. 1:1113, 1967.

14. BRODY, E. M.; KLEBAN, M.; WOLDOW, A.; AND FREEMAN, L.: *Survival and death in mentally impaired aged.* J. Chronic Dis. 28:389, 1975.

15. BROSIN, H. W.: Contributions of psychoanalysis to the study of organic cerebral disorders, in Alexander, F., and Ross, H. (eds.): *Dynamic Psychiatry.* University of Chicago Press, Chicago, 1952.

16. BUCHWALD, J.: *"Just an Old Crock"* (Editorial). Psychiatric News 4:2, 1969.

17. BUSSE, E. W.: Psychoneurotic reactions and defense mechanisms in the aged, in Hoch, P. H., and Zubin, J. (eds.): *Psychopathology of Aging.* American Psychopathological Association Proceedings, 1960.

18. CAMERON, D. E.: *Discussion of paper by Lorge, I.*[52] Res. Publ. Assoc. Res. Nerv. Ment. Dis. 35: 57, 1956.

19. CH'IEN, L.; HATHAWAY, M.; AND ISRAEL, C. W.: *Seronegative dementia paralytica.* J. Neurol. Neurosurg. Psychiatry 33:376, 1970.

20. COBLENTZ, J. M.; MATTIS, S.; ZINGESSER, L. H.; KASOFF, S. S.; WIESNIEWSKI, H. M.; AND KATZMAN, R.: *Presenile dementia. Clinical aspects and evaluation of cerebrospinal fluid dynamics.* Arch. Neurol. 29:299, 1973.

21. CORSELLIS, J. A. N.: *Mental Illness and the Ageing Brain.* Maudsley Monograph #9, Oxford University Press, London, 1962.

22. DETRE, T. J., AND JARECKI, H. G.: *Modern Psychiatric Treatment.* J. B. Lippincott Co., Philadelphia, 1971.

23. DIMASCIO, A., AND GOLDBERG, H. L.: *Managing disturbed geriatric patients with chemotherapy.* Hosp. Physician 11:35, 1975.

24. DODGE, P. R.: Syphilitic infection of the nervous system, in Beeson, P. B., and McDermott, W. (eds.): *Textbook of Medicine,* ed. 14. W. B. Saunders Co., Philadelphia, 1975.

25. DREYFUS, P. M.: Nutritional disorders of the nervous system, in Beeson, P. B., and McDermott, W., (eds.): *Textbook of Medicine,* ed. 14. W. B. Saunders Co., Philadelphia, 1975.

26. EARNEST, M. P.; FAHN, S.; KARP, J. H.; AND ROWLAND, L. P.: *Normal pressure hydrocephalus and hypertensive cerebrovascular disease.* Arch. Neurol. 31:262, 1974.

27. EDITORIAL: *Care of elderly people with dementia.* Br. Med. J. 1:434, 1973.

28. EPSTEIN, L. J., AND SIMON, A.: *Organic brain syndrome in the elderly.* Geriatrics 22:145, 1967.

29. FISHER, C. M.: *Dementia in cerebral vascular disease.* Transactions of Sixth Congress on Cerebral Vascular Diseases. Grune and Stratton, New York, 1968, pp. 232–236.

30. FREEMON, F. R.: *Evaluation of patients with progressive intellectual deterioration.* Arch. Neurol. 33:658, 1976.

31. GILROY, J. G., AND MEYER, J. S.: *Medical Neurology,* ed. 2. Macmillan Publishing Co., New York, 1975.

32. GOODMAN, L. S., AND GILMAN, A. (eds.): *The Pharmacological Basis of Therapeutics,* ed. 5. Macmillan Publishing Co., New York, 1975.

33. GUTHE, T.: Treponemal diseases, in Beeson, P. B., and McDermott, W. (eds.): *Textbook of Medicine,* ed. 14. W. B. Saunders Co., Philadelphia, 1975.

34. HAASE, G. R.: Diseases presenting as dementia, in Wells, C. E. (ed.): *Dementia,* ed. 2. F. A. Davis Co., Philadelphia, 1977.

35. HACHINSKI, V. C.; ILIFF, L. D.; ZILHKA, E.; DUBOULAY, G. H.; MCALLISTER, V. L.; MAR-

SHALL, J.; RUSSELL, R. W. R.; AND SYMON, L.: *Cerebral blood flow in dementia.* Arch. Neurol. 32:632, 1975.

36. HENDERSON, R. H.: *Syphilis: USPHS guide to treatment.* Human Sexuality 10:107, 1976.

37. HERBERT, V.: Megaloblastic anemias, in Beeson, P. B., and McDermott, W. (eds.): *Textbook of Medicine,* ed. 14. W. B. Saunders Co., Philadelphia, 1975.

38. HOLLISTER, L. E.: *Drugs for mental disorders in old age.* J.A.M.A. 234: 195, 1975.

39. HORENSTEIN, S.: Amnesic, agnosic, apractic, and aphasic features in dementing illness, in Wells, C. E. (ed.): *Dementia,* ed. 1. F. A. Davis Co., Philadelphia, 1971.

40. KAHN, R. L.; ZARIT, S. H.; HILBERT, N. M.; AND NIEDEREHE, G.: *Memory complaint and impairment in the aged. The effect of depression and altered brain function.* Arch. Gen. Psychiatry 32:1589, 1975.

41. KAPLAN, E. A.: Personal communication, 1970.

42. KATZ, L.; NEAL, M. W.; AND SIMON, A.: Observations of psychic mechanisms in organic psychoses of the aged, in Hoch, P. H., and Zubin, J. (eds.): *Psychopathology of Aging.* American Psychopathological Association Proceedings, 1960.

43. KATZMAN, R.: Personal communication, 1975.

44. KATZMAN, R.: *The prevalence and malignancy of Alzheimer disease: A major killer.* Arch. Neurol. 33:217, 1976.

45. KATZMAN, R.: Normal pressure hydrocephalus, in Wells, C. E. (ed.): *Dementia,* ed. 2. F. A. Davis Co., Philadelphia, 1977.

46. KATZMAN, R., AND KARASU, T. B.: Differential diagnosis of dementia, in Fields, W. S. (ed.): *Neurological and Sensory Disorders in the Elderly.* Stratton Intercontinental Medical Book Corp., New York, 1975.

47. KILOH, L. G.: *Pseudo-dementia.* Acta Psychiatr. Scand. 37:336, 1961.

48. LEWIS, A.: *Amnestic syndromes: The psychopathological aspects.* Proc. R. Soc. Med. 54:955, 1961.

49. LIJTMAER, H.; FULD, P. A.; AND KATZMAN, R.: *Prevalence and malignancy of Alzheimer disease* (letter to Editor). Arch. Neurol. 33:304, 1976.

50. LORANGER, A. W.; GOODELL, H.; McDOWELL, F. H.; LEE, J. E.; AND SWEET, R. D.; *Intellectual impairment in Parkinson's syndrome.* Brain 95:405, 1972.

51. LORANGER, A. W.; GOODELL, H.; McDOWELL, F. H.; LEE, J. E.; AND SWEET, R. D.: *Parkinsonism, L-Dopa, and intelligence.* Am. J. Psychiatry 130:1386, 1973.

52. LORGE, I.: *Aging and intelligence.* Res. Publ. Assoc. Res. Nerv. Ment. Dis. 35:46, 1956.

53. MALAMUD, N.: Organic brain disease mistaken for psychiatric disorder: A clinicopathologic study, in Benson, D. F., and Blumer, D. (eds.): *Psychiatric Aspects of Neurological Disease.* Grune and Stratton, New York, 1975.

54. MARSDEN, C. D., AND HARRISON, M. J. G.: *Outcome of investigation of patients with presenile dementia.* Br. Med. J. 2:249, 1972.

55. MARSDEN, C. D., AND HARRISON, M. J. G.: *Presenile dementia* (letter to the Editor). Br. Med. J. 3:50, 1972.

56. MARTIN, W. A., AND SMITH, A. O.: *The evaluation of dementia.* Dis. Nerv. Syst. 35:262, 1974.

57. McDOWELL, F., AND WOLFF, H. G.: *Handbook of Neurological Diagnostic Methods.* The Williams & Wilkins Co., Baltimore, 1960.

58. McHUGH, P. R., AND FOLSTEIN, M. F.: Psychiatric syndromes of Huntington's chorea: A clinical and phenomenologic study, in Benson, D. F., and Blumer, D. (eds.): *Psychiatric Aspects of Neurological Disease.* Grune and Stratton, New York, 1975.

59. McNAMARA, J. O., AND APPEL, S. H.: Biochemical approaches to dementia, in Wells, C. E. (ed.): *Dementia,* ed. 2. F. A. Davis Co., Philadelphia, 1977.

60. NODINE, J. H.; SHULKIN, M. W.; SLAP, J. W.; LEVINE, M.; AND FREIBERG, K.: *A double-blind study of the effect of ribonucleic acid in senile brain disease.* Am. J. Psychiatry 123:1257, 1967.

61. NOTT, P. N., AND FLEMINGER, J. J.: *Presenile dementia: The difficulty of early diagnosis.* Acta Psychiatr. Scand. 51:210, 1975.

62. PAULSON, G. W.: The neurological examination in dementia, in Wells, C. E. (ed.): *Dementia,* ed. 2. F. A. Davis Co., Philadelphia, 1977.

275

63. Pincus, J. H.; Reynolds, E. H.; and Glaser, G. H.: *Subacute combined system degeneration with folate deficiency.* J.A.M.A. 221:496, 1972.

64. Poser, C. M.: *The presenile dementias.* J.A.M.A. 233:81, 1975.

65. Post, F.: Dementia, depression, and pseudodementia, in Benson, D. F., and Blumer, D. (eds.): *Psychiatric Aspects of Neurological Disease.* Grune and Stratton, New York, 1975.

66. Prinsley, D. M.: *Psychogeriatric ward for mentally disturbed elderly patients.* Br. Med. J. 3:574, 1973.

67. Reichel, W.: *Organic brain syndromes in the aged.* Hosp. Practice 11:119, 1976.

68. Reynolds, E. H.: Rothfeld, P.; and Pincus, J. H.: *Neurological disease associated with folate deficiency.* Br. Med. J. 2:398, 1973.

69. Roth, M.: *The natural history of mental disorder in old age.* Br. J. Psychiatry 101:281, 1955.

70. Salzman, C.; Shader, R. I.; and Harmatz, J. S.: *Response of elderly to psychotropic drugs: Predictable or idiosyncratic?* Psychopharmacol. Bull. 11:48, 1975.

71. Shenkin, H. A.; Greenberg, J.; Bouzarth, W. F.; Gutterman, P.; and Morales, J. O.: *Ventricular shunting for relief of senile symptoms.* J.A.M.A. 225:1486, 1973.

72. Shenkin, H. A.; Greenberg, J. O.; and Grossman, C. B.: *Ventricular size after shunting for idiopathic normal pressure hydrocephalus.* J. Neurol. Neurosurg. Psychiatry 38:833, 1975.

73. Sklar, J., and O'Neill, F. J.: *Experiments with intensive treatment in a geriatric ward,* in Hoch, P. H., and Zubin, J. (eds.): *Psychopathology of Aging.* American Psychopathological Association Proceedings, 1960.

74. Snowdon, J.: *When is dementia presenile?* (Letter to the Editor). Br. Med. J. 2:465, 1972.

75. Strachan, R. W., and Henderson, J. G.: *Psychiatric syndromes due to avitaminosis B_{12} with normal blood and marrow.* Q. J. Med. 34:303, 1965.

76. Strachan, R. W., and Henderson, J. G.: Dementia and folate deficiency. Q. J. Med. 36:189, 1967.

77. Sweet, R. D.; McDowell, F. H.; Feigenson, J. S.; Loranger, A. W.; and Goodell, H.: *Mental symptoms in Parkinson's disease during chronic treatment with levodopa.* Neurology (Minneap.) 26:305, 1976.

78. Tomlinson, B. E.: The pathology of dementia, in Wells, C. E. (ed.): *Dementia,* ed. 2. F. A. Davis Co., Philadelphia, 1977.

79. Tomlinson, B. E.; Blessed, G.; and Roth, M.: *Observations on the brains of demented old people.* J. Neurol. Sci. 11:205, 1970.

80. Walshe, J. M.: *Penicillamine.* Practitioner 191:789, 1963.

81. Wang, H. S.: Dementia in old age, in Wells, C. E. (ed.): *Dementia,* ed. 2. F. A. Davis Co., Philadelphia, 1977.

82. Wang, H. S., and Whanger, A.: Brain impairment and longevity, in Palmore, E., and Jeffers, F. (eds.): *Prediction of Life Span.* D. C. Heath and Co., Lexington, 1971.

83. Wells, C. E.: *Dementia reconsidered.* Arch. Gen. Psychiatry 26:385, 1972.

84. Wells, C. E.: Delirium and dementia, in Abram, H. S. (ed.): *Basic Psychiatry for the Primary Care Physician.* Little, Brown, and Co., Boston, 1976.

85. Wells, C. E.: Dementia: Definition and description, in Wells, C. E. (ed.): *Dementia,* ed. 2. F. A. Davis Co., Philadelphia, 1977.

86. Wells, C. E.: Unpublished observations.

87. Wells, C. E., and Buchanan, D. C.: The clinical use of psychological testing in evaluation for dementia, in Wells, C. E. (ed.): *Dementia,* ed. 2. F. A. Davis Co., Philadelphia, 1977.

88. Whybrow, P. C.; Prange, A. J., Jr.; and Treadway, C. R.: *Mental changes accompanying thyroid gland dysfunction.* Arch. Gen. Psychiatry 20:48, 1969.

Index

277

280

282

Ventricles
  size of, pneumoencephalography in, 228
  stasis of, in normal pressure hydrocephalus,
    76–77
Virus(es), 93–112, 139–143
  slow, 95–100
Visuomotor performance, tests of, 197–198
Vitamin B$_{12}$ deficiency, 45
  diagnosis and therapy in, 265

WAIS Block Design and Digit Symbol
    Subtests, 198
Wernicke-Korsakoff syndrome, 44
  EEG findings in, 215–216

Wernicke's encephalopathy, 39
  pathology in, 116–117
Wechsler Adult Intelligence Scale, 16,
    193–194
  on elderly, 17–18
Weschler Memory Scale, 195–196
Wheeler-Reitan Modification of Halstead-
    Wepman Aphasia Screening Test,
    198–199
Whipple's disease, 54
Wilson's disease, 38, 137–139
  diagnosis and therapy in, 262
  pathology in, 116
  putamen in, 138